TELL EVERYONE

A PEOPLE'S HISTORY OF THE FACES

TELL EVERYONE: A PEOPLE'S HISTORY OF THE FACES

BY THE SAME AUTHOR

The Who – I Was There

Pink Floyd – I Was There

Jimi Hendrix – The Day I Was There

Led Zeppelin – The Day I Was There

The Smiths – The Day I Was There

The Jam – The Day I Was There (with Neil Cossar)

Black Sabbath – The Day I Was There

Rush – The Day I Was There

The Wedding Present – Sometimes These Words Just Don't Have To Be Said (with David Gedge)

Orchestral Manoeuvres in the Dark – Pretending To See The Future

Simple Minds – Heart of the Crowd

Shaun Ryder's Book of Mumbo Jumbo

Cream – A People's History

Queen – A People's History

Jethro Tull – Lend Me Your Ears

The Rolling Stones in the Sixties – A People's History

Gonna See All My Friends – A People's History of Fairport Convention

The Stranglers – Live (Excerpts)

All Down The Line – A People's History of the Rolling Stones 1972 North American Tour

The Wedding Present – All The Songs Sound The Same (with David Gedge)

TELL EVERYONE

A PEOPLE'S HISTORY OF THE FACES

Richard Houghton

Spenwood Books
Manchester, UK

TELL EVERYONE: A PEOPLE'S HISTORY OF THE FACES

First published in Great Britain 2023
by Spenwood Books Ltd
2 College Street, Higham Ferrers, NN10 8DZ.

Copyright © Richard Houghton 2023

The right of Richard Houghton to be identified as author of this work has been asserted in accordance with Section 77 of the Copyright, Design and Patents Act 1988.

A CIP record for this book is available from the British Library.

ISBN 978-1-915858-03-0

Printed in the Czech Republic via Akcent Media Limited.

Design by Bruce Graham, The Night Owl.
Front cover design: Bruce Graham
Rear cover images: (clockwise from top left) Bruce Kahn, Eduard Bühler, Peter Smith, Anthony Dew, Len Webster, Henry Race
All other image copyrights: As captioned

TELL EVERYONE: A PEOPLE'S HISTORY OF THE FACES

It's a well known old secret
Go and tell everyone…

TELL EVERYONE: A PEOPLE'S HISTORY OF THE FACES

TELL EVERYONE

I saw Rod Stewart and the Faces on telly. Rod was obviously pissed and having a fantastic time. I thought: 'That's something I could do.' So that was my dream, singing along to the mirror in my bedroom.

Fish (Marillion)

There may have been better bands, but there was never a band to make you feel so good... They were the only band who were actually invited to my wedding, and their roadies, and they all came too.

John Peel (BBC Broadcaster & DJ)

I lived in Kensal Green. Sandy Sargent, one of the dancers from *Ready Steady Go*, lived a couple of streets away. All us kids went round there on our bikes to watch one of the Small Faces come to take her out. When I met Ian McLagan I told him this and he said, 'You can't have had much to do.' I said, 'Mate, I was ten years old at the time. Give me a blinkin' break.' He said, 'I didn't take her out. I lived there. I used to drink in the Mason's Arms.' The Mason's Arms is where I had my first pint, so I go way back with the Small Faces.

Glen Matlock

ACKNOWLEDGEMENTS

I'd like to thank everyone who contributed memories for this book and in particular Dee Harrington, Sandie Ritter, Mike Walton and Glen Matlock.

I'd also like to thank the following for their help: Neil Drysdale at the *Aberdeen Press & Journal*; Graeme Strachan at the *Dundee Courier*; Jane Silvester at Lancaster University; Georgia O'Keeffe and the Alumni Relations Office at Loughborough University; admins for and members of the following Facebook groups: Faces: Had Me a Real Good Time, Who Remembers the Boston Tea Party, Liverpool Stadium, Ron Domilici; Rick Burton (check out his rainbowhistory.x10.mx website); Nico Zentgraf, whose Ronnie Wood database nzentgraf.de was an excellent point of reference; ronnielane.com; Richard Marsh.

For permission to use the images on pages 182-183, 200-201, 212-213 and 396-397 from his Faces collection, I'd like to say a special thank you to Matt Lee. If you have any Faces memorabilia for sale, please contact Matt at mattleeuk@gmail.com.

And I'd like to thank web wizard Bruce Koziarski, design guru Bruce Graham and the woman without whom none of this would be possible, the lovely Kate Sullivan.

INTRODUCTION

Some bands are measured by the records they sell. Others by ticket sales. With the Faces, you'd probably just count the number of empty Mateus Rosé bottles.

The Faces were famous for being boozy, playing loose and having a good time. For the Faces, it mattered less whether they hit a bum note than whether they were having a laugh, and whether the audience was too. Modern day bands wouldn't get away with it. Nowadays, there are curfews which require you to start on time, pre-programmed lighting sequences based on the set list you've already determined to play and all manner of health and safety conditions to be borne in mind. And as for smoking cigarettes on stage – well, where can you still do that anymore?

Rather like 'legend', the phrase 'much mourned' is over used. But if there was ever a band for whom the term much mourned was appropriate, then it's the Faces. Their reputation for giving a rousing performance in concert was such that the phrase 'best live band I ever saw' litters the 500-plus accounts of seeing them in performance that make up this book. From 1971 to the middle of 1973, perhaps the only band anywhere in the world that could touch them as a live act was the Rolling Stones.

By the time the Faces entered my teenage consciousness, they had already called last orders on their career. I did get to see the three surviving members of the original line up play at Kenney Jones' polo club on a freezing cold September evening in 2014, when they did seven numbers as part of a charity fundraiser in aid of tackling prostate cancer. Seven numbers that conjured up for me a little bit of the magic that between 1969 and 1975 hundreds of audiences around the world got to enjoy.

The story of the Faces is not the tale of a group of school friends rehearsing in a back bedroom and then bursting onto the music world fully formed. Ronnie, Mac, Kenney, Ron and Rod all had musical CVs before performing together as the Faces. This book attempts to knit together some early memories of the five of them up to and including the seven shambolic, booze-drenched years in which the Faces sang, danced and did everything before a paying audience or three.

TELL EVERYONE: A PEOPLE'S HISTORY OF THE FACES

As with the other fan-centric books I have compiled, this book does not claim to be a complete history of the band. It is woven together from the memories of those who have kindly shared their recollections with me, so inevitably it is lopsided in places. But no history of any band can be entirely balanced. Editing these memories has been a bitter-sweet experience. It has been fabulous to read recollections of the Faces in their prime and the way in which they could command a stage and an audience. But it has also been heart-breaking to learn of the constant tension between Rod and Mac, how early and ultimately how severely Ronnie Lane's health was impacted by MS, and just how pale an imitation of their former selves was the band that carried on post his departure.

I would have loved to see the Faces live and witnessed one of their slightly chaotic, slightly dishevelled, slightly drunken performances, in which all the individual parts came together to produce the magic to which so many people in this book give testimony. If I was offered a trip in a time machine and a golden ticket for just one concert, a performance by the Faces in 1972 is the act I'd cash that ticket in for. Just to experience the atmosphere, the excitement and the fun that some of the lucky so-and-sos who tell their stories in this book got to enjoy back then.

The one official live album released during the Faces career is, by all accounts, not at all reflective of the band in concert. A prime motivator behind this book was a desire on my part to capture the essence of the Faces live.

I wish I'd been there. By reading this book, you can be.

Richard Houghton
Manchester, February 2023

STUDIO 51
OCTOBER 1963, LONDON, UK

Rod Stewart's first performances on stage are with Jimmy Powell and the Fifth Dimension, mainly at Studio 51.

I did two numbers a night – then I went home.
Rod, talking to the *NME*

TWICKENHAM RAILWAY STATION
5 JANUARY 1964, LONDON, UK

After watching Long John Baldry perform at a club, Rod is singing a Muddy Waters song and playing harmonica whilst waiting for a train. Baldry hears him and asks, 'Would you like to join the band?'

TWISTED WHEEL
11 JANUARY 1964, MANCHESTER, UK

Rod performs with Long John Baldry for the first time.

RAILWAY HOTEL
1964, WEALDSTONE, LONDON, UK

I WAS THERE: VALERIE DUNN
Rod the Mod at the Railway Hotel! He used to have back-combed hair and wear a bit of make-up. He was really sweet. He was the Mod, but he would get up and sing with Alexis Korner and Cyril Davies, who had Dick Hextall-Smith on saxophone. They'd do all this really great Blues Incorporated bluesy stuff and he would just join in. He had that lovely raspy voice and he was such a character, really cute, and they all loved him. He was like the

cheeky lad who would get up and sing with these well-established musicians.

And Long John Baldry, of course. He was probably more the instigator of the whole thing at the Railway. He was the one that got it going and noticed musicians, and got them in and invited them, etc. He'd be there and he'd just get up and sing a few numbers, which was really great. Everyone would love it because he had a bit of charisma and it was a bit different, to see this back-combed guy prancing around on – well, it wasn't even a stage really, it was just sort of a flat area.

MARQUEE JAZZ CLUB
16 APRIL 1964, LONDON, UK

I WAS THERE: DAVID COLYER

I just have a few memories of seeing Rod Stewart at the Marquee Jazz Club in Wardour Street, in the early Sixties. He was a regular singer with Long John Baldry and the Hoochie Coochie Men. He chose to sing blues songs by Muddy Waters, John Lee Hooker and Sonny Boy Williamson.

EEL PIE HOTEL
JUNE 1964, LONDON, UK

Ronnie Wood's band The Birds (sometimes appearing as The Thunderbirds) begin playing the London club circuit semi-professionally. They stay together until February 1967, when Ronnie leaves to join the Jeff Beck Group.

CORONATION GARDENS
1964, LEYTON, LONDON, UK

I WAS THERE: BRIAN WILLIAMS

I live in Leyton in East London. There was a place around the corner from me called the Coronation Gardens and in the early Sixties, Rod Stewart played there with the Hoochie Coochie Men. I used to help out in there and I got to meet Rod. He came on as the guest singer with Long John Baldry and the Hoochie Coochie Men. They introduced him and he came on and he sang. I liked him but I thought he was unusual. Then, next thing, he was in this little shed that was attached to this pavilion where they sold tea and biscuits, just chatting away. He wasn't well known. He was just a weird-looking guy. People looking sat him thinking 'wow', because he was a real stylish Mod.

(There is no verifiable record of this gig, but another person also remembers it.)

CENTRAL HOTEL
1964, GILLINGHAM, UK

I WAS THERE: LORAINE SMITH
I remember seeing Rod Stewart, Julie Driscoll and Long John Baldry playing at a venue called The Central Hotel in Gillingham. I stood next to Rod at the bar – and he didn't buy me a drink!

Loraine Smith remembers seeing Rod in action in Gillingham

TOWN HALL
25 JULY 1964, HOVE, UK

I WAS THERE: KAREN TYRRELL
The first time I saw or heard Rod Stewart was when he was in Long John Baldry's Hoochie Coochie Men at the first Hove Town Hall! I remember my friend and I said to each other 'one day he's going to make it!'. Seven years later he released 'Maggie May' and, well, say no more. I still have the advertisement from Brighton's *Evening Argus* advertising that gig. It is on the back of a photo of me amongst in a crowd of mad teenagers swarming around Gerry Marsden's car outside the Hippodrome in Brighton!

RENDEZVOUS CLUB
3 OCTOBER 1964, PORTSMOUTH, UK

I WAS THERE: PAT STURCH

I saw Rod many times around 1964. He was living in and around Southsea for about six months. He was at the Rendezvous Club often and sometimes at the Birdcage Club. He would turn up and sometimes get on stage with whoever was playing. The stages were small and only about one or two feet off the ground, so at the end of the evening all of us at the front would be up on the stage. There was no alcohol at the Rendezvous so in the break everyone, including the band, would go in the pub next door. Rod was with Long John Baldry and then with Julie Driscoll and Brian Auger, but he was always hanging around the blues clubs.

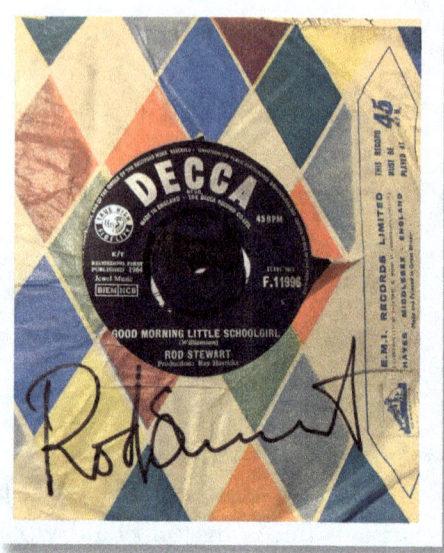

Pat Sturch bought Rod's recording of 'Good Morning Little Schoolgirl' in 1964

I bought this record back in 1964 (I had to order it) after Rod told us he'd made his first record. I finally got it signed in Vegas in 2018. Rod looked at it and said, 'Blimey, that must be worth a bob or two.'

Rod leaves the Hoochie Coochie Men in October 1964, performing as 'Rod Stewart with the Soul Agents', but often still sharing a bill with Long John Baldry.

RUSKIN ARMS
27 JANUARY 1965, MANOR PARK, UK

The Small Faces – including Kenney Jones and Ronnie Lane – begin rehearsing for the first time. They go on to have seven UK Top Ten singles, including a number 1 with 'All or Nothing', and a number 1 album with Ogden's Nut Gone Flake.

OASIS
11 JUNE 1965, MANCHESTER, UK

I WAS THERE: MICHAEL KINGSLAND
I saw Ronnie Wood's group The Birds a couple of times at the Oasis Club on Lloyd Street off Albert Square. It was a great time for Manchester. The Who played there, as did the Pretty Things and another fine band called The Action, from London. Great times.

ODEON THEATRE
16 JULY 1965, EXETER, UK

Rod joins Steampacket, fronted by Long John Baldry and Julie Driscoll. Their first show is on a package tour headlined by the Rolling Stones and featuring The Walker Brothers and Elkie Brooks. Rod performs over 200 gigs with them in 15 months.

ORFORD CELLAR
3 AUGUST 1965, NORWICH, UK

I WAS THERE: DEREK BURROUGHS
I saw Rod at the Orford Cellar in Norwich when he was with Steampacket. Rod was in his Mod period, with back-combed hair, etc., and appearing with Long John Baldry, Brian Auger and Julie Driscoll. The music was excellent, very blues-influenced. The Orford Cellar was really small, but 300 packed in on a good night. One small staircase led down from the alley above, and there was a small bar in the corner, a small stage in the opposite corner and a large net strung across the ceiling which dripped with sweat (there was no health and safety in those days). I remember standing at the bar at half time and exchanging a few words with Rod while he was waiting for his beer; he looked very young and quite thin.

(Rod may have appeared at the Orford on three other occasions with Steampacket.)

THE DANCING SLIPPER
21 AUGUST 1965, WEST BRIDGFORD, NOTTINGHAM

I WAS THERE: PAULINE SILVESTER

During my misspent youth in Beeston, Nottingham in the early Sixties, I used to go to a nightclub called The Dancing Slipper in West Bridgford – then a rather nondescript suburb of Nottingham but now a rather posh and trendy one! Although it didn't seem at all unusual at the time, this nightclub was above a street-based petrol station with a single pump and to say the premises were small is rather understating the case. The only room contained a minute stage and dancefloor and was about the size of the average front room!

Every few weeks there was a gig there put on by artists collectively known as The Steam Packet, which comprised the Brian Auger Trinity, Julie Driscoll, Long John Baldry – and a very young Rod Stewart. The room probably only held about 30 people including the artists, so it was a very intimate affair. Rod was an amazing entertainer even them and there was always a special buzz on the weeks that he performed. I'm proud to say that I was amongst those who were there at the very start of his long career in music.

BLUE MOON
25 AUGUST 1965, CHELTENHAM, UK

I WAS THERE: JANE MAISEY, AGE 16

We saw a lot of now famous names at the Blue Moon, which was only open for two years. Rod Stewart was there with Long John Baldry, and also Brian Auger and Julie Driscoll. A friend remembers Rod asking him to lend him £2 for fags, but another friend said he cadged a cigarette off her, so the general consensus is he was a bit tight. We went to a bar with Julie Driscoll and Rod Stewart. I was only 16 and they asked me my age (which was really embarrassing) but it was to me just an ordinary night, with the added extra of being in the company of people that were playing at our local night club. If only I'd known who he would become.

I've been to Rod's concerts and so wanted to get to see him and tell him how I met him – and see his reaction!

(Steampacket also played the Blue Moon on 20 October 1965 and 4 December 1965.)

CORN EXCHANGE
14 SEPTEMBER 1965, BRISTOL, UK

I WAS THERE: GEORGE BURFORD

I saw a really excellent show given by Long John Baldry, Julie Driscoll and the Trinity and a very young Rod Stewart. The concert took place on a Tuesday night at the Bristol Corn Exchange under the auspices of the so-called Chinese Jazz Club night. Long John Baldry asked us what we thought of his 'new discovery' and we looked up to him and said we were impressed and that we'd keep an eye out for his future career.

MARQUEE CLUB
30 SEPTEMBER 1965, LONDON, UK

I WAS THERE: JOHN KERNOT

I grew up in Finchley and Rod in Highgate. I never met him, but I saw him a few times at the Marquee when he guested with Long John Baldry. At that time, he was probably known as Rod the Mod! He duetted several songs with Baldry, singing in unison. He had a special stage presence. The crowd at that time had several other musicians on the way up, eg. Paul Jones. The Marquee was a very intimate place at that time.

Another memory of Rod comes from a friend who played pub league Sunday football in North London. Usually there was nobody watching, but at this match (in the 1970s) there were hundreds of girls! Along comes a Ferrari and Rod gets out with a net of footballs. That match was a bit unusual, with Rod on the opposing side.

FLORAL HALL
19 OCTOBER 1965, GORLESTON, UK

I WAS THERE: PAUL TAYLOR

We went to see the Small Faces at The Floral Hall, Gorleston (now known as the Ocean Room) at the time that their debut single, 'Whatcha Gonna Do About It', was in the charts and Jimmy Winston was the organist. They were only able to play live both sides of the single and about one other number, all of which they played twice to spin it out! Not surprisingly, Winston was soon replaced.

BLUE MOON CLUB
20 OCTOBER 1965, CHELTENHAM, UK

I WAS THERE: GORDON EWING

Rod Stewart had become an acquaintance of mine and he arrived in Cheltenham to play with Steampacket at the Blue Moon in Cheltenham. After the show, we all gathered on the pavement and Long John Baldry went off with some local talent while we chatted with Rod. They were staying overnight and not leaving till late, so Rod agreed to meet for a lunchtime drink. I was working at the brewery, loading lorries to deliver Devenish Ales to the deepest West Country and had a short lunch break, so Rod agreed to come round to the brewery pub, which I believe was called the Stonehouse, for a swift couple of pints. He was sitting there alone when I arrived. If that pub still

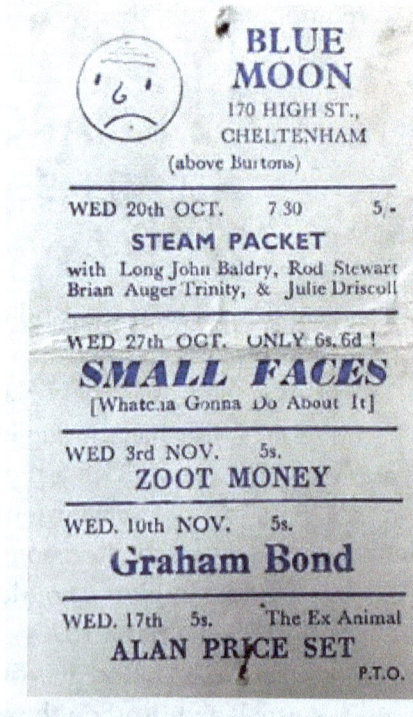

Rod Stewart was a regular performer at the Blue Moon Club in Cheltenham as a part of Steampacket

exists, they should maybe erect a plaque to the man who would later be ennobled as 'Sir Rod'.

(The Stonehouse Inn was located on Swindon Road in Cheltenham but no longer exists.)

MAJESTIC BALLROOM
1 NOVEMBER 1965, READING, UK

I WAS THERE: LYN COLLIN

I saw Rod the Mod at the Majestic Ballroom in Reading when I was at school. It was a very small venue. I'd gone with schoolfriends to see Long John Baldry, and in the background were Rod and Julie Driscoll. John was this big giant of a man and Rod looked quite little in comparison. That was the first time I ever saw him and I

When Lyn saw the Faces at Hurtwood Park it was 50 years since she'd first seen Rod

didn't realise who he was. And we heard that he (John) was going to be in Reading, where we lived, and went along to see him on what I think was a Monday night. That was probably one of the first gigs I went to, apart from The Beatles when I was younger. And then Rod pretty much disappeared from view until he appeared in the Faces. I was aware of the Small Faces, because a friend who lived round the corner used to play their music. Whenever I went round there, that was all you would hear.

When 'Maggie May' came out, I had a Rod poster on my bedroom wall. The Faces were at Reading Rock Festival and I lived in Reading. The stages then were a rickety piece of wood with a bit of scaffolding. When you see the stages that bands perform on now, you wonder how on earth did they stay alive back then? Those early Reading rock festivals were quite basic.

I then saw the Faces at the Sundown in Edmonton. I lived in London by then. They played two nights at the Sundown in Edmonton and I went with a friend from work. I only did one show. I was so excited to be there. And Hurtwood in 2015 was amazing. Again, I went with a friend from work. It was so exciting to know that they were going to be on, and that it was actually going to happen.

LYCEUM THEATRE
2 NOVEMBER 1965, LONDON, UK

Ian McLagan plays his debut gig with the Small Faces after replacing Jimmy Winston in the band's line-up.

LEOFRIC HOTEL
21 NOVEMBER 1965, COVENTRY, UK

I WAS THERE: JAN SHARP

I remember seeing Rod the Mod in the Jazz Club at the Leofric Hotel ballroom. I went with my mates, all girls who were Mods who also loved Rod. It was packed in there and a fantastic atmosphere. The place erupted when he sang 'In the Midnight Hour'.

THE BEACHCOMBER
25 NOVEMBER 1965, PRESTON, UK

I WAS THERE: SHIRLEY RAWSTORNE

I have many memories of Rod Stewart playing at a club in Manchester called the Twisted Wheel. I have all the dates in my diary. We loved him and he happened to play at a club in Preston, so we hitched along. When we got there, we didn't have enough money to pay for admission, but Rod came along as we were trying to get in and promptly lent us two and six (13p).

TOWN HALL
6 DECEMBER 1965, TORQUAY, UK

I WAS THERE: LIONEL DIGBY
The Small Faces were signed to Don Arden, the rock and roll mafia, as he was known. They were a virtually unknown group and he put them on a wage of £20 a week. When they got a hit record (with 'Whatcha Gonna Do About It') he was putting them out at £200 plus a night and they were still on £20 a week wages.

I remember when they came to me in Torquay, they had a roadie/minder with them and the instructions were, 'You don't pay the band, you pay Don Arden or his representative.' As soon as they arrived, they were set on getting the money. They wanted paying and I said no. 'You have to go on stage and you don't get paid until afterwards.' Don Arden was very strict. They were arrogant little Mods. I didn't get on with them at all. But they went on.

ST GEORGE'S HOTEL
18 DECEMBER 1965, HINCKLEY, UK

I WAS THERE: GRAHAM AUCOTT
I saw Rod Stewart at the St George's Ballroom with Steampacket – Brian Auger, Julie Driscoll, Long John Baldry, etc. It was a good night, although most of our crowd were not familiar with most of the artists. He was very much in the making, with Brian Auger the main man with his Hammond valve organ and Lowry sound cabinet, a sound never bettered in my opinion.

PLAZA BALLROOM
6 FEBRUARY 1966, HANDSWORTH, BIRMINGHAM, UK

I WAS THERE: KEN FORD
I was in a band called The Bitta Sweet, formed by Al Atkins in 1966 as a

four piece. Al was on vocals and drums but we recruited a new drummer and Al became the front man. We auditioned at the Adelphi in West Bromwich and were second on the bill to Robert Plant and the Band of Joy, who borrowed our new Shure mics. We passed an audition for the Plaza circuit with Ma and Pa Regan, They owned three dance halls, which were all converted cinemas – the Plaza in Handsworth (now a Sikh temple), the Plaza in Old Hill (which became a bingo hall and is now a wedding venue) and the Ritz Ballroom in Kings Heath (which became a bingo hall and then a shop before being destroyed by fire). All the dance floors were upstairs with the bar and cloakrooms below. The Regans' gigs were fantastic – four bands a night with top artists on the bill including Cat Stevens and Dave Dee, Dozy, Beaky, Mitch and Titch. We shared a bill with a young David Bowie but were asked to do a double that night and passed him on the road!

We supported Long John Baldry on a Sunday night. There were just two bands that night, with records played in between. I think Al our singer had a drink with Rod at the bar afterwards but he cannot remember now. Only later did we discover who Rod was, and that the pianist – who wanted to take me home with him – was to become Elton John. That night Albie met his future wife, a real beautiful girl, and the band broke up. It was our last gig and the end of my involvement with bands.

ZAMBESI CLUB
18 MARCH 1966, HOUSLOW, UK

Rod's last appearance with Steampacket, although whether he quits or is sacked is disputed. He joined Shotgun Express.

TOP OF THE WORLD BALLROOM
11 JUNE 1966, STAFFORD, UK

I WAS THERE: PAUL SMITH
I recall telling my friend Charlie about the Small Faces appearing at the Top of the World and he replied that he'd just seen the Yardbirds

and the Spencer Davis Group, and that Steve Winwood fell off the stage. The first concert we went to at Top of the World was Davy Dee Dozy Beaky Mick and Titch. They were an awful band, but we had a great time. I remember being shocked by the line-up of girls in the parking lot after the concert, waiting to be admitted to the band bus to be serviced by the group.

Top of the World was pretty exotic for provincial Stafford, but expensive. In the autumn our little group worked on Saturdays as beaters for the Ingestre estate and our hard-earned shekels would pay for a night out. One Saturday, Charlie found a £10 note on the estate. He was rich. Such was the pricing power in those days that it not only covered our entrance fee to Top of the World but a few rounds of drinks as well. I can't recall much about the Small Faces performance though.

SOUTH PIER THEATRE
7 AUGUST 1966, BLACKPOOL, UK

I WAS THERE: NEVILLE LEE

In 1966, the Small Faces played a gig at South Pier. I was there to take photographs and remember there were a few girl fans. The band ran down the pier until we had shaken them off and then stopped for us guys and signed autographs except, I remember, Steve Marriot who for some reason would not. Ronnie Lane signed with his nickname Plonk rather than his name. It was unusual for bands not to sign, because no one was aware that these signatures would be worth anything in five years, never mind 50. The idea was that they had 18 months of fame and then would be forgotten. Nobody knew we were on the cusp of the rock revolution.

A friend of mine called Sue went to see the show and handed in her autograph book. She did obtain Steve Marriott's signature, perhaps helped, she said, by buying him a packet of cigarettes for his birthday.

In March 1967, I saw the band on a package tour with Roy Orbison in the days when the bills were somewhat bizarre, no doubt to attract as many different tastes as possible. They were very good.

26 OCTOBER 1966
ABC THEATRE, NORTHAMPTON

I WAS THERE: PAULINE LEVER, AGE 15

The Small Faces were supporting the Hollies, along with Paul Jones, Paul and Barry Ryan and The Nashville Teens. I fancied Steve and I liked the way they dressed. When the Small Faces came on, we ran to the front. I lost my friend Kay amongst the crowd and a policeman pulled me away from the edge of the crowd and pushed me over, hurting my knee. Another policeman pulled me up and pushed me to the back, so I moved over to the other side of the stage. Aa load of fans rushed forward so I joined them. We rushed the stage and a bouncer grabbed me. I fell flat down.

When I got up, I was still at the front. I knew I could vault the stage from having done so on a previous visit. A few of us got into the orchestra pit and two bouncers jumped in and just seemed happy to let us stay there although they kept us off the stage.

I stood at the side and leaned on the wall, screaming and holding my hand out. One of the Small Faces reached out and briefly held my hand. Steve looked my way and I think he smiled at me, I remember them singing 'Whatcha Gonna Do About It' and 'Sha-La-La-La-Lee'. They were fantastic, and Steve was very cute close up.

At the end, I found Kay. I was limping and my sister, who had come with us, was furious. I was totally exhausted on the bus home. At home, Bridget told Mum she wasn't going to any more shows if I was going, Mum was more concerned about my swollen knee. My Dad thought it was pretty good my being able to vault the stage.

JEFF BECK'S FLAT
JANUARY 1967, SUTTON, LONDON, UK

First rehearsals for the Jeff Beck Group, featuring Ronnie Wood on guitar and Rod Stewart on vocals.

MARQUEE CLUB
11 APRIL 1967, LONDON, UK

The first performance by the Jeff Beck Group is at London's Marquee Club.

THE BENN HALL
SPRING 1967, RUGBY, UK

I WAS THERE: JOHN PHILLPOTT

It was one week in the spring of 1967 and I was an 18-year-old trainee reporter on the *Rugby Advertiser*. The Small Faces were playing the local Benn Memorial Hall that Saturday night – I think it was around April – and I asked chief reporter Len Archer if I could cover the event and also interview the band. Len gave me a disapproving look and said, 'As far as I'm concerned, they're just a bunch of long-haired layabouts. But if you must, then all right – just make sure you cover the Rugby and District Angling Association annual general meeting at the Peacock Inn first. And no sneaking out early, boy!'

John Phillpott saw the Small Faces once he was off the hook for the angling AGM

That Saturday evening, I went along to the Peacock, notebook and pencil in hand. The meeting dragged on and on, members discussing such vital issues as the fall in the gudgeon population on the Oxford Canal or whether to use coloured maggots or not. And then, finally, it ground to a halt – and I was out the door in a flash, heading straight for the Benn Hall. I rushed through the doors, flashed my Press card, strode across the dance floor, and within seconds was in the presence of the Small – and, it has to be said – rather spotty Faces.

In those days, I modelled my questioning on the *Melody Maker's* lifelines style of questions and answers, so I asked singer Steve Marriott about his musical influences, favourite food and drink – usually scotch or rum and Coke with all the stars – and also requested that he gave me what was essentially a set list of numbers the band was going to play that night. Imagine that these days!

Anyway, they were soon onstage, and were absolutely electrifying. They blasted through 'Whatcha Gonna Do About It' and Otis Redding's 'Shake', while coasting through the slower soul covers, the titles of which now escape me. I've been to hundreds of gigs over the years, but that night at Rugby's Benn Hall was sheer magic, absolutely electrifying. It's half a century ago but the cliché still rings true… it could have been yesterday.

Postscript: The Editor of the *Rugby Advertiser* used more of my angling association AGM report in the next week's edition than my Small Faces piece. Ah well, c'est la guerre!

CITY HALL
19 MARCH 1967, NEWCASTLE-UPON-TYNE, UK

I WAS THERE: ROGER LUND

I was sent by my company, Shell Tankers, to South Shields in February 1964 to complete my Marine Engineering apprenticeship. I spent seven months at the Marine College and eight months at Greenwells Ship Repair Yard in Sunderland. I met my late wife Maggie, who was training to be a nurse in South Shields General Hospital, soon after I arrived and we married in February 1967. I had been on a long ten month trip and managed to get home five days before the wedding. We were both aged 23.

I remember going to City Hall to see the Small Faces. Also on the bill were Roy Orbison and Paul and Barry Ryan. We went in the afternoon as there were two performances that day. Paul and Barry Ryan were at loggerheads at the time and for some reason one of them stormed off, leaving his brother in the middle of the stage.

KINEMA
24 APRIL 1967, DUNFERMLINE, UK

I WAS THERE: ALAN WATTERS

When I was in my late teens and early twenties, I worked part time in the Kinema ballroom in Dunfermline and on Sunday nights we always had big bands play. My mate Bob Smith and I would help the bands set up on stage on a Sunday afternoon to be ready to play in the evening so we met lots of the top names. One Sunday, we were setting up for the Small Faces and Ronnie 'Plonk' Lane asked if I would like to fill in when they were rehearsing, as another band member hadn't turned up yet. So my claim to fame is that I jammed with the Small Faces! I was only learning guitar at the time so he showed me what chords to play and I just strummed away, hopefully in time with the others! What an amazing feeling that was.

On another occasion, Joe Cocker and the Grease band were playing in Dunfermline and we met them in the pub beforehand. Their road manager came in and said that they had been thrown out of the City Hotel but that he was trying to find them somewhere else to stay. We ended up arranging with the band that me and my mates would take one each home that night and give them a bed. I was the one who was to host Joe Cocker! In the end, I said they should try the Pitbauchly Hotel and they did get rooms there so they didn't stay with us after all. Funny thing is, my mother was the manager of the City Hotel at the time and I didn't half give her a hard time when I got home that night (there were no mobile phones in those days).

UNKNOWN VENUE
22 MAY 1967, COPENHAGEN, DENMARK

I WAS THERE: JANNIE JENSEN

I saw the Small Faces in Copenhagen when I was very young and it was a fantastic evening. I had to stay on the dancefloor because I didn't have enough money to buy a beer, and you had to either had to buy something to drink or dance to avoid being thrown out!

DOUGLAS HOTEL
9 JUNE 1967, ABERDEEN, UK

I WAS THERE: ARTHUR WYLLIE

Rod Stewart once appeared at the Douglas Hotel, Aberdeen with the Jeff Beck Group. I took the chance to write to Jeff Beck and ask for their autographs which I received almost by return post. Rod's was amongst them and I still have them.

Arthur Wyllie was at the Douglas Hotel

The Jeff Beck Group played Aberdeen's Douglas Hotel

I WAS THERE: IAIN WOLSTENHOLME

I saw the Jeff Beck Group featuring vocals by Rod Stewart, bass by Ronnie Wood and drums by Aynsley Dunbar. The 'growing ever-heavier sound' was something else and quite physical at the time, especially in a hotel lounge setting where there was little divide between band and audience pressed nose-to-nose. In Aberdeen, the main talking point was when Rod Stewart came face-to-face with local stalwart of the soul scene, Gordon Lemon, who is sadly departed. (Lemon Soul was the band name.) Rod is reputed to have said, 'Snap!'

TOWN HALL
15 JULY 1967, TORQUAY, UK

I WAS THERE: LIONEL DIGBY

I booked the Jeff Beck Group for Torquay Town Hall in 1967. Jeff had recorded 'Hi Ho Silver Lining', his big hit, with session musicians. The band he went out on the road with wasn't the band that had recorded it. The band that went out on the road consisted of Rod Stewart on vocals and Ronnie Wood on bass.

The Jeff Beck Group played Torquay Town Hall

Rod Stewart turned up in a denim jacket and jeans, with his knees hanging out of them, and he went on stage like that. The rest of the band dressed up a bit but he didn't. I'm sure he was a bit smarter when he was in Long John Baldry's band. Rod was stoned out of his bloody head. He was facing the band and dancing about and he stepped backwards. The stage at Torquay Town Hall is about four feet high and he went straight off that and fell into the crowd. They pushed him back on again and he carried on.

NEW CENTURY HALL
2 SEPTEMBER 1967, MANCHESTER, UK

I WAS THERE: MICHAEL KINGSLAND

As well as seeing Ronnie with The Birds, I also saw Ronnie Wood with Jeff Beck and Rod Stewart at the CIS buildings, New Century Hall, in Manchester. They were amazing. Beck was bending the strings of the neck of a 12 string Vox Phantom.

FILLMORE EAST
14 & 15 JUNE 1968, NEW YORK, NEW YORK

The Jeff Beck Group kick off their first full US tour with four shows in two days in New York at the Fillmore East, below the Grateful Dead. The tour runs until 3rd August 1968, taking in 33 shows. The New York Times proclaims that they upstage the Dead.

STEVE PAUL SCENE
18 – 22 JUNE 1968, NEW YORK, NEW YORK

I WAS THERE: FRED FISHER
My friends were huge Yardbirds fans so when we heard Jeff had a new group, we got down to Steve Paul's Scene and grabbed a table up front. We enjoyed Mick Waller on drums, Ronnie Wood on bass, Jeff with a Les Paul and Rod singing. We knew Rod was going places. At one point while Jeff was soloing, the strap came off the bottom end, he swung his guitar around with his left hand (still playing), planted the bottom end in the ceiling tile above him, finished the solo and put the strap back on. Pretty impressive. We came back the next night and got the same table. I went back to Boston and two nights later saw them again at the Boston Tea Party.

I WAS THERE: RON ADCOCK
When I was in college in California in 1968, I spent six weeks in New Jersey and New York. I had seen the Yardbirds in Hollywood with Jeff Beck probably two years before. In the summer of 1968, Jeff was playing in New York for the first time with his new band, the Jeff Beck Group. This was before the *Truth* album was released, but I was already a huge Jeff Beck fan. I had been the drummer in a band in San Diego. The bass player was my older neighbour. The guitarist and singer were from New Jersey. The singer returned to his home in Elizabeth, New Jersey.

It was a one day trip from New Jersey to go and enjoy New York, riding the ferry boat and subway, and I had never gone east of Texas, but that summer I decided to go visit the singer. I stayed for six weeks. I worked from Monday to Friday at a discount department store, visiting New York City on the weekends. I went to the Fillmore East to see the Grateful Dead. I went to the Cafe Wha? where Chas Chandler had discovered Jimi Hendrix. The Jeff Beck Group concert was at a small but very famous club called Steve Paul's Scene. It was hard to get in because so many people wanted in. But we made it.

The show opened with a new Boston group called Earth Opera. They really impressed me. The Jeff Beck Group had a new face singer named Rod Stewart, and Ronnie Wood was the bass player. When I saw the Yardbirds, it was in a club that used to be an adult club. There were tables in front of the stage. But Steve Paul's Scene was smaller and we sat on the floor on the same level as the band. There was no raised stage. I was in the very front and Al Kooper was sitting next to me. I couldn't believe it – I was an Al Kooper fan and I loved the Blues Project – but I didn't want to bother him. He was there to watch the show like me.

I was a small town boy and being in New York City was overwhelming. I was so close to the band that I could almost touch them. I was hearing the *Truth* album songs live before the album came out. It was beyond amazing. There was a break between the Jeff Beck Group's two sets. My friend was a good talker and, to my amazement, he brought Jeff Beck over to me and introduced us – 'It's nice to meet you.' I was too shy to tell Jeff how much I loved his music. But it was so unbelievable that I met him and shook hands. He was a very nice guy.

Then the second set began. Jimi Hendrix was on stage with the Jeff Beck Group. Jimi played bass. They had an amazing jam session. Jimi had a very magical aura. Cosmic energy was emanating from him. This was the most memorable live event I have ever witnessed. Yes, Jimi made it special. And having Al Kooper sitting next to me. But the Jeff Beck Group's playing just blew me away. And this was my first time to hear Rod the Mod sing. Hearing Jeff Beck play guitar live in a small club was beyond amazing – and unforgettable. Finally, the *Truth* album was released, and at first I was disappointed because it didn't have the overwhelming power of what I had heard live. Of course, later I began to appreciate the album and it is truly a classic!

The drummer was Micky Waller. The whole band was cookin'! I've been to many concerts at many different venues, but to see a band live in a small club can't be beat, and Jeff Beck live in a small club...well, it doesn't get any better than

that. When I met Jeff, I didn't tell him that I'd seen him two years before with the Yardbirds in Hollywood, because he had been fired by them so I was afraid that he wouldn't be happy if I mentioned them.

At the time I saw the Jeff Beck Group in New York, only Jeff was well-known. Rod Stewart and Ronnie Wood were unknown in America. Of course, they would both later become very famous. The *Truth* album hadn't been released yet so my first time to hear Rod sing was live in that small club in New York. What a glorious voice! It doesn't get any better than that. I'd heard Steve Marriott, Steve Winwood and Joe Cocker. But now Rod Stewart – wow! Young, white British boys who sounded like old, black bluesmen!

ST LUKE'S COLLEGE
28 JUNE 1968, EXETER, UK

I WAS THERE: GEORGE BURFORD

I attended a dance concert at St Luke's College in Exeter where the Small Faces featured, in 1968 or '69. It was an eventful occasion because to begin with the group disputed whether they were booked for half an hour, or an hour as the college claimed. The result was a ramshackle performance where the band was loudly booed, and the group became quite abusive. The drummer was dragged off his stool by a rugby player student. The dance was saved by a storming performance by Adge Cutler and the Wurzels!

GRANDE BALLROOM
5 & 6 JULY 1968, DETROIT, MICHIGAN

I WAS THERE: PJ FREER, AGE 17

I saw the *Truth* band at the Grande Ballroom. All the great bands wanted to play at the Grande Ballroom, because all the fans knew the band members' names and the lyrics to all their tunes, plus it was a great sounding room. Everyone in our neighbourhood had the *Truth* LP and we played it over and over, so to see them live was such a rush. The lights got low and, all of a sudden, they broke into 'Shapes of Things'. It frickin' blew my head off! Jeff's wah-wah work was incredible. He could make his guitar talk. I was with The Red White and Blues Band and we played on the same bill, so I was in the Local Bands dressing room and got to drink some wine with Rod Stewart. Micky Waller was like a Mitch Mitchell clone.

SHRINE EXPOSITION HALL
26 JULY 1968, LOS ANGELES, CALIFORNIA

I WAS THERE: SEPP DONAHOWER, CONCERT PROMOTER

I was always a music nut, collecting records and following what was going on. I was in graduate business school at USC, where I saw what was going on in San Francisco with Family Dog, at the Emerald Ballroom and with the Fillmore just firing up. There were a few shows here and there in LA and I went over to the old Shrine Exhibition Hall, which was adjacent to the USC campus, and made a deal with a company called Highbury Corporation, who had a lease on the exhibition hall from the Shriners, for the beautiful auditorium that adjoined it. It had an all-wooden floor with a balcony going all the way around it and it held about 5,000 people. It was a killer ballroom. I made a deal with them for a paltry amount of money to have exclusivity to put on rock concerts, never having done one in my life. But we were young and dumb and we started putting on shows as Pinnacle Productions. Our very first show was the Grateful Dead, Buffalo Springfield and Blue Cheer and it was a big success. We kept doing them; we got Pink Floyd, Jefferson Airplane, Moby Grape, Country Joe, Cream, Jimi Hendrix, Traffic… we did everybody.

I got into a relationship with the agents in New York who were just starting up, such as Premier Talent. I would guarantee two weekends to an agent for them to bring a British band over, and then they'd get a couple of guarantees from somebody in New York and perhaps Bill Graham in San Francisco, and then they would have enough for maybe eight dates, which meant they could just barely afford to put the band on the plane and get them over here. A lot of times they couldn't even afford to bring the gear, and so sometimes you'd have to supply the backline for the bands. On the first date we did with Fleetwood Mac with Peter Green, they were the opening act and they couldn't bring any equipment, so I went and got them to deal with the guy that ran Acoustic Control to sponsor them and then all of a sudden they had their own amps rather than having to rent something every time they went into a city.

I remember talking to Frank Barsalona or one of the other agents and guaranteeing a couple of weekends to bring over Fleetwood Mac and the Jeff Beck Group. Being a Yardbirds nut, I was panting. And then I got a test pressing of the *Truth* album and went 'holy moly!' I put them on on a few dates and saw immediately the star quality of Rod Stewart as a front man and I got to know him a little bit. But the company tanked in 1968 and so I took a breather.

TRUTH
RELEASED 29 JULY 1968, USA

The first album by the Jeff Beck Group, credited solely to Jeff Beck, is released. It reaches 15 in the US album charts. Its UK release takes place some months later.

KINETIC PLAYGROUND, ELECTRIC THEATRE
11 OCTOBER 1968, CHICAGO, ILLINOIS

The Jeff Beck Group embark on their second North American tour, concluding on 8th December 1968 at the Fillmore West in San Francisco after 33 shows.

I WAS THERE: DANNY DRAHER, AGE 15
When I moved up to Chicago from Indianapolis, the neighbourhood I lived in in Chicago was full of Jeff Beck fans. There were a couple of good guitar players in my neighbourhood, and people who liked music and who were fans back from The Yardbirds days. We saw everybody that came through

there. Led Zeppelin, Johnny Winters, Alvin Lee, The Who. They were the best shows I ever saw. Jeff had the *Truth* album out. The line-up was Rod, Nicky Hopkins, Ron Wood and Micky Waller on drums. I didn't know anything about the group, but it was good singing, good playing, good blues. That group was an important step in Rod's career. It really propelled him on. I saw Led Zeppelin at the same venue a few months later. Jeff knocked me out a little bit more than Jimmy. It was a big sound on a big stage with a lot of heavy guitar stuff. If I had to choose my guy it would be Jeff Beck. I respect all the stuff that Jimmy does but he was just a different personality.

The site of the Electric Theatre is now apartment buildings.

ALEXANDRIA ROLLER RINK
20 OCTOBER 1968, ALEXANDRIA, VIRGINIA

I WAS THERE: NANCY DOUGHERTY

I lived in DC metro area, and we saw Jeff Beck at the Roller Rink in Alexandria, Virginia. We had to sit on the wooden floor because there were no seats. Rod Stewart was the singer. Nicky Hopkins was playing piano. The other band playing was Jethro Tull, and Ian Anderson was fine, but I couldn't take my eyes off Beck and his guitar. I particularly remember their clothing… tight bell bottoms on those skinny bodies.

BOSTON TEA PARTY
24 – 26 OCTOBER 1968, BOSTON, MASSACHUSETTS

I WAS THERE: LARRY CRONIN, AGE 18

I was 18 years old and I thought it was the best thing I had ever heard. It was Jeff Beck with Nicky Hopkins, Ron Wood and Rod Stewart. I can't remember who was on drums. But I do remember 'Beck's Bolero' stunning me, along with 'Shapes of Things' and 'Morning Dew', which stuck out for me with Rod singing. What really impressed me was his timing and how he blended with the band. I'm not sure if 'Beck's Bolero' was the encore. I remember thinking about the superior musicianship and how much better they were than the local groups I was accustomed to. I got a little buzz in the balcony.

I WAS THERE: BRAD CARDINI
I saw Rod at the Boston Tea Party with the Jeff Beck Group and with the Faces. Jeff was a guitar maestro and Rod's vocals are legendary.

SHRINE EXPOSITION HALL
29 & 30 NOVEMBER 1968, LOS ANGELES, CALIFORNIA

I WAS THERE: BABO GRUNDITZ
I heard the Jeff Beck Group in 1968 at the Shrine Auditorium. Rod Stewart was the lead singer. It was a very good show. They played 'Ain't Superstitious', 'Rock My Plimsoul' and 'Morning Dew'. It was hard blues rock à la psychedelia.

ALEXANDRA PALACE
31 DECEMBER 1968, LONDON, UK

During a Small Faces show, Steve Marriott walks off stage saying he's going to quit the band.

Halfway through the set, (Mariott) just threw his guitar down and walked off, leaving us like three lemons.
Kenney Jones

STONY BROOK, STATE UNIVERSITY OF NEW YORK
7 MARCH 1969, NEW YORK, NEW YORK

The Jeff Beck Group embark on their third US tour, playing exclusively East Coast shows.

SPRINGFIELD THEATRE
8 MARCH 1969, JERSEY, UK

The Small Faces play their final concert. Post-gig, Mac confirms that the Small Faces are over.

RON WOOD'S COTTAGE
APRIL 1969, HENLEY-ON-THAMES, UK

Ron Wood jams with Ronnie Lane, Ian McLagan and Kenney Jones.

FILLMORE EAST
2 MAY 1969, NEW YORK, NEW YORK

The Jeff Beck Group's fourth US tour is a week-long visit focusing on the East Coast and ending on 9th May in New Haven, Connecticut.

WOOLSEY HALL
9 MAY 1969, NEW HAVEN, CONNECTICUT

I WAS THERE: TONY DESILVIS
I was lucky, because in a three-month period I saw Jimi Hendrix, I saw Cream and I saw the Jeff Beck Group. Hendrix kicked ass – don't get me wrong – but I saw the Jeff Beck Group at Woolsey Hall too, and in my opinion they were better than Hendrix. Jeff was class. The way you see him play now is the way he played back then. Stewart on the other hand? I don't know how to explain Rod Stewart at the time, but everybody I ran into in the weeks and months after who were at the show all said the same thing – it was a great show. Jeff Beck kicked some serious ass. The opening band was meant to be a band called Rhinoceros but they were late so Jeff came out first and killed it. And when Rhinoceros came out,

people wanted to hear their first album with 'Apricot Brandy' on it, but they mainly played stuff off their second album, Satin Chickens, and nobody knew the songs. It was the middle of the show before they played 'Apricot Brandy'. They got booed off stage.

OLYMPIC SOUNDS STUDIOS & LANSDOWNE STUDIOS
JUNE 1969, LONDON, UK

In just one and a half weeks, Rod records the tracks for what will become his first solo album release. Ronnie Wood plays guitar on the album.

AERODROME
2 JULY 1969, SCHENECTADY, NEW YORK

The Jeff Beck Group embark on their fifth and what proves to be their final US tour.

SINGER BOWL
13 JULY 1969, NEW YORK, NEW YORK

I WAS THERE: NIC REEGER
I saw a show at the Singer Bowl with The Edwin Hawkins Singers, Ten Years After, The Jeff Beck Group with Rod Stewart and Ronnie Wood and headliners The Vanilla Fudge. When Jeff Beck came on, he did amazing stuff from *Beck-Ola* and was joined on stage by Carmine Appice, Alvin Lee's drummer Ric Lee and Jimmy Page, Robert Plant and John Bonham – four drummers playing! I had to pinch myself to see if I was dreaming. They did 'Train Kept A-Rollin'' and Bonzo stripped down to his Union Jack briefs. He had to be carried out on his drum stool because he wouldn't stop playing. He was still swinging his drumsticks!

TELL EVERYONE: A PEOPLE'S HISTORY OF THE FACES

I WAS THERE: STEPHEN WARNE

I grew up in Queens, a borough of New York. I wanted to see the Jeff Beck Group. I had first heard them on FM radio which in 1968, '69 was new in my house. I was lying on the floor in the living room when everybody was sleeping because overnight they played more underground-type stuff. I didn't hear it introduced but 'Plynth (Water Down ihe Drain)' came on, from *Beck-Ola*. When I heard that I said, 'Oh man, this is the greatest thing. Who's the black guy singing? Maybe it's one of the guys from The Temptations.' I just thought it had to be a black guy with that kind of throaty, very macho voice. Turns out it's Rod the Mod.

Then I saw that they were playing this gig at Singer Bowl, a large arena at Flushing Meadow which was originally built as part of the World's Fair but which has been rebuilt several times and is now used for the US tennis open. Sometimes they had these fairly large outdoor rock 'n' roll shows there on weekends, where they would put two or three groups together. The Jeff Beck Group played there on 13 July 1969. Vanilla Fudge headlined and the opening act was a gospel group called the Edwin Hawkins Singers – famous for 'Oh, Happy Day' – and they were followed by Ten Years After. I loved Alvin.

The show started in the late afternoon around 6.30pm and went on into the evening, finishing around 11pm. When Jeff Beck came out it suddenly seemed to get dark and the spotlights came on making it appear like a polished kind of performance. I remember Rod Stewart wore a cream-coloured suit and looked great. The way they looked and the way they were groomed reminded me a little bit of the Stones. Ron Wood wasn't famous then, but I said 'he's a really good bass player'. His bass playing stood out because it stayed close to the music as opposed to a jazzier Cream-type situation. And Micky Waller was on drums. I understood later that Rod made his first Rod Stewart solo album – *An Old Raincoat* – with Micky and with Ronnie.

They did numbers that I knew from the Jeff Beck Group and then a couple of what I thought were blues. I thought everybody wrote their own songs in those days. I thought The Beatles wrote 'Rock and Roll Music' until I started reading about them. Jeff Beck did a slow blues thing and in the middle of it started the theme from The Beverly

Hillbillies which was a real kitschy thing like 'Dueling Banjos' before going back into the blues song. That knocked me out.

Right towards the end of their set they started to play 'Jailhouse Rock', which was also on *Beck-Ola*. Jeff Beck wandered behind his amplifiers and brought a guy out and it was Jimmy Page, holding an old-fashioned martini glass. Zeppelin were really new at the time but I had seen them at the Fillmore East the previous winter. Jeff Beck put one of his guitars around Jimmy, who began laughing and put his cocktail down and started playing. So now they're both playing guitar and who steps out but Robert Plant? So now Robert Plant is sharing the microphone with Rod Stewart. This is a dream situation for a young rock 'n' roll fan. I was just blown away.

Then John Bonham came out. He must have been pretty wasted because he was falling all over the drum kit. He started playing drums but also taking his clothes off. So he's playing and laughing and throwing his shirt off, and then he started taking his pants off revealing the black stretch shorts he had on for underwear. It looked like a bathing suit. He carried on playing, sat down at the drum kit, and then someone came up behind him and pulled his shorts down, so now his ass was hanging out. It was just this cacophony of colours and sounds. And then Alvin Lee came out, and this was not even the main band!

Right towards the end of 'Jailhouse Rock', Rod Stewart was singing about the cops in the prison. Now this show had cops in front of the stage like security. They didn't like any of the music but they were always at these outdoor shows. One of these guys was leaning against the stage and Rod Stewart was behind him and came over and – wham! – knocked the guy's hat off. The cop's hat went flying. The cop turned around like he was going to kill Rod Stewart but Rod just laughed, backed up and kept on with the song. The energy was incredible.

I saw that they were booked to play Woodstock and I said, 'I've got to go to this festival.' As soon as I told my parents what it was, they said 'you're not leaving the house'. I thought, 'These guys are great. They're going to be around for a long while.' And about a month later they split up. They never played Woodstock because they split up right before then, and this only a month after I had seen them.

GRANDE BALLROOM
26 JULY 1969, DETROIT MICHIGAN

The Jeff Beck Group's final US show. Ronnie Wood is then sacked by Beck, and Rod decides to quit, Jeff having flown back to England.

BERMONDSEY
AUGUST 1969, LONDON, UK

The Faces (without Rod) rehearse at the Rolling Stones rehearsal space.

ROD & RONNIE JOIN THE FACES
18 OCTOBER 1969, LONDON, UK

Rod Stewart and Ronnie Wood are officially unveiled as members of the Faces.

NEW LEAD SINGER JOINS THE FACES

ROD STEWART, formerly with the Jeff Beck Group, has joined the Small Faces as their new lead singer — thus filling the role previously occupied by Steve Marriott. In an attempt to present a new image, the group is to change its name, but a new title has not yet been set. As we close for press, the NME understands that the Faces have left Immediate and have signed a lucrative world-wide deal with the giant Warner-Reprise company.

October 18, 1969

Press cutting announcing Rod 'joining the Small Faces'

OLYMPIC SOUND STUDIOS
OCTOBER 1969, LONDON, UK

The Faces – Rod Stewart, Ronnie Wood, Ronnie Lane, Ian McLagan and Kenney Jones – record three demos with Glyn Johns producing/engineering.

HANWELL COMMUNITY CENTRE
OCTOBER & NOVEMBER 1969, LONDON, UK

The Faces begin rehearsals.

UNKNOWN VENUE
10 NOVEMBER 1969, ILNAU-EFFRETIKON, SWITZERLAND

In the space of eleven days, the Faces perform nine shows in Switzerland, including shows in Basel, Bern, Geneva and Lausanne.

I WAS THERE: SANDIE RITTER

I was a Small Faces fan but I had an inkling that the Small Faces were going to split up before it happened. I was 14 or 15. I don't really think it clearly through at that stage. I remember going to what I think was the last Small Faces gig in England, although I gather they played one or two more shows in Europe after that. Ronnie Lane seemed very drunk that night. He was hitting his bass guitar and not making that much sound at all, but with hindsight that could've been the multiple sclerosis. They gave me and my friend a lift to the station. We had to argue for that, otherwise we wouldn't have caught our train back to London, and it was obvious that things weren't right. I remember sitting on the train with my friend Cathy and saying, 'It's like the end of the holiday.' So, yes, I knew the Small Faces were coming to an end. But I didn't know what was happening next.

TELL EVERYONE: A PEOPLE'S HISTORY OF THE FACES

Life at that point was a lot of fun because I lived in a suburb of London and I was going out to listen to a lot of music. I got very into underground music amongst other things. Occasionally I would go to Steve's (Marriott) and take him a present on his birthday or something. He would invite me in and Jenny, his wife, would make me a cup of tea and all the cats would sit on my lap, and he would play me some music. He got me interested in people like Spooky Tooth and Janis Ian that I would never have known about otherwise, because it just wasn't part of my world. Because I was that much younger, and I didn't have any siblings so there was no one to influence me or inspire me. My mum was into classical music and Frank Sinatra and stuff like that.

When the Small Faces ended, Steve created Humble Pie and I went to their first concerts, in Belgium and Holland. By then I was 16, but my parents were very liberal and let me do more or less what I wanted.

The Faces came along maybe six months later. The first time I saw the Faces was when they did their first official concerts in Switzerland. By then it was a normal thing for me to do so I said, 'I'll go over to those concerts. It must've been in the music press, because I don't know how else I would've known, although I might have been phoning the management, because I did find out which flight they were catching to Switzerland and made sure I was on the same flight. I remember being at Heathrow Airport and the bar was this tiny thing where maybe five or six people could stand at the bar. It's not like Heathrow now. Mac introduced me to Rod and Ronnie, who were propping up the bar. They seemed very different to the others, looking or pretending to look more worldly. Of course, they had travelled to the States with Jeff Beck and so I guess they had reason to feel that superiority. They looked at me like, 'Well, who do you think you are?' and I ignored them and just thought, 'How stupid.'

I had seen the Jeff Beck Group a few times in London. I'd been a Jeff Beck fan since the start. The show I remember most is one at the Lyceum, because I was recording it on a silly little tape machine, and Rod looked at me and said, 'Oh, look at that little boy down there,' and I thought 'thanks very much'. And I must've seen them at the Marquee as well, because at that point I was at the Marquee practically every night of the week. I saw King Crimson, The Nice and you name it.

When they were in Switzerland, and I have no idea how this happened, I was sitting in Ronnie Lane's bedroom and he was lying on the bed resting and Ronnie Wood came in. We were having this conversation and I remember saying to Ronnie Wood, 'You know, you're my favourite bass guitarist. You play so well.' And he said, 'I will play the guitar as well as that.' He was still working on his guitar playing then. Thinking back, it was probably not the best of things to say in front of Ronnie Lane, but Ronnie Wood was a more accomplished musician than Ronnie Lane. I wasn't criticising his guitar playing. I was just saying that when he was in Jeff Beck, he was a brilliant bass player.

They were playing stuff off the first Faces album on that tour. They didn't play any Small Faces material whatsoever. They weren't billed as the Small Faces, as I recall. But in Switzerland, I probably wasn't paying much attention. I was trying to get from one place to another, which was quite a challenge. At one point I hitchhiked across a mountain! My German and my French were very, very basic, but somehow or other I was able to make myself understood. But it was mad, and I didn't really think it through clearly. My parents didn't know that I was hitchhiking around Switzerland.

I only went to three or four of the concerts. They might have done one or two more. And then, when they started touring England, I saw them a lot. They started off playing in small clubs and universities. It was wonderful. I love the first album. It's probably my favourite one, because of Ronnie Lane's influences.

THE GREYHOUND
29 NOVEMBER 1969, CROYDON, UK

The first ever UK performance by the Stewart-Wood-Lane-McLagan-Jones line up. The Faces go on to perform three more shows (in Lucerne, Switzerland and in Molesworth, Cambridgeshire and in London) before the year is out.

BOSTON TEA PARTY
10 JANUARY 1970, BOSTON, MASSACHUSETTS

I WAS THERE: SANDY FAULHABER

There was a surprise birthday party for Rod – and my 25th – January 10 1970 after their appearance at Tea Party. The birthday cake had 25 joints in it.

Rod was on a publicity junket for his first solo album, entitled **The Rod Stewart Album** *in the US.*

MOTHERS
25 JANUARY 1970, BIRMINGHAM, UK

I WAS THERE: PHILIP TARMEY

I saw them at Mother's in Birmingham. Ronnie Lane got down from the stage and danced with one of the bar staff.

I WAS THERE: BRIAN REES

We had so much music and there were so many bands. I don't know how we did all we did at that age, but we did. I was a soul boy at first. And by the age of 14 I was going out at least once a week to a club or to see a band. When I was 15, I was just out all the time even though I was still at school. In 1966 and '67, the music scene was changing dramatically. I was a Mod so I got into the Small Faces. I saw them at a place called Bearwood Ice Rink, which they used to cover over for concerts, and it was fantastic. I used to go down and visit Moss Bros and get measured up for a suit. That's what being a Mod was all about. At 15 I had three suits which were all hand made. You'd go up every Saturday and pay two and six (13p) on your suit. It was totally about the look.

    I loved to dance because Mods loved to dance. The boys would stand around the outside and the girls would dance. But Mods tended to dance. I got in with this famous DJ, Bobby Childs, and because me and my mates could dance, and because of my contacts with him and with this promoter called Pete Martin, we used to get in everywhere for free, which is a great bonus when you're a kid. We'd turn up and we'd get the guys dancing. We'd get everybody dancing.

You're a Mod so you're into the Small Faces, you're into The Who, you're into this, that and the other. And then you got a bit older. I think I was 17 when I saw the Faces at what I believe was their second ever British gig, at Mother's Club in Erdington. Everything in music has happened there. Pink Floyd recorded *Umma Gumma* there, in front of 69 people. Can you believe that? It was only a small place.

Pre-Facebook, pre-YouTube, pre-anything really, your bible every week used to be the *NME*. There were gigs everywhere, especially in Birmingham. You could see a band every night of your life and I very often did. I saw the Faces were playing at Mothers, which I used to go to a fair bit. So being a Small Faces fan, and because I already knew Rod Stewart through Jeff Beck, I thought I'd go and see them.

I would say there was no more than 200 people there, because I stood right in front of Rod Stewart, two foot away from him, and I wasn't crowded out. I thought, 'He's got a canny voice.' I was just transfixed. He was in a pink suit with some nasty embroidery on it. And he even played the banjo on one track, but don't ask me what that was. I hadn't bought the album, *First Step*, and so I didn't know any of the songs on the night.

We were going from being Mods into hippies, so I went out and bought the album. I worked out that they'd played 'Flying' and I thought, 'Christ, this boy can sing.' They had the dress sense that Mods had mixed with the rawness of the hippy scene, R&B-ish, like the Mod life was all about and just slightly away from what the hippy scene was becoming – the Genesis and the Pink Floyd. That suited me down to a tee and I started following them.

REFECTORY HALL, UNIVERSITY OF LEEDS
7 FEBRUARY 1970, LEEDS, UK

I WAS THERE: GERALD CLEAVER
I was studying at Leeds University. The refectory was, and still may be, where Leeds University Students Union promoted live bands for their

students on Saturday nights. On weekdays it was, as the name implies, used as a place for feeding the students. But on Saturdays the dining tables were stacked up at one end of the room as a makeshift stage and bands would play to the students, either sat on the floor or stood up. Bands like The Who, Rolling Stones, Led Zeppelin, Pink Floyd, Humble Pie and even the many members of Ginger Baker's Airforce were able to fit onto these tables and play their music. And the Faces.

As I recall, when the Faces gig was advertised nobody had heard of them. Unlike other bill toppers, who were well known to students or had had hit singles and/or albums, the Faces were an unknown band. I am not too sure whether they were even billed as the Faces in the advertising. Anyway, nobody knew who they were, but we all were aware of the support act, the Keef Hartley Band. They were a jazz rock band, had played Woodstock, and had also been played on John Peel's *Top Gear* radio programme. So lots of students attended the gig to see them play. It wasn't expensive, probably no more than seven and six – 35p in pre-decimal money!

So the audience went to see Keef Hartley Band, and very good they were too. Many members of the audience had already resolved to either stay in the bar or leave the students union building after their set, and not bother with the Faces. That's what I did. I left and went to a party; it was Saturday night after all. So many people had left, the band were playing to only a small crowd. The doors were open, presumably to let others in to swell the numbers. My friends and I, on our way to the party, actually popped back in to listen. The audience were pretty unruly and jeering, slow handclapping. Keef Hartley Band were a pretty tight band, with well-arranged songs. No insult intended, but the Faces weren't like that. They were pretty sloppy, or loose – inebriated even. They would go on to sell records and sell out large venues and entertain thousands of fans. But not that night.

My abiding memory is of Rod Stewart appealing to the small audience, 'Come on, give us a chance.' I am still ashamed to say that we didn't.

SCANDINAVIAN TOUR
14 – 22 FEBRUARY 1970, DENMARK & SWEDEN

The Faces travel to Scandinavia to play five dates.

'FLYING'
RELEASED 20 FEBRUARY 1970

'Flying', released as a precursor to the first Faces album, fails to dent the UK singles chart.

LYCEUM BALLROOM
1 MARCH 1970, LONDON, UK

I WAS THERE: JIM PILCHER

My love for the Faces grew out of admiration for the Small Faces who I was lucky enough to see twice in Wellington in 1968. Steve Marriott and Ronnie 'Plonk' Lane were the heart and soul of that group and together wrote some classic songs that still stand the test of time to this day. Sadly, the Small Faces never made it big in the States but 'Itchycoo Park' made the charts for them. When Steve left to join up with Peter Frampton to form Humble Pie, the other three lads were at a bit of a loose end of what to do as far as forming a new group was concerned. Enter Ronnie Wood who had been playing bass guitar with the Jeff Beck Group. Still short of a vocalist, as only Plonk could sing a bit, they started to look for a potential front man when Ronnie Wood brought Rod Stewart along to a practise session and from that the Faces were born. I first saw them live at the Lyceum in London in 1970.

The place was packed in anticipation that something special was about to unfold – which it did. These guys really turned it on that night with a set of songs, some of which I knew and some I didn't. They were helped along by several bottles of various alcoholic beverages from wine, spirits, beer and whatever else was available. The music produced that night still resonates with me to this day – songs like 'Cut Across Shorty', 'Three Button Hand Me Down', 'Plynth', 'Stone', etc.

I was lucky enough to see the Faces eight times in London – twice at the Marquee Club and the other six times at the Lyceum. Over that time, the music changed as Rod's solo career started to gather momentum and some of his songs were incorporated into the Faces set list, and I think it was at this stage that Ronnie Lane starting looking at other opportunities. The band was also beginning to be known as Rod Stewart and the Faces.

Over the 18 months I saw them, they were an unpredictable excitement machine, one that only comes around very rarely. As a band, they always had so much fun on stage and interacted so well with their audience, which can be witnessed on some live DVDs that they recorded. The band became huge in the States, but as a live act rather than a chart-topping group. And as Rod's solo songs began to chart in America, Ronnie Lane left the group to form his own band, Slim Chance. He was replaced in the Faces by a Japanese bass player, Tetsu Yamauchi.

The songs changed during this time and the magic was gone when Ronnie left. But they left some classics in their wake, the biggest being 'Stay With Me'. As we know, Rod has gone on to have a massive solo career from his humble beginnings, as has Ronnie Wood with the Rolling Stones – who Ian McLagan sometimes played with – and Kenney Jones had a brief spell with The Who. Sadly, Ronnie Lane and Ian McLagan are no longer with us.

Steve Marriott, after enjoying huge success in the States with Humble Pie, returned to England to front another couple of bands (including a Small Faces reunion). He sadly died in a house fire at his London home. RIP all those that rode the magical journey that was the Small Faces and the Faces. I was so lucky to have seen both groups live and to have lived to tell the tale.

The new revitalised Faces are even better than the older and smaller variety. That is the glad tidings I bring from their performance at London's Lyceum. The group sounds heavier and tighter than of old and much of the credit must go to guitarist Ronnie Wood. Rod Stewart not only sounds just right as the new singer but is one of the best pop showmen.

Melody Maker review of the Lyceum show

COOKS FERRY INN
16 MARCH 1970, LONDON, UK

I WAS THERE: SANDIE RITTER

I saw them in clubs and I'd go to some universities to see them, mainly around the London area. They were playing so many places around London that there wasn't any need to travel any further. Then Pete Buckland, who was the sound engineer, said, 'You're always here early queueing. Just knock on the backstage door and ask for me and I'll let you in.' So from there on in, I'd sit at the side of the stage watching the concerts, except in London, because of all the music industry people and family and friends and so on.

I didn't have to pay for a ticket after that. In hindsight, that probably wasn't the best of things because it separated me from the rest of the fans. I never knew any of the fans that went, because I never in the audience. Also, I didn't drink very much then. I was on more of a spiritual path, so I was a bit out of sync with everybody because I wasn't drinking. I was taking drugs and smoking hash. I felt that alcohol dulled the senses and everything was about raising one's consciousness, as it pretty much was for a lot of people in that era. Ronnie Lane was on that wavelength too, although he was drinking heavily. But the rest of the band were just not on that level at all. They were just having fun and partying.

I saw a few concerts where they were 'a bit dishevelled', but it didn't matter. It was part of the music. The only thing I noticed that was a bit odd was that Mac's hands would sometimes go down on the keyboards quite heavily, and it would almost sound like his hands were going through the keyboard. But I thought I was just hearing it because of whatever drug I was on. Now I think it was probably the influence of alcohol, but it didn't upset the sound. It was part of the sound. They still played very well. It's rock 'n' roll. It's not like going to a Yes concert where you have to be completely on the ball and everything has to be just so. It's pretty straightforward music. And Ronnie Wood was used to playing in that sort of state. He'd grown up in that kind of environment where people drink and play. It was just like one big party.

FIRST STEP
RELEASED 21 MARCH 1970

Credited to the Small Faces on the North American release (and subsequent reissues), the cover of the first Faces album shows Ronnie Wood holding a copy of Geoffrey Sisley's guitar tutorial, First Step: How to Play the Guitar Plectrum Style.

The album reached number 119 on the Billboard 200, Rolling Stone describing the band as 'highly derivative' and playing 'with more control than soul… They know exactly what they are doing and they do it well, as good musicians should, but the precision and purity of their sound seems a little sterile, and they lack the drive and power to make their music work without subtleties.'

MOTHERS CLUB
21 MARCH 1970, BIRMINGHAM, UK

I WAS THERE: MIKE NEWEY

I saw the Faces live at a small venue called Mothers in Erdington, Birmingham in 1970. Mothers Club in Erdington High Street, Birmingham was a well renowned venue for some very big acts but was only open from August 1968 to January 1971. A number of us used to spend much of our time there and it was Saturday 21st March 1970 when the Faces were on there. There were two support acts. One name escapes me but the other was a band called Clarke Hutchinson Band, who were a really good blues rock outfit. Mothers was only a small club (previously called the Carlton Ballroom) and it was situated on the first floor above a furniture shop. It probably only held around 150 people.

Mike Newey saw the Faces at Birmingham's legendary Mothers Club

TELL EVERYONE: A PEOPLE'S HISTORY OF THE FACES

My friend Fred and myself were literally at the very front, no more than two metres away from the band. Rod came out wearing a banjo around his neck and the banjo strap was just a length of sisal string! They were exciting and sounded terrific. Ronnie Wood (I was reminded) was playing a pink Strat. I particularly remember listening intently to Ronnie Lane's bass playing. He reminded me of the style of Andy Fraser of Free. They were a very melodic and tuneful rhythm section. Fred remembers that they were a smart looking band – well dressed, polished shoes and sharp looking, not like the usual dress code. 'Flying' had just been released and was in the charts at the time.

I WAS THERE: FRED ROBINSON, AGE 16

My school friend, Mike Newey, and myself were just 16 at the time, seriously getting into progressive rock, blues and good guitar-based bands. We were both learning to play guitar, and watched bands whenever we could. It was an amazing privilege to have such a special venue, Mothers, within three miles of our homes. All we talked about was 'who's appearing this week?' Regulars were The Groundhogs, Bakerloo Blues Line (Clem Clempson was from nearby Tamworth), Fairport Convention and DJ John Peel. This list was endless. The venue was always busy, but comfortable. The musicians would be chatting and drinking at the bar. Then we saw the Faces advertised. We couldn't miss that one.

Fred Robinson's membership card for Mothers

That night, Mike and I sat on the floor (I think), about three rows from the front of the stage. The support band were Clark Hutchinson Band. We watched them set up, pulling curly guitar leads out of big brown paper bags. There were no flight cases in those days! I also remember the guitarist's amp failed at sound check and Ronnie Wood let him plug into his amp. Their set was amazing – powerful electric blues projecting from their sweaty long-haired and scruffy image; all very normal!

When the Faces took to the stage, the first thing I was struck by was Rod Stewart's smart shiny brogue-styled shoes and the band's image, which was smart compared to most of the other bands. Whilst I can't recall their entire set list, I remember that it was powerful rhythm and blues, soulful and very special. The one song that I recall clearly was 'Flying', which was in the charts at the time, or just had been. I always liked that song and we don't seem to hear it played much.

The atmosphere was buzzing the whole evening. Sitting near the front, we were able to watch the band's every move. The band members all communicated with each other so well, and it was all so much fun, slick and professional. It was a great concert and a night that I'll never forget, and which I still talk about often.

Mothers continued until January 1971 and we saw some great bands there during those special formative years of our teens. The premises are still there today, now being a furniture showroom. The owners are aware of its history, and it is possible to work out the location of the stage. I took my wife there a few years ago, just to show her – and I didn't buy any furniture! I still have my Mothers' membership card.

VARSITY ARENA
25 MARCH 1970, TORONTO, CANADA

The Faces embark on their first North American tour, concluding on 30th May 1970 after 28 shows.

We just went on and played rock 'n' roll and relaxed, because as an opening act you've got nobody chewing your heels and nobody to follow.
Ronnie Lane

We organised the first tour so that the places of most importance – the gigs that had to be really good – came at just the right time… if we had gone straight into the Fillmore East and given a dud show it would have had a bad effect on the band.
Ronnie Wood

A FARM
MARCH 1970, PEACHAM, VERMONT

I WAS THERE: MARK RICHARDSON

In early 1970, before the band kicked off their US tour, they took up residence in a small Vermont town. It was all hush hush, but one of my friends knew who owned the farm and we drove over a few times in my '64 VW bug from Montpelier to sit in the barn and watch them rehearse their set. The band was so new that some of their gear was still stamped Small Faces and other pieces of equipment were stamped Jeff Beck Group. We knew not to do anything but listen and applaud their performances, and we felt privileged to be there. It was fun indeed to occasionally talk with the guys during a break or when they were finished for the night. For a bunch of locals, we certainly didn't want to wear out our welcome. Before they left, we heard their set from beginning to end, and I remember loving every minute of it. I was back in Boston when they played there. Being a fan in the crowd was a little bit sweeter knowing the work they had done to make it happen.

TEA PARTY
26 – 28 MARCH 1970, BOSTON, MASSACHUSETTS

I WAS THERE: STEVE BREMNER

Rod Stewart had just joined when I saw them, at a small place in Boston called the Boston Tea Party. This was a great place that brought in major acts. They were the opener for Lee Michaels, a keyboard/drummer duo who were hot at the time. That was my time period; I got out of high school in '70 and saw Pink Floyd, Jethro Tull, ELP, Yes, Savoy Brown and others. I saw Jimi twice too, something I still brag about!

At the Tea Party in 1970, Rod was already getting top billing

TELL EVERYONE: A PEOPLE'S HISTORY OF THE FACES

I WAS THERE: ALICE DALY

I saw them at the Tea Party. I think they were passing a bottle of Irish Mist around onstage and they were having more fun than any band ever. They were very loose and happy.

I WAS THERE: RICH FINKEL NIEDEL

What I remember beside the fantastic music was that both Rod and Ron were wearing clogs. At that time, clogs were not really popular especially for men. I thought, 'How cool is that?'

I WAS THERE: DAVID KINSMAN

I saw them with Rod Stewart at the Boston Tea Party. I think it was their first US appearance with Rod. I don't remember a lot about the show except that Rod was pretty drunk. The Faces sounded good. I had been a fan of the Small Faces and especially liked the album *Ogden's Nut Gone Flake*. I was with the band Ill Wind and that album was a favourite at the band house.

I WAS THERE: FRED JEFFERY

I saw them at one of the March 1970 Tea Party concerts. Zephyr opened, and Lee Michaels followed the Faces. It was an amazing performance. I remember Ron Wood, with a sublime smile on his face, playing slide on 'Around the Plynth'. Back then it was so intimate as we were within several feet of the stage. At some point, Rod split the rear of his pants and went off and changed. I love that first album. I still have the poster.

I WAS THERE: LAURENCE TREGLIA

I saw them in Boston and Rod Stewart split his pants!

I WAS THERE: FRED JOHANSON

I worked at the Lansdowne Street Tea Party as, among other things, the janitor. The Faces were playing a three day stand and were doing a sound check/rehearsal one day while I was working. They took a break and Rod Stewart said 'let's play' and tossed a soccer ball out on the floor. The band and I scrimmaged for a while and I was way over my head. I didn't know then how good a footballer Stewart was. I was smoked, as were other things with them.

I WAS THERE: STANLEY KASTNER

I played soccer with the Faces in the empty Boston Tea Party after a sound check. Wow!

YOUTH CENTER
31 MARCH 1970, WHEATON, MARYLAND

I WAS THERE: ROSS NICHOLS, AGE 12

I saw Faces in 1970 and again on their farewell tour in '75. The 1970 show was in a small gym. I stood just a foot away in front of Rod. The stage was only a foot high. I saw Iggy and the Stooges at the same place, which was also wild. Grin with Nils Lofgren opened the Faces show. Nils is a local hero and I saw him many times. The Faces were seemingly intoxicated. The gym was in a residential area and Rod and Woody played soccer on the lawn the next morning.

EASTOWN THEATER
3 & 4 APRIL 1970, DETROIT, MICHIGAN

I WAS THERE: BILL LONGACRE, AGE 18

I saw the Faces a few times at the Eastown Theater. I was a young 18-year-old. We lived three hours away in Kalamazoo, so the trip alone was a good time. I was playing in a band so we just snuck into Detroit for a few hours. Eastown was amazing with all the limos and city chicks... Nobody from my area really was into feminine guys like these and guys like Bowie. The whole first (ground) floor had the seats removed so you could work your way up to the stage. Rod shared his champagne. The Faces were great and Rod's best back up. It felt kinda wrong for him to be with anyone else after that.

The Eastown Theater was an awesome and rather small, intimate venue. Large stadiums just are not the same. You can get better seats at home now, watching a show on TV. And there are no crazy huge crowds to watch a screen hanging above you.

TELL EVERYONE: A PEOPLE'S HISTORY OF THE FACES

I WAS THERE: MICHAEL SPICER

They were my favourite band. I first loved the Small Faces – Ronnie Lane was my hero. When Marriott left, I gravitated to the Faces after Ron Wood and Stewart joined. I saw them eight times. Most fans liked Rod as leader, but for me it was Ronnie Lane. I saw them in Detroit mostly, several times at the Eastown Theater but also at the Crisler Arena in Ann Arbor and one time in Cincinnati. Somehow, I missed them at my favourite venue, the Grande Ballroom in Detroit, which I hear was epic. (*They never played the Grande.*) We sat right with the bands of the day, up close and personal. I cannot pinpoint the first show I saw exactly – it was at the Eastown Theater in Detroit in 1970 and the Faces played there seven times in total that year. They had a bar set up on stage with the band, I recall, complete with bartender. The *First Step* album had just come out.

I also saw the *Long Player* tour and then the *Nod's as Good as a Wink* and *Ooh La La* tours. I also saw the tour in support of the *Gasoline Alley* album and the *Every Picture Tells a Story* tour. And in '75, after my hero Ronnie Lane quit, I saw them at Cobo Hall in Detroit. But I missed Ronnie – the band was not the same.

In '79, I saw the New Barbarians in Ann Arbor, Michigan, featuring two Faces – Ronnie Wood and Ian McLagan – along with Keith Richards and Stanley Clarke. Two Faces were better than none.

I WAS THERE: KEN PHELPS, AGE 14

My first gig of theirs? The *First Step* tour in Detroit. I was 14. I saw them between 44 to 50 times as I can remember, not having all of my tickets. I used to hitch hike all over North America to see them if I did not have travelling money. I first met them in 1970 at a Holiday Inn, where I was introduced by my girlfriend, who loved them. I was scared to talk to them at first, but my girlfriend back then and who was a few years older than me introduced me. I was hooked from then on. They were nice, fun lads, all funny buggers, and very approachable. I saw them a lot and partied with them. Holiday Inns were a blast. I never saw anything like it. One thing they liked doing in the early days was putting all the furniture in the hallway and then setting it up to use it like it was one big room. It was a blast.

Their live show was not like other rock bands, as Faces came out and grabbed you with their energy from the flowing music. It was incredible and infectious. There is no doubt they were the best, in a time when bands were great. Their live show was so powerful; it pulled you in with every tune!

I WAS THERE: JAMES KELLEY

Back in the day my band Lincoln Zephyr opened for them a few times up in the north east. As an upstate New York regional act, we opened for a lot of big name bands. The Faces were a great group of guys. At the time I was the only guy in our band without a wife. Woody at the time was also single. Because of this, after gigs we found ourselves hanging and trolling together and we had some crazy chick adventures. One time, somebody stole his leather jacket from the dressing room. It was a city where I knew a lot of people and, with the help of friends, I was able to track it down and get it back for him. The thief had a bad night. Ah! The good old rock and roll road days. Wild times.

I WAS THERE: SACH DRAFFEN

They played the Eastown Theater about the same time that Joe Cocker, Leon Russell played there on the *Mad Dogs & Englishmen* tour. I was a fan of Jeff Beck and Rod Stewart and it was a great experience for me. The theatre had all of the lower floor seats removed, so you could be right there within five feet of the stage. There were a lot of real hot groups coming though Detroit in that era, and Motown was rocking.

FILLMORE NORTH
5 APRIL 1970, TORONTO, CANADA

Mac, with a conviction for drugs, is held at customs and strip searched, after which he is moved on to New York. He misses the Toronto show: 'That's the only Faces gig I didn't play.'

TELL EVERYONE: A PEOPLE'S HISTORY OF THE FACES

PALLADIUM
17 & 18 APRIL 1970, BIRMINGHAM, MICHIGAN

I WAS THERE: DAN MURPHY

I used to move gear for many rock 'n' roll bands when they came to Detroit. I was known as Detroit Dan. Whilst working with Faces, I was backstage with Rod Stewart, Ron Wood and their manager at the Birmingham Palladium. They were looking for more songs to do. I suggested they do 'I'm Losing You', which was originally done by The Temptations and also by Rare Earth. I thought it would be a perfect fit. I told them to listen to both versions. They did, and put it on their next album. Rod did many Motown songs after this tip.

I WAS THERE: BILL LYNN

The band Julia opened for them. I remember very little about the Faces, except that Rod Stewart was fairly new.

I WAS THERE: NORM LYLE

The Palladium was a small, 800 capacity club run by Punch Andrews, Bob Seger's manager. The Faces were touring under the original name of the Small Faces. It was an amazing performance, and included material from the first Faces albums plus Rod's two solo efforts.

I WAS THERE: HERMAN DALDIN

I was a musician and close friends with many bands and performers of that era. I was close to Badfinger and met the Faces in 1970. I was closest to Ian but I also was friends of Rod and Ron. I saw them first at a club in Birmingham, Michigan called the Palladium. They were in town regularly as it's a Detroit suburb and Detroit was home to many other venues as well, including the Grande

Herman Daldin with Rod

Ballroom and the Cobo Hall. When they were in town, I would go and hang out with them.

I was at Rod's birthday celebration in the Ponchatrain Hotel following a show at Cobo Hall. They were a party band, drank a lot and I even traded a cheap bottle of Boone's Farm Apple Wine with Rod for Courvoisier. We ended up cutting the cake and later tossed pieces from the window of the very high floor room onto unsuspecting pedestrians walking far below. I loved their music and passion as well as the fun, playful performances they gave. They were very professional for such young men but also so playful, energetic and young at the same time.

ACTION HOUSE
24 & 25 APRIL 1970, ISLAND PARK, LONG ISLAND, NEW YORK

I WAS THERE: RANDY DANNENFELSER

Late April 1970, a cold and rainy late afternoon on the South Shore of Long Island New York. Barb and I were bored ornery in our garden apartment, feeling trapped by the bad weather. We had been married 16 months and Barb was pregnant for the past six, already carrying large. We were in our early twenties, babies having a baby, a couple of kids living the sentiment of the Beach Boys' 'Wouldn't It Be Nice' while navigating the harsh realities the song didn't mention. The 'morning sickness' phase of Barb's pregnancy had morphed into the 'constantly uncomfortable' phase. She needed something to put her discomfort in the back of her mind for a little while and I needed something to forget about the bad mood her incessant complaining about it was putting me in. That something turned out to be the Small Faces.

There in the local entertainment newspaper I'd picked up at the record shop downtown was an advert for the upcoming roster of bands at the Action House, a boxy music-and-booze joint 30 minutes by car from our L-shaped hole-in-the-wall. The first band listed was the Small Faces 'with Rod Stewart', playing their second of two nights there, and commencing in just a few hours.

I'd been a Small Faces fan from when I first heard Steve Marriott belt out 'Sha-La-La-La-Lee' on a local FM radio station's weekly half-hour *Things from England* segment three years earlier. I thought Marriott's voice and Ian McLagan's rock bluesy Hammond organ through a trippy Leslie tone cabinet were the most awesomely distinctive rock sounds I'd heard since The Who became my favourite band in the mid-Sixties. I was aware that Marriott had left the group a little over a year earlier, and that the remaining three members had merged with members of the Jeff Beck Group and pruned the contingent down to five members. ('Took two good musicians to replace little Stevie,' said I, ever the Marriott supporter.) But the new band were only calling themselves the Small Faces on this, their first American tour, at the insistence of their record company; the thinking being, they would pull in maximum name recognition for the new album they were supporting with the 'familiar' name. In actuality, Rod Stewart's voice changed the sound of the band so much that they couldn't do any numbers from the Marriott days even if they'd wanted to – which clearly, as it turned out, they didn't.

And even knowing all this, I'd hoped they might try a Marriott song or two anyway, which is why I suggested to Barb that we break loose from our digs and check them out. Barb, not being too familiar with the Small Faces but being very much the adventurous type said, 'Sure, why not?' After a TV dinner and a soft drink, we were off in the rain to the show.

Did I mention that we'd never been to the Action House before? From the muddy parking lot, the place looked like a converted factory warehouse. Once inside, the atmosphere was that of a huge high school gym but with liquor. When I squeeze my memory, I see a long bar in the back of the room and at the opposite end a small stage more suited for a small-town grange hall, with a small staircase to the left and an old red velvet theatre curtain partially drawn on either side. What the room didn't have were chairs. It was standing only.

We entered the hall to the blare of the opening band. It immediately became difficult to hear a spoken word. Barb made a beeline for the ladies room. I made my way to the bar and somehow communicated my drink request through the din. When Barb returned, we sipped our Seven and Sevens and after a few minutes she asked me to find her a chair. The warm-up band ended and the Small Faces crew began setting up. After casing the room, I determined that there were no chairs to be had and told same to Barb. She gave me a look of desperation and told me I *had* to find one – she couldn't remain standing much longer. I went to an assistant manager – a short, thin ferret just beyond college age – and pleaded for help. When he saw how wobbly my pregnant wife had become, he put the chair hunt into high gear. No luck. We went to his boss, the manager, a mob-dressed type in his mid-thirties, who looked over at Barb and came up with an instant solution.

There was one seat in the house he knew of – it was the bench in front of the piano, just off stage right. By now, the Small Faces had begun their set (with what might have been 'Three Button Hand Me Down'). They were excruciatingly loud, and this was back in the days when earplugs were considered uncool. The mob-dresser took us all the way to a back corner of the room so that we could at least barely hear him and asked if we would mind sitting close to the amps. I said 'no' and Barb just shook her head. Then he led us to the stage, moving patrons out of his way with determination, up the stairs, and then to the bench seat – mostly behind the drawn curtain but no more than 15 feet from Rod Stewart's mic stand.

Barb sat and I stood next to her as the band played 'Wicked Messenger'. The stage area was small and the equipment was so bunched in, I couldn't make eye contact with McLagan or Ronnie Lane on stage left, or Kenney Jones on a low riser; however, Stewart and Ron Wood were in direct sight, in front of us to our left. Because they were cramped, Rod couldn't do his usual dancing and strutting around the stage. He spent most of the night shimmying up and down behind his mic stand.

Amazingly, my ears began to adjust to the assault. We still couldn't understand speech, but at least there was no pain accompanying the sound, which had been my fear. Probably, it was because we were now positioned to the side of the amps.

Rod and Wood glanced over at us as we were being seated but neither paid any attention to us for the next couple of songs. Somewhere in the set, I think I remember hearing 'Devotion', but I wouldn't make book on it. I do know for sure they didn't play any Marriott-era Small Faces music, but from where we were located, I no longer cared. And we were acclimating, becoming more comfortable with our surroundings. So were Rod and Ron Wood. After the band launched into 'Pineapple and the Monkey', Rod glanced over at us quizzically, as if to ask, 'What are you doing up here?' Before I had a chance to react, he moved over to Wood and they went into the bonding musicians act that all rock bands do, digging each other's moves. Rod wriggled back and glanced at us again and, maybe it was the drink, or maybe it was the moment, but I pointed at Barb's belly and then I pointed at Rod and my lips formed the word 'yours'.

Rod's reaction was one of immediate shock, followed by a smile, and then an exaggerated head shake, 'No, no.' He wheeled and wriggled back up to his mic stand. Barb and I laughed, but we were drowned out by the din of the music. Rod glanced over at us again and pantomimed another 'no, no' with his hand over his heart. Barb and I laughed harder and so did he. It was going to be fun chatting with him and the rest of the Small Faces after the show.

But almost immediately after our Rod Stewart moment, a horrible thought entered my mind. Panicking, I leaned into Barb's ear and yelled, 'We have to leave RIGHT NOW. Follow me!' She tilted her head with a look of 'why?', but my gravity convinced her to exit with me right away. I grabbed her hand and we headed for the stairs and out the stage door into the parking lot. The cold rain fell on us as we rushed through the slop to our Mustang. We slid into the bucket seats, our ears still suffering the ringing deafness Rod the Mod and his band had caused.

Barb asked, 'What was that all about?' Still panting, I answered, 'What if all that super-loud music was damaging the baby in some way? Suppose his or her little eardrums were being destroyed by all that volume? Look at us – we can hardly hear anything now. Isn't it possible our baby could be born deaf?' Barb railed at me for suggesting such a thing. 'How could you...?' I defended myself. 'No, no, we had to get out of there. We had to play it safe.'

Two days later, Barb's gynaecologist told us to try not to worry, that the amniotic fluid had most likely shielded the baby from harm. But he also said we wouldn't know for sure until after the baby was born. And he also ordered that until after the blessed event took place, 'No more concerts!' Not very reassuring.

Two and a half careful months later, our first child, a boy, was born. Ten fingers, ten toes – and two good ears in fine working order. And I know what you're thinking – did we name him Rod after you-know-who? The truth is, his name is Peter, after Pete Townshend of The Who. Although we'll always have the wonderful memory of our night at the Small Faces show and our Rod Stewart moment, Barb and I will forever be Who fans, first and foremost.

FILLMORE WEST
7-10 MAY 1970, SAN FRANCISCO, CALIFORNIA

I WAS THERE: VIC VALDES

The boys were so young yet full of confidence. I have two strong memories of their first show. At one point, Ron's guitar became unplugged during a solo but he continued to play while reattaching the chord back to his guitar and the crowd and band loved it. And at the end of the final song, when Rod announced that he had heard so much about the women of San Francisco and how he and Ron were looking for 'dates', they jumped off stage and walked through the crowd ever so slowly. I don't know the outcome, but I'm thinking they were successful…

It was an outstanding, high-energy show and they were very personable.

I WAS THERE: JEFFREY KILE

It's one of my favourite shows of all time. They came on stage and played three or four tunes. Either the audience wasn't responding well, or for dramatic effect, they said 'goodnight' and left the stage. People freaked out and we made a lot of noise for a good 20 minutes – I think; my perception of time had been chemically altered. When they returned, they played straight through for two and half to three hours, and kicked ass.

EAGLES BALLROOM
15 & 16 MAY 1970, SEATTLE, WASHINGTON

I WAS THERE: GREG PACKHAM, AGE 15

They were awesome, particularly when they did 'Maybe I'm Amazed'. The hair stood up on the back of my neck when Ronnie Lane started singing. I had seen Ron Wood playing bass with Jeff Beck and was shocked to hear how good he was on guitar. I was 15, a gigging musician, and still am. I remember Ron Wood's Dakota Red Strat, and when he did 'Around the Plynth' with Rod. Great stuff.

UNIVERSITY OF MICHIGAN
24 MAY 1970, EAST LANSING, MICHIGAN

I WAS THERE: MILENA BIX'S HUSBAND, AGE 17

I was a music fan from seeing The Beatles on *Ed Sullivan*. And as the young will do, I was a bit of a snob by then. I was a big fan of Beck's *Truth* when that came out, but I never saw the Jeff Beck Group live. I liked *Beck-Ola* just as much, and it was a big disappointment for me when the Jeff Beck Group split up. Steve Marriott's Small Faces were not big here in the US, apart from 'Itchycoo Park' on the radio.

This was a three day festival. They were drinking wine from the bottle, lots of wine. Rod was wearing a black sports jacket with white piping on the lapels and white pants. Woody already had his Zemaitis and he also played a Les Paul Gold Top. He also had a black Tele with a round metal pick guard that he used on one song for a show-stopping slide intro. For me, the Faces were the best live band and I saw a lot of bands, always from the first five rows. They were having more fun than we were! I saw them every chance I got until the Cow Palace in San Francisco in September 1973. They went from being the best-dressed band to just ridiculous, as Ronnie Lane had gone.

I WAS THERE: PAUL HEATH

The first time I saw them was an all-day concert in East Lansing, Michigan. The PA was blown out and it took them an hour to rewire the mics through the amps. Rod picked up his mic stand and shoved it in the speaker that wasn't working. They played 'Wicked Messenger', 'It's All Over Now' and 'Maybe I'm Amazed'. It was a great night. I saw them five or six times after that and they always rocked, but that night when he shoved the mic stand in that blown speaker is a great memory!

FANWOOD HIGH SCHOOL
28 MAY 1970, SCOTCH PLAINS, NEW JERSEY

I WAS THERE: KAY STEVENS-DAILEY

I discovered the Faces on the radio, starting with the Small Faces. I remember being mesmerised by Rod Stewart's voice. At this show, I walked right up to the stage and stood in front of him. I could not get my friend to come with me. Her loss!

CAPITOL THEATER
29 & 30 MAY 1970, PORT CHESTER, NEW YORK

I WAS THERE: SUSIE SMITH

The first time I saw them was at the Capitol Theater in Port Chester, New York. I believe it was their first time in the US. I was with my boyfriend at the time. We went to see them, although Mountain with Leslie West was top bill. I had a huge crush on Ronnie Wood (I still do). Even though Rod was front man, I was always watching Ronnie. I loved watching his hands playing some of the best guitar I ever heard.

We had balcony seats on the right side, third and fourth seats in from the aisle. The first two seats were never filled. I was in the seat closest to the aisle. Right after Mountain started playing, someone sat in the seat to my left but I was watching Mountain so I didn't take notice. In between songs, I turned and realised that Rod Stewart was sitting next to me also watching the show. I was so star struck that I could not even look at him after that. He only stayed for a couple of songs and then left. Ugh! I was so disappointed in myself.

We followed the Faces every time they were in the New York area. I saw them several times at the Fillmore East, sometimes catching every show for that venue. I don't think I ever sat further back than fourth row back then. I also saw them at Pocono Downs in PA one summer. I used to have a fantasy band in my head, with Ronnie Wood and Keith Richards playing, so I was in heaven when Ronnie joined the Stones.

The Faces returned from their first US tour to play a handful of UK dates in June 1970.

CASTLE ROCK FESTIVAL, DUDLEY ZOO
5 JUNE 1970, DUDLEY, UK

I WAS THERE: DAVID SMITH

I saw them twice. The first time was at an open-air gig in the grounds of Dudley Castle. They were third on the bill below the Edgar Broughton Band and T.Rex. I seem to remember they played a bosting set, despite being pissed. The second time I saw them was at Birmingham Town Hall. They were top of the bill that night and were supported by Osibisa.

I WAS THERE: PETE SMITH

In the summer of 1970, the year I got married, we attended the 'Rock at the Castle' event at Dudley Castle on a very moist Friday evening, with T. Rex, Black Sabbath and Rod Stewart. They all performed wonderfully and we chatted with all the performers as they sat huddled in their cars on site whilst 'In the Summertime' by Mungo Jerry and 'All Right Now' by Free blasted out of the soaking wet speakers. It was a good – but very wet and cold – summer's night.

Records suggest the Edgar Broughton Band rather than Black Sabbath were in the line-up. Following the Edgar Broughton Band, the Faces found the audience unreceptive and booing them after three numbers. One eyewitness described the band as 'actually quite drunk'. Robert Plant guested as vocalist on one song.

THE WAKE ARMS
6 JUNE 1970, EPPING, UK

I WAS THERE: NIGEL MONEY

I was there, along with six or so friends, for both nights. It was a long time ago, but I seem to remember it was on two consecutive Thursdays.

I WAS THERE: BRIAN 'BRUNO' BURNS

A few of us followed the band after the Small Faces split. I was at both the Faces Wake Arms gigs in 1970. I also saw them at the Sundown in

Edmonton plus the Weeley concert in Clacton in '71. I lived in Harlow at the time. Our local school youth clubs plus the local nightclub, The Birdcage, showcased all the bands of the '60s and '70s – Family, Love Affair and Alan Bown to name a few. Rod was one of the vocalists with Zoot Money and Brian Auger's band with Julie Driscoll and Long John Baldry. It was a fabulous time to enjoy live music. If we wanted something different, we would go to the Rhodes Hall at Bishop's Stortford where I saw the early Floyd (with Syd), Free and Chicken Shack, plus Peter Green's Fleetwood Mac. I also got to see Jimi at the Saville Theatre in Shaftesbury Avenue in early '67. They had some fantastic gigs there.

The Faces also played the Wake Arms on 22 November 1970.

GASOLINE ALLEY
RELEASED 12 JUNE 1970

Rod's second album, **Gasoline Alley**, *is released. Mercury had given co-producer Lou Reizner £12,000 to produce the album, saying Rod could keep any underspend. Rod produced the album for £3,500.* **Melody Maker** *said of the album: 'Rod's voice is an extraordinary tool, seemingly shot to pieces and at times barely seeming to exist, yet retaining a power and depth of communication with which few can compare.' The album only reaches 27 in the UK charts.*

GREAT HALL, LANCASTER UNIVERSITY
19 JUNE 1970, LANCASTER, UK

THEY WEREN'T THERE: BARRY LUCAS
I was a student doing the social secretary job at Lancaster University. My first gig as an Ents Sec was The Who in May 1970. The Faces didn't actually appear at Lancaster. I have got an advert in a student newspaper with the Faces on it but they didn't turn up. They were among about half a dozen acts who were scheduled to play at a grad ball. I don't know whether it was because of illness or the van

breaking down or whatever. It happened, not regularly, but it wasn't unusual for gigs to get cancelled at the last minute in the late Sixties and early Seventies.

I was a fan. I did see them about that time in Blackpool at the Opera House. And while I was away at uni, my parents moved to Oadby in Leicester and I went and saw them at Leicester University Students Union. It was a three-floor building and they were on the top floor. It could hold 500 people on each floor so they let 1,500 people in who were all trying to get in to see the Faces. I was on the stairs. I could hear them but I couldn't see them. Halcyon days!

The Faces returned to the US to play a handful of East Coast dates in early August 1970.

GOOSE LAKE INTERNATIONAL MUSIC FESTIVAL
7 AUGUST 1970, LEONI TOWNSHIP, MICHIGAN

I WAS THERE: PHIL WALROTH
At Goose Lake Festival in Jackson, Michigan, they announced 'Rod Stewart and Faces' and the band wouldn't come out until they just introduced them as 'Faces'. It was a rip-roaring set, with the band having lots of fun and bottles all over their set.

I WAS THERE: DAVE GORDON
Most of my memories of the concert are rather hazy. (Like they say about the Sixties, if you remember them, you weren't there.) I really can't say I remember the Faces performance. There were so many things going on and I was very young. I was busy with the opposite sex. But it was a very good time indeed!

I WAS THERE: MICHAEL WALSH
Goose Lake was the only time I saw them. I'm told by my friends that we had fun…

> *The biggest audience the Faces ever played to was at Goose Lake. 250,000 people. It was a starry night and once the stars faded, looking out from the stage, it was like you were playing in space.*
> **Kenney Jones**

FILLMORE EAST
8 AUGUST 1970, NEW YORK, NEW YORK

I WAS THERE: RISA ROSENTHAL

I saw them at the Fillmore East and at Ungano's in New York. I saw them many times, probably every tour. They knew us and would get us in to gigs and we'd hang out with them at Loews Midtown Motor Inn or go to Nobody's (a music bar hangout) with them. I'm bad with dates but I was probably about 17 or 18. I was already in awe of the Small Faces because of Steve Marriott, and I loved Rod because of Jeff Beck's *Truth* album. I'm a singer songwriter and used to sing 'Rock My Plimsoul' and copy Rod. You knew what you saw was special! I even got a snog off Mac once, which made my day.

I WAS THERE: JIM FISHER

I saw Faces around five times at the Fillmore East in 1970 and '71. I lived a few blocks away. They were – and are to this day – the greatest smaller venue rock band of all time. They were blatantly drunk every performance and still managed, with excellence, to deliver the entirety of what always seemed to be three-to-four hour concerts. Each night, their love of the stage and the crowd was evidenced by four to five encores at the end of the night. There were so many encores and they played so beyond the normal closing time that Fillmore management would finally have to turn on the theatre lights and demand an end to the show. Rod is/was – along with Mick Jagger and Roger Daltrey – the greatest rock lead singer ever. All of them – the Ronnies, Ian and Kenney – were the ultimate!

THE SCENE
9 AUGUST 1970, MILWAUKEE, WISCONSIN

I WAS THERE: BRAD MORRIS
I saw them four times. The first time was in 1970 in Milwaukee, Wisconsin, at a venue called The Scene. I'm not positive about how many bands played, although Fuse from my hometown of Rockford, Illinois (one of Rick Nielsen's early bands) were there. They had trouble with their PA so only played a short set. Bummer. The whole thing with Steve Marriott leaving the Small Faces and Rod and Ron Wood arriving was weird timing. The album *First Step* was released in the US as by the Small Faces whereas everywhere else it was the Faces. They were absolutely fantastic.

THE GREAT MEDICINE BALL CARAVAN, CHARLTON PARK
31 AUGUST 1970, BISHOPSBOURNE, UK

I WAS THERE: ROBERT HAYWARD
The Faces appeared at Charlton Park as part of the filming for *The Great Medicine Ball Caravan* – a French movie that was never shown. The movie purported to show a group of travelling bands crossing the USA, playing at various venues and open-air festivals, and concluding with the Isle of Wight festival in the UK. Unfortunately, they could not get permission for some of the bands to play the Isle of Wight, or for filming. The production company's answer was to host a free concert elsewhere in the UK and pretend it was the Isle of Wight!

They were offered a country house park just outside Canterbury. They flew bands like Pink Floyd, Mott the Hoople, etc. in by helicopter, often straight from the Isle of Wight. The audience of around 2,000 local hippies, including myself, heard about it by word-of-mouth and a last-minute announcement on local radio. We were treated to Wavy Davy, Stoneground and a free barbecue, and (in some cases) free dope and beads to sit up front and be enthusiastic. That was actually very easy, especially when one of my mates, Colin White, was invited by Pink Floyd to sit in on drums on one number. Floyd were absolutely incredible that day. Local band Caravan played, and facilitated access to the performers. Daddy Longlegs were playing that night at Folkestone, and they too fetched up.

The most interesting fact was the clothes worn by the Faces. Whilst all the American bands were in faded Levis and dungarees, the Brit progs in flared jeans and tasselled jackets, sporting leather wide brimmed headgear or beads, Rod and Co were wearing tight-fitting satin trousers and velvet jackets. The Yanks were wearing open-toed sandals, moccasins and the like but the Faces were in stack-heeled shoes and flouncy shirts. You must remember that Glam had not yet happened. The Yanks and most Brit bands were hairy, grimy and worn. They took acid and smoked dope. Rod bounded on stage clean and shiny, with a bottle of wine in his hand.

All of the bands – particularly Stoneground, Caravan and the Floyd – were great, but it was Rod's lot that really energised the cross-legged crowd and brought them to their feet. That many of us could have reached out and touched them really enabled connection-making. They really won over the crowd with their energy and enthusiasm. Great setting, great weather, great drugs!

I WAS THERE: DAVE RADFORD, AGE 18

I was at the *Medicine Ball* show. A friend of mine says he saw Edgar Broughton walking about but they didn't play, and yet everybody says they did play. But Pink Floyd definitely did. The Faces definitely did. There were only about 200 people there. It was only advertised on the previous Friday in the *Kentish Gazette*, and if you took the newspaper with you, you got in free. But you didn't even need a newspaper. It was the same weekend as the Isle of Wight Festival. Everything was free, but there was just nobody there. I don't know why. It was a really lovely atmosphere. I think Floyd thought it was the best gig they played that summer as far as festivals went. It's also suggested that Caravan played, but I'm absolutely certain they didn't. It was called the *Great Medicine Caravan* and I think people got muddled up as a result. Daddy Longlegs played and I've got a feeling Al Stewart did too, but that never gets mentioned. Stoneground were on the bill. They were very similar to the Faces in terms of their rocky style.

I was 18 and went with my wife. We'd just had a baby and were going backwards and forwards so we could feed the baby, because it was quite newborn and she didn't want to take it with her. There were loads of people on *Easy Rider*-type motorbikes riding around. There was free food and all of the stage was tie-dyed. It was brilliant. We were sitting cross-legged on the floor. It was very open.

Dr Kildare actor Richard Chamberlain was sat in front of us and a friend of ours asked him for his autograph, which I was a bit embarrassed by. My friend Peter went with his brother. They lived in Thanet, went on their bikes and got a right bollocking from their parents when they got home because they took the wrong road and went towards Folkestone instead.

It was an amazing day.

I WAS THERE: PETER HARDEN

In the early Seventies I was living in Canterbury and attending the local tech college. I, along with virtually everyone else, was invited by a fellow student to a party at his house. His home turned out to be a magnificent Grade II country house set in extensive grounds. Charlton Park had been let to an American film company (director Richard Chamberlain/ Dr Kildare) to film the follow-up to Woodstock, called *The Great Medicine Ball* and bankrolled by Warner Bros. A host of rock bands had been booked for the event. Although we were guests we also acted as extras for the film.

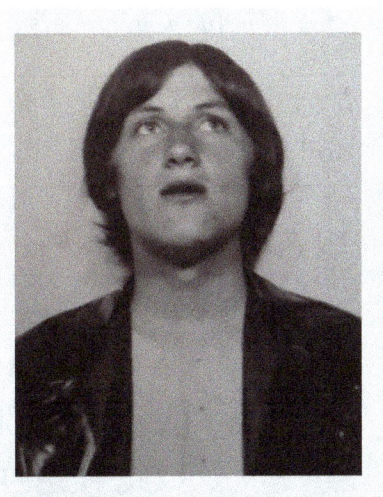

Peter Harden saw the Faces at the Great Medicine Ball

I remember initially being a little disappointed that it was the Faces and not the Small Faces on stage, but the music and the phenomenal stage presence of Rod Stewart changed all that. Other than that, all I remember about their set is the clothes they wore. If my memory serves me well, each member of the band wore a different and brightly coloured suit – pink, yellow, etc. I think Rod wore white.

The event happened at the same time as the famous 1970 *Isle of Wight Festival* (Dylan, Hendrix, The Who, etc.) and, as a result, the attendance at the Canterbury event was low. It's hard to put a figure on attendance but it was probably somewhere between 500 to 1,000. I had no problem sitting with friends on the edge of the stage while Pink Floyd performed the entire soundtrack to *Atom Heart Mother* (the finale!).

LOVE AND PEACE OPEN AIR FESTIVAL
4 – 6 SEPTEMBER 1970, FEHMARN, WEST GERMANY

The festival is sadly remembered for being the last gig Jimi Hendrix ever played but it was also badly organised, with some bands pulling out due to non-payment of advances, German bikers inadvisably hired to act as security (no lessons having been learnt from Altamont) and very poor weather. The Faces played on Saturday.

It was dreadful. It peed down with rain.
Rod Stewart

The Faces embarked on their second US tour on 1st October 1970.

QUAKER CITY ROCK FESTIVAL, SPECTRUM
23 OCTOBER 1970, PHILADELPHIA, PENNSYLVANIA

I WAS THERE: SANDY RYDEL
I saw them with Eric Burton and War and they had to turn the lights off on Eric because he would not get off the stage. Grand Funk

Sandy Rydel saw Faces at the bottom of a bill topped by Grand Funk Railroad

Railroad were top billing and Faces were the warm up band. They were better than the other two and that's how we got introduced to Faces. I saw Rod there three more times. Once, he had about 15 old men with violins, and another time he was kicking soccer balls out into the audience.

I WAS THERE: NEIL MINNUCCI

The poster said 'Small Faces' with 'featuring Rod Stewart' in small letters below it. The opening act was Eric Burdon and War. Eric Burdon was well known as the Animals' front man and Rod Stewart was not yet well known. Eric Burdon was so phenomenal that cheers kept him on stage. He wanted to keep singing and he heard that they were going to cut his microphone off. So he told the crowd to be quiet and he sang using only his voice and no amplification to a silent crowd who adored him. They had to turn the lights out to get him off the stage. Don't get me wrong, the Faces were fantastic as they always were, but I'll bet Eric Burdon never opened for them again.

AGRODOME
1 NOVEMBER 1970, VANCOUVER, CANADA

I WAS THERE: LARRY PATTENAUDE

It was the early Seventies, just after *Gasoline Alley* had been released. The Faces played a great concert that night whilst drinking Mateus on stage and having a blast. Terry David Mulligan, a local DJ and actor, hosted the night. Later, my buddy and I met the band back at the Holiday Inn. Rod was in the middle of trying to settle a small argument with some of the guys about the gig but Ronnie went with us into the coffee shop and sat for an hour or so, talking with my buddy who had filled in for the drummer with the Big Three. Ronnie recalled going to see the band and even sang a couple of tunes. Great night!

Larry Pattenaude hung out with Ronnie Wood after the Vancouver show

CHAPIN HALL
6 NOVEMBER 1970, WILLIAMSTOWN, MASSACHUSETTS

I WAS THERE: DAVID LOEHR

On November 6, 1970, Williams College in Williamstown presented a concert with Rod Stewart and the Small Faces. Poco were the opening act. The show took place at Chapin Hall. The brick structure, built in 1912, was actually a lecture hall lined with white marble columns, carved wood panels and crystal chandeliers. It was probably the first time the ornate room had been used for a rock concert.

The elegant showplace was filled to capacity with 1,200 people. The show opened with the country-rock band Poco. After a short intermission, Rod Stewart

David Loehr saw the Faces play the beautiful Chapin Hall

and the Small Faces were introduced and the whole feeling in the room changed. Stewart's voice was raspy, and he danced and pranced around the stage singing, and spinning the microphone over his head. Songs that evening included 'Gasoline Alley', 'Country Comforts' and 'An Old Raincoat Won't Ever Let You Down', all from Stewart's solo albums. They performed the Small Faces song 'Flying' and got a huge audience response to Paul McCartney's 'Maybe I'm Amazed'. The show ended with the Rolling Stones song 'It's All Over Now', a song that Rod covered on his *Gasoline Alley* album.

Their look and style was in complete contrast to Poco. Rod and the Faces all wore brightly-coloured outfits of silk, velvet and corduroy and they had the awesome hip British shag haircuts. Many of the Poco fans began leaving the hall when they saw the dancing and prancing group of colourful musicians. It was a show to remember, and to see it in beautiful Chapin Hall made it even more special.

OLYMPIC STADIUM
7 NOVEMBER 1970, DETROIT, MICHIGAN

I WAS THERE: TOM CARUSO

I became familiar with Rod and Ronnie during their time with Jeff Beck. I heard potential but didn't think their talents meshed with such a virtuoso guitar player. Of course, I became familiar with the Small Faces during the Marriot era. Again, there were no 'barn burning' songs, but the tightness of Lane, Ian and Jones merited close listening. When Rod and Ronnie joined said trio, the impact to me was immediate. They had tight yet 'sloppy' instrumentalization, allowing Rod's voice to roam where it fit, and the choice of songs was very good.

I loved Rod's first solo albums and I could feel those songs come alive with the Faces band (personally, I loved Micky Waller's drumming over Jones). I finally saw them in concert second on the bill at the famous Olympia Stadium in Detroit, where the Beatles played in '64. Johnny Winter opened with a blistering blues and rock set, which Detroiters eat up like late night pizza! The headliners were Three Dog Night who, at the time, were one of the biggest acts in American music. But after Johnny, the Faces came out, looked at the audience and collectively smiled at us as if to say, 'OK, Detroit, we know what you like,' and they transformed the mammoth stadium into a cozy, little pub full of rock, blues, soul... and personality to spare.

Loose but tight, scattered but together, singing that was all over the place but in harmony... and their dancin' and prancin'... They weren't putting on a show; they were enjoying themselves and let the audience in on their joy. It was an amazing night, an amazing debut and we became instant, lifetime fans. My faves continue to be Woody and that little giant, Ronnie Lane.

Three Dog Night did not come out on stage for over an hour due to the ovations after the boys left the stage. We left midway through the Dog show (who we liked) and the next day sang ourselves to our favourite record store and bought whatever we could with the boys playing on it. I still have my records and best of all, the eight or nine times I saw them in small venues in and around Detroit. A nod is as good as wink!

I WAS THERE: DAWN MEDLEY, AGE 14

I wasn't familiar with their music and only went to see the headliner, Three Dog Night. I remember was how electric their performance was. Watching Rod Stewart and Ron Wood interact on stage was mesmerizing. And Rod's voice! For a girl who grew up listening to country music, Elvis and The Beatles, Rod Stewart's voice was something I had never experienced before but I knew I wanted more! It wasn't just the gravel and grit in his voice. It was the emotion and how he and the whole band put everything they had into his music. After their set, my friends and I looked at each other and said, 'Three Dog Night is going to have to really rock it to make the crowd forget what we just saw!'

I was 14 years old when I attended that concert. That night started a lifelong love of Rod Stewart. I've been with him from 'Maggie May', through the disco years, the 90s hits, his *American Songbook* period. I loved every phase. I can't count how many times I've seen him and every time was amazing.

Earlier this week, my husband and I were talking about favourite songs and he asked me to name my favourite Rod Stewart song. I thought and I thought and I thought. Then I told him this, 'I can tell you my favourite Beatle song. I can tell you my favourite Three Dog Night song. I can tell you my favourite Rolling Stones song. I can tell you my favourite Bob Seger song (I'm a Detroit girl!). But I can't for the life of me tell you my favourite Rod Stewart song. They are all such a part of my life that naming one would be impossible.'

FILLMORE EAST
10 NOVEMBER 1970, NEW YORK, NEW YORK

I WAS THERE: ROB FERRI

Back then, during the week the Fillmore East in New York was pretty user friendly. It was five bucks or so to get in and I went quite often. I have two memories from this night. A very unknown Black Sabbath opened, and Mr Stewart and the Faces passed bottles of Mateus Rosé wine whilst providing one kick butt performance. I don't even think an audience was necessary for them. But I'm glad I was there.

SYNDROME
13 NOVEMBER 1970, CHICAGO, ILLINOIS

I WAS THERE: VERA WATKINS

I went to see them at the Syndrome (formerly known as the Coliseum, located at 15th and Wabash) in Chicago. This venue hosted Cream, Hendrix and other big names between 1968 and 1971 in addition to boxing events. It was a dark and dingy dump of a place, with very little lighting. It was basically just a huge old gymnasium with an upper level balcony. It was standing room – no seats – and general admission. Many of the fans rushed the entrance gate and crashed through. They handed fans a 45rpm single of 'Gasoline Alley'. I thought the concert was great, but I don't remember all the songs they played. I wish I had taken photos.

COMMODORE BALLROOM
15 NOVEMBER 1970, LOWELL, MASSACHUSETTS

I WAS THERE: DEBORAH MITCHELL

My first ever concert, somewhere on the north shore, maybe Lowell. I told my mother it was a sleep over. Such a bad girl!

PARIS THEATRE
19 NOVEMBER 1970, LONDON, UK

The Faces return from the US to record a radio session for John Peel's **Sunday Concert**, *followed by a clutch of UK club and college shows in the run up to Christmas.*

THE WAKE ARMS, EPPING FOREST
22 NOVEMBER 1970, EPPING, UK

I WAS THERE: ANDREW HEIGHT

I can't remember how I started to go to the Wake Arms on a Sunday evening, but for a period from the late 1960s into the mid-1970s, it was the place to go to if you valued good music. The hall where the bands played was at the back of the pub and was like a large garden shed, with an apex roof, medium sized stage and a small bar. All the walls, ceiling and fittings were painted black. Sunday nights were for the up-and-coming bands of that time and nearly all would go on to become very famous. One of those was the Faces. They had started life as the Small Faces but Steve Marriot had moved on to form Humble Pie. When the Faces were formed, Ronnie Wood and Rod Stewart joined. The transformation was huge. The Small Faces had been known for their light and brilliant pop songs, but the Faces were blues, soul, boogie and something that became known as country rock. The sound they created was raw, very funky and you either liked it – or you liked it! It was very infectious and compulsive.

Andrew Height was at the Wake Arms

I had seen the Small Faces play and when the Faces appeared at the Wake Arms, it was the gig to go to. Needless to say it was packed. Not unusual then, as on most Sundays, maximum numbers were admitted, carefully controlled by a couple of unusually friendly bouncers, who were weekly regulars and became friends with just about everyone there.

Because the Arms was fairly small, you were close to the band when they played and it was impossible not to be caught up in the atmosphere of the evening. This is what I remember the most, that everyone was into the band and having a great time. There was a slightly larger bar between the entrance and the hall and it was easier to get to for a drink. And in the interval, most of the bands that played there would be at the bar too, the Faces included. And they would talk to everyone who was there. Yes, there were girls who wanted to get to close but the bands all managed to avoid being jumped on. I cannot recall screaming females trying to crawl all over Rod and the rest of the band. I think everyone then was a bit more respectful. If you could talk to the band members, why spoil it?

The Faces on stage were, to me, just downright dirty. By that I mean the music. It was very much a case of, 'We'll play this, let's see where it goes'. Most of their numbers were self-penned blues or soul songs and they would ad lib and extend the songs as they pleased. More obscure blues numbers were played, all with a mean and thundering bass line, which was a sure way to get everyone there going! At that time, they were just starting out and hit records were yet to come. When they got down to boogie on the blues and soul numbers that was what the people really liked. With everyone jammed into the hall, shoulder to shoulder, even on a winter's night, it got really hot and sweaty, and the music only increased the heat. The Faces made sure that you went home wet! It was very good music and the audience loved it.

If I remember rightly, the band would do two sets of around 45 minute each, finishing at around 11.00pm. Sometimes it was later which was never a problem as the Green Line bus route was outside and the last one was at 12.01am on Monday morning!

I attended the Arms on many Sundays at that time and saw Stone the Crows, Sam Apple Pie, Genesis, Chicken Shack, Curved Air, Hawkwind, Brinsley Schwarz, Arthur Brown and Deep Purple there amongst others.

Sadly, the Wake Arms has gone, and the bands that made the music are slowly going too. But we have vinyl, CDs and other forms to allow us to carry on hearing that music. And best of all, we have volume controls, because bands like the Faces need to be heard – loud and proud!

I WAS THERE: HOWARD PAAR

If you were 14 in 1969 and cared more about music than anything else, Sunday nights at the Wake Arms were a dream come true. I'd been lucky enough to be at the Hyde Park show that Pink Floyd did in June '68 and the one the Stones performed, two days after Brian Jones died in July '69, but they were outdoors with thousands of people. The Wake Arms was a small, sweaty, in your face, back room in a pub, a bus ride away from

Grange Hill and Chigwell where my friends and I grew up. If you looked 'sort of' old enough, getting a drink was not a problem and of course we'd always have a spliff on the way.

It was blisteringly loud, especially if you stood right up front by the speakers, which we always did, and having ringing ears for two or three days after was a source of pride when discussed at school. It was always packed with hippies and heads, along with a fair amount of bikers whose numbers swelled if bands like Status Quo, the Edgar Broughton Band or the Groundhogs performed. (Watching the Groundhogs load in one night as they'd arrived late and roadie-less, humping their own equipment, wearing donkey jackets and with one or two members balding was my first glimpse and realisation that being in a band maybe wasn't quite as fun and glamorous as I'd thought.

If you stayed for the encore, it usually meant you'd miss the last bus which meant walking five miles home while hoping to hitch a ride on the mostly deserted road. Which occasionally happened, like the night Joe Brown pulled up in a big red Cadillac and asked if 'you boys want a ride home?'. I actually met my lifelong best friend, Ross Curtis, waiting in vain for the last bus that never came one night.

I'd loved the Small Faces and went to the Faces show out of curiosity, as I wasn't familiar with Rod Stewart then. My recollection of the Wake Arms show is of initial shock when I realised that the band were as drunk – or drunker – than we were. They were clearly having a good time. Although it was very sloppy, I liked that they all seemed to be mates, which made it pretty infectious. Long John Baldry ended up doing lead vocals on at least one and maybe more songs towards the end.

The Faces brought a much-needed injection of fun into rock and roll again and I feel lucky to have witnessed the beginning of the Seventies at such a truly great venue. I came to love the Faces, and saw some amazing shows at the Edmonton Sundown in '73, where they were in all their ragged glory. Sadly, those were the last with Ronnie Lane.

I WAS THERE: RAY SPARX

Going to a concert was like going to the pictures. You could just turn up and buy a ticket on the day. I'd just started as an apprentice in 1963 and a lad that worked there who was a couple of years older said, 'Do you like music?' Well, I liked any pop music at the time. And he asked if I liked blues music. I didn't really know a lot about it but I said I liked the bits I had heard. And he said, 'Well, come with me on the weekend and we'll go to this place, Eel Pie Island.' There was just a little bridge you went over and it was in a hotel. That was '64 or early '65. It was about 50p to get in. It wasn't expensive, and you didn't have to queue up. You just went in. It was a different world. The Yardbirds were on, and the Stones, and I was just absolutely blown away by the Yardbirds. Eric Clapton was with them then, and lead singer Keith Relf was absolutely amazing on harmonica. They were an absolutely terrific group, way way better than the Stones. Which is crazy.

Then I used to go to a club called the Goldhawk in Goldhawk Road, Shepherds Bush, and the Small Faces used to be on every couple of weeks. The Who used to be on quite a lot as well, and another group called The Action. Geno Washington was another band I saw there. The Goldhawk was a Victorian house. You went through the front door and walked through the house to a massive shed at the back. The room at the Goldhawk wasn't massive. The first thing you noticed as you went through the door is that if you had a white shirt on, your clothes changed colour the moment you went through the door because of the ultra violet lights.

The groups used to come in through the front door as well. The stage was about a foot high and they just performed and you could chat to Kenney Jones and Steve Marriott when they had a break. They would just have a pint with people and it was so easy going. It was just a good laugh. There was never any trouble. Obviously, they weren't famous then. It was the equivalent of about 50p to get in. They'd just started to become a bit bigger. They were all local lads, from Acton, Shepherd's Bush or Chiswick, which was nice. I was a Mod. I had my Vespa and my Parka and I'd go down to Brighton and Margate and Hastings. I just never went to Southend, because that's where all the ones on the motorbikes went.

And as the Small Faces got a bit too big for the Goldhawk, it was up to the Marquee in Wardour Street. The Marquee also had a low stage and they weren't massive crowds. It would hold 150 to 200 people at most, but you could chat to everybody that was there. Every Tuesday night was up-and-coming groups like Spencer Davis and John Mayall's Bluesbreakers. Mayall would give kids a chance, so you had these really good singers coming through like Stevie Winwood, who was then with Spencer Davis. There were just so many terrific groups coming through at the time. And then on a Friday or Saturday would be the groups that were becoming a bit more established. So the Marquee became the place to go.

It was all very casual. I remember Steve Marriott leaving the Small Faces and I found that very sad, because Steve Marriott's voice was to me the best voice you would ever hear. For a fellah that was probably about five foot five, you could not believe the voice that came out of him. It was just crazy. It was so powerful. They took their music seriously, but they laughed at themselves and a lot of their songs were just happy songs. It was as if they were playing for a laugh, not to earn millions out of it. They just enjoyed it and they looked as if they enjoyed it. In the Goldhawk, they'd sometimes forget the lyrics. You could see the progression as the weeks went by. They were getting better and better.

Steve Marriott was the lynchpin of the group. Once he'd gone, he started to go down different routes and he wasn't as successful, but the whole of music changed and as you get older your tastes start to change. I started following other people, like Chris Farlowe. A lot of the groups were not that great live. The Kinks were awful live, and you wouldn't go and see the Stones once they became famous, because you couldn't hear them. It was just this row of girls screaming.

And then after that it was out to the Wake Arms. We used to drive out to the Wake Arms because it was in Epping. You've grown up a little bit and you started to wear a suit to go out in. You wanted to dress up on a Saturday night. On a scooter it would be white t-shirt, Levi's and your desert boots and your Parka. I think 1970 was the first time I took my wife out there. I think we saw the Faces there twice, in '70 and '71. The Faces didn't really inherit a Mod audience from the Small Faces. It changed.

It became a bit more serious when Rod Stewart joined, obviously, because he was quite established by then. There was a complete change in the dynamic in the band with Rod joining. They were expected to be a lot better and a lot more professional.

I WAS THERE: MICK HOLDER

They were awful, completely off their heads and totally disinterested in the gig but it seemed like they were having a great time, which pissed me off doubly.

However, Long John Baldry was also there (he lived locally) and he got up to sing one or two numbers at the end and they pulled themselves together. I think they played 'Let the Heartaches Begin' and 'Rockin' Pneumonia and the Boogie Woogie Flu' with him and they sounded like a proper band. I later read in Mac's autobiography about their 'fuck the gig' habit.

The Faces and the Rolling Stones top my 'worst band live' list. It's like Dave Dee says in *The Great Rock 'n' Roll Swindle*: 'They were so bad I had to back and see them a second time to check they were actually that bad.' It's a great shame because I really love much of their recorded stuff.

I was a very underage teenager when I started going to gigs, as many were. I was a very big kid but got away with it. Groovesville at The Wake Arms, generally on a Sunday, was my home until it closed. And I was spoilt rotten with the fantastic music that came through it. Apart from the Faces.

There would be an informal gathering at Epping Green on Sundays of various members of Humble Pie, the Faces, Uriah Heep and, I think, Pink Floyd, where they used to play football.

I WAS THERE: MICHAEL FARROW, AGE 18

I visited the Wake Arms every weekend. I didn't know how lucky I was! John Peel kept going on about the Faces, so we knew about some of their music. I don't remember too much about the gig except that Long John Baldry came on with them. I also saw the Faces at Crystal Palace Bowl, The Oval and the Great Western Festival.

KIRKLEVINGTON COUNTRY CLUB
27 NOVEMBER 1970, KIRKLEVINGTON, UK

I WAS THERE: ANN WOODWARD

Rod Stewart was a regular in the North East before he was famous and very friendly with John McCoy, owner of the famous Kirklevington Country Club. My friend even went to his house after he invited her down. When he stayed at the Red Lion Hotel in Redcar, Rod borrowed the landlady Doris Foster's rollers for his hair. Tony Hargon, the well-known disc jockey in Middlesbrough, even suggested to him that the jocks were playing the B-side of his record 'Maggie May' and not the A-side.

THE GREYHOUND
29 NOVEMBER 1970, CROYDON, UK

I WAS THERE: KEITH SPILLETT, AGE 16

I saw the Faces shortly after they formed, after the split of the Small Faces. They were doing a gig at the Greyhound in Croydon. The Greyhound was pretty much my second home at the time. So many up-and-coming bands played there in the late '60s and early '70s and it was only a short bus ride from where I lived. I went with a girlfriend and we were all kept waiting so long for the band to appear that we nearly gave up and went home, but eventually they hit the stage. It was a great gig with good knockabout rock and roll. I remember in particular 'Three Button Hand Me Down'.

I WAS THERE: GEOFF MANGER

I left school the summer of '69 when 'Something in the Air' was competing with 'Jumpin' Jack Flash' for number 1. I saw Family play at Bromley College of Technology as the first major gig I attended. Music had always been a serious part of my life. I was in the local St Luke's church choir, a solo soprano in the senior school choir – Bromley Technical School for Boys, which a certain David Jones attended along with Peter Frampton's old man, Ollie, who attempted to teach me art. I learned to read music and always 'got it' when I heard a decent voice, no matter the musical genre. I enjoyed listening to The Hollies just as much as Eric Clapton's 'Badge' sent chills down my spine. The Greyhound in Croydon was the obvious venue for us Bromley boys and I first went there towards the end of 1969 to see Mott the Hoople. Life changed that night.

I went to the Greyhound with my pal Billy Ryder as he was going on endlessly about the Faces. Now to get to Croydon required us to get a 119 bus from Bromley North station terminus and they ran every half hour on a Sunday, if that. We got to Bromley North station, got on the 119 bus when all of a sudden someone on the top deck was having an epileptic fit. We had only just left school but we knew this was serious shit. The driver wanted to get the bus going to keep to his schedule, but we said an ambulance had to be called for. Someone had to find a phone box and the bus had to wait for the ambulance, etc. I'm adding this flavour because it was necessary to get to the Greyhound well before the doors opened to get in and get down the front. Eventually, an ambulance arrived at the bus terminus and the poor chap who'd had the fit was looked after properly. In high anticipation, we set off for Croydon.

Even in July, it was freezing cold in the wind tunnel of the alleyway leading to the entrance to the Greyhound, so imagine what it was like wearing tie-dye t-shirts and little else in winter. A line of chairs was arranged across the hall, about 15 yards from the apron of the stage, so that the first arrivals could sit on the floor while the 'heads' all stood behind the chairs.

I have no recollection who supported Faces that night. It seemed pretty rammed in the hall. The Faces lived up to all the hype, this despite the size of the stage appearing to be no larger than a snooker table. Rod Stewart had an amazing range, which was of particular interest to me as a somewhat-trained singer. The set standouts were 'Maybe I'm Amazed' and a sensationally elongated version of 'Stay With Me', which funnily enough has done just that.

I WAS THERE: LIZ KNOX

I saw them quite a few times at the Greyhound and at lots of other places. The Greyhound was a huge music venue on a Sunday night and they had so many greats on there – T.Rex, David Bowie, Uriah Heep, Arthur Brown, Queen, Hawkwind, Roxy Music, Status Quo, Suzi Quatro and loads more. We used to try and go every Sunday.

TOP OF THE POPS STUDIO
2 DECEMBER 1970, LONDON, UK

The Faces appear on the BBC's premier music programme to play 'Had Me a Real Good Time', recording a performance that is broadcast the following day.

We were pissed out of our minds when we did it... we stayed in the pub until it shut at three o'clock and then went in to record the programme.
Rod Stewart

NORTH EAST LONDON POLYTECHNIC
4 DECEMBER 1970, LONDON, UK

I WAS THERE: DAVID SIMPSON

I studied Architecture at North East London Polytechnic from 1968 to 1971 and the Faces appeared there during that time. I remember a large bedsheet hanging upon the college canteen advertising 'The Faces (Small Faces plus Jeff Beck)'! Having been a fan of the Small Faces and the Yardbirds, I obviously knew how that mistake arose…

I remember being in the student bar before the gig with members of the Faces happily drinking there. It was a great concert. I'd already bought their first album so knew what to expect. I saw them numerous times after that, including at the famous Roundhouse in Camden, and with The Who at the Oval. I live in Hove and Ian McLagan played one of his last UK gigs in the Prince Albert in Brighton. Sadly, I found out about it too late and couldn't get in.

LOWER REFECTORY, SHEFFIELD UNIVERSITY
5 DECEMBER 1970, SHEFFIELD, UK

I WAS THERE: MEL HARRISON

I was already a fan of Rod's as I'd seen the Jeff Beck Group at the same venue about 18 months earlier and was raving to anybody who would listen about the singer. I was also a fan of the Small Faces, who I saw at Queens Hall in Leeds in 1968. They were amazing as well, so when the Faces came along it was a no brainer. On that freezing cold December night, I and my girlfriend at the time were full of anticipation.

When the band came on stage, it was very (very) obvious that they were extremely well oiled. As they were ripping through the set, they were taking drinks from big glasses of what looked like Ribena. I learned much later that the band's favourite tipple was actually brandy and port. Yikes! The one thing above all that stands out in my memory is Ronnie Wood. He took the stage dressed in what I can only describe as a Monty

Python 'Gumby' outfit, even down to the wellington boots. His playing and his drunken asides became more and more erratic until, after about the fifth or sixth number, he passed out. I'm not joking! After about 15 minutes, the announcer came on stage and told us the gig was over as Ronnie Wood was unable to continue. Oh dear, but just like them!

I still have my ticket in a frame with those of other gigs I attended over the years. Unfortunately, the doorman tore it in half so all I have left is a ticket that says 'THE FA…'.

There is a whole genre of music now called Americana which I love and Rod's early solo stuff slots right into it. He's never mentioned when anybody speaks of that particular kind of music and that is just wrong. In my opinion, it's equal to if not better than anything by, say, Gram Parsons.

THE MARQUEE
7 DECEMBER 1970, LONDON, UK

I WAS THERE: MIKE HAYWOOD

I came of age in London during the Mod scene. I can still remember my Parka with rabbit fur across the back and on the lapels, a Union Jack on the back and a bull's eye on the front, and the day I upgraded my Lambretta Li 150 to an SX 225... the power! I wish I still had the Parka today. It was proper US army surplus. I grew upon the Isle of Wight and used to help out a friend

Mike Haywood remembers a Marquee gig

who did the lights at a couple of venues in the late '60s, including Ryde Pier Head, Disco Blue and Ryde Pavilion, plus Portsmouth Guildhall and Black Cat Club. I moved to London for college and used to frequent the Middle Earth Club, Chalk Farm Roundhouse, the Marquee Club and Eel Pie, as well as Hyde Park concerts and quite a few music pubs around Putney and Hammersmith. Home was still very much on the Isle of Wight and I was able to get into the pop festivals so I saw most of the hot bands; who I saw where is a bit difficult to tie down. It was the '60s, after all!

I remember seeing the Long John Baldry road show with Rod Stewart in Portsmouth, and my mate sneaked me into the Marquee Club for the fantastic Faces gig just before Christmas in 1970. The Faces were taking the piss out of the film crew. (The show was being filmed by German WDR-TV and aired on German TV on 15th January 1971). There were so many great venues where you could see bands. One of the best was the Half Moon in Putney, where the Small Faces and the Who both appeared in the same week!

BBC STUDIOS
8 DECEMBER 1970, LONDON, UK

The Faces appear on John Peel's **Top Gear** *radio show, performing 'God Rest Ye Merry Gentlemen', 'Good King Wenceslas', 'Silent Night' and 'O Come All Ye Faithful' along with Marc Bolan, Peel, Robert Wyatt, Mike Ratledge, Ivor Cutler, Sonja Kristina, Bridget St John, Faces road manager Pete Buckland and with composer David Bedford on piano. Rod also does a solo version of 'Away in a Manger'. The recording is broadcast on 26th December.*

CITY HALL
20 JANUARY 1971, NEWCASTLE-UPON-TYNE, UK

I WAS THERE: BRIAN HOLDMAN
It was so early in their history the band still had Small Faces stencilled on the PA, which was also used to balance bottles of brown ale to refresh the band. There was no sound mixer then so the band adjusted their own amps up! That meant the sound balance was poor. But it was a great show, the highlight of which was 'Maybe I'm Amazed'. I seem to remember Rod wearing a white suit and a basketball top, but that may

TELL EVERYONE: A PEOPLE'S HISTORY OF THE FACES

be 'recovered memory'. I went with my then girlfriend who became my wife in 1972. We went to the City Hall a lot, usually on Sundays, as I preferred live music to the cinema. Everybody on tour did the City Hall, so there was somebody on most weeks.

I WAS THERE: STEPHEN SPENCER

I saw them twice, first at Newcastle City Hall when the support was, I think, Dorris Henderson's Eclection. I was very much a City Hall regular and this gig was attended out of curiosity rather than being a big fan. This was an early Faces gig. It was an enjoyable concert. I was impressed by their version of 'Maybe I'm Amazed' and Rod was not yet into his prancing around the stage.

I WAS THERE: HENRY RACE

Like everybody else, we loved the Small Faces. They just looked like us. They were into their clothes, they were into their music. They just seemed like a gang; a little bit naughty and always up to mischief, with great pop sensibility. I had Jeff Beck's *Truth* album with the personnel that went on to play on every picture, tells a story. We used to scour the enemy. But it came out. This news that two guys from the Jeff Beck group were joining

Henry Race saw the Faces at an almost empty Newcastle City Hall

the small faces that was quite an exciting thing. John feels advocacy his promotion, his enthusiasm for the faces he used to gush about them. That was really infectious because we liked John Peel as well.

They played Newcastle City Hall. Admission was twelve shillings (60p). We would've bought our tickets in advance because we always used to do that, but we didn't sleep outside for tickets or phone up the box office on the day they went on sale. My ticket was A20, so we were right smack bang in the middle of the front row. Newcastle City Hall holds 2,400 people and the place was absolutely empty. There were 100, perhaps 200 people there. But the Faces just went for it.

Rod Stewart was going to be Rod Stewart, swinging the mic whether it was in front of 20,000 people or 200 people. We were right in front of Ronnie Lane and during a little break he lit a cigarette, flicked his match away and it hit me, because we were right in the front. And he saw this, and he came across to the edge of the stage and put his hands together, gave a little bow and said 'ever so sorry'.

Ronnie Wood was playing an orange Stratocaster with a white scratch plate. I've never since been able to find a picture of him playing an orange Stratocaster – I don't even think that was a standard colour – but that's what I remember him playing. And he had a big crocheted scarf around his neck. I remember them playing 'Maybe I'm Amazed' and 'Three Button Hand Me Down', one of boogie six/eight shuffle songs off *First Step*.

TRENT POLYTECHNIC
22 JANUARY 1971, NOTTINGHAM, UK

I WAS THERE: TREVOR FOSTER

I 'borrowed' a poster for this gig which was advertised as 'The Faces featuring Rod Stewart', with a price of 8/- (40p). It was just as we were going decimal with our money. We arrived relatively early, unlike the band. A bloke kept coming on and announcing the band had broken down on the motorway and were on their way. They eventually took to the stage about 9.30pm and Rod Stewart said they'd not broken down – they'd been in the boozer! I was dead keen as I'd grown up being a Small Faces fan and so was watching Kenney, Ian and Ronnie Lane all the time. I only remember one song really well, 'You're My Girl'. God, I wish I'd still got that poster.

Trevor Foster saw the Faces at Trent Poly

I WAS THERE: CHRIS PRICE

The band were incredibly late going onstage. One of the roadies told us that the band's vehicle had broken down. At about half past eleven, they rolled onto the stage and Rod apologised, saying that they'd been detained in a particularly good pub in Leicestershire! They were well lubricated when they came on, and pissed as farts by the end of the show, but gave us the best night of rock 'n' roll you ever heard. I loved the Faces, the best rock n roll band ever in my book. As a musician, Ronnie Lane was the heart and soul of the band, Mac the finest Hammond player I ever heard and Kenney Jones just a great drummer.

CROYDON GREYHOUND
24 JANUARY 1971, LONDON, UK

I WAS THERE: ARFER APPLE

The Small Faces were the first band I ever saw live, at the Starlight Ballroom in Crawley. I was blown away. Jeff Beck brought in Ronnie on bass and Rod on vocals on the *Truth* album, which I still play today. It was strange working as a chef; Jeff would often come for dinner on a Monday night. We always had a chat after his dinner. Steve Marriott left the Small Faces and Ronnie Wood joined and then Rod. The blend of music was a step up. I remember seeing the Faces live for the very first time in Croydon, in a place opposite the Fairfield Halls. They were an hour late. There was no support band and people were pissed off but then out came the band and the footballs and we all soon forgot about waiting so long to see them. I travelled to see the reunion in 2015 all the way from Darwin, Australia. I didn't have a ticket but showed up at 9am at the gate. A security bloke said 'I'll get ya a ticket' and he did. I also scored a ticket to see Rod in Hyde Park the following Sunday. Was it worth travelling all that way to see them again? Yes, it was!

DEVONSHIRE HOUSE, UNIVERSITY OF EXETER
29 JANUARY 1971, EXETER, UK

THEY WEREN'T THERE: PHIL MERCER

I have a poster of the social events at Exeter Uni for the spring term in 1971 advertising the Faces gig. But the day before the gig it was cancelled which is why I haven't ticked it off on the list I kept. I think Rod cried off because he was sick or lost his voice.

THEY WEREN'T THERE: MIKE WATTS

I was there as much as anyone was there…

In 1970/71, I was Social Secretary of the Students Union. Rod and the Faces were one of the first acts I booked

The Faces were a no show at the University of Exeter

for the spring term, having been a big fan of their first album. I think the agreed fee was £370. As it got close to the date it became clear the signed contract had not been returned. This was not unusual in those days but I kept chasing the agent, who eventually admitted on the evening before the gig that the band were not coming. Without any chance of booking a replacement I asked the support act, Gentle Giant, if they would play two sets, which they did. The mood on the night was not the best we'd ever seen at a Devonshire House event when the word got round that the main act wasn't appearing. We had to rebate part of the ticket price. Fortunately, the rest of the term – The Kinks, Pink Floyd, Mott the Hoople, Lindisfarne, Slade, Family and Roxy Music – was not such a let down!

WINTER GARDENS
31 JANUARY 1971, BOURNEMOUTH, UK

I WAS THERE: DAVID LONG

I saw the Faces four times in Bournemouth, at the long since demolished Winter Gardens and at Starkers, on the site of O2 Academy in Boscombe. I only liked Rod Stewart when he was a Face, and as soon as they started to believe the publicity and aimed for chart success, I cooled on them. I had done Bath Rock Festival in June 1970 and the Isle of Wight later that year, but picked up on the *First Step* album. I had already liked *Old Raincoat* and *Gasoline Alley* and the Faces debut was, and still is, great.

In January 1971, they had two supports, or maybe just the one, a band called Steamhammer. The place was half full and the Faces just strolled on and were great! The material I still remember includes 'Flying', 'Three Button Hand Me Down' and, best of all, 'Around the Plynth'. Those that were there moved to the front from their seats and I can recall how good they were. Better still, nobody I knew had heard of them.

I WAS THERE: MICHAEL FEASEY

I was a Navy brat. I grew up in the Weymouth area because my dad was stationed at Portland. Most of my musical appreciation was formed as a teenager at the Weymouth Pavilion. It tended to be mostly soul bands but round about '68 it changed to what they called in those days progressive rock. There was no warning. It was literally just on a poster – 'appearing this week', and the price went up from five shillings to seven and sixpence so everybody was 'phwoar, a bit pricey' – but we saw Eric Bell's Thin Lizzy live and direct from Dublin supporting Yes, which was quite a change in musical direction. It tended

Michael Feasey was already a fan of Rod from the Jeff Beck days

to be mostly pop bands, so to occasionally see what we considered a 'big' band, we'd have to go to Bournemouth Winter Gardens, where we saw bands like Emerson, Lake and Palmer.

The Faces stood out for me because I was a blues rock fan. I'd grown up through that backdrop of John Mayall's Bluesbreakers and Clapton, and I liked the heavier kind of sound. I was very fond of the Rod Stewart-Jeff Beck combination, so when the Faces arrived their reputation preceded them, although we'd never heard them play live.

It was a stonking show and delivered on all points from the point of view of atmosphere and the sound quality was good. There was rapturous applause from the audience and a couple of encores, and the audience kept clapping and stomping their feet and they kept coming back on. It was a Saturday night, but there was a local council by law that said no noise after midnight. I think promoters were only licensed to use the venue until midnight. But the band kept playing. They really seemed to want to deliver to the audience.

The venue management came down and were gesticulating – 'that's enough, cut it, cut it' – but they wouldn't. To our delight they kept on playing. They had two warnings which they basically ignored and so the management cut the power to the stage. It all went dark and there was a big 'ooooh' from the audience. But the band carried on playing with acoustic instruments, so we had drums and acoustic guitars and the harmonicas came out. Meanwhile the roadies laid some big thick power cables down the side corridors and connected them up to the emergency lighting which illuminated the exit signs and ran the whole show again from these side lights. So we kept on rocking! There was a lot of singing along from the audience as well. It was just a party atmosphere at the end.

It was a great gig – and we were sticking it to the man, which for a teenager ticked a lot of boxes. It was a mini revolution. They carried on playing until eventually someone threw the circuit to cut the lights off. The lights had to go on again for legal reasons, but people with torches were then in amongst the audience saying 'right, leave your seats' and we were turfed out. I've seen a few late ones, but I've never seen one that went as late as the Faces.

MARQUEE
1 FEBRUARY 1971, LONDON, UK

I WAS THERE: PAUL BRUHIN PRICE

In 1971-72 I worked for Polydor Records in Stratford Place in London W1, in the sales and promotions department. 'Comps' (free tickets) were constantly coming into the office and I probably went to three or four gigs every week. The Marquee was a favourite because we got to mingle with the bands pre and post gig in the bustling bar. When tickets for the Faces gig came in it was a must-see gig – their first album was excellent and the Small Faces/Jeff Beck Group heritage meant a great show was on the cards. The boys were renowned drinkers and my pal and I were in the bar early, only to find we were standing back-to-back with Rod and Ronnie, who were in fine, chatty fettle and downing copious triple vodkas, while the warm up act played a medium to average set. In between acts, the triple vodkas kept flowing. Just as the boys ordered another round, a voice on the tannoy announced that they'd be on stage in ten minutes and we should move into the auditorium.

As the announcement finished Rod said, 'No we fucking won't!', which got a cheer in the bar as we all ordered another round. Around 40 minutes later, Rod and Ronnie strolled to the stage, as did the rest of the band. We dutifully followed. The following hour and a half or so was a brilliant blur as they pounded through an incredible chaotic set and rightly received a rapturous response. One of the best gigs ever? For sure. The best gig I've ever seen by a bunch of total drunkards? Indeed.

LONG PLAYER
RELEASED 1 FEBRUARY 1971

Highlights of the second Faces album are live versions of Paul McCartney's 'Maybe I'm Amazed' and 'I Feel So Good' (both recorded at the Fillmore East on 11 October 1970) and the wistful 'Richmond', while a combination of Rod's voice and the languid pace of the song make the beautifully careworn and seemingly throwaway 'Sweet Lady Mary' so essential. A studio version of 'Maybe I'm Amazed' was released as a 45 in advance of the album. In 2015, the album was reissued in a remastered and expanded form, including two previously unreleased outtakes, 'Whole Lotta Woman' and the instrumental 'Sham-Mozzal', along with two more Fillmore East live tracks.

The Faces are the best rock 'n' roll band in the world today.
Record Mirror, reviewing Long Player

It's by no stretch of the imagination going to save anybody's soul.
Rolling Stone, doing the same

5 February 1971 sees the start of the Faces third North American tour, supported by Savoy Brown and the Grease Band.

THE MOSQUE
5 FEBRUARY 1971, RICHMOND, VIRGINIA

I WAS THERE: GAITHER KENNELL

When Steve Marriott left the Small Faces to form Humble Pie, Rod Stewart and Ronnie Wood joined the band. I was already familiar with both from their days with the Jeff Beck Group and I was a huge Rod Stewart fan. Rod's voice was pure rock 'n' roll. His raspy, high, soulful voice and great phrasing and showmanship made him the best front man in rock 'n' roll. The first time I saw the Faces, at the Mosque in Richmond, Virginia, Rod was cavorting about the stage and the band delivered a great, rock-solid performance. I saw them again later that year, in December, at the College of William and Mary in Williamsburg, Virginia. They would walk around on stage with a bottle of whisky and put their arms around each other while singing and playing. You felt like you were in a pub with a bunch of friends, drinking and singing songs. They were a professional rock 'n' roll party band, who also happened to be great musicians and singers.

MUSIC HALL THEATRE
9 FEBRUARY 1971, BOSTON, MASSACHUSETTS

I WAS THERE: BOB FALANGA, AGE 19

I was backstage with them at the Music Hall in Boston. My father was the promotion man for Warner Bros and Reprise Records. After the show, they left the stage and Ronnie remembered that he'd left his leather jacket on the stage. He asked me to go back with him to get it. The thing I'll always remember is in the dressing room, while they were being interviewed, Rod was drinking Mateus from the bottle.

STANLEY WARNER THEATRE
10 FEBRUARY 1971, JERSEY CITY, NEW JERSEY

The Jersey City show runs late, with the cops turning the power off to prevent the band playing an encore. Rod throws his mic stand into the stage backcloth and the crowd pelt the stage with coins.

FILLMORE EAST
16 & 17 FEBRUARY 1971, NEW YORK, NEW YORK

I WAS THERE: LYNN LAGERSTROM

They were so amazing live and their recordings never really put through their energetic impact. I absolutely loved them but of course it was so long ago I can't really remember everything. I remember them covering 'It's All Over Now', which I loved. I do remember that were indeed small men, as so many British were who were born right after the war due to the food rationing and shortages. The thing was, even though they were small, when they started to play and sing, in my eyes they became giants of talent and presence.

I WAS THERE: CAROL ANDERSON STRANO

I saw the Faces three times at the Fillmore East. Me and my besties Billy,

Tommy and Craig tried to go weekly either to the Capitol Theater, the Nassau Coliseum, Asbury Park Convention Hall, etc. Tickets were $5 to $5.50. Imagine! There's only two or three great bands we missed back then. I saw Led Zeppelin (five times), the Floyd, Moody Blues, Mott the Hoople, Cream, everyone... All we had was Joe's Lights (the Joshua Light Show) playing on a screen. It was nothing like today. It was just good music and there was so much pot smoking going on. Even if you didn't smoke, you still got buzzed! As good as the Faces were – and they were great – who could take their eyes off Rod? He really overshadowed them. He was so sexy. I saw him two years ago and he's still got it.

CAPITOL THEATRE
18 FEBRUARY 1971, PORT CHESTER, NEW YORK

I WAS THERE: STEPHEN WARNE

A little bit down the road after the Jeff Beck Group split up, I heard the solo Rod Stewart stuff and said, 'This isn't bad but I kind of miss the guitar of Jeff Beck.' Then I found out that Ronnie Wood was now playing guitar. I didn't know he was a guitarist. I just thought he was a great bass player. And when I heard that first Faces record, I thought they were a heavy, underground band. I didn't realise they were so much fun.

I bought the Faces' *First Step* album, and at the same time I was buying Rod Stewart's solo records, and I noticed that some of the Faces were on some of the tracks on his solo records.

As I got to know the new version of the band, I thought the secret weapon in the Faces was Ronnie Lane. And then I went back and listened to the Small Faces stuff with Steve Marriott, which we hadn't got in the US at all except maybe 'Itchycoo Park' got played.

I only saw them once, in upstate New York in 1971. My memory of that show is the energy of it. They were colourfully dressed, almost like cartoon characters.

I remember them doing 'Street Fighting Man', which Rod did as a cover on a solo record, and maybe 'Gasoline Alley' and even 'Country Comforts', the Elton John song. They mixed these up with songs from *First Step*, one of which was a remake of that Jeff Beck tune called 'Plynth'.

By the time they did 'Street Fighting Man', Rod Stewart went up behind Kenney Jones and somehow disappeared. The next thing, he jumped over the whole drumkit and landed on his feet on the stage, knocking over a hi-hat on his way down. The whole audience was all over the place because it was hard to follow these guys. They were so much fun.

I'm a big Dylan fan, so when they started off with 'Wicked Messenger' I thought, 'Boy, these guys are serious. They're going to be a great, great band.' But by the second album they were already falling down. Musically, they sounded like they were laughing and singing at the same time. But that had its appeal, and that became their reputation – these crazy, sloppy Brits. When I saw the Faces, as raucous as they were, bumping into each other and laughing, they never missed a note. People say they were sloppy players but they weren't. They had the camaraderie and the musical chops that gave them a cohesiveness. They could do things really, really well.

The Faces really weren't together that long. I remember them coming to New York a number of times, but all of a sudden Rod got really big with his solo stuff and they sort of took a back seat. I think they were hoping to last for a while longer. Rod Stewart is a great singer but he kinda went downhill after that Faces era. There was a loose kind of craziness that was very appealing and they were such great musicians. When Ronnie Lane left they really lost something. There was a kind of magic missing. The new bass player was okay, but the camaraderie wasn't the same.

One time, my wife and I went to see Ronnie Wood give a talk at Town Hall in New York. There was no band. It was just Ronnie. He walked out with his electric guitar and one amplifier and a lady with a microphone. And for 90 minutes he sat there, reminiscing, and then he played a couple of songs. It was billed as 'A Night with Ronnie Wood'. It was a little weird. I felt a little ripped off because there was no rhythm section, you know?

When Ronnie Lane had the ARMS benefit gig, my wife and I went to Madison Square Garden. Ronnie Wood played and he lived in New York at the time. I said to my wife, 'We're seeing three of the Faces. All we need is for Rod Stewart to walk out.' Whatever beef he had with those guys, Rod never did much with them after they split up, which I thought was sad. When Ronnie Lane left the Faces, they really just became the Rod Stewart machine right towards the end. But they still sounded great. Every song was terrific.

Rod never really mentions the Faces. He seemed to have a good time at the time. He just seems to brush it off. Maybe he's more comfortable in Vegas. But he's still got the voice. Because they're your heroes, you think they're going to be around forever. You don't realise that they have the same lifespan as the rest of us.

COBO HALL
23 FEBRUARY 1971, DETROIT, MICHIGAN

I WAS THERE: BOB BRISCOE

They were fabulous. Mostly I remember the way Rod tossed the mic stand around. Like an obedient dog, it always returned to his hand. It was an excellent show and we had great seats. They were super tight with an awesome sound. There's been many a great show in Detroit. It's the home of rock 'n' roll, regardless of what they say in Cleveland.

I WAS THERE: CHUCK MYERS POOLE

I grew up in Florida as a kid and moved back to Michigan in the summer of 1970. My first taste of Rod was 'Maggie May'. I just loved that song. And the album *Every Picture Tells a Story* was the greatest. It's one of my all time favourite albums. I saw the Faces twice at Cobo Hall, on 23 February 1971 with Savoy Brown and again on 30 April 1973 with Jo Jo Gunne. I just remember a great couple of concerts. Back

Chuck Myers Poole saw the Faces twice at Cobo Hall

then everything was very pure. There were no big shows like nowadays, just great music. Ron Wood and Rod were amazing. I have to admit being a bit high. And I believe mescaline was my choice at that time.

THE WAREHOUSE
27 FEBRUARY 1971, NEW ORLEANS, LOUISIANA

I WAS THERE: WEBB WILDER

They blew my mind. I saw them again somewhere else in New Orleans in '75, with the string section and Tetsu. I am embarrassed to admit I don't remember seeing Jesse Ed Davis there, although he was supposedly on that tour. I loved – and still love – the Faces and Rod's Faces-era solo stuff, but felt very betrayed by most of his post-Faces musical choices.

I got to know Mac a bit and loved him. The coolest guy I ever met! And Ronnie Lane's

Webb Wilder backstage with Mac at 3rd & Lindsley in Nashville

widow called me after I did an all-covers album called *Town and Country* that contained our cover of the Small Faces' 'My Mind's Eye' by Marriott/Lane. She told me Ronnie loved my stuff and the Georgia Satellites, a very Faces-influenced band, all of which made me ache to have met him as he lived in Austin for a time. Sadly, I didn't meet him. She and Ronnie may have heard our version of 'My Mind's Eye' on KGSR radio in Austin, whose programme director told my (then) Austin-based label that they really liked that album but didn't normally like my albums and probably wouldn't like the next one!

I met Mac backstage during the Americana Festival in September 2014. He passed a few months later in December, when I filled in for him on two of Nick Lowe's Christmas tour dates. Mac was supposed to open all the shows as a solo artist and sit in with Nick and Los Straitjackets on the whole tour, but died within a day or two of its start.

INGLEWOOD FORUM
10 MARCH 1971, LOS ANGELES, CALIFORNIA

The Faces play their biggest show yet at the 18,000 capacity Forum. The LA Free Press wrote of the gig, 'The Faces delivered their unique and distinctive brand of rock, transforming and extending the rich, warm spirit of good old bar room drinking music into the monumental proportions of R&B-based killer rock 'n' roll.'

COMMUNITY THEATER
11 MARCH 1971, BERKELEY, CALIFORNIA,

I WAS THERE: MICHAEL LAZARUS SCOTT

My first knowledge of Rod the Mod Stewart came on 12th July 1968 when I ventured to the Fillmore West to see the Jeff Beck Group. I had seen Jeff with the Yardbirds in 1965 and had been informed by a Sunset Strip scenester friend that Jeff had a dynamic new band, with a singer that should not be missed. All became true very fast when Jeff took the stage with Micky Waller on drums, Nicky Hopkins on piano, Ronnie Wood on bass and a tall gent with a rooster cut shag and a distinctive sandpaper soul voice who strutted his stuff. His name of course was Rod Stewart and my girlfriend Marlene and I had never heard or seen anyone quite like him.

Flash forward two years… During which time the Faces were formed and Marlene and I found ourselves, along with our trusty buddy Mike Mecartea, at Mr Stewart's birthday party, produced by Warner Bros at Bimbo's 365 Club in San Francisco, a beautiful art deco setting. My high school friend Ed Takitch (RIP) was doing PR work for the label and got us into the festivities. Warner Bros pulled out all the stops as there was a large ice sculpture spelling out 'F-A-C-E-S', the debut performance by the incredible Stoneground, and an hilarious risque drag review by the outrageous Cockettes.

TELL EVERYONE: A PEOPLE'S HISTORY OF THE FACES

Birthday boy Rod and his band of merry men showed up in all their rock star glory with Stewart in a pink three-piece suit with clunky platform shoes that had just become popular. Woody was in a three-piece red ensemble and the two of them with their rooster topknots towered over the little Small Faces dudes. They looked more rock star than anyone I had ever seen. They took their seats in front and proceeded to get drunk and act their given roles, throwing around the catered food and drink and seemingly having more fun than should be allowed. They appeared to especially enjoy the Cockettes.

At some point, a three-layer cake arrived appeared and Rod graciously cut and served it to the multitudes. Our little group had tied three well-tailored joints with a ribbon which we gave to the comely Marlene and sent her to get a piece. When Rod passed her the plate, she in turn gave him his present. With a devilish smile he stuffed them in his vest pocket and, giving a wink, said, 'This will most certainly be of use later!'

The following night the Faces played the Berkeley Community Theatre, another beautiful art deco palace that was four blocks from where I was raised. Marlene and I had front row seats off to the right side. The opening band was Kim Simmonds' Savoy Brown, who rocked the house and primed us for Rod and the boys, who took to the stage to the bass thumping 'You're My Girl'. Rod was resplendent in a purple and navy blue crushed velvet outfit. I always thought his vocal chords must be lined with that velveteen material, giving it that certain grit. The show was the best bawdy, rowdy, impassioned performance I could ever have wanted. They were having more fun than anyone ever, but as mesmerising is it was, it was about to get a whole lot better for Marlene. The German-born fraulein was in a contour-hugging, see-through full-length coral coloured lace gown, with embroidery over her intimate places. When you first looked at her, she appeared nude. She was ravishing!

As the band went into their rendition of 'Maybe I'm Amazed', Rod must have noticed her and, after Ronnie Lane sang the first verse, he ambled across the stage, planting a mic stand directly in front of us and sang the remainder of the song to the lovely Marlene. Their eyes interlocked and Marlene seemed to melt into the plush seat. It was one of the most beautiful, soulful, heartfelt moments that I've ever witnessed. Something I, and especially Marlene, shall never forget. Thank you, Rod Stewart, for your amazing grace, and thank you Marlene, wherever you may be.

PAVILION HALL, SANTA CLARA COUNTY FAIRGROUNDS
20 MARCH 1971, SANTA CLARA, CALIFORNIA

I WAS THERE: BRENT FUTRELL

They were great fun to see live. They came out before Savoy Brown. They encored several times as the audience loved them. They had a curfew, and because the Faces were on so long the promoter cut off the power to Savoy Brown. Savoy Brown were pissed and for a while they refused to leave the stage. It was quite a night for teenager me.

Poster for the Santa Clara show

KINSMEN FIELD HOUSE
23 MARCH 1971, EDMONTON, CANADA

I WAS THERE: BRIAN BINGHAM

This was the third ever concert I had attended in my life. I very impressed by the blues-based riffs employed by the Faces. I was already a fan of the Jeff Beck Group before this. And I had been keenly aware of the music of the Faces since their earlier days as the Small Faces. I was also a big fan of Humble Pie in 1971. I have always been a fan of British progressive blues since 1964, with bands such as The Animals and The Yardbirds and, by extension, Rod Stewart and John Baldry.

March 23rd, 1971 was my 19th birthday and I remember the Faces performing music from *Gasoline Alley* – 'Gasoline Alley', 'It's All Over Now, 'Cut Across Shorty' and 'You're My Girl (I Don't Want to Discuss It)'. My younger brother David was collecting many of the contemporary Rod Stewart 45rpm singles at the time. I also recall hearing them perform renditions of numbers that later appeared on the *Every Picture Tells a Story* album – 'Maggie May', '(I Know) I'm Losing You', '(Find A) Reason to Believe' and 'Mandolin Wind'. The performance of both the Faces and Savoy Brown were impeccable, and I can only speak of that concert in superlatives. I was very fortunate to be in attendance.

PNE AGRODOME
24TH MARCH 1971: VANCOUVER, CANADA

I WAS THERE: ED BILAWCHUK, AGE 16

This was my absolute very first concert. My older brother took me to see Savoy Brown and the warm-up band was a group from England with a supposed up-and-coming singer by the name of Rod Stewart with his band, The Faces. I have only just realised, 50 years later, that I also saw a young Ronnie Wood and Kenney Jones and whoever else was in the band!

CAPITOL THEATRE
2 & 3 APRIL 1971, PORT CHESTER, NEW YORK

I WAS THERE: PETER GERSTEN, AGE 15

It was the late show, so they pulled out all the stops. They had cases of wine and handed out bottles to the crowd constantly, not giving a shit about any age restrictions. They were clearly drunk, but not so drunk they couldn't play. They yelled to each other throughout the night. Rod kicked some soccer balls out into the crowd. I think he clipped a woman in the head with one. They played for three hours. You really felt like you were part of their family and it was as much fun as you can possibly have at a rock show. They loved the fans and the fans loved them.

'MAYBE I'M AMAZED'
RELEASED 6 APRIL 1971 (USA ONLY)

Released in the US as a single, this studio version of the McCartney song is not released in the UK as the band are unhappy with the final version.

The Faces return to Europe and, after a handful of German shows in mid-April, gig around the UK.

Rod and the two Ronnies meet fan Marianne at the Zircus Krone Bau, Munich

UNIVERSITY OF NOTTINGHAM
24 APRIL 1971, NOTTINGHAM, UK

I WAS THERE: JOHN PEAKE
I remember seeing them at Nottingham University. As we were waiting for them to appear, this young kid came on who can't have been more than 15. He sat down at the drums and played this absolutely astonishing solo for ten minutes or more. It was mind blowing.

TOP OF THE POPS
BBC TELEVISION CENTRE
28 APRIL 1971, LONDON, UK (AIRED 29 APRIL 1971)

The band appear on Top of the Pops, performing 'Richmond' and 'Bad 'n' Ruin'. Woody plays his famous toilet seat-shaped guitar.

I WAS THERE: SANDIE RITTER

Rod and Ronnie were very close. They were friends from the Jeff Beck Group days. They walked into a situation with three people who had been in another band together, and they had a different world view to the others. The Small Faces had a real teenybopper following, irrespective of their roots, whereas the Jeff Beck Group didn't. Jeff Beck's audience now is mainly men, unless their girlfriends are going with them. Very few women go to see Jeff Beck because they are fans of his. That must've been true then too, so it was a different culture that Rod and Ronnie came from, a whole different world in terms of their experience of being on the road to the Small Faces, because their audiences were very different. So they felt more sophisticated. The Faces weren't a teenybopper band. Most of the Small Faces fans were banished, or if they were there, they were listening to the music rather than just screaming, so it was a different culture and the culture was more like the Jeff Beck Group culture. Audiences weren't like Small Faces audiences anymore. The audience wasn't full of crazy young teenage girls anymore.

And they became more accomplished as musicians. I saw a video the other day of Ronnie Wood singing 'Richmond' on *Top of the Pops*, and it was just so touching. You could see how pleased Ronnie Lane was. It looked to me as if Ronnie Wood had just taught it to him and there they were, doing this thing together, and he just looked so pleased that it worked. Ronnie Lane singing 'Maybe I'm Amazed' was one of the highlights of going to see them. Even though he only sang part of the song, that really was so beautiful. It was like the end of the band for me when he left. He was the heart and soul of the band. It wasn't the same without him.

ROUNDHOUSE
29 APRIL 1971, LONDON, UK

I WAS THERE: CHRIS WHITEHOUSE

I saw Rod Stewart and the Faces at the Roundhouse in Chalk Farm. I was working there at the box office and they ran out of follow spot operators one night and so I was roped in as a follow spot operator. I was sat up in the roof of the Roundhouse, on one of the girders, as the follow spot for Rod. It was quite fun. They provided us with talkbacks, but as soon as the group started you couldn't hear a bloody thing. I had to wing it from then on.

For a live show, it has long been my opinion that The Who couldn't be topped – but watch out Who, the Faces are breathing down your necks.
Chris Charlesworth, *Melody Maker*

The overall effect sounded a bit ragged and disjointed and it all added up to less than what you'd expect from a band with such strong individual personalities.
Sounds

GREAT HALL, UNIVERSITY OF LANCASTER
30 APRIL 1971, LANCASTER, UK

I WAS THERE: JILL WESTERGREN, AGE 14

I went my then boyfriend. I remember they were pissed before they came on. But Rod was brilliant, a real showman. The details are all very vague now. I know I was far too young to go but my parents allowed it, as long as I came straight home after.

MAY BALL
LEICESTER POLYTECHNIC
8 MAY 1971, LEICESTER, UK

I WAS THERE: PAUL GENT

I saw them in concert at Leicester Polytechnic, set up in a quad in the student union. I would have been 19 or 20 years old. I went with a couple of mates who were about the same age. One thing that sticks in my mind was the security guys on the roof, in case anyone was foolish enough to try to climb over! They were amazing and obviously had as good a time as we did. It was open air so it made the local paper, the *Leicester Mercury*, as the sound was picked up and then dumped some miles away, where of course there was lots of confusion as to where the 'concert' was. I got a chance to chat to them at the bar. What a brilliant evening! It was one of the best gigs – if not the best gig – I ever went to and I saw a fair few bands in both my home town of Leicester and in Nottingham.

I WAS THERE: JENNY JOANNOU, AGE 18

I cycled down to the Poly in Leicester to watch Rod Stewart on my own. They were fantastic and I seemed to be very close to them. I was wearing a long night dress as they were cheap to buy and the long ephemeral look at the time was the in thing. I cycled home and was stopped halfway by a police officer who wanted to know what a young girl on a bike was doing out at 11pm on her own? I told him I had just been to see the Faces at the Poly. He let me go on my way with a 'be careful'. I have never forgotten that night. It was a very special part of my growing up.

I WAS THERE: CHRIS PRICE

As a school kid I'd been a Small Faces fan. That said, I only really knew their singles and I didn't know much about them. That would change when I heard 'Lazy Sunday Afternoon'. I was impressed by Steve Marriott, who came across as a great singer and a hell of a character, so I started to learn more. I didn't get into *Ogden's Nut Gone Flake* until shortly after the band had split, but what an album that was!

I was aware of the new line-up from the start and bought the 'Flying' single as soon as it was released. It was a great song though the flip-side, 'Three Button Hand Me Down', gave us more of a clue of what was to come. I thought Rod Stewart was the perfect choice of singer to replace Marriot. He had a similar vocal range and was clearly influenced by the same people.

I bought the *First Step* album as soon as it came out. I wasn't entirely won over by it, but there were some nice moments. It was Rod's second solo album, *Gasoline Alley*, that really did it for me. The Faces played on most of that album and they were playing quite a few songs from it when I first saw them live. I then bought *An Old Raincoat Won't Ever Let You Down*, Rod's first solo album. It's one that's often overlooked and yet is as good as anything he did. His take of Mike D'Abo's 'Handbags and Gladrags' was brilliant, while his version of 'It's All Over Now' would become a Faces standard.

It was in 1971, just before I finished school, that my stepdad took me to Leicester and dropped me off at the Polytechnic. I'd asked my school mate Simon to come along to this concert, as his knowledge of all things rock 'n' roll had been an inspiration to me. But he declined, dismissing them as 'a bunch of puffs'! I think he might have been wrong about that. What I saw was life-changing.

They were brilliant, and very loud too. Their clothing, along with Stewart and Woody's barnets, was certainly considered to be camp back then, but that was all part of it. When they first took to the stage, a lot of guys wolf-whistled and took the piss. But by the end of the night, everyone was stunned and in great spirits. I didn't know quite a few of the songs but it didn't matter. I do remember them playing 'Flying'. The single didn't really capture it, but live it was an incredible song. The bit where it slows and Woody does that unusual guitar fill (it happens a couple of times) absolutely made my hair stand on end. 'Maybe I'm Amazed' was glorious and very funny in places. Rod and Ronnie's antics were hilarious. I hadn't heard it before so I didn't know that it was a McCartney song, and Paul liked the Faces version, which is good enough for me.

'I Don't Want To Discuss It', 'Country Comforts' 'Around The Plynth', 'Feel So Good' and 'All Over Now' were songs I recognised but there were others too. The night also introduced me to the concept of a band getting extremely pissed on stage! The Ampegs had umpteen bottles of Mateus Rosé lined up on top, all of which were consumed by the band

and a few lucky souls at the front. As a budding musician myself I would try and emulate their behaviour, which did me no good at all!

I WAS THERE: KELVIN WHITE

Me and friends used to travel all over the country seeing live bands in the Sixties and Seventies and one of our favourites was the Faces and Rod Stewart, who we saw many times. The most memorable was the May Ball at Leicester Polytechnic. It was an outside gig. We were standing on the corner of the stage and Rod Stewart came across and asked where the toilets were. When he came back, he kicked us off the stage and we ended up watching the show from up a tree next to the stage.

PARIS CINEMA
13 MAY 1971, LONDON, UK

The band record a set for John Peel's Sunday concert, transmitted ten days later, including performances of 'Love in Vain', 'Had Me a Real Good Time' and 'Feel So Good'.

CRYSTAL PALACE BOWL
15 MAY 1971, LONDON

I WAS THERE: STEPHEN CARLETON, AGE 15

I was volunteering for the St John's Ambulance Brigade and went to my first outdoor concert at the Crystal Palace Bowl. The line up was Quiver followed by Mountain and then the Faces, with Rod Stewart in a pink suit. Pink Floyd headlined. I went to other concerts at the Bowl, but as a normal punter. St John's Ambulance Brigade cadets were banned due to there being 50 plus overdoses at this show, and the influence that was deemed to be having on us youngsters!

Photo: Michael Farrow

Programme for Crystal Palace Bowl

TELL EVERYONE: A PEOPLE'S HISTORY OF THE FACES

I WAS THERE: BRIAN REES

I saw them at Crystal Palace Bowl. Pink Floyd were headlining a one day festival. That was the worst I ever saw the Faces, because they were totally fucking pissed. Totally out of it. The thing is about the Faces, if anybody can remember the set list or what everybody wore and what the weather was, etc., on any gig, they weren't there. Because if you were a Faces fan, you were as pissed as the band. That's what it was about. That's what the Faces were all about. It was a party. It was like you'd gone to somebody's house and you were having a party.

I WAS THERE: IAN MCEWAN, AGE 16

The first time I saw the Faces was at the Garden Party at Crystal Palace Bowl. I had really gone to see Pink Floyd and don't remember being overwhelmed by the Faces, but maybe I just wasn't ready for the raunch. 'Had Me a Real Good Time' and 'It's All Over Now' stick in my mind. Maybe a pink suit was involved. Next time was the *Goodbye Summer Concert* for Bangladesh in September at The Oval. What sticks in my mind about this gig is Rod's suit, which I think was leopard print. That was a great show on a great day. The last time I remember seeing them was at the Reading Festival, on 25th August 1973. I think this was a slicker performance than the other two, and the clothes seemed glitzier somehow. As I recall, the Faces were on in the dark, and I had a great time. A standout memory is of us, my and some pals, getting into the backstage area and up on stage after the show had ended for the day. Memory is a strange thing though, and it may be that I saw them more times than I remember, because I have a definite and clear memory of Rod Stewart in a yellow vest and wearing a boa.

EDWARD HERBERT BUILDING, LOUGHBOROUGH UNIVERSITY OF TECHNOLOGY
21 MAY 1971, LOUGHBOROUGH, UK

I WAS THERE: CHRIS PRICE

I bought *Long Player* as soon as it was released and was delighted that it included a live version of 'Maybe I'm Amazed'. This is my favourite Faces album. I think it's the only one that comes even close to capturing what they were all about. 'Had Me a Real Good Time' features Woody's first shot at playing a Stones-type riff, and what a great song! I took a girlfriend to see the band at Loughborough University. She had no idea what to expect but was completely blown away. They played much of the same set I'd seen before, and were in blistering form. 'Had Me a Real Good Time' was wonderful. Several more uni/college gigs followed that year and it was more of the same. I used to have a recording of the Loughborough gig because I smuggled my cassette recorder in!

I WAS THERE: ANTHONY HUDSON

I and a couple of people I am still in touch with from my Loughborough days attended this gig, but I can't remember much else about it other than the odd visual flash of Rod on stage. We were very lucky at Loughborough to have an excellent Ents team who managed to book some really big bands. I had seen Rod Stewart many years before when he performed with Long John Baldry's Steampacket along with Julie Driscoll and Brian Auger at Richmond Rugby Club, probably around 1966. I was also a fan of the Small Faces, being a Mod at the time. That's about all I can remember, apart from remembering that I always had a good time. Perhaps that's why I can't remember very much else!

I WAS THERE: PETER JOHNSON

Sometime before the concert, I remember being in the Edward Herbert Building, or EHB as we called it, with friends and seeing a poster promoting 'The Faces featuring Rod Stewart'. I said, 'Who the hell is Rod Stewart?' as he was not well known at the time. At one point during the concert, Rod left the stage – apparently unexpectedly, because he said to Ronnie Wood something like, 'I'm going for a pee, take it away Ronnie.' Ronnie looked like a rabbit caught in the headlights, but he carried on playing guitar for what seemed a very long time until Rod eventually reappeared. I think they played 'Maggie May' but I can't be sure. I do remember it being very popular in the summer.

TELL EVERYONE: A PEOPLE'S HISTORY OF THE FACES

I WAS THERE: BRIAN JOHNSON

I went to lots of gigs there and this wasn't one of the most memorable ones. It actually put me off Rod Stewart because he was very big-headed, and at the time the Small Faces were just as well known as he was. He behaved as though it was totally his band. This dislike of Rod stayed with me until I heard that, although the Faces had broken up, Rod had actually paid for Plonk Lane's hospital treatment, when Plonk became ill and was just about penniless. I liked Rod a little more after hearing that! He had been singing for Jeff Beck of course, who I did like. Pete

Brian Johnson was a townie who saw the Faces at the university in Loughborough

Day was the chap who booked the bands for the university and he was very good at predicting who would be good to have well in advance. He never managed his main aim of booking The Who though, as they always cost a bit more than the uni could afford.

I WAS THERE: PETER MURCH

If I remember rightly, they opened up both ends of the Edward Herbert Building. This enabled more people to see the group from both ends of the stage. The gig was great and Rod Stewart was excellent. I have seen him since, including at the old Wembley, and he always works very hard for his audience. The guy who ran the Students Entertainment Committee was Rob Dickins. He was a year or two older than me at Loughborough. He went on to be a very big name in the entertainment industry, and went on to manage Rod.

I WAS THERE: PAUL DUNSTAN, AGE 18

I had long been a Faces fan but was somewhat confused by a short blond-haired youth in the bar before the gig, bugging up how many people had come to see 'him'. I'd gone to see the Faces and paid little attention to the 'featuring Rod Stewart' on the promotional material.

TELL EVERYONE: A PEOPLE'S HISTORY OF THE FACES

Who knew the impact 'Maggie May' would have the next year? The Faces were outstanding!

I WAS THERE: TONY HOLT

I was an undergraduate at Loughborough studying Chemical Engineering from 1970 to 1974. I recall seeing the Faces at both Nottingham University and the EHB at Loughborough in the spring of 1971, although my recollections are a bit fuzzy.

I was introduced to the Faces by a course mate, John Hamlin, who also introduced me to Santana and Jethro Tull, probably earlier in 1971. Having bought *Long Player*, we went off in someone's car to Nottingham to see them play live. I recall arriving late to a full hall and being allowed to watch the performance from the side of the stage. I can't see that happening now. A few weeks later I saw a repeat performance at Loughborough, although John did not. Ents Secretary Rob Dickins sported a full, dark-haired 'Rod' haircut for several terms.

We did not realise at the time how lucky we were at a provincial university to see such talent every week, including Fleetwood Mac in December 1970, The Sweet, Thin Lizzy, America and many, many more. My wife Carole still has the ticket from a Faces performance at the Kings Hall at Belle Vue in Manchester from November 1974 that she went to before I met her.

'Maggie May' was number 1 just a few months after I saw the Faces. At my local disco/club in Derbyshire, and for the only time in my life, I asked the DJ to play it as a request. The answer? 'Sorry mate, we don't play progressive on Sundays.'

I WAS THERE: ROBERT WARR

My memories of the Faces gig at the Edward Herbert Building in 1971 are still clear today after all these years. I was 19 at the time and working for Riker Laboratories (pharmaceuticals) in Loughborough. Two work colleagues, Chris Barsby and Eddie Crich, were both Faces fans and by association I was also drawn into following the band, so when they were booked to appear at the local uni, it was a done deal that we would be there. The Saturday evening would have followed its usual routine, where the group of us would meet in the town centre market place, usually in the Nelson public house, followed by a tour around the locals including the Black Bull cellar bar (a Berni Inn steak bar serving half pints only) before moving next door to the then prestigious hotel the King's Head who, by its very status, refused to stock mild beer.

Walking up Forest Road to the uni was probably my first insight into life on a campus and what a strange (but exciting) diverse kinds of people I was thrust into. The gigs at EHB were always pretty well sold out, as pre-television

Robert Warr has clear memories of the gig over 50 years later

coverage (bar *Top of the Pops*) and videos, there was very little opportunity to see live bands, and particularly very, very good live bands. We arrived at the EHB in good time and had to mill about before the doors were open, which worked in our favour as we were able to pick a spot standing right at the front of the stage.

When the band arrived on stage, the first thing that struck me was their wardrobe. Rod the Mod certainly was an impressive dresser, complete with immaculately spiked hair. Like thousands of others in those early years, being unable to research too much info on the band members apart from *Melody Maker* and *NME*, I thought that Rod and Ronnie W were related. I can still picture Rod's outfit today, a corduroy two piece suit in deep pink (blush?) and which obviously hadn't been bought in C&A. Two things I remember about the suit were firstly the fit and then 'why corduroy?', because up until then I had always viewed corduroy as a working (poor?) man's material. But it was much better quality and less coarse a thread than that awful elephant cord material that had either just started or was about to be in vogue.

The gig was shortly before the band went meteoric, and not long before 'Maggie May'/'Reason to Believe' was released. The one song that keeps coming back to me was the Temptations number, 'I'm Losing You'. I seem to recall it was quite a big stage number and performance from the band, with Rod's vocals, Woody's guitar and a rousing drum solo from Kenney Jones. I also seem to remember that as well as piano keyboard being played by Ian McLagan he also had a Hammond organ type keyboard played to great effect. Another song I remember them playing was the title track from *An Old Raincoat Won't Ever Let You Down*.

Besides Rod's unique voice, I was impressed how professionally sounding the music came through the speakers. I had been to other named gigs where the very opposite was true regarding sound quality at the gig versus studio recordings. But the Faces lads were spot on. Although all members of the band gave a real tight performance, Ronnie Wood's stood out. I had never really heard a guitar sound like his and probably still haven't to this day. It was pure bristles standing-up-on-the-back-of-your-neck time. I don't know why he joined the Stones (apart from the cash), as in my humble opinion his early guitar work has never been bettered.

I never saw Kenney Jones at all during show. Because we were right at the front of the stage and therefore looking upwards, he was completely out of sight all night. And at the end of the show, after the encore, Rod came to the edge of the stage, knelt down and proceeded to sing 'Auld Lang Syne' with us, allowing us to share his mic.

COLLEGE OF EDUCATION
24 MAY 1971, BRIGHTON, UK

I WAS THERE: STEVE ANDREWS

When I was about 13, I spent a lot of time wishing I could have been that crucial six years or so older. That way I could have enjoyed the fruits of the permissive age, or so I told myself as I knuckled down to failing miserably at Dorothy Stringer Secondary Modern in Brighton as the 1960s morphed into the 1970s. My dad worked as a printer at the prestigious Tinsley Robor company in Lancing, where they produced the gatefold sleeves for many of the top-drawer rock albums of the day plus the musician's trade magazine, *Beat Instrumental*. Spare copies of *Beat* would find their way home and I was gutted to read in the spring of 1969 of the 'Small Faces last gig', already old news apparently. Then, in early 1970 I heard Johnnie Walker or someone similar on Radio 1 announce 'a new single by the Small Faces – or just the Faces as they're now calling themselves', and when I heard the finger-picked descending chord sequence of 'Flying', I was hooked.

I soon purchased *First Step* with accrued pocket money and, as the band put in many appearances on *Radio 1 in Concert* and John Peel sessions, I would listen eagerly to the differences between versions, the Rod Stewart solo tunes and – most importantly – the warm band banter. Their evident mateyness filled a gap in my life and it's maybe no surprise that when they came to play at the College of Education in Falmer in the spring of 1971 I bunked off school, leaving behind acts of theft and vandalism that I'd have to answer for later.

I shouldn't big up my street cred too much. My dad drove me there and collected me later and helped initiate a conversation with the head roadie (who I recognised from a few photos in the music press) whereby I got the cover of *First Step* autographed. The snooty 'hipper than thou' Student Union reps on the door sneered under their collective breath at this point, but not too loudly as Dad looked (and still does) A Bit of a Geezer. I remember one of the support acts were called Beggar's Death, because they kept announcing the fact rather too often in an attempt to be humorous. I recall nothing about their music but I know they were local, because as the years rolled by the members would show up in bands like Krakatoa, who went on to have some connection with Saxon.

I recognised some rock celebs of the day filing in on the right and being allowed to go through double doors to some sort of inner sanctum, John Peel among them. I watched like a hawk the Faces' equipment being set up and was curious that the tall WEM speaker columns still had 'Small Faces' stencilled on the side. What history – and they made gear to last in those days! Soon there was a bit of a hubbub at the back of the stage where various pineapple hairdos could be seen bobbing about for a while behind the amplifiers. It was a Monday evening, all very casual.

Everyone who wanted to be at this Faces gig and therefore 'in the know' was there, and lights dimming and stage management wasn't really in it. The university campuses on the edge of Brighton had uniformed porters with peaked caps keeping things on an even keel as grumpy old meters 'n' greeters. One of them was patrolling the back of the stage area like a sitcom traffic warden and was attempting to make his diminutive presence known to the wine-quaffing trio of Ian McLagan, Ronnie Wood and Rod Stewart by hovering nearby. I suppose part of the porter's role was ensuring that acts got on in accordance with schedule, but as he stared up at them (he was shorter than Mac) the punchline of a joke or filthy story so appalled him that he grimaced, turned on his heel and stomped off. I regret that I don't recall what the band started with but I know they played 'Plynth' because I got up and shouted, 'G'wan ma Ron!' at Woody and he grinned. I felt very grown up and part of something, like the kid who wanted to run away with the circus.

The staging had separate moveable sections which had become a bit too movable halfway through the performance and Rodders asked the nearest members of the seated (on the floor) audience to collectively move the straying sections back with their feet, which they gladly did. 'Cheers', he went. A gent.

During minor disruptions to the equipment, a mic stand fell off the reorganised stage and hit a student. He wasn't mortally injured but clearly wasn't a Faces fan either as he sulked like a spanked baboon and glared up at Plonk, who was also a gent and made apologetic gestures and – er – faces, even though he'd been nowhere near the offending stand. It was a great gig and more than lived up to my expectations.

NAG'S HEAD
27 MAY 1971, WOLLASTON, UK

I WAS THERE: BOB BILSON

After attending Lanchester Polytechnic (now Coventry Uni) from 1966 to 1970, I returned home to Northampton where I was a regular at local venues including the Nag's Head in Wollaston, which was run by Big Bob Knight. I saw one of the earliest performances of the Faces, but can't

Bob Bilson saw the Faces at Wollaston's Nag's Head pub

remember any details of that evening other than the whole place was really rocking. The best venue at the time was the Blisworth Hotel, run by a Danish man called Van. Every Sunday, Radio 1 DJ John Peel would turn up in his little van, introduce the band and then drink with us all in the hotel bar afterwards.

I WAS THERE: GEOFF TOYER

I was at the Hurtwood Park reunion. My only other claim to have seen them – or not – was at the Nag's Head in Wollaston, Northamptonshire. The first time they were booked, they failed to turn up. Under threat of suing by the promoter, Bob Knight, and with a word from John Peel, the resident DJ at the Nag's Head, they acquiesced to a request to return a couple of weeks later, on 27 May. This time the word was out so I couldn't get in the place. I had to listen to them in the car park. They threw copies of their album, *Long Player*, into the crowd. I didn't get one but the sister of a mate of mine did!

The Nag's Head gig was advertised but the Faces famously didn't make the gig

I WAS THERE: ROY SALMONS

The gig at the Nag's may never have taken place. Big Bob Knight and John Peel had a sister venue at Blisworth Hotel, which was just off the old main road from Northampton to Towcester. Sunday night was John Peel's night to be the DJ and he invited bands to play there as well as at the Nag's Head. The Faces were booked to play Blisworth in February 1971 but it was called off because – and I am sure this was the story – Rod had laryngitis. I knew very little about the Faces at that point apart from reputation. I didn't buy many albums, because I couldn't afford both to go to gigs and to buy albums. The next we heard was that the band was playing the Nag's, in April. We were a bit disappointed because we lived about eight miles from Blisworth but 25 miles from the Nag's, and we had to go through Northampton and Wellingborough to get there.

We got off work early to get to the gig and, of course, they famously didn't show until we had been given our money back. We were in the car park cursing them when a big black old car pulled in and the band jumped out. John Peel met them at the top of the stairs and gave Rod a piece of his mind in colourful language. He panned them on his radio show.

The Nag's Head in Wollaston where the Faces were invited to play by DJ John Peel

The free gig that they did by way of recompense meant taking time off work to make sure we were there on time and could get in. It was a magnificent performance, complete with handing out free pints to the audience. It was a very small room, with maybe 150 crammed in, so many of us got a freebie. They were oiling their throat with Mateus Rosé which they drank copiously from the bottles, lobbing the empties behind the speakers. Mateus got a credit on *Every Picture Tells a Story*!

After the gig, I followed them as far as their music was concerned but didn't get to see them again. They were not a studio album band as they really came alive on stage, but the live album *Coast to Coast* didn't do them justice. Having said that, 'Stay With Me' is possibly the best song of all time and came from the studio. But *Ooh La La* showed the splits that were emerging and it was clear that they were heading for an end.

Rod reportedly called for a tea break mid-set and pints of beer were passed to the band through the crowd.

EVERY PICTURE TELLS A STORY RELEASED 28 MAY 1971

Every Picture Tells a Story, *Rod's third solo album, is released.* **Melody Maker** *concludes, 'You won't hear a better rock and roll album in 1971.'*

MAYFAIR BALLROOM
28 MAY 1971, NEWCASTLE-UPON-TYNE, UK

I WAS THERE: ROBERT WALKER

John Peel was really in their corner and brought them to my attention on Radio 1 although I remember them on *Top of the Pops* doing 'Had Me a Real Good Time' and chucking paper airplanes around (although that might have been 'Flying'?). My mate bought the *First Step* album and I was hooked. I'm also a massive Stones fan because it's the energy in the music and performance that attracts me. The day that *Every Picture...* was released, they played the Mayfair Ballroom in Newcastle and to this day this is still in my top three all-time gigs. They were back from America and on the way up and the atmosphere was electric.

The venue was a Mecca establishment and had a revolving stage, so they were playing as the stage turned. Rod Stewart was wearing a pink satin or maybe linen suit. They were touring the *Long Player* album. In those days, people sat on the floor but one memory that will stay with me (no pun intended) forever was during Mac's piano intro to 'It's All Over Now' and the crowd rising as one, such was the boogie-woogie sound. It was an unforgettable night and they were fantastic. I saw them a further four times, but that show was truly memorable.

HARD ROCK CAFÉ
14 JUNE 1971, LONDON, UK

I WAS THERE: SEPP DONAHOWER

I came back with some new partners and a new company, Pacific Presentations, in 1970. Originally, the Faces were still called the Small Faces in the US. I knew they were going to be huge because Rod is a star. We were a little fledgling concert company out of Los Angeles and we bought every date we could get our hands on – Pittsburgh, Boston, all over the place – just taking a flyer on them. Then the records were released – the Faces and Rod's solo albums – and then suddenly, bingo, they were a headline act. The ATI agency out of New York was clever.

They put together unmissable three band packages – Rod Stewart with the Faces, Savoy Brown and Deep Purple – for anybody who was into British rock and blues-rock. They did some great packaging, and they liked us out of all the promoters around the US, so we ended getting tours for the whole of the US. We'd take whatever dates we wanted to produce and co-produce the other ones with certain promoters in certain markets. We were working hand-in-hand with (Faces manager) Billy Gaff, and with ATI routing their tours, putting them on and promoting them, it all worked out. We fell in love with the band.

'MAGGIE MAY'
RELEASED JULY 1971

Arguably the biggest single of Rod's career, with Woody on guitar and bass and Mac on Hammond organ, 'Maggie May' tops the UK and US charts and becomes the second bestselling single for 1971 in both countries (beaten to the number 1 slot by Dawn's 'Knock Three Times' in the US and George Harrison's 'My Sweet Lord' in the UK).

I WAS THERE: HENRY LAWRENCE

I know Mike Bobak very well. He was the engineer at Morgan Studios who recorded 'Maggie May'. Rod Stewart gave him £100 after 'Maggie May' charted. I also knew Kevin Westlake, the drummer with Blossom Toes. Kevin was playing guitar at a jam with the recently disbanded Small Faces, with Kenney Jones on drums, when Rod Stewart dropped by and said he urgently needed a band to go into the studio to record his new song, 'Maggie May'. 'Sorry mate,' he said to Kevin, 'we already have a guitarist.' Kevin thought no more about it until 'Maggie May' came out. 'You win some, you lose some' was his philosophical take on it.

I WAS THERE: ANNABEL MARSHALL

I was in Leicester when I first heard Rod Stewart. Radio 1 DJ Johnnie Walker played 'Maggie May' on the radio. I was on the landing at my grandparents' house in Marston Road in Leicester. It's almost like 'you always remember where you were when Kennedy was assassinated…' Well, I clearly remember where I was when I first heard Rod's voice and music, and I've been a firm fan ever since that momentous moment, thanks to Johnnie Walker. Since then, I have gone on to see Rod ten times and have all the albums. I've always wanted to catch a football at his concerts, but I have never been successful!!

One of the girls at school had a dad who was a policeman. He told her that when Rod and the Faces played at the Hippodrome in Bristol, they stayed at the Holiday Inn, which subsequently had to be fumigated after they left. They trashed it! I remember regretting even more that I couldn't go to see them as it sounds like it was an amazing concert!

It'll never happen again. I couldn't turn out another hit single to save my life.
Rod, on learning 'Maggie May' had sold one million copies in the US

KINGSTON POLYTECHNIC
3 JULY 1971, KINGSTON-UPON-THAMES, UK

I WAS THERE: ROBERT HAYWARD

In 1971, I was living above a plumber's shop on Muswell Hill Broadway that overlooked the Broadway roundabout and toilets, where the W7 bus from Finsbury Park would turn around. From the first floor windows, we could look down on urban life as people scurried to and fro. Sometimes we would see the patients in their pyjamas who had absconded from Friern Hospital hanging about awaiting re-capture. Occasionally, first thing in the morning, we would espy Rod Stewart entering the Unigate Dairy across the way to purchase a pint of milk on his way home to Cranwell Gardens. He'd be greeted by a fully amplified track from *Truth* or *Beck-Ola* from Flat 2 where my neighbour, Geoff, would crank up the volume with the windows open in order to see that beaky nose and famous floppy mullet crane to see where the music was coming from. We did this every time we saw him. He never spotted us.

We saw the Faces twice that year. The first time was at Kingston Polytechnic. We travelled down from N10 by public transport. The gig was fantastic – nearly two hours on stage and all the usual antics on stage and banter with the crowd. Afterwards we hung about and asked Rod for a lift back to Muswell Hill, which he declined to give us. Geoff and I then walked all the way across London, back to Muswell Hill, getting home about 6am.

Two or three weeks later we went to the Roundhouse to see them again. In the intervening few weeks the Faces had been on *Top of the Pops* and were celebs – or at least, Rod was. This time they were on stage for about 45 minutes, went through the motions of having a good time with lots of swigging from wine bottles, little contact with the fans and a fairly lacklustre musical performance with no encore. I think they were shedding the fans who had followed them from the Jeff Beck Group, via the two Stewart albums, for a larger constituency prepared to shell out for 45rpm singles. The Roundhouse, of course, was to be exchanged for the later stadium venues.

I WAS THERE: WILLIAM H JONES

I saw them at Kingston Polytechnic. It was shortly after the release of *Every Picture Tells a Story*. Rod was complaining about a sore throat but the students were not impressed with that excuse and he carried on in the best way he could. The suspicion was that he thought he was too big for the college circuit.

SPECTRUM
9 JULY 1971, PHILADELPHIA, PENNSYLVANIA

The Faces fourth US tour has Deep Purple as support, although in places like Ohio, Florida and Texas, Purple are the headliners.

It ought to be a lot of fun and a really good tour because the Faces are a good band and no one will be trying to blow anyone off.
Ian Paice, Deep Purple's drummer (before the tour)

The Faces were lovely guys but they were always so arseholed that they didn't play well at all. They were already sitting back on their laurels.
Ian Paice (after the tour)

PUBLIC AUDITORIUM
10 JULY 1971, CLEVELAND, OHIO

I WAS THERE: ANNA REINHARD

The first time I saw the Faces, I was in my first year of college and an old high school buddy asked me to go to a concert with him. It was in Cleveland, Ohio and the band and its lead singer made the place crazy! Nobody sat in their seats and I eventually got close to the stage, locked eyes with Rod and magic happened. I was swimming in those doe-like eyes as he reached down for a bottle of Blue Nun. I just stared at it and then back at him when someone else grabbed the bottle before I could regain sense. The unceasing thunder of the band and the raw sexiness of the band's presence and funny antics left my suburban Doris Day personality longing for something, I knew not what. All I knew was I wanted to see them again.

HARA ARENA
17 JULY 1971, DAYTON, OHIO

I WAS THERE: TOM GALLAGHER

I've been a big Beck fan since the Yardbirds. In 1968, my father passed away and my mom moved from Columbus to Philadelphia, where our families were. I was a junior in high school. The upside was that I got to see all the great bands of the era, mostly at the Electric Factory and the Spectrum. I saw Beck with Rod Stewart at the Spectrum. They were the opening act of about five that night, including the Mothers of Invention, Sly and the Family Stone, the Grateful Dead and Savoy Brown, who were supposed to play but didn't. Beck was good but he broke a string on the second or third song. A roadie ran out with another Les Paul and a Stratocaster but he decided to finish the set with five strings. He was pissed off. I'm not sure if Ron Wood was in the group that night. It was towards the end of that band. Nicky Hopkins was not there. Rod Stewart was great. He was wearing a pink velvet suit. He hid behind the amps all night, which was hard because it was a concert in the round with a rotating stage in the middle of the arena.

It was a good show but not nearly as good as the rough and ready band I saw in Dayton, Ohio when I was in college. I had about five people with me. We sat right up front. There was maybe 300 – 400 people there, in a large arena.

SPORTS ARENA
18 JULY 1971, TOLEDO, OHIO

I WAS THERE: DENNIS GWYNNE

Toledo is a small town, about 50 miles south of Detroit, where the Faces often played, so we're a stop between Detroit and Cleveland or maybe Chicago. The Sports Arena in Toledo was not a favourite of bands, having no dressing rooms so to speak, as the bands had to use one of the extra long restrooms as a pre performance area or green room. The concert that night featured Matthews Southern Comfort, Faces and Deep Purple. Faces were the middle act and I remember them totally rocking out and being very enjoyable. Rod launched numerous soccer balls off the stage and the band looked like they were having an extremely good time. The crowd obviously loved them. I had Rod's solo LPs and all the Faces albums that were out so I was ready! I've been a musician for over 50 years now and the Faces with Rod are one of my all time faves.

I WAS THERE: GLYNN WILSON

I saw them at Goose Lake. I remember a calm Rod Stewart and a lot of colourful lighting for them as they played. I saw them again in Toledo, Ohio. Yes opened the show followed by Deep Purple and then the Small Faces (as I think they were called then). I sat close to the front and we stood on our chairs. They were very intense musicians. I enjoyed the guitar solo, and again it was another very calm Rod Stewart. After the concert ended, he invited the audience to come to the hotel after and we went. They were asking everyone who came in the door if they had any downers (sedatives).

One other memory that stands out from the Toledo concert is that during one of the numbers, Rod had paused singing for the guitar solo and was walking to the right of the stage. The spotlight was still following him, and he stopped and got the attention of the operator and strongly pointed to the lead guitar in a commanding way, to signal to the audience to give Ron Wood his well-earned due. The spotlight quickly went over. Rod continued to proceed to circle around behind the drummer and take a short break, while the guitar sparked out with intensity. Ronnie's body language strained on the pick for all the right notes.

AUDITORIUM THEATER
21 JULY 1971, CHICAGO, ILLINOIS

I WAS THERE: WAYNE KEDSCH
Rod Stewart and the Faces was the headliner along with Deep Purple and Southern Comfort at the Chicago Auditorium in July 1971. They also played a makeup show at the Auditorium because Rod was sick and couldn't perform. He was supposed to headline a concert with Savoy Brown and the Grease Band at the Chicago Syndrome.

I WAS THERE: TONY ROZENSKY
I saw the tour in Chicago at the Auditorium Theatre with Rod and Ronnie. It was an incredible show. I remember how incredibly loud Deep Purple were.

PIRATES WORLD AMUSEMENT PARK
23 JULY 1971, DANIA, MIAMI, FLORIDA

I WAS THERE: ANDY MOORE, AGE 15
This was my first big show. I saw them at a now defunct amusement park outside Miami called Pirates World. Except for Rod in the Jeff Beck Group and 'Itchycoo Park' by the Small Faces, I wasn't familiar with the Faces at all before that night. They followed Matthews Southern Comfort and Deep Purple and they played their asses off. Woody played a great slide solo, and my friend and I both agreed they had a good bass player. The first time I ever heard 'Maggie May' was that night. It was

very loud this place – good loud! Deep Purple played before them. Faces were good but Purple were better. Blackmore was on fire. I can imagine it would be very tough for anyone to follow Deep Purple back then. Two different kinds of bands really – a 'what if Led Zep opened for the Stones?' type of thing – but they and Deep Purple were both in their prime. If I remember correctly, we had to leave before it was totally over. Someone's dad was waiting with our ride. I wish there was a good live album of the Faces from around this time.

SAM HOUSTON COLISEUM
28 JULY 1971, HOUSTON, TEXAS

A photograph of the crowd is taken which is later used for the cover of **A Nod's as Good as a Wink**…

LONG BEACH ARENA
30 JULY 1971, LONG BEACH, CALIFORNIA

I WAS THERE: DEE HARRINGTON
My girlfriend Patsy and I were living in Los Angeles with a guy called Jack Oliver. Jack ran Apple Records in Savile Row and he'd moved out to LA to work with Peter Asher, who managed James Taylor and Linda Ronstadt. I was 20 when I was there and very young. Patsy and I were both models but struggled to get work in LA because we didn't have green cards, so I used to do the cooking in the house and Patsy did the cleaning. The only work I could get was doing photographs for the centre page of *Playboy*, and the only reason I did that was because it paid five thousand dollars for one picture.

One day Jack said to me, 'There's a friend of mine in town who's from England and he's touring – would you cook him a roast dinner?' That was Kenney Jones. Kenney came round and I cooked the dinner and he said, 'We've got an after show party at this particular club and would you like me to put all your names down?' I didn't really know the Faces at that time, but we said 'yes' and we went down to the club, which was called Bumbles, and that's where I met Rod.

All these very glamorous women were throwing themselves at him and the Faces. I didn't know it at the time but they were LA groupies. I was shocked by everything that went on. But Rod asked me to dance, took me out of the building and I never went back to rejoin my friends in the club. That was it for five years.

Two days later the Faces were playing at Long Beach Arena. Rod asked if I'd like to come and see the gig. That's the first time I ever saw the Faces. Rod had organised for me to be at the side of the stage. The stadium was very dark and they put the house lights on near the end. I was amazed at how many people were there. It was a fabulous show. Rod and I also went up to San Francisco and I saw them play there. They were touring, so they went on to Seattle and a few other places while I stayed in LA.

America in 1971 was a fabulous musical time in all respects, and the Faces were very entertaining, had a very exciting sound and were very well received in America. This was before Rod had released *Every Picture Tells a Story*, so he hadn't had his solo success with 'Maggie May'. I thought, 'Wow, this is brilliant music.' I loved the Stones and a lot of the Sixties bands. Then I got into black American music – soul and R&B, that kind of thing.

At the end of their tour, Rod and the Faces went back to the UK from the States and after a few weeks, I had Rod on the phone saying 'why don't you come back here?' and so I went back to the UK to be with Rod.

SUMMERTHING
6 AUGUST 1971, BOSTON, MASSACHUSETTS

I WAS THERE: ROBERT SHEA

I saw them at *Summerthing* on the Boston Common. It was a great show. They were running all over the stage. It must have been their soccer past coming out. They were the minor league for the Stones.

I WAS THERE: ANDREW ARSENAULT

I sat on stage at *Summerthing* on Boston Commons. It was a fine show. I leaned against a leg of Ian McLagan's Hammond B3 until Rod pulled so many audience members on stage that, when he and Ronnie turned to leave, they were swamped. Then it was all hands on deck to pull them out of the soup!

I WAS THERE: DARRYL HOPKINS

I can still see Rod in his cherries jacket at *Summerthing*. That was one rockin' show.

After their North American tour wraps in Washington DC on 7th August 1971, the Faces head back to Europe for several festival shows.

MAYFAIR BALLROOM
27 AUGUST 1971, NEWCASTLE-UPON-TYNE, UK

I WAS THERE: JOHN LOGAN

I had always been a Small Faces fan, and I was a fan of the Jeff Beck Group, mainly for his virtuoso playing but also because he had a great vocalist in Rod Stewart and bass player in Ron Wood. I watched with interest when I heard that Ron and Rod had left Beck's group to throw their lot in with ex-Small Faces Ronnie Lane, Ian McLagan and Kenney Jones. There was a band right there!

I had the *Beck-Ola* and *Truth* albums and *Ogden's Nut Gone Flake* by Small Faces. I waited eagerly for news of gigs under this new band, who I'd heard were just called 'Faces' on account of fact that the two new additions were not 'small', ie. Rod and Ronnie.

My first Faces gig was at Mayfair Ballroom in my home city in the summer of 1971. It was a pay on the door gig. The Mayfair was an iconic rock venue and all the geat bands played there – Led Zeppelin and Free to name but two. The Faces had played the same venue just three months previously but sadly I couldn't get to that one. The August gig was just before 'Maggie May' entered the charts and the *Every Picture Tells a Story* album was charting too, both later to go to Number 1 on both sides of the Atlantic simultaneously. Rod was the first solo artist to achieve this feat.

The Mayfair was made for the Faces. It was a small 1,500 capacity ballroom, and it had a great atmosphere. They played a great set, mainly from *First Step* and *Long Player*, with 'Three Button Hand Me Down', 'Maybe I'm Amazed', 'Love in Vain', 'Feel So Good', 'Bad 'n' Ruin' and a soulful rendition of 'Richmond' with Ronnie Lane on vocals as Rod took a breather with what looked like Mateus Rosé side stage. It was a short set as I recall (they were infamous for that in the early days) after a late arrival. It was not surprising as they seemed well inebriated, in keeping with their image in years to come. It was packed to the rafters.

I WAS THERE: JEFF SPENCE

Jeff Spence and wife Mandi were both Faces fans

The Small Faces were a band I really liked as I entered my teens and I admired Steve Marriott's vocals. Strangely, 'The Universal' was my favourite song by them as it was just different. Around the same time my mate, John Snowball, introduced me to *Truth* by the Jeff Beck Group, an album that I still listen to today. I loved Rod's vocals and the incredibly bluesy feel to the record. I bought the next album, *Beck-Ola*, as soon as it was out too. Not long after, John told me that the band had split and 'that singer you like' had joined the rest of the Small Faces. He never mentioned Woody so it was a nice surprise when I found out that he was in there too… on guitar? Once again there was a slight twist when I found a copy of *An Old Raincoat…* in my local record store and loved it and then my mate told me that the new band were playing in Newcastle soon. The band played on *Top of the Pops* around that time with 'Flying', ensuring that I needed to go and see them live.

Over the next few years, I saw them at Sunderland Top Rank Club and the Locarno Ballroom, several times at Newcastle Mayfair, at Newcastle City Hall and Newcastle Odeon as well as catching them in London in 1973 and a couple of gigs in Scotland, particularly at Glasgow Playhouse and somewhere in Edinburgh and the Caird Hall in Dundee, again in 1973. I actually followed them from Newcastle Mayfair in August 1971 down to Weeley for a weekend festival. They stole the whole show and, at that point, hadn't had anything like a 'hit' single but had a massive live following.

Lindisfarne were good that day and T.Rex got showered with bottles and cans and didn't like it. The Edgar Broughton Band suffered a similar fate at the same festival or perhaps at the Great Bardsley Festival sometime later. The Mayfair gig was a bit of a revelation. The Faces had previously played to a half empty City Hall and a fairly full Mayfair just a few months before, but this time you could tell that something was ready to happen. 'Maggie May' was introduced as a song about 'a schoolboy that fell in love with a prostitute' and 'Losing You' contained the drum solo. The venue was packed and Rod was treated as the star, although the whole band was always well loved.

WEELEY FESTIVAL OF PROGRESSIVE MUSIC 1971
27 – 29 AUGUST 1971, CLACTON-ON-SEA, UK

The Faces share a bill with Colosseum, King Crimson, Heads, Hands & Feet and T.Rex. A reviewer for the **New Musical Express** *writes, 'After they'd finished my sympathies were with the follow-up band, T.Rex. After all who could possibly follow or match the sheer brilliance of the Faces who were undoubtedly at their best.'*

I WAS THERE: CHRIS PRICE
It was on the way to see them at a festival that a gang of us listened to 'Maggie May' on the radio in my Morris Minor. We knew right away that it was going to be a huge hit and to see them do it live was a delight. *Every Picture Tells a Story* was Rod's third solo album, although it again featured members of the Faces throughout. I didn't actually rate it as highly as his first two, but he was clearly going to be famous in a big way. For me it also marked the beginning of the end. Yes, that early.

TELL EVERYONE: A PEOPLE'S HISTORY OF THE FACES

I WAS THERE: GRAHAM MCANDREW, AGE 15
It was my first major gig. Obviously, I knew about the Small Faces (I enjoyed them and still do) but I hadn't really heard of Rod Stewart then. 'Maggie May' had come out just a few months before. My sister had heard of Rod. She had come across 'Handbags and Gladrags' and she definitely said, 'Catch the Faces – they'll be brilliant.' They were, and blew everyone away. I can't remember if they were before or after T.Rex, but I do remember them being superior to Marc Bolan's band, who initially got jeered at for 'selling out'. I do recall thinking how the Faces really knew how to work the audience with a more devil-may-care and fun approach than practically all the preceding bands, and without having to flaunt their obvious good musicianship. Rod is, and has, been fantastically charismatic right from the start.

I WAS THERE: ALAN BUTCHER
When T.Rex came on the crowd was split, as most booed them for selling out and I saw young hippy girls crying as they begged fans to give Bolan a chance. Rory Gallagher was as brilliant as ever, and the Faces were awesome. There was trouble between the Hell's Angels and the caterers, but I was there for the music and kept well away from all that stuff.

I WAS THERE: NIALL CORBETT
I liked The Small Faces and always loved their singles. I heard them on the radio and saw them on *Top of the Pops*. The first I heard of Rod Stewart was when I saw his LP *Gasoline Alley* in the window of Town Records on the Kings Road, Chelsea, a few hundred yards from The World's End. The shop Granny Takes a Trip was close by and Sophistocat, complete with famous pet lion, was just across the road. Older friends often spoke about 'Rod the Mod' but it didn't mean much to me at that time.

I first heard *Long Player* in 1970 and was completely smitten with it. The lazy and loose rock 'n' roll was fantastic. I couldn't wait to see the Faces live. My first opportunity was at the Weeley Festival. There was a massive crowd, most of whom were completely knackered by the time the Faces came on to play. There was such a huge number of bands booked to play that, in order to fit everyone in, a decision was made to start the programme around 7pm to 7.30pm on Friday and continue non-stop through to Sunday afternoon! I was desperate to see Rory Gallagher on Friday night, but I crashed out and missed him. There was a huge outcry as many had done the same. The organisers got him to play again on the Saturday night, and guess what? I missed him again!

But I was wide awake for the Faces. It was broad daylight. They were fantastic and I loved their performance. There was, however, a distraction. An enormous food fight developed amongst the crowd near me and my friends, with foodstuffs flying in all directions! It was hard to look at the stage, as one was likely to get a banana or a hotdog in one's earhole. A neighbour commented, 'By the way, the Faces are playing.' That brought my attention back to the stage. I honestly cannot remember anything of the set list.

I WAS THERE: CHRIS RYMER, AGE 17

I had not long passed my driving test and this was my longest drive so far. I arrived early on the Friday to the maddest, baddest festival to be held on British soil. At least my old Zephyr Mark III got myself and a couple of mates there without letting us down. But what had I let myself in for? My memories of the festival itself consist of a huge crowd, well in excess of the 110,000 estimate. I also remember the dreadful latrines, which consisted of eight foot deep trenches and a couple of scaffold poles to lean against, burning tents, living on yoghurt for three days and Hell's Angels doing security! I wanted to see the Edgar Broughton Band. The festival had just started at midnight on Friday and they kicked off at about 1.30am. Although you could hear them about 10 miles away in Clacton-on-Sea, I fell asleep and missed the gig.

The standouts for me were Barclay James Harvest, Mott the Hoople, Curved Air (with their famously named drummer, Ariel Bender) and Status Quo. T.Rex were due to headline, but most wanted the Faces. They played before T.Rex on the Saturday evening. Rod was very good, he sang his heart out. 'Maggie May' was the stand out song. Yes, he nailed it. It would have been the largest audience he, Ronnie Wood and the rest had played in front of, and we had several encores. I was 17, Rod 25 and Ronnie 23. We will probably all never forget that crazy weekend.

TELL EVERYONE: A PEOPLE'S HISTORY OF THE FACES

I WAS THERE: STEVE WARREN

Allegedly, this is where they first performed 'Maggie May'. I can't vouch for that fact but I do remember Rod, Ronnie and the boys performing a superb set which was one of the highlights of the weekend. I was directly below the stage as I had a press pass (I wrote a record column at the time in the *Durham Advertiser* series). Rod was resplendent in a pink satin suit, with no shirt. I also saw

Steve Warren was at the Weeley Festival

him back stage in deep conversation with Marc Bolan. Marc was booed by the crowd for being too 'pop'. The Weeley experience was amazing as it had been organised by Clacton Round Table to replace their donkey derby and they were expecting around 10,000 but well over 100,000 turned up. There were fires, fights with Hells Angels and great bands, but the toilets (a trench with scaffolding) left a lot to be desired

The B reg 1964 Mini I drove there was an old wreck and had no reverse gear due to gearbox problems which meant my girlfriend (now my wife) Val had to occasionally jump into the driver's seat while I jumped out to push the car backwards. When we eventually arrived at Weeley, the cornfield had been mowed but all the hay just left on the ground. I covered the Mini in straw for privacy and other festival goers made straw 'igloos' where they slept. Occasionally, a fire would break out and people would run out to stamp the flames out. At one point, the blaze got out of control and burned out several cars. Fortunately for us, this was on a different part of the site. The Round Table organisers were using a van stocked with handheld fire extinguishers they had borrowed as a make shift fire engine. It is a miracle no one died.

I WAS THERE: WILLIAM H JONES

After Kingston Polytechnic I saw them at the Weeley Festival, which wasn't as good as people like to say. Most of us were the worse for wear on booze and cannabis.

I did see Rod arrive by Bentley in his pink suit on my way to the toilets.

As for the performance, I seem to recall they played pretty good set but how good is open to interpretation. My most vivid memory is the journey home. Our transit van broke down and we had to push it, all of us with shoulder-length hair, and getting loads of abuse from the rest of the vehicles.

PURCELL ROOM, QUEEN ELIZABETH HALL
5 SEPTEMBER 1971, LONDON, UK

I WAS THERE: MARK BRADY

I saw the Faces twice, at the Queen Elizabeth Hall and then at the Rainbow. The gig at QEH was a lot more sedate. It's a classical music concert hall situated in the Festival Hall complex, a lot smaller than the Rainbow, and it seemed a bit soulless. There was certainly not as much leaping around and raucous behaviour as I witnessed at the Rainbow. I don't really remember any specifics other than there were a lot of tartan scarves. This was my second ever gig, with the first being Creedence Clearwater Revival at the Royal Albert Hall.

I WAS THERE: ALAN WESTWOOD

I was in my final year of school in London in 1971 before starting at the University of Exeter in September. My school friends and I were hippies and loved the rock and blues scene around London and going to the Rainbow and to small clubs, seeing bands like Family, Yes, Led Zeppelin and so on.

One of the best ever was Rod and the Faces at the Purcell Room on London's South Bank. It was special as the tickets were sold before *Every Picture Tells a Story* was released and before 'Maggie May' was a hit. It wasn't a huge venue so this was a small group of perhaps 300 fans who knew Rod for albums like *An Old Raincoat* and *Gasoline Alley* as well as, in my case, Jeff Beck's 1968 album, *Truth*. Rod knew it was going to be the last time they ever played to such a small audience.

The concert started off normally enough with a familiar run of songs from his older albums. But then, after about an hour or so, he stood on stage and looked at us and said how this would be special because, since these tickets had been sold, he had become a major star. He laughed when he said, 'I'm not doing anything different to what I was doing a year ago.' Meaning, I guess, how suddenly life can change. He called those at the back to come on down to the front and sit on the steps in the aisles and then brought out a case of Scotch whisky. Bottles were handed out and passed around.

He then said, 'We are going to just keep playing all night!' which raised the loudest cheer of the evening. This 90 minutes or so gig turned into well over three hours and had us all singing along. I seem to recall him saying his parents were there. I have been to hundreds of gigs over the years and the atmosphere on that night has never been equalled. My friends and I had a long walk home as buses and trains had long since finished and I recall arriving home around five in the morning.

I went to see Rod and the Faces twice more that summer. One was at an all day event at The Oval, when they were second only to The Who that night and where they were still firing on all cylinders. But, of course, it was impossible to recreate the intimacy of the Purcell Room. I also saw them at the open air festival at Weeley in Essex in August. As with most festivals of that size, it was hopeless.

I WAS THERE: ROBERT WARR

After watching the Faces at Loughborough University in May 1971 and with the band starting to receive a heck of a lot more media attention (did that phrase even exist in the 1970s?), myself and a few of the lads started asking around our peer group if anyone (boys only) would be interested in a trip down into London for a Faces concert at the Queen Elizabeth Hall, which I seem to recall was near the Thames Embankment. The selling point for most of the guys wasn't in seeing the band, but in getting the chance to have a good time in the capital. Therefore the necessary arrangements were made for transport, tickets to the show and a loose itinerary around seeing the sights. Upon reaching London, it was a glorious sunny day which worked very much in our favour, as the girls were very much displaying their many charms wearing mini-skirts and hot pants. I remember that although we had very many attractive girls around Loughborough, it seemed that the streets of London were certainly paved with a more cultural and worldy-wise group of young, free-spirited people. It wasn't just legs that were on show as, whilst waiting to cross the King's Road, one of our party noticed something and suddenly called in a muted style almost under his breath, 'Eyes right!' Upon instinctively looking right, we were joined at the crossing by a guy (who I don't remember too much about) and his girl, who was so much more prominent as she was wearing no top. In fact, as I remember it, she was very prominent in a couple of places!

I recall a certain amount of nervousness and trepidation from within our group as to what we should do to not bring attention to ourselves. For my part, I think I just looked at my shoes until she moved on. Now that never happened back in Loughborough or, at least, never when I was around – bugger!

The other recollection of that time spent on Kings Road was seeing Tony Blackburn cruising past in his E-Type Jag complete with open shirt, a cravat and a big cheesy grin. He was obviously milking the looks and stares as he went by on numerous occasions. Before making our way to the concert, which was in the afternoon or early evening, we did the touristy bit around Carnaby Street where we happened upon a music shop with Keith Moon's drum kit for sale, which had some massive ticket price on it like £1,000. The hippy brigade were out in force (albeit well-heeled as in having obvious cash to spend) and the transport of choice was the open topped Mini Moke.

Upon entering the Queen Elizabeth Hall, it was quite a culture shock, being well upholstered and comfortable with excellent views of the stage with pretty good sound systems reaching out to all of the hall. On the bill before the Faces was a band called Cochise, which I seem to remember were a late replacement for the originally booked act. Both bands gave an excellent account of themselves, but sadly it was the last time I was able to see the Faces as superstardom was about to embrace the singer and the rest of the band would soon be no more.

I have followed Rod Stewart's career since those early days but for me he has never musically achieved the same rawness and musical excitement as when the Faces were together. The up-tempo rock stuff was replaced by the slower paced ballads which did not have the DNA of the original band. I think it was a great disservice to music and to Kenney, Ian and Ronnie Lane when Rod and Ronnie Wood went their separate ways.

THE OVAL CRICKET GROUND
18 SEPTEMBER 1971, LONDON, UK

The Faces appear at the Goodbye Summer concert at the Oval cricket ground in South London. The music press herald The Who as the winners, but a Faces fan writes in to Melody Maker to say 'the Faces were ten times better'.

I WAS THERE: CHRIS PRICE

I last saw the Faces at The Oval cricket ground. They had just released 'Stay With Me'. I didn't enjoy the gig all that much. I thought The Who were bloody awful. The Faces were still a great band, but I didn't think it came over well on such a big stage. It was at this point that I jumped ship so to speak. I continued to love them but I didn't think their later albums really did them justice. The point was totally lost when Ronnie Lane left. Tetsu was the wrong man to replace him. Rod Stewart's later commercial stuff doesn't work for me at all, but you can't argue with that level of success! The reunion shows were a waste of time in my book. You can't recreate something like the Faces. It was of the moment. Mac in particular wanted it, yet his Bump Band were great. I know because we supported them at a gig in Nottingham in 2008.

'Goodbye Summer' programme

TELL EVERYONE: A PEOPLE'S HISTORY OF THE FACES

I WAS THERE: ANGUS DUNBAR

I got into the Faces by luck really. I lived in Vauxhall, close to the Oval cricket ground. I sneaked over the wall.

I WAS THERE: HOWARD GARDNER

15 of us piled into my mate Dale's small furniture van. We put a mattress or two and some blankets in the back and set off from Leeds the night before the concert, stopping off in Barnsley for a beer or two before driving through the night to London. We managed to get parked just opposite the main gate.

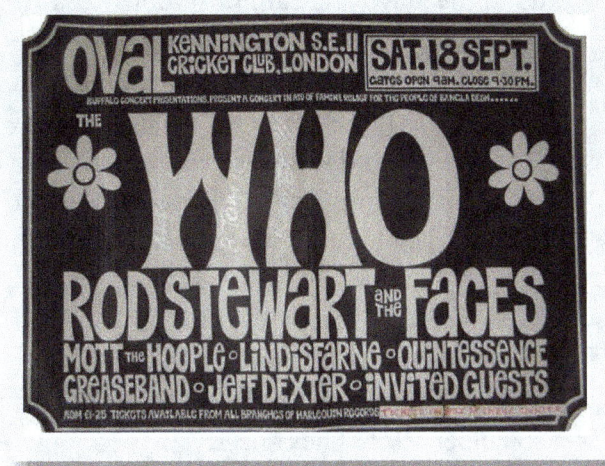

Poster for the Who and Faces 'Goodbye Summer' show

The date marked the first anniversary of the death of Jimi Hendrix, so there were quite a few things going on in memory of Hendrix. There were a number of bands on that day, including America, Pentangle, the Grease Band, Mott the Hoople. The Who were the main act. The atmosphere had been a bit sombre most of the day. People just sat around listening to the music, drinking and eating, and there was a lot of polite applause. But when the Faces came on in the early evening, the whole atmosphere changed within a couple of songs. Everyone was up dancing and clapping along with the music. 'Stay With Me' had just been released and that brought the house down. The whole set was complete fun from start to finish. It was a close call as to who was the best band that day, but The Who just shaved it.

Rod wore a tiger-skin suit which he later auctioned for charity, raising £500 for Bangladesh.

I WAS THERE: MARILYN KENNEDY

I first saw the Faces at the *Goodbye Summer* concert for Bangladesh. Next day I went straight to a record shop and bought *Every Picture Tells a Story*.

TELL EVERYONE: A PEOPLE'S HISTORY OF THE FACES

I started going to as many concerts as I could get to around the London area. What appealed to me most, apart from loving the music they performed, was the fun the Faces were having and this transferred to the fans. The concerts were singalongs, with everyone joining in. The music made me want to dance. I could never have sat down at a Faces concert, and to this day I still cannot sit down at a Rod Stewart concert.

I remember the Faces having a bar on stage at some concerts and the band drinking from the bar throughout the concert. The Faces were having a good time on stage, while the fans were doing exactly the same in the crowd. Rod's dress sense and hairstyle made him stand out. At a time of 'supergroups' and 'progressive music', the Faces were a breath of fresh air. Happy, fun and where you just went a bit crazy for a while.

I WAS THERE: NIALL CORBETT

After Weeley, the next time I saw them was at The Oval in September 1971. The concert was called the *Goodbye Summer* concert for Bangladesh. There was a terrific line up and The Who headlined. The Faces were magnificent. Rod wore a leopard skin pattern jacket and Woody was equally dressed to the nines. There were people selling acid and dope in the crowd, just like selling ice creams. There was some bad acid there and some people near us had bad trips. The third time I saw them was at the Rainbow in February 1972. It was another great show. There was some fabulous loose playing and lots of booze was taken. I left the theatre thinking to myself, 'Wow, top that!'

Batting order for The Oval 'Goodbye Summer' show

TELL EVERYONE: A PEOPLE'S HISTORY OF THE FACES

I WAS THERE: WILLIAM MARTIN

This was a great concert, presented and promoted by the people who put on the 1970 Isle of Wight Festival, the Foulk brothers of Fiery Creations, which I also went to. On the bill were Cochise, the Grease Band, Lindisfarne, Quintessence, Mott the Hoople, America, Eugene Wallis, Atomic Rooster, the Faces and headlined by The Who. It was a brilliant day; sunny, dry and warm. The Faces came on at 6pm and played for well over an hour, and what a brilliant show they played. They played tracks from their first two LPs. I remember Rod wearing a leopardskin printed stage suit, and he used that mic stand to full effect. They were brilliant. I saw Rod Stewart solo many times after that night. Sadly, I never saw the Faces again.

I WAS THERE: SANDIE RITTER

It was difficult to know what was happening with Mac. He'd been my favourite in the Small Faces, although I knew Steve better than any of them. Rod and Ronnie are both very extrovert. Ronnie has always been very flamboyant on stage, including in the way he dresses, and you can see that in the videos of the Faces and how he moves around. I'd go into the dressing room and he would talk over me. And I just couldn't be bothered. He was quite loud, and Rod was very loud, whereas the others weren't. Kenney was very quiet and Ronnie Lane was more introspective, and I think Mac probably was too. Rod and Ronnie took over just because of being themselves. And, of course, Rod's success meant that people began looking towards him more than the rest of the band.

Things changed once 'Maggie May' hit the charts. The audience changed. Everything changed. They were plummeted into success. It wasn't theirs. It was Rod's. Cracks were bound to show up at some point, although you don't see things as a fan unless you're looking for them. I certainly didn't know that Ronnie Lane's health was deteriorating, yet it was probably quite obvious by then.

And they were all so young. It must've been a very exciting time for them to have that success, to be going to America, to be breaking in America. Even for Rod and Ronnie, even though they'd been there before. It must've been different not to be doing this as part of someone else's band but in their own right. Because at the end of the day, when he was in the Jeff Beck Group, Rod was Jeff Beck's singer.

And with success they could have all the drink, they could have all the girls, they could have all the everything. What is there to complain about? It's only after a number of years that they woke up and realised 'this is all rather shallow'. That was when Ronnie started doing too much and he's now been sober for getting on for ten years.

But then it was the lifestyle. It was a very hedonistic time. We were living in very different times and our parents wanted us to have so much that they couldn't have because of the war. They wanted us to have more freedom. And the pill came along and it changed everything. There was a lot of experimentation. And LSD suddenly became popular, that and other drugs.

Things went bad when cocaine took over. That I did see in the Faces. I did see things disintegrate through cocaine, because I wouldn't take a drug like that ever. When he became a solo act as well, Rod turned quite horrible. He became a nasty piece of work and I'm sure that cocaine must've had a big influence on that. But it was popular and I guess it still is with a lot of people. Bands would have requirements on their riders as to what should be in the dressing room, and cocaine may have been one of their requirements.

Cocaine started to take a grip of the Faces when they could to buy afford it. Certainly, people from council estates weren't taking cocaine. It wasn't cheap. My hippie friends were taking speed but not cocaine. Maybe it meant the Faces could play music with alcohol in their system, because one would balance out the other. But they certainly didn't seem sober very much of the time.

I don't think Rod and Ronnie tried to take over. I think it was just unfortunate for the Faces that Rod had that solo success and that Rod actually had a recording contract in place before the Faces had begun. Rod must've hoped for solo success, but he saw himself as very much part of the band. He didn't see himself as a solo act until Ronnie Wood went off with the Stones. Yes, there was a lot of Rod's solo stuff on the last UK and US tours, but the band had been on his records. It was all mixed into one.

I'm not sure what Mac thought at the time, and what he thought at the time and what he said later may not always be the same. He seemed quite happy with his lot in life back then. He was earning good money. Things were in place for him in terms of his career, whereas when the Small Faces split up, they weren't. None of them knew what the future was. When Rod had success, it was good for all of them.

TOP OF THE POPS
29 SEPTEMBER 1971, LONDON, UK

The Faces back Rod on his appearance on the legendary BBC television show to promote 'Maggie May'. Musicians' Union rules require the band to mime. BBC DJ John Peel appears on stage 'playing' the mandolin. The same union rules that stop bands performing live mean non-musician Peel should not be on stage and BBC cameramen are instructed to keep him out of shot. Rod responds by taking every opportunity to stand behind Peel during the taping so that he's captured on screen.

ROYAL BALLROOMS (AKA STARKERS)
8 OCTOBER 1971, BOURNEMOUTH, UK

I WAS THERE: BAZ MORT

They were supported by Thin Lizzy and Cochise. I believe that this was the tour when the Faces employed a roadie just to keep their wine at the right temperature. This was a night that got so rowdy and out of control – both the Faces and the audience – that the management turned off the power during 'I Feel So Good', bringing the gig to an abrupt end. However, to give him his due, Rod came back on to carry on singing unaccompanied until he was hustled off.

Baz Mort was at the Royal Ballrooms

When we arrived, it was getting very messy in the bar. It seemed like it was everyone's ambition to get as pissed as possible. Consequently, we missed all of Cochise and most of Lizzy as we were busy catching up. The room was packed with mostly standing or staggering clientele. When the Faces came on, it was clear that the rumours about the wine roadie were true. They all looked like they'd had a few. But it was all great fun. Their set list was pretty varied, including 'Three Button Hand Me Down', 'Maybe I'm Amazed', 'When Will I Be Loved', 'It's All Over Now', 'Stay With Me', 'Around the Plynth', 'I Know I'm Losing You', 'Maggie May' and 'I Feel So Good', during which the plug was pulled. There was also a Ronnie Wood interlude so he could show off all his guitar tricks. To sum up, a great night was had by all and it was a real pleasure to see such a great band in their prime.

I WAS THERE: DAVID LONG

The next time I saw them was 26th May 1971, again at the Winter Gardens. There were lots more in the audience. It was a similar setlist but you started to notice Rod! After that, they moved to a place called Starkers. This venue put on many great shows (all standing) including Led Zeppelin, Bowie, Fleetwood Mac and a personal favourite of mine, the Keef Hartley Band.

I was upstairs and the support was Thin Lizzy, who were amazing. Phil Lynott was sending the fans mad, particularly my girlfriend. Looking back, he blew Rod off the stage. The Faces had just had a hit out, and it was a slicker show with time being of the essence and less standing around and smoking, etc. My recollection was of Ronnie Wood, with solos he still plays, and Ian McLagan and that great organ sound. (I saw Mac in Dylan's band at Wembley Stadium where he played liked a member of The Band!) The show was great. The place was packed out. The Faces had arrived.

They were due to play the Winter Gardens on 19th December 1972, but I think it was pulled. They were known to pull a few gigs if *Top of the Pops* wanted them. The last time I saw them was December 1974, again at the Winter Gardens, when they were at the top of their game. They were beginning to muck around to excess, no doubt assisted by Boots the Chemist.

A few years back at the Borderline, I managed to share a coffee with Ian McLagan, who was there to see Buddy Miller, and we discussed the development of all things Faces. He was back in the UK from the States. What a great bloke, and sadly missed.

REFECTORY HALL, UNIVERSITY OF LEEDS
16 OCTOBER 1971, LEEDS, UK

I WAS THERE: CHRISTINE PINDER (NEE GIBSON)

I was a postgraduate student at Leeds University. In mid-September, I bought tickets to see Rod Stewart and the Faces in the Union building. At that time, they weren't particularly well known, but by the time the gig came round, Rod had gone to number 1 in the charts with 'Maggie May'. Tickets for the gig were changing hands at three or four times the original cost, but I hung onto mine and went to the gig. It was absolutely heaving, and they did 'Maggie May' as their encore. We all went wild, bellowing every word of the song, and after the long instrumental bit towards the end of the song, yelling the last 'Maggie May' even louder and right on cue. What a gig!

I WAS THERE: TIM SULLIVAN, AGE 20

I was a mere lad of 20 when I saw the Faces. 'Maggie May' had been released and it might have been number 1 in the charts. I remember that it was a brilliant gig and Ronnie Lane was well gone. I went with a friend, Martin, who I had been at school with. I was working in 1971 and in 1970 and 1971 we seemed to be going to gigs on a regular basis. I remember they did 'Maggie May' but also 'Twistin' the Night Away' and the Paul McCartney number they used to do, 'Maybe I'm Amazed'. My lasting memories of the gig are of how much the band enjoyed playing, which of course influenced how the audience reacted. And despite how Rod Stewart's career developed, he was a damn good lead singer in a good rock band.

KINETIC CIRCUS
22 OCTOBER 1971, BIRMINGHAM, UK

I WAS THERE: BRIAN REES

I think I saw them nine times. I saw them at a fantastic place in Birmingham called the Kinetic Circus which was also known as the Mayfair Suite, where they were totally pissed and all over the place. It was a bit shambolic but in a good way and they kept it together somehow. They were brilliant. It was just a riotous night. Rod gave me a sip of his Blue Nun! And I saw them at the Town Hall in Birmingham, and at the Odeon in Birmingham. Two great gigs. The Town Hall gig was just epic. They were as tight as two coats of paint, and the whole crowd was up for it.

At the Weeley Festival, Rod was in a pink satin suit with a cut jacket, and they were just awesome. And at Reading, Rod was in a gold or silver matador's top. They blew the place apart. They were absolutely brilliant. At Dudley Zoo, where they played with the Edgar Broughton Band and T.Rex, Robert Plant got up and did a song with them.

The music scene was getting extremely dull and I wanted to go out and have a party. And that's what you did with the Faces. I remember going to see Led Zep play at the Odeon and Robert Plant telling the crowd to quiet down: 'You're like a football crowd. Quiet down. Listen.' What's he saying? You're in a rock crowd and you've got to sit down? That's not what it's about. It's about cracking on and having a good time.

I met them once. They'd played in Nottingham somewhere. We all bowled over there. On our way back at a motorway service station there they were in this Rolls-Royce kind of car – the kind of car the Queen drove, one of those long old cars with loads of seats. We had a great chat with them. They were drinking Blue Nun. How classy!

The Faces were the right band at the right time, and more so. When you went to see the Faces, you knew you were going to have a good time. I saw them play badly a couple of times and I know they could be hit and miss. But when they were 'hit'? Bloody hell, that was something else. There's never been anybody else for me that's done it like that since. I've seen Rod, either with the Faces or solo, about 85 times. I've seen him on every tour, and multiple gigs on a tour. He's my main man. Bands like the Black Crowes and the Quireboys have tried to imitate them, but you'll never touch the Faces. Never.

FREE TRADE HALL
25 OCTOBER 1971, MANCHESTER, UK

I WAS THERE: MELANIE DOUGLAS

I had just started university in Manchester. I was living in residence and had made a few friends – Gill, Stella and Jayne. I don't remember how or through whom, but Gill and I met a girl called Lynn. I can't even remember if she was a student, but I got the feeling she was older than us. We were very tuned into the latest music and we loved the Faces and Rod Stewart. 'Maggie May' was number 1 on the charts and we could sing every word (I can still do that today).

Melanie Douglas got in for free thanks to her friend Lynn

Lynn said she knew the Faces and could get us into their upcoming concert at the Free Trade Hall in Manchester. Gill and I were sceptical and quite naïve 18 year olds, but we were away from home and didn't need permission, so we went into Manchester with Lynn and she led us to the back of the building to the stage door. Up until this point, we were still very unsure that anything was going to happen. We thought we had been 'had'.

It wasn't long after arriving that a limousine pulled up, and out poured the Faces and Rod Stewart! Dressed for the stage, they were long-haired, skinny and fashionably dressed. I remember satin and sparkles. As they walked by Lynn and me and Gill, Rod greeted Lynn and said, 'Come on, follow us in. We'll get you a seat.' Now we were excited, knew it was for real and followed Lynn. We ended up in the dress circle, with no seats per se but a fabulous view. We rocked out all night to the music and when they started the opening bars of 'Maggie May', the place went wild. Everyone sang and knew every word! Rod kicked footballs into the crowd and we went wild too.

I still can recall the excitement and thrill I felt that night, nearly 50 years ago, and remain a huge fan of Rod. I love whatever he sings, but those early songs still take me back to my student days. The mandolin, 'played' by John Peel on 'Maggie' on *Top of the Pops*, always sends a thrill through me. My husband knows it, my kids know it and it will always be my favourite song.

I WAS THERE: LESLIE MURPHY, AGE 14

I first saw the Faces at the Free Trade Hall in October 1971. It was my second ever concert, the first being the vocal quartet The Spinners (don't ask! My ex liked them). The venue was heaving with Faces fans and every song was greeted enthusiastically. As I had a pretty good view, I made a point of looking at the whole band and what each member was contributing to the evening's performance. I couldn't see that much of Kenney Jones even though his kit was on a drum riser, but I certainly heard his drumming! Ronnie

Leslie Murphy's previous concert experience was seeing The Spinners

Lane had a permanent grin all night and was superb on the bass, with his vocals complementing Rod's lead. Ronnie Wood was playing the Tony Zematis Mother of Pearl guitar I had admired previously only in pictures in magazines, and he was wearing a waistcoat and flares whilst either smoking his cigarette or sticking it in between the strings on the guitar's headstock. Pure class!

Ian McLagan wore a white suit with cherry red Doc Martens boots.

He had a bottle of Jack Daniels and numerous plastic cups on top of his white Steinway piano. One of the highlights was Mac playing the piano during 'Memphis', using his foot a la Jerry Lee Lewis. Total sacrilege on a Steinway, surely? Nevertheless, the crowd loved it!

Even back then at the age of 14 I thought Rod was a supreme showman, in blue sparkle top and yellow satin flares and 'that' barnet constantly being ruffled between songs using a towel, and grabbing a drink near Kenney's drum riser. At several points, Rod did his trademark of throwing the mic and stand in the air, catching it on the way down, and doing a version of the splits. The whole show seemed to be over so quick because it was so brilliant. What a first rock concert to attend!

After that I was a devotee, cutting my hair into an approximation of Rod's feather cut and buying satin pants, silk girls' blouses, etc. and strutting my stuff in nightclubs at the tender age of 15! Later on, I even had a copy of the ruffled shirt Rod wore on the cover of the Smiler album, hand-made as I recall by Nicholls the bespoke Manchester shirt maker, who normally made shirts for the likes of Mike Summerbee and George Best of City and United fame. Three or four of us would venture uptown on a weekend, decked out as Rod and getting lots of attention from the girls. It was a fabulous period in my life and I'm still a lifelong fan of the band and the individual members.

I WAS THERE: DAVID GARRITY

I remember a tight band. And then Rod came on, brandy bottle in hand, and he was tight. I loved the Faces but I thought Rod was a let down.

ROD STEWART DAY
HILTON HOTEL
5 NOVEMBER 1971, AMSTERDAM, THE NETHERLANDS

Record execs throw a party for Rod and present him with six gold discs, two silver discs and a platinum disc, the latter representing 1.5 million sales.

FILLMORE
10 NOVEMBER 1971, FILLMORE, SUNDERLAND

I WAS THERE: ALLAN STOREY

In 1971 Rod was number 1 in the hit parade with 'Maggie May'. Myself, my girlfriend Dawne and my friend John got tickets to see the Faces at the Rink in Sunderland. The price of the ticket was a really expensive one pound! While we were queuing to get in, there were whispers that Rod might not be with the Faces. But we went in and saw the support act, who were called Byzantium. After a while, the Faces came out and there was Rod. I don't remember the first song, but for the last song of the encore Rod said, 'This song is called 'Twistin' the Night Away'.' This was the first of many times I was to see the Faces or Rod solo.

After the gig at Sunderland, Dawne and I hitched from Durham to Barney in Lincolnshire to see the Faces at the Great Western Festival in May 1972. Also performing were Rory Gallagher, Status Quo, Lindisfarne, the Beach Boys (the first gig for Brian Wilson after coming out of the Betty Ford Clinic), Slade and Spencer Davis, who got booed off. The Faces came on after Maggie Bell of Stone the Crows. It was rumoured Rod was friendly with her. (Well, it began with an 'f'…) While we were watching the Faces, an extremely big lady who was stood next to me turned to me, handed me a long homemade cigarette and said 'have some'. She then crouched down, lifted up her ankle-length skirt and emptied about a gallon of fluid from her bladder.

Since then, I've seen Rod at Ibrox (I bet that was a really happy time for him) when his support act was Gary Glitter. And my (now third) wife and I saw him at Maine Road, Manchester in the round, where he was wheeled from the changing rooms to the stage in a wooden box. His support there was Belinda Carlisle and the brilliant Mike and the Mechanics. My wife and I were running a pub in Eccles at the time. We got lost on the day near the Scottish and Newcastle brewery. We saw a police car and asked the way. The copper told me: 'Go past the traffic lights and turn left onto Claremont Road. Then lock the doors and windows and don't fucking stop until you get to Maine Road!'

I have also seen Rod at Gateshead Stadium with support from

Status Quo and Joe Cocker. The last time I had the pleasure of seeing him was at the Newcastle Arena.

From the first time I saw him at Sunderland Rink to the present day, Rod has been one of the greatest entertainers. After the first time I saw him, I bought a green jacket with brown patches on the elbows and shoulders and got myself a spikey hair cut. There was only me who thought I didn't look a prat.

KIEL AUDITORIUM
23 NOVEMBER 1971, ST LOUIS, MISSOURI

The Faces embark on their fifth North American tour, playing 17 shows through November and December 1971.

MEMORIAL CIVIC CENTER
24 NOVEMBER 1971, CANTON, OHIO

I WAS THERE: ANNA REINHARD

My next Faces adventure was in Canton, Ohio at the Memorial Civic Center. Four or five girlfriends and I decked ourselves out and went to the concert. We were determined to find the boys after the concert and do – what? We didn't have a clue, being all too young to know anything about anything. Anyway, the concert was incredible! How was it that they were able to create this freight train sound that drove everyone mad?

Rod and the Faces were belting out 'Stay With Me' when suddenly the folding chairs we were sitting on became fodder under our feet as we rushed towards the stage – a rather low one. People were jumping on stage and my best friend told me to casually walk up the side steps where we found ourselves face-to-face (no pun) with Woody, Rod, Ian and Kenney. Rod gave me the once over and looked me in the eyes and the same thing happened again. The earth stood still. I had to speak to break the spell so I asked him what the matter was. He waved at the stage scattered with fans and said, 'They won't let me perform.' It was so cute and funny to see his exasperation over his own fame. It was one heart-pounding moment before we got swept off the stage by the inexperienced, understaffed security. Apparently, the venue had no clue regarding the effect the Faces were having on the USA and its young women and men.

After the gig, we finally arrived at a Holiday Inn of sorts to look for the band. We split up into a couple of groups and my group looked for late night lights in rooms with a party going on. My one friend came running up to us and said that Ian 'Mac' McLagan had just gone into the men's room. I, being brave, went in after him and when he saw me, I asked him, 'Did you aim correctly?' (Where did I get such cheeky nerve?) Never to miss a beat, he replied, 'Can you?' I explained, 'I don't use one of those' and walked over to the regular toilet and sat on it and said, 'See?' He said, 'Don't you usually pull your skirt up?' I was slow to realise how forward I looked but finally figured out the consequences of my situation and let out a large cheerleader-style scream! Mac ran out and my friends ran in, saying, 'Rod and Woody are in the bar, so hurry!'

We walked, as cool as we could, into the motel bar and saw the guys sitting there casually drinking and laughing. All of a sudden, drinks came our way and we were behind Rod and Woody, playing with their spikes of hair and saying they felt like feathers. It was exciting fun while it lasted but eventually, because of parental restrictions on the car, we had to head home. Needless to say, I was again moonstruck. I had never seen such cool guys with funny little smiles, like they just swallowed a couple of canaries. I had to find out more...

From then on, each time we knew the Faces were touring we tried to round up funds to go to as many shows as possible. We sold blood plasma, returned Christmas gifts for cash and I did a very bad thing – I used monies set aside for school tuition. I would have graduated with a Fine Arts degree and perhaps landed a teaching job or become a curator of a museum, but instead I worked the rest of my life in retail or customer service. Regrets? Not for long. Life has it way of working out for the best.

My wild years of chasing the Faces were full of small and big events. Here are a few of the more memorable ones:

1. Somewhere in Indiana, we were dancing at the front of the stage and I don't know what was so special, but I looked up and the whole

band was looking at me. I was a good dancer, I knew that, but what? Then, all of a sudden, some guy grabbed me and tossed me on his shoulders. Good grief! I started hitting him in the head to let me down because I was afraid of falling and being paralysed for the rest of my life. And it was the first time I had anyone's head between my legs so my modesty hit the panic-o-meter! Crazy insane! The rest of the audience were like the Israelites reviling while Moses was on the mountain getting the Law from God. Sheeesh!

2. Then there was Detroit... We only had enough money for the airfare and the tiniest room I ever saw in a hotel. We lucked out when we took the elevator to the main floor lobby and who should be getting on but Rod and some of the Faces! Rod's butt was exactly at hand level and I couldn't resist the invite to pinch it. Always the pro, he just rubbed it in to ease the sting! Eventually, we ran into the road manager, Peter Buckland, and let him know we had no seats. He said if we could get to the stage door we would be led to offside seats. It was incredible. Cobo Hall? The Faces? Free seats for us?

After the show, someone gave us a ride to a small venue where Ron and Woody had gone to see Muddy Waters perform. It was a quick stay then back to the hotel. That same night, in Rod's penthouse suite, we saw Rod's protective side when Peter came over to us, telling us we had to leave because the party may get a little rough. Rod knew we were innocent and didn't fit in with the hard-core groupies who were there. I'll never forget him for that. We were pretty obviously babes in the woods, and he wanted to protect us.

The final take from all of the Faces concerts, and what kept bringing us going back and spending our money, was the joy and happiness, the incredible music, the comedy, and the absolute love we felt from Rod and the gang. We always walked away with a smile on our faces.

The 'we' I refer to in my story was my very best friend, Pam. She was only four foot eleven and I was five foot six, so we made a rather odd entrance. I think that's why we were remembered by Rod and the band. My other friends had more serious things to take care of in their lives, but Pam stuck it out with me and was game for anything. I became close to her after her lovely mother died from breast cancer. Pam had a rough time of it from the beginning of her life – she was given a naturally red afro, big bosom and short legs. There we were, both virgins, both orphans and both willing to investigate the music world. Rod was always very kind to her in little ways, like mussing her afro as he passed by.

There could be 30 good-looking women in the room and he would ignore them and show Pam that kind of attention. Pam knew I had an unrealistic crush on Rod, but she never criticised me for it. She was a real saint and went on to be a monk of some sort with the highest degree back belt available. I'm sure it was for her own protection, because she had her fill of bullies.

MADISON SQUARE GARDEN
26 NOVEMBER 1971, NEW YORK, NEW YORK

The Faces performed to a sell out crowd of 20,000, with scalpers charging $100 for tickets.

I WAS THERE: LARRY PALEY

I remember seeing them at MSG. They were one hell of a fun band with the drinking and the interaction between the mates. You could tell they really enjoyed each other. After that I saw Rod five or six more times. The last time was at the Providence Civic Center, Rhode Island. I took my young daughter to the *Forever Young* tour. She has all my ticket stubs and programmes. Rod is one hell of a frontman.

I WAS THERE: MICHELE GORMLEY, AGE 16

I lived in New Jersey and so I waited on line at the Army Navy Ticketmaster in Hackensack, New Jersey to get mediocre seats; I went with four of my girlfriends – we were kids with no money. 'Maggie May' had just been released. Going to the gig was the most exciting night of my life so far. We went to McSorley's Bar in NYC and got served for the first time. At the show, Rod walked up a ramp that went halfway up into the audience until he was about 20 feet from us. I looked right into his eyes and fell in love…

The Faces' music became the soundtrack of my teen years. *Never a Dull Moment* is my favourite album of all time. I keep one copy in my car and still play it in full a few times a week. If I am having a bad day, it instantly brings me joy.

Since the Faces split up, I have continued to follow Rod. I have seen 108 of his shows, the last one being at Madison Square Garden in August 2019 which is, as Rod put it when I finally met him in June, 'where it all began'. I have danced with him on stage at MSG in 1993, where he kissed me on the lips with Racheal Hunter there. At Miami in 1997, he stopped the show and went under the stage to bring me up a soccer ball which he signed in front of me. In June 2018, I went backstage in Hollywood, Florida with my husband and met Rod and Penny. Rod autographed my back and I went immediately to the tattoo parlour and got my first tattoo at the age of 63. Rod is the soundtrack to my life. My love of him has outlasted two husbands.

Michele Gormley has been a fan of Rod since the age of 16

A NOD'S AS GOOD AS A WINK... TO A BLIND HORSE
RELEASED 17 NOVEMBER 1971

The Faces third album reaches number 6 in the US album charts and number 2 in the UK.

SPORTS ARENA
28 NOVEMBER 1971, SAN DIEGO, CALIFORNIA

I WAS THERE: RONNY JONES, AGE 14

I saw the Faces three times in San Diego. The first time stands out. *Nod* had just come out and 'Maggie May' was climbing the charts. They had reflective flooring on the stage which looked like a mirror and black and white video screens. The venue was a sports arena but only one fourth of it was used for the show, so they weren't huge yet. They were on top of their game. They looked like they were having so much fun. That made a big impact on me. I'm sure the bartender on stage helped the mood a bit as well. It was maybe 20 years later that acts started using video screens at shows, so the Faces were ahead of their time on that one.

I went with a group of friends from my neighbourhood who were all older than me. They were all getting high and I just wanted to see the bands. One of the 'older' kids I went with became my wife 30 plus years later. The middle show was also great. It was Ronnie Lane's last tour. Rory Gallagher was the opening act and I was a big fan of his too. My dad took me to that one, which made it a bit uncomfortable, but while they played, they were great. This time the arena was full.

My wife-to-be was at the last show too. The last tour was boring in comparison to the first. Ronnie Lane was gone. Rod was a star. Woody had one foot in the Stones. They looked like they were going through the motions. The chemistry was gone.

Still to this day that first show is one of the best shows I've ever seen, and I've seen a lot.

MADISON SQUARE GARDEN
26 & 28 NOVEMBER 1971, NEW YORK, NEW YORK

I WAS THERE: DEE HARRINGTON

In the UK I went to quite a lot of Faces concerts and saw the British public fall in love with them. Then in November 1971, three months after Rod and I got together, I went to Madison Square Garden to see them play. Me and Krissy Wood went out to New York. Me and Rod and Ronnie and Krissy Wood shared a suite at the New York Sheraton and while we were there, Rod asked me to marry him. That was three months after we'd been together. Then we went over to LA, after which I came home and they carried on with their tour. I didn't go on any more of the US tours, and neither did any of the Faces wives. Longer US tours were replaced by ten day tours. Rod had his solo success and was producing two albums a year and so there was more studio work to do. When you become more successful you can't just keep touring. You've got more promotion and that sort of thing to do.

They were quite big on the stadium circuit, and the stadiums just got bigger, particularly after the Rod solo stuff. He became so successful. He was making two albums a year and he was number 1 for six weeks both sides of the Atlantic with 'Maggie May' and *Every Picture Tells a Story*.

We were at home a lot except for these quick American tours. Even then he would be in the studio. He used to record in Willesden in north London at Morgan Studios, while the Faces would record at Olympic Studios in Barnes. I'd go to Morgan Studios quite a lot, and not so much to the studio with the Faces.

When Rod did vocals, he always wanted me to sit in the vocal area with him. It was a very relaxed atmosphere. He always had the same engineer – Mike Bobak – a very quiet, nice guy. Rod knew what he wanted to do and he'd just get him to do it. Ronnie Wood played a lot on Rod's solo stuff and Ronnie Lane did a bit. But he used Micky Waller on drums because Rod had been with the Jeff Beck Group with Ronnie Wood and Micky. They obviously worked well together. Rod never stopped working, and the band were always getting together to write and rehearse and record. It was a full-time job.

SWING AUDITORIUM

30 NOVEMBER 1971, SAN BERNARDINO, CALIFORNIA

I WAS THERE: RICHARD DANNELLEY, AGE 17

I was 17 and highly impressionable. It was one of the first rock shows I had been to, and I was dosed up on mescaline and got close to the stage. The stage had like a dozen Marshall cabs in a semi-circle, which were upholstered with tuck and roll silver glitter material, and a big piano. It was Ron Wood who really got my attention, and he put the rock and roll right in to me for life. He smoked continuously, sometimes hard, and particularly (I noticed) while he played hard with two slides on his left hand.

The truly famed Swing Auditorium was sometimes referred to as The Barn. Every single rock band we talk about today played there and it was often the first show of the tour, before the bands went on the 90 miles to LA. The last act to play it was Ted Nugent, and I was there. Ted sucks; he is a violent madman but he is an excellent musician. (I was only there for the chicks.) Right after that, a plane crashed into that old WWII aircraft hangar. I blame it on Ted.

CENTER COLISEUM
1 DECEMBER 1971, SEATTLE, WASHINGTON

I WAS THERE: SHANNON COBERLY

I got to see the Faces one time only, in Seattle. They delivered. A group called Cactus opened for them. Ronnie Wood used the mic stand as a slide numerous times and did a damn fine job of it. Usually when that happens it's sloppy, but he was right on. To this day their music is still with me. I listen to them weekly if not daily. Understanding that all good things come to an end, I was very disappointed that they broke up as a band and that Rod discovered spandex.

I WAS THERE: STEVE PORTTEUS

They put on a great show. I remember Rod marching with his mic stand and twirling the mic around, and being blown away by Ron's guitar playing. The whole band was fantastic though. I was only in my early teens, but saw many concerts and the Faces were one of the best. They had a connection that set them apart from the others.

'STAY WITH ME'
RELEASED 3 DECEMBER 1971

'Stay With Me' reaches number 17 on the US Billboard chart and number 6 in the UK.

VETERANS MEMORIAL AUDITORIUM
4 DECEMBER 1971, DES MOINES, IOWA

I WAS THERE: GEORGE SMITH, AGE 17
I was in my last year of high school. I went with my wife and another couple. It was about 110 miles from home. We just bought tickets on the door. I saw them with Bull Angus and Cactus supporting. *A Nod's as Good as a Wink…* had just been released, 'Maggie May' was still being played on the radio and I swear they were as good live as the Stones. They had a big black guy on stage with a handkerchief tied on his head like a gypsy who was dancing while they played. He wasn't someone from the audience. They sounded great, as did Cactus.

FORUM
10 DECEMBER 1971, MONTREAL, CANADA

I WAS THERE: LISA MCKEAN, AGE 15
Rod strutted onto the stage wearing a white satin suit and no shirt! The back drop was a huge fabric panel that said *A Nod's as Good as a Wink to a Blind Horse*. They were on fire. 'I'm Losing You' really stands out as particularly good.

WILLIAM AND MARY HALL
14 DECEMBER 1971, WILLIAMSBURG, VIRGINIA

I WAS THERE: VAUGHN DEEL
I saw the Faces at William and Mary Hall. Even though I was leaning against the stage the entire time, I really don't remember much of the show after 48 years. I took pictures at the show and, due to not changing the

Vaughn Deel's 'terrible' picture of Rod and Ronnie

ASA on my camera, all of my pictures were pretty bad. I only printed out one picture of Rod Stewart and Ronnie Lane. That was the best of the lot – and it was terrible!

MEMORIAL AUDITORIUM
16 DECEMBER 1971, BUFFALO, NEW YORK

I WAS THERE: STEPHEN GRAHAM, AGE 17

I got food poisoning the night they played, so I spent most of the show in the loo. I was in my junior year of high school in Buffalo New York. My girlfriend Barb and her friend Helen picked me up after I had dinner, a bologna sandwich with salmonella. But it was one of the most memorable evenings of my life! I was so looking forward to them and I did see some of the show. A British band called Audience and another band called Cactus (two guys from Vanilla Fudge) opened for them. 'Stay With Me' had just been released as a single a few weeks earlier and I was absolutely taken by it. I was already a fan of Rod Stewart's from his time with Jeff Beck so I was very familiar with his voice, and

Stephen Graham's enjoyment of the show at the Aud was interrupted by the call of nature

when he teamed up with Ronnie, they exemplified my style in music and fashion circa 1971.

We had pretty good seats pretty close to the stage, the second tier up in Buffalo Memorial Auditorium. When the Faces came out, it blew me away. Rod was interacting with the people down in front, kicking a soccer ball around and sharing a bottle of Mateus wine with them. He had his tripod mic stand, not with the usual big heavy base, and wielded it in a way that was lighter and looser than anybody I'd seen.

It seemed like the auditorium was much smaller than it had ever been, and they turned it into an intimate party. Unfortunately, I had to run back and forth from my seat to the men's room, never knowing what was going to happen... I was so angry, because the band represented my sensibilities more than any other band at that time, and I was missing most of the show due to my condition. I would come back to my seat, and Barb would tell me how pale I looked, and after five or seven minutes, I'd have to get back up and run to the loo again.

I did buy *A Nod's as Good as a Wink to a Blind Horse* from Columbia House Records in my first selection with my new girlfriend, Jamie, and we played the grooves out of it. And, to this day, when 'Stay With Me' comes on the radio, it gets cranked up to 11.

I WAS THERE: TERRY SULLIVAN

I saw the Faces at the Buffalo War Memorial Auditorium on their *Nod's as Good as a Wink* tour and it was amazing. They basically changed my overall landscape as a rock 'n' roll performer at the time.

I WAS THERE: DENNIS THOMANN

My friends and I had front row seats but as soon as the band started everyone rushed the stage so we had our arms on the stage at the foot of Ron Wood. I remember being spellbound by his amazing guitar mastery and also by Rod's singing. Ron played at the edge of the stage only a foot away. I remember thinking he was one of the best guitarists I've ever seen. Then suddenly there was a naked hippie running around on one of the upper levels, which caught the attention of the entire audience. The police began chasing him but he was jumping down four or five rows of seats whenever they got close and the audience would respond with 'aaaws'! The band kept playing but were watching also. Eventually they did catch him and I remember Rod made some remark. It was a fantastic concert and I will never forget it.

INTERNATIONAL AMPHITHEATER
17 DECEMBER 1971, CHICAGO, ILLINOIS

I WAS THERE: DAVE ROGER

As they dimmed the lights the girl in front of us with the beehive hairdo pulled a bobby pin from her hair, reached inside her mound of hair and pulled out her bag of joints and lit up. She then replaced the bag in her mound of hair and we all rocked on. Greatest and loudest rock band ever!

I WAS THERE: LARRY RUDOLPH

This was the last show of the tour and the whole band was drinking throughout the show. I think they may have had a bar on stage. It was a great show and lots of fun. I remember the opening band was a great forgotten band called Audience.

I WAS THERE: PAUL DUBIEL

They always had a bar on stage and, yes, the opening band was excellent. And, yes, the Faces were one of the funniest bands to see! I saw them many times in the Seventies – at the Chicago Auditorium, the Amphitheater and at Mar y Sol in Puerto Rico. They would roll out a bar and actually passed out bottles of wine and bags of pot! It was the only rock show that made you feel like you were at a large party with great old friends. The band was always rocking and would occasionally take audience requests, sometimes doing covers, eg. 'It's All Over Now', better than the original. Me and my friends decided to cut our hair like Rod and Ron Wood.

'Maggie May' is the second biggest selling US 45 of 1971 (behind 'My Sweet Lord' by George Harrison) while Every Picture Tells a Story is runner up to Simon and Garfunkel's Bridge Over Troubled Water in the best selling US album stakes.

The Faces begin 1972 with a mixture of British, Irish and mainland Europe shows.

TELL EVERYONE: A PEOPLE'S HISTORY OF THE FACES

TOP RANK SUITE
7 FEBRUARY 1972, BRIGHTON, UK

I WAS THERE: TONY HARVEY-GIBSON, AGE 18

I had just left grammar school so I was earning money. I went with my friend Bruce who had grown up two doors away. He was a year younger at 17. We lived in a newly-built council estate in Portslade. We were both fanatical about Rod Stewart, even to the point that we went to a renowned barber in those days, at the bottom of North Road in Brighton, called Richards, who gave us the spikey top, layered long sides, etc. We thought we looked great. My Dad said we looked ridiculous (but boy we broke some hearts!). I can't remember how much the cut was, but it was expensive, and it had to be cut every six weeks to keep the look.

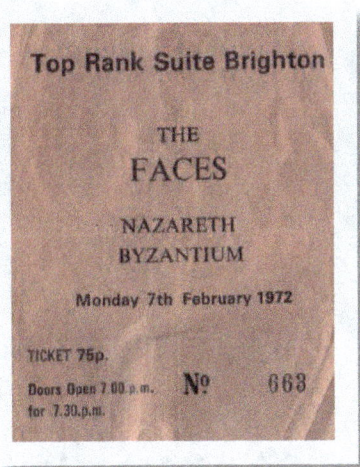

Tony Harvey-Gibson saw the Faces at Brighton's Top Rank Suite

In those days you had to go to the booking office to buy tickets. I seem to remember we bought them about six weeks before the concert. The night eventually came and we had a few beers in The Bosun on West Street, a very popular watering hole at the time. The support acts were Nazareth and Byzantium, the latter crucified for the amount of swearing they did. We were there for the Faces, so we were in and out of the bar while they were on. The boys didn't disappoint. They were loud, raw and highly entertaining. It was always the voice and the rawness that drew me. It was an unforgettable concert.

I saw Rod a further three times but I feel his best was in the early Seventies, both with and without the Faces. It was great to see Kenney Jones and Ronnie Wood get the opportunity to join two of the greatest bands ever in The Who and the Stones, sadly only as a result of the deaths of the genius that was Keith Moon and the enigmatic Brian Jones.

I WAS THERE: PHILIP PLUMMER, AGE 24

As a 24-year-old I went to this gig with a pal, Derek Marr. The Top Rank was full to bursting. Nazareth were the support band and the PA system kept breaking down. After four attempts to carry on, the band gave up amidst some choice Glaswegian language. By the time Rod and the Faces came on, the crowd had got a bit lively and Rod seemed quite concerned about the safety of people near the stage. He asked the audience to behave and said they would not start until things had settled down. Commendable behaviour from a young rock star!

The set was brilliant and the Faces were very good musically. Strangely, I remember Rod singing 'Underneath the Arches', the old music hall song made famous by Flanagan and Allen. In later years I met one of Rod's management team who said he was great fun to work with. Hopefully my memory of events some 50 years ago is still accurate, and I still think 'Maggie May' is one of the best records I ever owned.

I WAS THERE: STEVE ANDREWS

Eight months is a long time when you're young. After seeing them at the College of Education in May 1971, everything had changed with Rod Stewart's 'Maggie May' breakthrough and a new populist audience were all over it when the Faces came to town in early 1972, this time to the Top Rank. 'Are you going to see Rod Stewart?', girls would ask at school. 'No,' my rock chums and I would reply, 'We're going to see the Faces.'

As befits a venue in Brighton's West Street, the heart of testosterone and aggro-land as opposed to the semi-rural seat of learning I'd seen them in previously, the support bands were greeted with derision by non-regular gig attendees, whose teardrop collar shirts and feathered mullets marked them out as 'Smooths'. Byzantium were first on and were a bit 'Wishbone Ashy'. They copped for some heckling from people who would soon be drifting away to Lieutenant Pigeon or any other old chart crap. Nazareth didn't get the same reaction, mainly on account of Dan McCafferty's granite jaw, Glaswegian growl and convincing between-song rants aimed at whoever had turned his monitors down.

The Faces were great, but it wasn't the same. The stylists were out in force and barnets were looking more primpy. When a girl stepped away and, quite rightly, gazed in horror as I idiot-danced during the emotive Hammond break in 'Maybe I'm Amazed', I would come to regard the encounter as some sort of Frank Zappa/Katie Price interface whereas she probably thought I was an epileptic.

TELL EVERYONE: A PEOPLE'S HISTORY OF THE FACES

Later that year, I was disappointed in 'Cindy Incidentally' which, apart from being derivative of 'Memphis Tennessee', had my once-fave band sound like they were aiming for the *Sesame Street* market. As I perceived them trotting out silly melodies whilst playing to the Boot Boys, I found security in Afghan coats and Black Sabbath.

And Lieutenant Pigeon, of course.

The Faces play three shows at London's famed Rainbow Theatre.

RAINBOW THEATRE
10 – 12 FEBRUARY 1972, LONDON, UK

I WAS THERE: MARK BRADY, AGE 14

I went with my best mate from school. We were 14 years old. Living in London was a real boon in those days as we could get to gigs all over the city very easily, and relatively cheaply. This was the second time we had been to see the Faces. The first being at Queen Elizabeth Hall, part of the Festival Hall complex, maybe a year

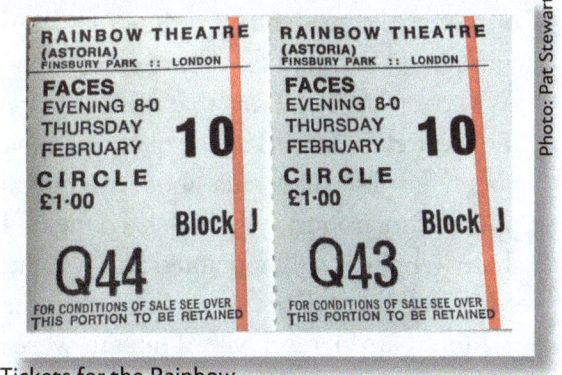

Tickets for the Rainbow

earlier. At the Rainbow we were in about the third row from the front. The band were fantastic. Rod was a real showman and he generated a fantastic party atmosphere. There were lots of singalongs to various hits, including the ubiquitous 'Stay With Me', and lots of footballs on stage which were dispatched into the audience. Ronnie Wood was wearing his Spanish matador outfit and that he constantly smoked on stage.

The funniest thing I remember was that my mate had had to have several teeth removed when he was younger and these had been replaced by a plate with a few false teeth. During one of the songs, we were singing along and leaping up and down when he inadvertently lost his plate and teeth. They had flown out of his mouth. Anyway, someone in the front row found them, handed them back to him and he put them straight back into his mouth, covered in fluff and dirt!

I WAS THERE: RICHIE DAVIES

As a 15-year-old in 1970, I used to go out with Kenney Jones's cousin Madeline. I was having a drink with the family, including Kenney (I looked older than 15) in The George in Commercial Road. Kenney gave me and Madeline a lift back to his mum's in his Jensen for a party. Although I knew Kenney, I never got any free tickets or albums. Madeline and I never lasted, but because of Facebook we have become friends again. I went to see The Jones Gang at Under the Bridge in 2016, where I met Madeline again and she invited me backstage where I met Kenney again. He is such a lovely, down-to-earth man. He never gives it the 'big I am'. I've since seen them twice more, and again had a chat with him.

A friend of mine turned me on to the Faces, although I was a big fan of the Small Faces. The first time I saw the Faces was at the Rainbow in Finsbury Park. I had to buy the tickets from there about a fortnight before. As I got off the bus, I saw that the queue for tickets went all the way around the theatre, so the end of the queue had joined the beginning of it. I duly got on the end when, after about five minutes, the doors opened and a guy put his arm around me and pushed me in. I was very lucky, because I'm sure there were lots of disappointed fans who were unable to get tickets.

On the night of the show, the Faces were supported by Byzantium and Ashton, Gardner & Dyke. The fans were getting restless as the Faces were, as usual, late. The eventually came on behind a cardboard cut out of a Rolls-Royce. As soon as they did so, everyone just ran to the front. It was the time of *Long Player*, and Rod's voice was superb. It was a great night. I wasn't with Madeline then, but a girl called Jean. Because the Faces were so late coming on, we missed the last Tube and I had to walk Jean home to Leyton and then on to my home in Mile End.

I WAS THERE: STEVE NIXON, AGE 15

I was 15 at the time so my recollection of the night may be a bit sketchy and a little over enthusiastic after 50 years, but it still remains one of the best shows I have ever seen. My first recollection is of buying the tickets. My friend Stephen Saunders and I travelled to unknown Finsbury Park

Station from south of the river to buy our tickets one Saturday morning. This was a time before you could pay on line with plastic and had to be prepared to stand, waiting in line to pay in cash at the box office.

When we arrived, the queue was enormous as tickets for other shows were also on sale that day. We joined the back of the queue that snaked around the Isledon Road side of the theatre and waited four or five hours before we shuffled into the foyer and arrived at the ticket kiosk. Once in the foyer, we had a crisis of conscience. We could now see the other gigs that were available. Did we stick with the Faces or go for Pink Floyd or Humble Pie? We only had enough money for one £1.50 ticket each. I seem to remember that Frank Zappa was also an option. Having queued for so long, we decided to stick with the Faces, which was the right decision, despite missing the chance to see Frank Zappa get pushed off stage by a 'crazed fan'.

The Rainbow Theatre was so unique that it felt special just being in the entrance hall. A dedicated rock venue was unheard of before the Rainbow opened. Tickets secured (Block E, Circle, seat D45), we headed back south. The show was due to start at 8pm on Friday 11th February 1972.

The bill included Byzantium and Ashton Gardner and Dyke (AGD) but I always thought Nazareth opened the show as I have no recollection of seeing Byzantium. Nazareth were a great band and I may have confused them opening this show with another I had seen at the Rainbow. AGD had one notable success, which was 'Resurrection Shuffle'. Once this was performed, their set went nowhere and someone from the audience suggested that they 'fuck off'. This advice became more widespread after each song and ended with Tony Ashton conducting the audience in a massive, triumphant 'fuck off!' at the end of the set. A Faces audience acted more like a football mob than any other crowd, ready to support the band from the first note played or mic stand spun.

Before the Faces took to the stage, the famous Joe's Lights show began. They were resident at the Rainbow. This consisted of psychedelic symbols illustrating the alternative, underground scene. The light show featured counterculture images straight from the pages of *International Times* or *Oz* magazine. It was very edgy and subversive at the time.

The air inside the Rainbow always crackled with energy. The ever-present buzz from the amps, the loud 'crunch' from a guitar lead being connected, roadies rushing to clear the gear from the previous act and the constant 'one-two, one-two' to test the mics.

The Faces exploded onto the stage. Rod Stewart wore a silver-and-black brocade jacket with Ron Wood wearing a matador outfit. This was all the more startling considering most bands at the time wore t-shirt and jeans, the same as their audience. The band reacted directly to the roar from the crowd and then picked up their instruments, as though surprised to find them on stage. Giving the impression of a band that had just come straight from the pub next door, they surged into the first number, just the right side of having had a few drinks (but only just). They were in the same condition as most of the crowd.

They made that night feel like New Year's Eve. The Faces made you feel that, if a thing was worth doing, it was worth doing to excess. The set list consisted of songs mainly from *A Nod's as Good as a Wink…to a Blind Horse* and *Every Picture Tells a Story*. Due to Rod Stewart's success with *Every Picture*, we were uncertain if it would be a Faces or a Rod solo show, but as soon as they started to play it became clear the two options blended into one. The band played sure fire crowd pleasers such as 'I'm Losing You', 'Memphis Tennessee', 'That's All You Need', 'Too Bad' and 'Maggie May'.

Ronnie Lane took lead vocals and centre stage on 'Debris', with Rod Stewart on harmony out of the spotlight. Ronnie never seemed overawed by Rod Stewart's huge stage presence and was a fundamental part of the band, taking lead vocals on three tracks on *A Nod's as Good…* From where I was sitting, it just looked like five good mates having the time of their life.

The lighting consisted of standard gantry lights and a massive spotlight from the back of the theatre. Nothing elaborate. Nothing elaborate was needed.

'Stay With Me' was saved for the encore and somehow everything went up a gear. Rod Stewart had footballs thrown on from the side of the stage, which he juggled, playing 'keepy up' before kicking them into the crowd. As a 15-year-old, I was amazed. Not only could he sing, perform and conduct a rabble rousing sing-a-long to raise the roof, but he could also play football!

Then it was over. House lights up, ringing in the ears and the downer that it had all ended. One of the shows from the three nights the Faces played at the Rainbow was recorded by the BBC and aired a few days later on 15th February. *The Old Grey Whistle Test* broadcast 'Stay With Me' (in black and white), but it was not like being there on the night. You just had to be there.

TELL EVERYONE: A PEOPLE'S HISTORY OF THE FACES

I WAS THERE: GLEN MATLOCK

When I was really little, my uncle had given me his old 78s, which came in a cardboard sleeve with stitching down the side. The first time I went down the Portobello Road, I found a record store and, flicking through the records, I found a record that looked like an old 78, with a cardboard sleeve with stitching down the side. It was an album and I bought it. It was *Long Player* by the Faces, and I didn't realise they were anything to do with the Small Faces.

Long Player opened the door to all different kinds of music. Round about that time, I was learning to play the guitar and listening to the blues and I noticed they had a Big Bill Broonzy song on there, so it all kind of slotted together. I got into Bobby Womack and The Staples Singers. I got into more of the blues and taking The Temptations seriously. The Temptations were always good, but it was a bit jive with the suits and the chicken-in-the-basket dancing. The Faces made you look beyond that. 'Why do they want to do '(I Know) I'm Losing You'?' Because it's a fantastic song. When you're 15, 16, you don't necessarily realise that.

The first time I saw them was at the Rainbow, when the power cuts were going on, in February 1972. They were supported by Nazareth and by Ashton, Gardner & Dyke. Tony Ashton was off his face, not singing, but squirting a water pistol into the audience. He got pulled off the stage, like in the old music halls, with a big long stick with a hook on the end. Then the Faces came on, kicking footballs around. They had a bar on the stage for the drum solo and a barman with a towel over his arm. The band had a drink during the drum solo. When Kenney Jones was getting out of puff, they ordered another round of drinks! I thought, 'I like these guys.' Then I saw them at Wembley, when the New York Dolls supported them. That was pretty good. And I saw them at the Reading Festival, with Tetsu. But it wasn't the same, because I was a Ronnie Lane fan.

I WAS THERE: PETER HIRD

I was a student in my first year at the London School of Economics when a group of us got jobs as ushers at the Rainbow. One of our friends talked his way into it. They gave us a silver bomber jacket each with 'Rainbow' on the back in red. We got paid about two quid a night which probably works out at about 20 quid now – mainly to watch bands! I saw The Who on the opening night of the Rainbow in November 1971.

TELL EVERYONE: A PEOPLE'S HISTORY OF THE FACES

I saw Rod Stewart and the Faces seven or eight times in all, including at the Rainbow. I remember Rod coming on at the start with a load of plastic footballs and drop kicking them into the crowd, which was obviously very popular. Rod came on and said, 'MAB it's a big horse. What's that mean, then?' It was a joke, because he meant the old music hall song, 'Maybe It's Because I'm a Londoner'. He sang a couple of verses of that and the audience joined in. Perhaps he had equivalent things for different parts of the country.

It was a particularly difficult show as an usher, because as well as getting people in the right seats, there were a lot of girls in the audience who took absolutely no notice of you. They'd just smile at you nicely and stand up or go where they weren't supposed to, in front of the stage. It was meant to be everybody sat down all the time, and the local fire officer was always there. I remember one particular girl getting inside the bass cabinet of the PA. She must've been absolutely deaf for weeks afterwards.

The idea was to have ushers, who were the same age as the audience and who looked a bit hippyish, who'd ask the audience to behave nicely. And then there was a second load of very big chaps who would physically remove people, virtually always male. In the culture of 1971, no one knew what to do with young females who didn't do what you asked them to, because grabbing hold of them and hauling them out wasn't to the taste of the beefy blokes.

For the London gigs the band hired Janet Webb, the very curvy lady from the Morecambe & Wise Show, to come on at the end of every night as the band were taking their bow. She would elbow Rod and Ronnie Wood apart and push her way to the front to do the same gag as on the TV show, where she'd give a little speech saying, 'I'd like to thank you for watching me and my little show.' That was always a good bit of entertainment.

I remember being told that there was going to be a party at the end for the staff, but the Rainbow was in Finsbury Park, and living in central London I always had to get home, so I was thinking 'I hope it's going to start soon'. Ronnie Lane, Kenney and Ian were there, so we said hello to them, but Rod and Ronnie Wood never turned up. They said Rod was in his dressing gown. I strongly suspected at the time that he might be 'entertaining' somebody. By the time we had to choose between getting the last Tube or stay on, we decided to get the last Tube so we never went to the party.

My sister was a huge fan. She saw them all over the shop. She even got to know Rod's driver by his first name. One time she couldn't get in because she didn't have a ticket and he got her into the gig.

The number one Rod Stewart impersonator lives round here, Stan Terry. He's done things like play at Rod Stewart's birthday party. Rod's sister booked him. Rod says that Stan knows the words to the songs better than Rod does now because he doesn't sing a lot of the old ones.

We always had to hand back the silver bomber jackets at the end of the night, so after not very many months, they'd all been nicked by bands. We ended up going in just Levi jackets or whatever. After getting paid to see bands like that, it's been downhill career-wise for me ever since.

I WAS THERE: DAVEY MAC

Ashton, Gardner & Dyke and Nazareth supported. It was the time of the three-day week and the power cuts, and they brought generators to augment the power supply. Everyone was there to see Rod and the Faces, so the support acts were getting a rough time. Tony Ashton was giving a bit back and spraying the front rows with a water pistol. I was near the front and have memories of Rod spraying saliva as he belted the songs out, finishing of course by kicking out footballs to the audience. I've seen about 40 Rod shows and never got near a ball...

TOP RANK
5 MARCH 1972, SUNDERLAND, UK

I WAS THERE: PETER SMITH, AGE 15

Rod was big. Really big in 1972. He had gone from semi-underground cult figure with *An Old Raincoat Won't Ever Let You Down* and *Gasoline Alley* to superstardom with the release of *Every Picture Tells a Story* in May 1971. The album and the associated single, the iconic 'Maggie May', were simultaneously number 1 in the singles and albums charts on both sides of the Atlantic. Whew. Heady stuff, which had not been seen since the days of The Beatles.

The Faces were doing alright too. The album *Long Player* had done well but the follow up, *A Nod's as Good as a Wink* had done even better. So all was well in the camp with everyone on top of the world and having an alcohol-fuelled good old time – with Rod often resplendent in a leopardskin suit. When the band rolled into Sunderland in the spring of 1972, it was a big deal, and a big gig for everyone at school.

I took time off one afternoon to go and queue for tickets; demand was huge as Rod Stewart and the Faces had just scored massive hits with 'Maggie May' and 'Stay With Me'. The anticipation for the concert was intense, with everyone talking about it weeks in advance. This was one gig that I queued up early for

Peter Smith was at the Top Rank in Sunderland

on the night, missing my tea and going straight to the venue from school. The Top Rank Suite (we knew it as 'The Rink') was a large ballroom in the centre of town, holding a couple of thousand people.

I was one of the first in the queue with some of my mates. We must have queued for two or three hours before the doors opened but the time seemed to fly byr; we were all so excited at what we were about to experience. As soon as the bouncers opened the doors, we handed our tickets in and rushed down the stairs to gain a vantage point down at the front. The small stage, which normally stood at the front of the Rink, had been replaced by a large wooden frame, which we quickly ran towards. We ended up at the front, crushed against the stage, where we stayed all night. I can think of nothing worse now; being crushed and unable to move, but at the time it felt great!

Support came from Byzantium, a psychedelic band with a soft rock/hippie vibe, who I saw a few times as support for other major acts in the early 1970s. They were always enjoyable, and built up their own small following, but never quite made it. One of their members, Chaz Jankel, went on to have success with Ian Dury and the Blockheads.

The gig itself is a bit of a blur. I was still at the stage of almost not believing what I was seeing, and how close I was to my heroes. Rod Stewart and Ronnie Wood were literally a few inches away from me. Rod was dressed flamboyantly and Ronnie Wood was playing a wonderful custom silverplated

TELL EVERYONE: A PEOPLE'S HISTORY OF THE FACES

Zemaitis guitar, of which I was very jealous. Ronnie Lane was looning about in his normal cockney Jack the Lad way, Ian McLagan seemed to be dancing around his keyboards and Kenney Jones kept the backline fully in order. They were running around in the drunken, beautiful ramshackle way that I expected of the Faces. This was simply fantastic to a young teenager.

The set list is also a blur, although I remember they played 'Maggie May' and 'Stay With Me' and I think the closer was their wonderful version of 'I'm Losing You'. The concert seemed to be over quickly, and we talked about it for days after at school.

After the show, some of us stood in a big queue to go backstage and meet the band. We waited for a long time but only the first few people were let in, including some mates from school who reported back that they partied with the band into the next morning. A great night. Happy, happy days.

I WAS THERE: JOHN HALL

The gig was the night before my English mock O level exam. I was a bit of a swotty kid and going out the night before an exam seemed like a bit of a risk. 'What the heck, they are only mocks – and it's only English!', so off I went. Not surprisingly, the place was packed to the rafters and the band put on a rollicking show, drawing material primarily from *Long Player* and *A Nod's as Good…* I can remember footballs being kicked into the audience and much general mayhem. Oh yes, and some great music!

I WAS THERE: STEPHEN SPENCER

The second time I saw them was at the Top Rank Suite in Sunderland. According to Geoff Docherty's book, *A Promoter's Tale*, the support band were Byzantium, of whom I have no recollection whatsoever! I had attended a great gig by Argent at the same venue three weeks previously and we were told that we should keep our tickets to allow us priority in purchasing tickets for the Faces. It was a cracking gig, the band were in full flow and Rod by then owned the stage. They were a good time band, who enjoyed themselves on stage and seemed to love entertaining the crowd. Embarrassingly, I had to keep an eye on my younger sister and her friends who were also there!

We have gone on sober, but there's not much chance of it.
Ian McLagan

DEUTSCHLANDHALLE
11 MARCH 1972, BERLIN, WEST GERMANY

I WAS THERE: AXEL SCHUMACHER

I saw the Faces in 1972. I had already tried to see them in 1970, at the famous Fehmarn Festival, but that event died in rain and disorganisation. I paid for tickets but only a few acts turned up. No Faces and no Jimi.

In the old days of the Cold War, when Berlin was a western island surrounded by East Germany, many acts flew in by plane and their instruments and stage construction were driven in by lorries on the autobahn. That way was cheaper, but it was also risky due to the weather or heavy traffic. So the Faces arrived early in the Deutschlandhalle but their equipment was late. The fans were kept waiting three hours and the lads did some partying with Berlin beer backstage. For a long time, I could see them behind the curtain, drinking and joking. When the stage was finally ready, they had problems staggering to their places.

Rod's voice was darker than ever and they were surprised by the unfriendly welcome of the audience. It became worse when a spectator, maybe as drunken as the boys, threw a beer-filled cup on stage. Rod immediately responded by throwing the whole microphone rig back to where the missile had come from. There was no 'boozer solidarity act' and so it was no wonder that the audience went wild and the Faces hastily left the stage in fear. After discussions backstage, a local DJ tried to calm the audience. It got even more silly but, in the end, the fans wanted the gig and the Faces delivered.

April 1972 sees the Rock & Roll Circus Tour, eight shows focused on the southern United States and their sixth North American visit.

MID-SOUTH COLISEUM
21 APRIL 1972, MEMPHIS, TENNESSEE

I WAS THERE: TOM HERROD

I saw them on the tour with Free opening, in Memphis at the Mid-South

Coliseum. They were at the height of their chemistry and incredible rocking fun. Free alone were worth the price of ticket! A great example of rock 'n' roll at that time. Faces were so cool and light hearted, and sharp dressers of course. Rod was in a leopard print jacket and Ronnie Wood looked like he was wearing a matador jacket. At one point, Ronnie Lane took off his jacket and Rod did a 'hah, look at those braces!' I loved it, and they were fabulous!

I saw them again at the Coliseum in 1975, in the overlapping period when Ronnie Wood left to join the Stones, so I saw him twice within a month or so, once with Faces and once with the Stones.

KENTUCKY FAIR EXPO CENTER, FREEDOM HALL
24 APRIL 1972, LOUISVILLE, KENTUCKY

I WAS THERE: SID GRIFFIN (THE LONG RYDERS), AGE 17

I first saw the Faces in 1972 on their *Rock & Roll Circus* tour of America. They had gone out on the road with various circus acts, acrobats and elephants and there was a scantily-clad lady who was twirling on a trapeze bar and who disrobed a bit, so it was really something for a 17-year-old high school male to witness. They played very well and really brought the audience into the show with them, unlike any act I have ever seen before or since. Another thing that was very noticeable was how colourful the act was, both musically and visually. This is before bands had a huge production going on behind them, where they showed films or slides behind the act as it played its hits. So what I'm talking about is that basically the band just performed its act while Rod threw the microphone around and Ronnie Wood paraded around the stage smoking a cigarette. But they were in very colourful clothing. Rod would be in canary yellow satin trousers with a purple satin top and a white feather boa, not typical street wear for a male anywhere in the Western World of 1972.

I maintain to this day that the Faces circa 1970-73 were the best band in pop music. Certainly they were the best rock and roll band in pop music, period. Their clothes were outstanding and really made it as part of the show. They were promoting the *A Nod's as Good as a Wink…* LP and they did some songs from *Never a Dull Moment*. Yet, of course, the largest applause was probably for their rather shambolic version of 'Maggie May', so you had the dichotomy in the band there already. People were buying tickets as much for Rod's solo stuff as for the Faces as a band.

I have a theory that's undoubtedly true. Simply put – why didn't Rod Stewart have a live solo band? And the answer is he is tight with his money and always has been. Therefore, if he used the Faces as a backing band, he could go out on the road and not be paying a backing band to do his songs like 'Maggie May' and 'You Wear It Well'. In fact, going out with the Faces, he made money as an individual band member and didn't pay anyone a penny to play his own solo songs. A wise move if you like to save your money.

Where it fell apart was twofold; the Faces versions of his solo songs didn't sound all *that* much like the records, they sounded like slightly sloppy enthusiastic fun versions of the Rod solo hits. Secondly, as Rod's solo career took off and the Faces only had the one single with 'Stay With Me', they began to be booked as Rod Stewart *and* the Faces. I was dear friends with the late, great Ian Maclagan from Mac's time in LA, when he lived with Kim Moon Maclagan near me, and I know for a fact this disturbed him greatly. I was also friendly with Ronnie Lane (and I have the photos to prove it) due to his caretaker being one of my fellow Long Ryders' band members best friends. So we saw Ronnie Lane a fair bit, frequently passing on messages from Ian Maclagan and certainly seeing Ronnie Lane every time we were in Texas on tour. And I know for a fact both Lane and MacLagan were upset at the increasing focus on Rod Stewart.

VETERANS MEMORIAL COLISEUM
26 APRIL 1972, JACKSONVILLE, FLORIDA

I WAS THERE: RICK FREEMAN
I was a Small Faces fan and was curious about Rod Stewart. I bought his first two albums and fell in love with his voice and the stunning work of Ron Wood. *Gasoline Alley* is so underrated. My favourite Faces album is *A Nod's as Good as a Wink to a Blind Horse*. The first Faces show I saw was in early 1972 in Jacksonville, Florida. The show was a dream come true for me. Free opened and everyone was in great form, having taken time

off due to drugs and egos. Paul Kossoff was on fire that night – and Paul Rodger's voice! Then the circus came out and performed while they set up for the Faces. Then out strolled the band.

Being general admission, I had five or six people in front of me. They started the show off with 'It's All Over Now' and 'Cut Across Shorty' after which my memory becomes hazy. I remember 'Maybe I'm Amazed', 'Stay With Me', 'Miss Judy's Farm' and 'Love in Vain' and them kicking soccer balls into the audience. It was just a solid two hours of possibly the best rock and roll I have ever heard. They did three encores and then told us they had nothing left to play. They played as if they were at someone's house. That's how cosy the evening went. Out of over 100 concerts I have been to, this show has to be my all time favourite.

When we were leaving, I told my friend that Ron Wood was a Rolling Stone and that he would one day be in the band. He asked me what would they do with Mick Taylor or Keith Richards? I told him he could play slide, much like Duane Allman counter playing against Dickie Betts' lead. To me it was a fantastic era. The Faces and Rod Stewart albums were just extensions of each other.

HOLLYWOOD SPORTATORIUM
28 APRIL 1972, PEMBROKE PINES, FLORIDA

I WAS THERE: NICK MORAN, AGE 30
The first rock concert I ever attended. The opening act was Free, later to become Bad Company. The show was excellent and one of the best I've ever seen. Admission was $10. I went with a good friend from Morgantown, West Virginia called Jim Farkus (aka Wizard) and his girlfriend, Cheryl, and on his recommendation. I had no idea who Rod Stewart was. The concert actually blew my mind.

I WAS THERE: RICK COLLINS, AGE 20
Free were the opening act and they had some circus acts as well. It was an excellent show. I was a big fan of the Small Faces, so it was not hard to be a Faces fan. I think I still have a recording of part of the show. I was surprised by how good Free were.

WINTER GARDENS
BOURNEMOUTH

Entertainments Manager: SAMUEL J. BELL   Telephone 26446

WEDNESDAY, 26TH MAY AT 7.45 P.M.

ARTHUR HOWES presents

FACES

featuring ROD STEWART : RONNIE LANE : RON WOOD
KENNY JONES & IAN McLAGAN

ATOMIC ROOSTER

TICKETS: £1.00   90p   80p   70p   60p

Box Office open each day from 10 a.m. to 5 p.m. (10 a.m. to 8.30 p.m. on Concert Days) Sundays 2 p.m. to 8.30 p.m. on Concert Days Only
Seats also bookable at Information Bureau, Boscombe Arcade

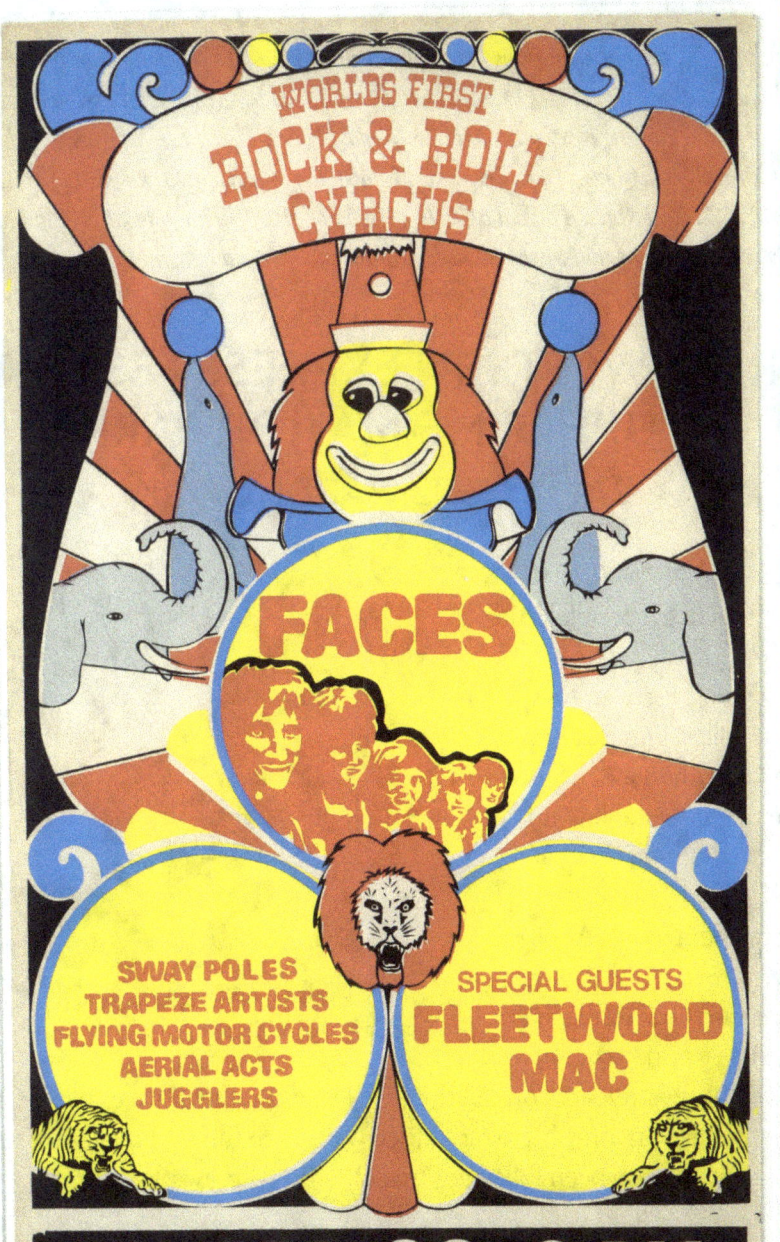

Back in the UK, the Faces headline the Saturday night of a four day festival in rural Lincolnshire put on by promoter Freddie Bannister. Hosted by deejay John Peel and with acts including Alexis Korner, Roxy Music, Helen Reddy, Focus, Slade, Lindisfarne, The Beach Boys, Genesis, Status Quo, Joe Cocker and Humble Pie and Monty Python's Flying Circus, the Great Western Express Festival attracts a crowd of 40,000 but typical British bank holiday weather means that by the Saturday evening the site is a quagmire, knee deep in mud.

GREAT WESTERN EXPRESS FESTIVAL, TUPHOLME MANOR PARK
27 MAY 1972, BARDNEY, UK

I WAS THERE: SUE OATES, AGE 22

I saw them live a couple times back in the early '70s. At the Bardney Pop Festival, myself and pals piled into a car and climbed through a hedge to go see the amazing line up. I also saw them in 1973 at the Top Rank, Doncaster. I also saw them at the Apollo in Manchester. I think all our gang at that time just loved their energy and how different

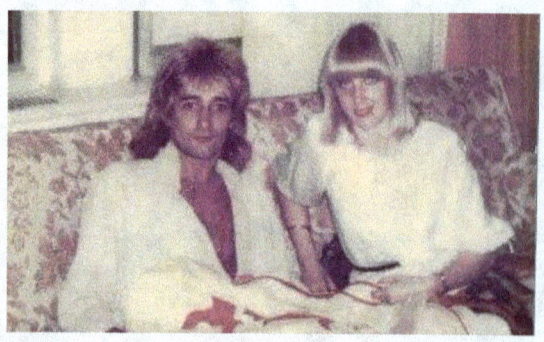

Sue has been a fan of Rod since crawling through a hedge at Bardney

they were. It was a follow on really, as we loved the Small Faces before them. They were just an amazing band – they were such fun and they were such amazing times. I've been following that Rod Stewart ever since!

I WAS THERE: PETER SMITH, AGE 15

I was so excited about going to a real pop festival. My dad drove me and a couple of mates down on the Friday night, after we'd been to the local Mecca ballroom. We arrived in the early hours of Saturday morning, having missed the Friday night bands, and slept in a big crash tent for a few hours. We soon ran into a group of other lads who had also come down from Sunderland,

and between us we built a cabin out of bales of hay and planks of wood which were lying around in the fields. I swear there were around 20 of us sleeping in there. We were quite close to the stage, and I pretty much stayed in that cabin all weekend. We could also stand on the roof and watch the bands.

There was a massive (and very empty) press enclosure which divided the crowd from the stage, so no-one could get that close, which seemed like bad planning. The weather was wet, with rain for most of the weekend. But I didn't care; this was a real pop festival, and I was determined to enjoy every minute.

Programme for the Great Western Festival

The Faces headlined the Saturday night, following Nazareth, Locomotive GT, Roxy Music, Heads, Hands and Feet, Wishbone Ash, The Strawbs and Stone the Crows with Maggie Bell. The Faces thus came at the end of what had been a musically varied and highly enjoyable day.

I remember Rod wearing a silver lame jacket and that they were pretty ramshackle, but great. The band had an authenticity to their performance and the raw energy they brought to their set rubbed off on the crowd. We were all singing along and Rod had us all captivated. Although not the most musically tight performance, for some reason the Faces set stayed with me for the rest of the festival. They managed to capture the raw intensity of rock and roll and the blues, whilst adding an element of fun. It was this less serious side which gave the band an edge and kept me wanting to catch them live whenever I could. They represented fun, drunkenness, ramshackle and dangerous performances. You always had a feeling that the music and the band could all fall apart at any minute, but they never did. It must have been great fun being a 'Face' in those days in the early 1970s. There was really no stopping them!

I WAS THERE: CLIFF BOND

They were awful. Rod was pissed, necking Blue Nun from a bottle. He smashed the top off on his mic stand.

TELL EVERYONE: A PEOPLE'S HISTORY OF THE FACES

I WAS THERE: TONY RAINE

In the summer of 1968, I was about to turn 13 and starting to seriously collect records. I had been the school DJ for two years, playing records at the dance club and at a couple of school dances. My mates who were a bit older had turned me onto soul music and a lot of Mod music. I clearly remember sitting around that summer fascinated by the Small Faces' 'Lazy Sunday' record, which was high on the charts that summer.

Living in Blackburn and having understood the 'breakthrough' acceptance of The Beatles and their northern Scouse accents, here was a new wrinkle. I understood the song was being delivered in a thick cockney accent, but to my young Northern ears it also needed serious translation. Firstly, I listened carefully every time the song was played; the tranny radio was ever present by then. I learned all the words and practiced the accent and soon understood 'suss', 'khazi', 'doing me crust in' and even 'yer mustn't grumble'. After such intense study, I began to delve into the history of the group and listen to their back catalogue and to explore more Mod sounds – The Who, Kinks and a lot of soul tracks on the Atlantic and Stax labels.

We adopted the hair dos and smart dress as best we could as working class schoolboys. We were now officially Mods.

I carried on spinning and collecting records through my schooldays and by 1969 had traded in my weekly comics for weekly deliveries of *Melody Maker* or *NME*, and – by 1970 – *Sounds* music magazines. I read those papers cover to cover and became fascinated by the music scene.

It seemed everything happened in London, and in particular in Chelsea, and followed Small Faces news through the breakup and changes and read about Rod Stewart and Ronnie Wood and their backgrounds. I was very interested in Rod's early albums and his knowledge of his influences. I remember thinking it was really cool that he would feature a Dylan song and Sam Cooke song on *Gasoline Alley*, *An Old Raincoat* and *Every Picture* and that he would 'celebrate' great tunes amongst his own material. The Faces concert reviews were gaining strength and the shows themselves sounded like a great party to this by now 16 year old reader.

In October 1970 I went to my first 'pop' concert, T.Rex at King George's Hall in Blackburn. This was poorly attended. We all bought cheap seats and were invited by Marc Bolan to 'come down to the front'. 'Ride a White Swan' was released the day after, and I still have the copy I bought that day.

Like so many lads of the day whose main interests of the day were 'birds, booze and football', the Faces' 'Stay With Me' single in 1971 was quickly adopted as our anthem. Now music was becoming a major part of our makeup and the Faces were front and centre role models. By September of 1971, I was in college and becoming more aware of prog-rock and adopting a hippy attitude towards life. The north of England felt desperate in the early Seventies and I was looking for change.

I also started going to rock concerts and by May '72, I had spent three days in the mud at the *Bickershaw Festival* in early May and was desperate to hit the *Great Western Festival* near Lincoln on the bank holiday weekend. The line-up was amazing, and the inclusion of the Faces – who were getting great reviews for their live shows – was an added incentive. The Faces followed Stone the Crows on the Saturday night. Maggie Bell had turned in a riveting performance following the recent death of guitarist Les Harvey, and I remember being a little disappointed in the Faces performance, but put it down to them following Stone the Crows and a day of great music.

I WAS THERE: TONY UNWIN, AGE 16

Sadly, I only saw the Faces on the one occasion, at a four day festival in Lincolnshire. It was a very early outdoor festival in the UK. There were some top bands playing, including the likes of The Beach Boys, Joe Cocker, Sha Na Na, Rory Gallagher, Slade as well as the Faces.

Me and a mate from school, Clive Davies, escaped from school sports day on the Friday afternoon and were chased into Coventry town centre by two facist prefects trying to recapture us. We got a bus to Leicester and hitched the rest of the way, getting a lift in an Austin A30 to the festival site.

The Friday night weather was appalling and we were too late to see any of the acts. Luckily, Rory Gallagher played again on Saturday so we didn't miss too much.

Of the other bands I remember: Roxy Music, unheard of at the time, being on at about 11 o'clock in the morning; Lindisfarne being brilliant; Status Quo swearing a lot; the Beach Boys saying they would play all night if we wanted them to; Monty Python performing live on stage for the first time; Sha Na Na doing their set without uttering a single word between each number; Slade, a band I previously didn't like, being the stars of the festival, encouraging an enormous straw fight; and Joe Cocker, stoned off his head.

The Faces were great that night. They were really sloppy, but it didn't matter. Rod wore a gold lame jacket and ended the show booting large footballs into the 40,000 strong crowd. They ensured a real good time was had by one and all. We went back to our tent to find everything had been nicked. We also refused to buy fish and chips for the rip-off price of 30p!

We managed to hitch home in a Morris Traveller, the driver very kindly dropping me off at the bottom of my street in Coventry. I opened the door at my parents house to find that Exile on Main St. had arrived, courtesy of Virgin Records.

Shows scheduled for the Free Trade Hall in Manchester on 31 May 1972 and Green Playhouse on 2 June 1972 are postponed to later in June.

FREE TRADE HALL
18 JUNE 1972, MANCHESTER, UK

I WAS THERE: PHILIP MAHON, AGE 14

The first time I saw the Faces was at a one-off concert they had scheduled at Manchester's Free Trade Hall. I managed to get a decent ticket from Hyme and Addison's (the usual ticket agent in Manchester at that time) after being tipped off by one of my mates. The night of the show arrived – 31st May – only for us to be told that the show was cancelled. It was actually postponed to a later date. The official line was that Kenney Jones' wife was giving birth but it was the night of the European Cup Final – Ajax vs Inter Milan – so our money was on Rod being at the match.

The rearranged date came around and off we went for round two. The concert opened with Byzantium, who seemed to be the support act for 50 per cent of gigs I went to in those days. Time was getting on and the band hadn't arrived. We were told that there had been an incident at Heathrow and the band would be delayed. They arrived and all was forgiven. They opened with 'Memphis' and carried on rocking. There were some new songs that were played that night, possibly for the first time: 'Angel', 'I'd Rather Go Blind' and 'True Blue'. I managed to blag a lift back to Bury with a mate's brother. The spell had been cast.

TELL EVERYONE: A PEOPLE'S HISTORY OF THE FACES

I WAS THERE: CECILIA WALKER

They were a fab live band and I have very, very happy memories. I saw them at the Free Trade Hall in 1972. It was my first concert and it was delayed by the Staines air crash (when an aeroplane crashed shortly after take off, killing all 118 people on board). I also saw them at the Kings Hall in Belle Vue, Manchester, and lots of other venues. I do recall that in 1972 Rod said, 'Our next song, you may know, is about a telephone conversation,' and in the ensuing lull I knew it was 'Memphis' and I yelled out 'oh yeah!', to everyone's amusement.

I WAS THERE: GARY CONSIGLIO, AGE 17

I had always quite liked the Small Faces. Then, in 1971, the whole country went Rod Stewart mad with 'Maggie May' and *Every Picture Tells a Story* being the number one single and album in America and England at the same time. This was the first concert I ever went to. It should have been on May 31st. I went by train from West Yorkshire with two school friends. We turned up at the Free Trade Hall to find it had been called off right at the last minute because Kenney was ill. There were hundreds outside and people weren't very happy. It was put back on again about three weeks later. I remember them playing stuff off *A Nod's as Good as a Wink...* and a lot of Rod stuff from *Every Picture*. *Never a Dull Moment* was just coming out and they played 'Angel' and 'Twistin' the Night Away'.

I followed them for the duration really, seeing them five more times – later that year at Leeds Town Hall and then Queens Hall in Leeds (with my younger sister), two of the Ronnie Lane farewell gigs at the Edmonton Sundown in June '73 and, after I went to university in Newcastle, at the Newcastle Odeon in 1974 with Tetsu. So, six times altogether.

The first time I saw the Faces, I didn't take much notice of how they played. They were just a party band. I saw them play with varying degrees of proficiency but nobody seemed to care. I don't think Ronnie Wood was as good a guitarist as he has since become with the Stones. I always thought Plonk was the best musician in the band by a mile. He was such a great bassist, he was almost like a second lead guitar and so melodic in the way he played. But they could be a bit shambolic, with songs falling apart.

The best I saw them play was the two gigs I saw at the Sundown. Because they were Ronnie's last gigs, I think they rehearsed those pretty hard. They were certainly pretty good the two nights I saw them. I'd have loved to have been the very last one.

A mate of mine was a stage manager for Rod's gig at Wembley Stadium. Ronnie Wood came on and they wheeled Ronnie Lane out in a wheelchair for one of the last songs. That was pretty emotional. He looked in a bad way. It was great to see him, but not that nice to see, if you know what I mean.

GREEN'S PLAYHOUSE
25 JUNE 1972, GLASGOW, UK

I WAS THERE: DAVIE LOGAN

I first heard the Faces on John Peel's radio show which was on around 6pm on a Saturday evening. One of the tracks was 'Maybe I'm Amazed'. I worked in Glasgow at the time and I went out on my lunch hour and bought *Long Player*. I'd just turned 18 and was brought up in a household with two older brothers who were into the Stones, Traffic, the Animals, etc. It took a bit of persuading to get them to listen to it but I eventually won them over. The Faces were due to play Green's Playhouse (later the Apollo) in the summer but Rod Stewart was ill and the gig put back until later in the year. The tickets were £1 and a great night was had by all. The only downside was we missed the last bus home, and had to walk or hitchhike the 15 miles home. The Faces gig is up there as one of the top gigs I've been to, and I've seen most of the greats.

CRANBOURNE COURT, WINKFIELD ROW
SUMMER 1972, ASCOT, UK

I WAS THERE: DEE HARRINGTON

Rod and I would get together from time to time with the Faces' wives. We'd go to Ronnie Lane's house over by Richmond Hill when he was married to Sue Lane. And we'd often go to The Wick in Richmond where Ronnie Wood bought that beautiful house off the actor John Mills. That house was always full of rock 'n' roll people like Led Zeppelin and the Rolling Stones and The Who. Ronnie had a bit of a studio and a pool room, so it was a meeting place for people to hang out. Pete Townshend lives there now.

We had a lovely house in Winchmore Hill in Southgate, north London. But after 'Maggie May' everybody wanted a part of Rod and suddenly it was like living in a goldfish bowl. People were outside the house all the time. We moved to the countryside so that he didn't have to feel, 'Oh, can I get out now? Let's have a look and see if anyone's there.' And we also moved also because his accountant said, 'You've got to spend some money on a house now and it has to be £100,000.' We might never have moved otherwise.

Perry Press, who was the estate agent to the stars, was taking us to places but we couldn't find anything we liked. We were driving back from some place that clearly wasn't suitable when Perry said, 'Well there is this house on the way back…' and Rod said, 'I want to have a look at it now.' It was in Winkfield Row in Berkshire. It had a very big driveway. We drove down the driveway, saw the house and Rod said, 'I want to see inside.' He loved it immediately. It was set in 20 acres so you never saw it from the road. It had a lodge house and gate and it was fenced. People didn't know where it was, because it was in the countryside, so although they'd come looking for the house, we didn't have as many fans turning up as we had with the previous house. We bought it from Lord Bethell. It didn't cost £100,000 but it was nearly that. So on January 1, 1972 we ended up living in this 'mansion in the sky'.

Because we were out of town it wasn't like we were out every night in clubs and bars. We'd go to Tramp a bit but we now had this beautiful and very large house that we spent two and a half years trying to get together. Rod would be doing his trains. His trains were his retreat from everything. His brother spent two and a half years in our house painting and getting everything sorted out. He'd also bash a hole in the wall and build a platform for Rod to build his train layout on. He didn't just buy a train and put it on the rails. We used to go to this place in Holborn where he'd buy railway stuff. We'd come back and I'd say, 'Can we have some people and horses?' and he'd go 'no!' He really got a lot of enjoyment out of it, and that time on his own helped to rejuvenate him for everything else.

We lived opposite Windsor Great Park and I had horses, so I rode in the park almost every day. I'd ride by the house and he'd pop his head up and wave, and on my way back he'd wave again, having been in that room working on his train layout all that time. He built his trains and the landscape. I rode to keep my sanity. Then we'd rush into London to try and buy something to fill the house with.

But there was always this studio thing going down. When you've got a recording contract you've got to supply material, and they were hot, so there was no hanging around. It was always, 'I'm going to the studio. We've got to get on and make the most of this and we've got to supply records, and then we've got to tour.'

Then there was the promotion in the UK and the promotion in Europe, so more TV interviews with a bit of travelling. I probably spent more time with Rod on his solo promotion stuff than with him on the Faces promotion.

I WAS THERE: PENNY BROWN, AGE 14

Me and my mate heard the 'Rod lives in a house owned by Lord Bethel' story. We got to Windsor, traipsed around asking people and finally found it. We walked up the drive and round to the front to find two yellow Lamborghinis, a two-seater and a four-seater, with the number plates LUC50K and LUC51K. We were lucky that Carlo the giant Alsatian guard dog wasn't out that day!

Dee came out and said, 'What d'you want?' We were so embarrassed, but said we had come to see Rod – as if the tartan scarves and spiky hair weren't enough of a clue! She said, 'He's away, but why don't you come in and have breakfast?' She cooked us bacon and eggs, gave us a tour of the house, including Rod's train set, gave us some of his t-shirts (I've still got mine!), took our names and addresses and then gave us a lift home in his Rolls-Royce!

Two weeks later, packages arrived with signed LP covers, photos, etc., plus an invite to meet her at the Edmonton Sundown pre-show later that year. We went back to the house twice before that, and sat in the garden with Rod drinking orange juice. And once, when he was away, we had lunch with Dee's parents.

We also traipsed around Richmond, Kingston, etc., and met Kenney at his house and Mac at his. Lots of times we spent ages sitting outside Woody's house, but he never came out, although we saw Ronnie Lane when he lived at the bottom of Woody's garden. The police came by one time, and then we managed to get pictures signed (and another lift home) but Ronnie still never came out. He must've been horrified when the policeman rang the doorbell!

I saw the band twice. The Edmonton concert was awesome. We met the band before it, Ronnie Wood gave us guitar strings and we sat in front of Rod's mum and dad. Dee sent us other tickets too, and was super nice. They were amazing live.

I saw the remains at Hurtwood Park, which was fab. They always seemed to be having so much fun. Treasured memories. I was gutted when the Faces split. Dee, you were the best!

WARNERS BROS RECORDS OFFICE
SUMMER 1972, LONDON, UK

I WAS THERE: NIGEL MOLDEN

I had the opportunity to see the Faces a number of times during the early 1970s, largely because they were one of the top touring bands of the period. Gigs at the Rainbow and the New Theatre in Oxford come to mind. I have read that they did not rate themselves as a band and that was the reason for their casual approach to performances. True or not, every appearance was happy-go-lucky. They were always late on stage – sometimes as much as 45 minutes, and invariably came on kicking plastic footballs and carrying a bottle of Mateus Rosé. It may have been their version of building up a rock and roll tension, as they certainly knew what they were doing. Exasperated to the point of leaving, I can remember the band eventually coming on stage at the New Theatre, Oxford with Rod Stewart saying, 'We'll make it up to you.'

However, the performances were not my principal reason for remembering them so clearly. In 1971, I had just been offered a job in London at Kinney Corporation, which was the early name for Warner Brothers Records. They had signed the Faces to a worldwide agreement although, in the early days of the corporation, it did not have many operational international companies. Having set up the London office they also installed Derek Taylor, the former press officer for The Beatles, as a local A&R man.

During 1972, Derek told me and my colleague in the Promotion

Department that the Faces would be coming in that afternoon and how they were all feeling very despondent. They were doing lots of gigs and getting hit records although not topping the charts. We all met in the gloom of the individualistic, art deco-inspired office that Derek had created. It was all pleasant enough with the kind of banter to be expected. However, I remember Rod Stewart lying on the floor quite close to me carrying on about having no money. Of course, he had a reputation for being tight but the drinking, clothes and lifestyle clearly played a part as well. The reason I mention this anecdote is that I remember seeing him being interviewed by Michael Parkinson many years later when he was asked how much he was worth. His answer was that he was told it was something like a hundred million. I do recall whether it was pounds or dollars but that is hardly the point. I could not help but think of the day he was laying on the floor, moaning about having no money!

The seventh North American tour, the Rock & Roll Circus Summer Tour, consists of eight shows starting in Boston, Massachusetts on 1st July.

GARDEN
1 JULY 1972, BOSTON, MASSACHUSETTS

I WAS THERE: SHAUN P MCCAUL
Did they have a circus act with a woman spinning around and axe jugglers? I was at that show. I remember kids throwing firecrackers at the girl, who was hanging by her hair or teeth.

SPECTRUM
2 JULY 1972, PHILDELPHIA, PENNSYLVANIA

I WAS THERE: DAVID MORESI
Growing up in Philadelphia was terrific for a concert goer like me since all the big names and all bands really played at venues throughout the city. I saw Rod and the Faces twice, both times at the Spectrum. The

one I remember the most was great. The bill was Rod Stewart and Faces, a Rock 'n' Roll Circus and Badfinger, who I also loved. One Badfinger band member, Joey Molland, had his left arm in a cast but sat down and played beautifully.

The Rock 'n' Roll Circus was very cool with trapeze artists and motorcycle riders in a big round cage riding and jumping over each other. For the circus finale, they had a woman hanging from her long black hair on a crane. She must have had on 50 kimonos, and took them off one at a time. Everyone was into that but she finally had on a one-piece swimsuit on at the end.

David Moresi saw Faces at the Spectrum

Rod and Faces were great of course. They played all their hits and Rod's, plus several songs from my all-time favourite Faces LP, *Ooh La La*. Of course, Rod was up to his usual stage routine of playing and kicking out soccer balls to the audience. Dang, I miss those days.

I WAS THERE: PETER DELLO BUONO

Philadelphia was a big Faces town. Whenever they played here, usually at the Spectrum, they would announce what hotel they were staying at and it would always turn into a big party at the hotel bar. The fellows would always come down and hang out, and there'd be plenty of girls and tons of fun. Most of the crowd were dressed up in clothing from Granny Takes a Trip (there was one in NYC). My good friends were the booking agent and stage manager

Peter Dello Buono (right) and his wife Betty (second left) got to meet Rod at the Spectrum in Philly

for one of the big concert promoters, Electric Factory Concerts, and through them I actually got to meet Rod at a backstage party. He was very friendly and it was his idea to have the photo taken.

I WAS THERE: JEFF GREGORIS
I saw them twice in the 1970s, and Rod Stewart many times afterward. The first concert was at the Spectrum in Philadelphia in the early Seventies. Badfinger were the opening act and then the rock 'n' roll circus with a stripper hanging from the ceiling as she performed. The Faces were on their A game, playing their stuff and some of Rod's. Wine was being passed around between the stage and the crowd up front. The second time I saw them, circa 1975, they played the Civic Center in Philly, and the story was the mayor of Philly at the time didn't want them playing at the Spectrum because of the boozing and rowdy behaviour. Once again it was a great show and Rod told the audience he liked the Civic Center and screw the Spectrum – and the mayor. They all worked and played well together. It was a blast.

I WAS THERE: ALAN SCHAFER
I saw them several times from '72 through to '75 and the last Faces tour. You always knew you were in for a great show with a good-time atmosphere that only the Faces could deliver! Everyone in attendance was there to have fun with Rod and the boys. The camaraderie they had was second to none. From the opening of the curtain accompanied by David Rose's 'The Stripper', you could feel the energy. It was something you had to experience live. Their entire show from wardrobe and stage through to lighting and equipment was always something to see... a class act in all respects. To this day, the Faces in my opinion were the best live show you could see. From the Faces hits to Rod's solo material and cover tunes, where in most cases I thought they outdid the original versions, they had it all. It was a shame they didn't continue as a band.

It was an amazing experience seeing the Faces for the first time. Rod was sporting a yellow satin suit with scarf. Woody was looking cool, the coolest guitarist of all time. And Kenney Jones was playing a set of tartan plaid drums. Midway through the show, someone on the floor in a wheelchair, somewhat near the stage, was being hoisted up in the air while in his or her wheelchair by people or friends in the area. Rod took the time to notice and comment on their presence and made sure that they too were having a great time!

Everyone attending a Faces show was there for a great time. They were without a doubt the best at providing that party atmosphere. In my opinion, Woody joining the Stones was a waste of his talents. Him and Mac sounded great together with Woody's unique style, and with him being the only guitarist.

RUBBER BOWL
3 JULY 1972, AKRON, OHIO

I WAS THERE: BARB YOUNG SALINSKY, AGE 17

It was my very first concert and I went with my friend Christine. I had won the tickets from a local radio station. My parents dropped us off at the entrance to the Akron Rubber Bowl and made an agreement on pick up time... midnight. The first band was Cactus, which I had only just heard of a few weeks earlier. Then Badfinger, who were big at the time. Rod and Faces were just totally awesome. I had never been exposed to such live energetic music before and it took over my soul. It changed my life inasmuch as I love live music so much, I wound up seeing over 100 bands live. There is nothing like the energy from seeing a band live!

I WAS THERE: CR KRIEGER

Cleveland promoter Belkin Productions started an early series of stadium concerts for 1972 at the University of Akron's football stadium, The Rubber Bowl. The Rubber Bowl was set into the side of a hill, forming one side of the seating, and had a normal seating capacity of over 35,000. With the concert stage in one end zone, a sell out crowd was nearer 40,000. The series included the Rolling Stones, Alice Cooper and Faces as headliners. The opening July 3rd line up started with Cactus, followed by Badfinger and then the Faces. My remaining faded memories are disjointed. I remember nothing of Cactus. Badfinger opened with 'Baby Blue', my favourite of theirs, which was disappointingly off key. I remember little more of their set except that it was a good one.

The Faces hit the stage with all the energy you would hope for. Rod was at his mic stand-twirling best, managing to hit the overhanging tarpaulin cover with it. The set was tight and rollicking. Rod wasn't doing his slow standards. They were playing Faces music! Midway through the set, they were beginning the lead-in to 'Memphis, Tennessee'. My friend Jim was on his feet, as that was his favourite Faces tune.

I noticed that my eyes were burning I turned to look at him. He was squinting at me through his glasses when we heard someone above us yell, 'GAS!' So there it was. We were being tear gassed. Some ticketless fans were trying to crash the gate at the top of the hill and the thoughtless Akron Police Department decided to hit them with gas, paying no mind that it spilled down into our seats below, clearing out a nice parabolic area of seats that we fled. It didn't take long to disperse and we returned to the general area of our seats for the rest of the show. I wish I could recall more.

CHRISLER ARENA
5 JULY 1972, ANN ARBOR, MICHIGAN

I WAS THERE: KEVIN DINGLE
Badfinger opened and rocked. There was quite a time between the two but when the Faces came out they tore the place up. It was a very high energy performance with Rod Stewart prancing all over the stage. Towards the end he did his traditional kicking soccer balls into the audience thing. I was too far away to have a chance of getting one. It was one of the greatest shows I have seen.

WAR MEMORIAL
6 JULY 1972, SYRACUSE, NEW YORK

I WAS THERE: CARL SCHAEFER, AGE 17
I grew up with an older brother and an older sister so music was always being played. When the album *A Nod's as Good as a Wink...* came out, I had to buy it. After I got out of school in my junior year, I travelled

back to Syracuse, New York and was visiting a friend when I noticed that the Faces were playing in Syracuse at the War Memorial. It was my first ever live concert. Badfinger played too. It was a great concert and afterwards I had to see the players whenever I got a chance, so have seen Rod Stewart three times since, Ronnie Wood six times (with the Rolling Stones) and Kenney with The Who. When the ARMS concert was in San Francisco, dedicated to Ronnie Lane and raising money for muscular sclerosis research, naturally I had to go. It was one of the greatest concerts, with Eric Clapton, Joe Cocker, Jimmy Page and Jeff Beck. I was able to take photos with my 35 millimetre camera without any flash.

POCONO INTERNATIONAL RACEWAY FESTIVAL
8 JULY 1972, LONG POND, PENNSYLVANIA

I WASN'T THERE: SUZY SOLTIS

My husband was at a three day concert in 1973 with the Faces with Rod along with Humble Pie and Black Sabbath. It would have been our first date had my mom let me go, but she didn't! There were 20 other bands over three days and it was eight bucks to get in.

Suzy Soltis didn't get to the festival

I WAS THERE: JOEL WATTERWORTH

The event attracted an estimated 200,000 people who were met with cold inclement weather, replete with rain and mud. The general atmosphere of the concert was compared to the Woodstock Festival of 1969. The Faces played at 5am. It was so wet when they finally came on. It was foggy and cold but they rocked it, big time!

UAC-DAYSTAR PRESENTS

THE FACES

FEATURING

ROD STEWART

RON WOOD · RON LAINE
IAN McLAGEN · KENNY JONES

— PLUS —

BADFINGER

WEDNESDAY JULY 5 — 8:30 PM
CRISLER ARENA

— TICKET INFORMATION —

TICKETS GO ON SALE THURSDAY JUNE 15
ALL TICKETS $5.00 — ALL RESERVED SEATS
— BEST SEATS WILL BE SOLD FIRST —
LIMIT 10 PER PERSON — NO CHECKS PLEASE
ON SALE THURSDAY & FRIDAY, JUNE 15 & 16 — 9:30 AM–3:30 PM ONLY
CRISLER ARENA BOX WINDOW

CIVIC ARENA
9 JULY 1972, PITTSBURGH, PENNSYLVANIA

I WAS THERE: MIKE GRALEWSKI

I saw many a show at the Civic Arena, which has now been torn down, and that Faces show one was one of the best. It was the *Nod* tour. Badfinger were the opening act. After 15 or 20 minutes, Rod instructed everyone to 'come on down'. It was just like the album cover. He kicked me a ball with a smiley face on one side and a frowning face on the other. They always finished the shows with 'Had Me a Real Good Time'. The most memorable song for me was 'That's All You Need'. The next time I saw them, Peter Frampton opened. It was promoted as a 'Rock & Roll Circus' with bagpipes and a girl suspended by her hair over the crowd. It was pretty theatrical.

I actually did a gig with Ronnie Lane at a club called the Decade in Pittsburgh. He was living in Austin at the time and in a wheelchair. I had to carry him upstairs to smoke some joints as the manager wouldn't let us smoke downstairs!

I WAS THERE: REESE SLATER, AGE 20

I was in college and just at the beginning of my rock 'n' roll 'career'. I played guitar in bands from 1972 to 1984. I was somewhat familiar with the Faces, but more so with Badfinger, with whom they were sharing the bill. I believe it was a Sunday. I was with three friends, just cruising around aimlessly as we were wont to do at the time, when we heard on the radio that Badfinger and the Faces were playing that night at the Pittsburgh Civic Arena. On the spur of the moment, we decided to head that way and bought tickets at the door. It couldn't have been much more than $5 as none of us had much money at the time.

The draw for us was Badfinger, who had a lot of radio play at the time, but it was the Faces that blew me away. I had never seen such raw energy, nor had I ever seen a band having so much fun while on stage. I recall them literally bouncing up and down while playing as if they were spring-loaded (it was probably speed, which hadn't arrived for me... yet). They had a bar set up onstage, replete with red-vested barman who was kept busy mixing cocktails and pouring beers, while they made trip after trip to the bar while continuing to play. We thought this was just fantastic!

At one point during the show, Rod kicked soccer balls into the audience while singing. It was just a night of great songs, great playing and pure fun. They made the audience feel like we were all in this together, and made a large arena feel like a small pub. I've seen hundreds of concerts and this show is still up there at the top of my list of best shows.

GOOSE FAIR FESTIVAL
22 JULY 1972, NOTTINGHAM, UK

A planned appearance at Nottingham's Goose Fair is cancelled.

SHERWOOD ROOMS
1 AUGUST 1972, NOTTINGHAM, UK

I WAS THERE: BOB BAXTER

I always enjoyed the songs of the Small Faces. My local pub held a disco every Friday night and the deejay played 'Had Me a Real Good Time' all the time so I went out and got *Long Player* and became a fan of the Faces. One of my mates, David Harrison from Blyth in Northumberland, was a mad Rod Stewart fan and he introduced me to Rod's back catalogue which then got me hooked on Rod. David has seen Rod hundreds of times and often gets a mention off Rod at his concerts, Rod calling him 'the crazy Newcastle guy'. He also has about a dozen footballs kicked into the crowd at Rod's gigs.

The Nottingham gig I attended was down to pure chance. Me and my mate John 'Lennie' Lennox were on our summer holidays and were driving around England and camping wherever. We just happened to be driving through Nottingham when we noticed a poster announcing a surprise concert by Rod and the Faces for that night and it was pay at the door – £1.00 entry. Apparently, they were due to play at an open air venue earlier in the year but cancelled because of illness to one of the band so it was payback time. We just looked for the venue, which was an older type of city hall next to a multi-storey car park, where we slept that night, and joined the queue. The concert was opened by Beggars Opera, a Scottish band who were excellent.

The Faces were very good on the night. Rod was on good form and people were throwing cigarettes to Ronnie Wood and he was smoking one whilst lighting another and wedging it between the strings of his guitar head so he always had one on the go, chainsmoking throughout the entire gig. Rod had dark hair in those days and he and other members of the band were constantly nipping behind the speakers to have a swig of wine or something else straight from the bottles. They got through quite a few that night!

Ronnie Lane singing 'Richmond' and Rod singing 'Maybe I'm Amazed' plus Ronnie Wood's guitar playing stick in my mind, along with his brilliant slide guitar. The atmosphere at the concert was raucous and fun. Everyone seemed to connect with the mood.

'YOU WEAR IT WELL' RELEASED 4 AUGUST 1972

Rod releases what is to become his second UK number 1 single. It reaches number 14 in the US.

TRENTHAM GARDENS
7 AUGUST 1972, STOKE-ON-TRENT, UK

I WAS THERE: ANDY DEAN

I think I might have seen them twice, but definitely '73ish at Trentham Gardens. I've still got the non-authorised programme, which was a piece of crap! The support band were Beggars Opera. My interest in the Faces started with either *Nod's* or *Every Picture*. I got into them via a school friend who was originally a Small Faces fan. I would have been about 15. I was hooked and then backtracked in no time at all to *Long Player* and *First Step*. I remember getting both on cassette for Christmas. They are possibly my favourite band of all time, along with (for different reasons) The Beatles, Steely Dan and Bèefheart.

NATIONAL JAZZ, BLUES & ROCK FESTIVAL
12 AUGUST 1972, READING, UK

I WAS THERE: PETE FISHER

Two musician friends and I drove up for the day from Hastings, as the bill featured quite a few favourites of ours. It was a pretty eclectic line-up – Man, Linda Lewis, Focus, Edgar Broughton, Johnny Otis, If, Electric Light Orchestra and finally the Faces. In my diary I noted that Edgar Broughton and Focus were the best supporting acts, although I remember also being impressed by Johnnie Otis and his teenage wunderkind guitarist son, Shuggie. I remember the Faces coming on and kicking a load of footballs into the crowd and generally fooling around before they actually played. They were obviously pretty tipsy. Rod had a glittery silver suit on and it was very much a party atmosphere. I wrote

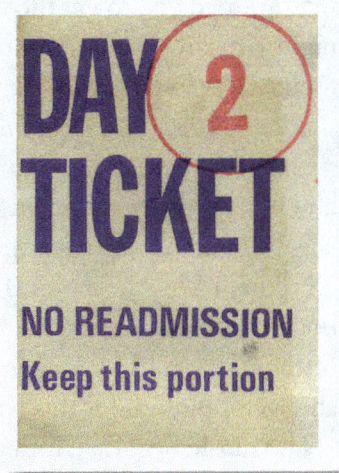

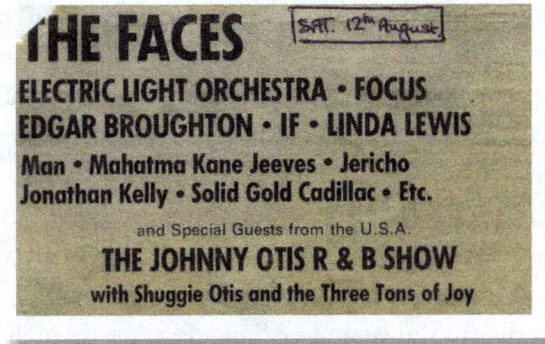

Pete Fisher was at the Reading Festival

in my diary that they were really brilliant, especially Ron Wood's slide solo. They did three encores before finally leaving the stage.

I WAS THERE: GARY JONES, AGE 17

I saw them at the Reading Festival. It was a double headliner with Status Quo – an incredible night!

I WAS THERE: PETER SMITH

I'd already attended the Lincoln Festival in May 1972, so as a 15-year-old

TELL EVERYONE: A PEOPLE'S HISTORY OF THE FACES

I felt I was already a hardened festival goer when I decided to go to the Reading Festival. I didn't know anyone else who wanted to go, so decided to go alone. My parents weren't keen on my idea of hitching so I agreed to go by train. Despite the festival starting on the Friday afternoon, for some reason I decided to get the train down to London early on the Thursday night, arriving around midnight. Having nowhere to spend the night I took a tube to Piccadilly Circus and found an all-night cinema that was showing Elvis films. I paid my money and sat close to the front. I watched six movies, *Kid Galahad, Fun in Acapulco* and *Girls, Girls, Girls* amongst them, and emerged, very tired, in the early hours of the morning and made my way to Paddington to get the train to Reading.

I didn't have a ticket for the festival, so on arrival I joined the queue and bought a weekend ticket. I stayed in the queue to get a good spot in front of the stage. All I had taken with me was a sleeping bag, no tent and no change of clothes for this hardened festival-goer.

The music began at 4pm and there were two stages set alongside each other to make for quick changeovers. I positioned myself close to the front somewhere between the two stages, so I had a good view of both. There was a press enclosure right down the front, and an area where the Hell's Angels would encamp, so you couldn't get that close to the stage. I got talking to a guy next to me; he was also alone, still at school and a similar age. We stuck together throughout the weekend, keeping each other's place in the crowd, and sleeping there on a night in our sleeping bags.

The weather was quite warm, sunny with a little drizzle now and then but nothing compared to the rain I had experienced at the Lincoln Festival earlier in the year. The Saturday line-up included Jonathan Kelly, Solid Gold Cadillac, The Johnnie Otis Show, Man, Linda Lewis, Focus, Edgar Broughton, and a Roy Wood-less Electric Light Orchestra. Then it was time for the Faces.

Rod and the guys were on great form. Rod's interaction was tremendous and we were all captivated by the band's energy. There were lots of footballs kicked into the crowd and the atmosphere was just right for the headlining act with the audience completely gripped by their performance. 'Twistin' the Night Away' and 'I'm Losing You' were big live favourites at the time and got a huge response, as did 'Maggie May' and 'Stay With Me'. DJ John Peel was a big fan, and no doubt enjoyed the set as much as the crowd did. Their set was over all too fast, as festival sets often are, but their performance stayed with us for the whole weekend and remained the high point of the festival for me.

By Monday morning I was stiff, tired and scruffy. I got the first train home and went straight to bed.

COTTON BOWL
19 AUGUST 1972, DALLAS, TEXAS

The Faces begin their ninth North American tour, with 15 shows that conclude at New York's Madison Square Garden.

I WAS THERE: BRIAN HERRINGTON

I saw them twice, once opening for Three Dog Night in 1972 at the Cotton Bowl, and then again at the Fort Worth Tarrant County Convention Center Arena in the fall of 1975 right before Woody became a full time Stone. All I can really remember is that the '72 show had relay speakers on the field as there was no floor seating in the Cotton Bowl while in '75 their intro was them coming out to the jazz tune, 'The Stripper'.

I WAS THERE: GREGORY HOLDSWORTH

I was in the army and stationed at Fort Hood, Texas when a friend and I got tickets to go see Rod Stewart and the Faces along with Three Dog Night and a couple of other groups playing at the Cotton Bowl in Dallas, Texas. It was a warm day and a fairly large crowd and we couldn't wait to see Rod singing 'Maggie May'. They were handing out Three Dog Night buttons for their new song, 'One is the Loneliest Number', and I still have several of those orange buttons with the number 1 on them. It was a lot of fun. We enjoyed the concert and we stayed until the end. I remember reading an article about the concert in the Greenville, Texas newspaper the *Herald-Banner*:

Last week Three Dog Night and Rod Stewart made a shambles of the Cotton Bowl, putting on a show to remember for the 40,000 screaming, stomping, bleary-eyed fans, myself included. Stewart was a little weird to say the least and the crowd didn't really get into what was he was doing. During 'Black Angel' (sic) he pranced across the stage and planted a kiss on the bass player... I mean, is that weird or is that... weird? But the shaggy-haired, gravel-voiced vocalist from England could tie a song up in a gag and throw it away. If R. Stewart didn't win total approval, and I think he should have considering the enormous problems of playing to a crowd that big in a football stadium, Three Dog Night came across like Washington on the Delaware...

There were over 40,000 wild, crazy fans there that night going nuts. They just kept screaming 'Three Dog Night! Three Dog Night!' Sorry, Rod. This was a great Three Dog Night show!

HOLLYWOOD BOWL
25 AUGUST 1972, LOS ANGELES, CALIFORNIA

I WAS THERE: NANCY BERMAN

They played 'Maggie May' and I recall it being an amazing concert but that's about it. It was such a long time ago and I'm sure that I was stoned out of my mind.

I WAS THERE: MARVIN STEWART STEINBERG

I saw at least ten shows when the Faces came to Los Angeles. I was in ninth or tenth grade at high school when *A Nod's...* came out and we would go into my neighbour's bedroom and he would put the record on and, even with his parents in the house, turn it up full blast. I would act like I was Rod Stewart and one of our brothers was Ian McLagan or Kenney Jones. That album just rocked and it still rocks today. When the Hollywood Bowl show was announced we said, 'No matter what, we're going.' My dad or a neighbour took us to Ticketron and we were able to get four tickets to see the Faces at the Hollywood Bowl.

I remember my friend Scott's mom drove us there. The memory I have of that show is them coming out to 'The Stripper' by Billy Rose. Rod would do the same at his early solo concerts. That song would start playing and it just got everybody in such a great mood. It was like an explosion. And when 'The Stripper' ended, they went into 'Miss Judy's Farm' and from there on in it was just an incredible show. We couldn't believe it. They even had a bar set up on stage with drinks and everything. It was just phenomenal.

Those live shows were just as big and exciting as what the Rolling Stones were – and are – from the Seventies on. The chemistry between all of them would be so playful, with Rod running around the stage with Ronnie. From one song to the next it was amazing. They did 'Maybe I'm Amazed' and 'Memphis' and the last song was 'Stay With Me'. And the soccer balls came out and they were all playing with them on stage and kicking them out into the audience. To this day, it's one of the best concerts I've ever seen in my life.

After that, they would come to the Inglewood Forum and I saw them there at least six times, and every time they played it was just as exciting. When *Ooh La La* came out, they came out doing 'Borstal Boys', which in my opinion is one of the all-time great rockers. When Ronnie Lane left, they brought in Tetsu and you could kind of tell that Ronnie was missed. But Tetsu did a good job and with the personalities of all the others, it was equally as exciting.

When I heard Mick Taylor was leaving the Stones and Ronnie was going to be the new member, I thought, 'Hey, that's great he's going to the Stones,' but at the same time, 'Hey wait – what about the Faces?' It was really hard to take.

A few years ago, Rod did a show at the Hollywood Bowl that was billed as 'Rod Stewart with special guest Ronnie Wood'. Of course, I had to be there. It was a great show. Halfway through the show, I noticed a grey-haired Rod/Ronnie-type haircut and it was Ian McLagan. And Rod got behind him and was playfully pointing down at him from an elevated position above and behind him, saying, 'Hey look, he's here.' It was so cool.

I found out Ronnie Wood was exhibiting his art in Sherman Oaks at this really high end gallery. My friend and I went and I brought along three of Ronnie's solo albums and a Faces album and I got to talk to him. Ian McLagan was there, and Jesse Ed Davis, and they all signed all the albums.

When they did the Hurtwood Park gig in 2015 I wrote on Facebook, 'Come and do it in LA. Everybody in LA loves you guys,' hoping that they were going to do more than just that one off show. But it never happened.

I WAS THERE: LOUIS VARGAS, AGE 15

I saw the Faces live nine times, twice with Ronnie Lane. The first time, I had turned 15 years old earlier that month. A group of us went to the concert. The songs I particularly remember from that show are 'Miss

Judy's Farm', 'Maggie May', 'Stay With Me', 'Angel', 'Maybe I'm Amazed' and 'Twistin' the Night Away'. What an absolutely fun concert that was!

Two days later, I saw them again at the much smaller and more intimate Hollywood Palladium. It was pretty much the same show as at the Bowl but the song order was changed a little bit. The concert was entitled 'The Faces Champagne Party' and there was a VIP section serving free champagne to anyone in that section. My brother and I snuck in and got a couple of glasses of champagne!

HOLLYWOOD PALLADIUM
27 AUGUST 1972, LOS ANGELES, CALIFORNIA

I WAS THERE: DAVID PRACY, AGE 15

I saw them when I was a kid. It was the first big show I saw, at the Hollywood Palladium, and they have been my favourite band ever since. I was with my cousin's very good looking early 20s wife, which was a big thing for a 15-year-old! She got us all the free champagne we could drink. The band supplied the champagne. We got a spot right up against the stage and it changed my life forever. I have been a sound engineer for the last 40 years and still play drums. I saw the Faces once more and have seen Ron Wood at least ten times, Rod five times and Ian six or seven times.

I met my wife because of Ron Wood and she convinced me to date her because of my love for Ronnie. When I was 35, I lived in San Francisco. I was walking down Geary Street and came upon an art gallery that had a drawing by Vargas and a self portrait of Ronnie Wood in the front window, so of course I had to go in. I met a lovely woman who ended up selling me a Ron Wood self portrait and invited me to an opening. She called me many times over the next year and, being recently divorced, I stayed away. Then Ron Wood was coming to San Francisco for his *Slide on This* tour, and she called me and said 'you can come to an opening at the gallery and meet him, if you would like to be my personal guest' and of course I had to do it. We have been together 27 years since that night!

OAKLAND COLISEUM
30 AUGUST 1972, OAKLAND, CALIFORNIA

I WAS THERE: DAN CUNY

This was one of the more anticipated shows that my friends – Michael Morton and Gary Hodges – and I attended that summer. Our other friend, David Miller, was on a backpacking trip. Boy, did he miss a great show! We always made an effort to acquire good seats, and for this show we were in the eighth row centre. I remember I had a 200mm lens on my camera, which allowed me to get a closer view of the stage and get tighter shots of the band.

When the lights went down and the band came on stage, it was truly electric. Rod Stewart was dressed in a silver sequinned midriff top and matching trousers. Ron Wood was in a red satin shirt and sequined pants. They started the show with 'It's All Over Now', which had Rod running from one side of the stage to the other, swinging his microphone and throwing it into the air. I had never seen anything like that before, so it was very exciting. Then they went into 'Miss Judy's Farm', one of the songs I was most looking forward to hearing because I love Ron Wood's playing on that one. The concert was a good mix of Rod Stewart's solo songs and songs from albums by the Faces.

Rod would run across the stage from one end, sliding on his knees at the other end. At one point, Ronnie Lane and Ron Wood were singing at one end of the stage, and while Rod was at the other end, Ronnie Lane let his microphone start to fall. Rod saw what was happening and ran to the other end, sliding and picking up the microphone just before it hit the floor, and continued singing.

There was a lot of fun on the stage, with the band joking around. I remember Rod Stewart walking over to a speaker cabinet and picking up a bottle, looking over at Ian McLagan and pointing to it. Ian shrugged his shoulders and Rod took a big swig from the bottle.

I clearly remember them playing 'Maggie May', 'Stay With Me', 'That's All You Need' and 'True Blue'. Ronnie Lane was a masterful bass player. Ian McLagan's playing on piano and organ was great, and Kenney Jones was powerful on drums. It was one of my all-time favourite shows, and one of the most enjoyable to photograph.

TELL EVERYONE: A PEOPLE'S HISTORY OF THE FACES

I WAS THERE: ERIC WEITZMANN

The Oakland Coliseum Arena probably seats about 16,000. The opening act was Oakland's own Tower of Power. The drink of choice on stage that evening seemed to be Mateus wine. They played a lot from *A Nod's as Good as A Wink…* and from Rod's most current solo record, *Never a Dull Moment*. It was Ronnie Lane's last tour with them and he had on a very nice dark sequinned suit. It was my first Faces show, but I saw them again in October of '73 with Rory Gallagher as the opener and Earth, Wind & Fire in the middle slot. Rory Gallagher owed the stage that night. He is, and always was, phenomenal. The Faces just weren't the same when Tetsu joined. I love the Faces – they were loose, but very tight too!

Eric Weitzmann saw the Faces twice

I WAS THERE: MICHAEL COLLINS MORTON

This was the first performance that I saw by the Faces. I saw them a second time, at the Cow Palace in October 1973, but the Oakland show was a better overall experience, which probably is why I can remember it more clearly. I also remember it as being the first time that I saw a man wearing a kilt, onstage right before the appearance of the Faces and playing 'Amazing Grace' on a set of bagpipes. The Faces delivered a performance that was as exciting, both musically and visually, and as casually polished as any performance of rock 'n' roll could ever be.

I was a dedicated fan of Rod Stewart, both with and without the Faces. In 1972, he was at his best, as were the Faces, and together they made a formidable team, boisterously playing music that was filled with friendliness and smiles. The public, perhaps inevitably, perceived Rod as the 'star', but all five members of the band, and particularly Ronnie Lane, had a strong hand in creating their unmistakable sound. Rod Stewart, it could be said, was 'first among equals'. He had become hugely famous on his own, but his fame had not unduly overwhelmed the other musicians, at least not to the extent that it did several years later.

Wearing an outfit of shiny silver, Rod was in lively form that evening.

He seemed abundantly fit, always in action, and his well-known hairstyle was in excellent condition, looking just the same as it did in photographs. He went through his loose moves with a smooth degree of easy perfection, happily strutting around the stage as if he owned it. He repeatedly threw his microphone upward, high in the air, catching it on the beat each time when it came down. Ronnie Lane was attired in a sharp suit, appearing extremely dapper, and he apparently had taken a drink or two (or more) before stepping onstage. Ron Wood displayed nearly as much flash as Rod Stewart, merrily sprinting back and forth as he offered one sprightly riff after another.

It was clear that the Faces enjoyed performing together. They drew their list of songs mostly from *A Nod's as Good as a Wink... to a Blind Horse*, with a handful of Rod Stewart's hits added for good measure. I am fairly certain that among the songs we heard were 'Miss Judy's Farm', 'Stay With Me' and 'Every Picture Tells a Story'. One moment is especially clear in my memory. When Rod Stewart was singing his greatest hit, 'Maggie May', his four cohorts acknowledged his words with an impudent chord as he looked at them and sang the line, 'Or find myself a rock 'n' roll band (*whump!*) that needs a helping hand.'

A wonderful performance by musicians who were talented enough to make it seem as if they were not even working at it.

MAPLE LEAF GARDENS
7 SEPTEMBER 1972, TORONTO, CANADA

I WAS THERE: DANNY SHIELDS

I was born in Scotland and came to Canada in 1963 when I was 12. Like Rod Stewart, I am a huge fan of Glasgow Celtic. I was born a mile away from Celtic Park. I first saw the Faces at Maple Leaf Gardens in Toronto. I went with my girlfriend (now wife of almost 45 years) and I remember paying $5.25 cents for tickets, 20 rows from the stage. It was a great show. The Faces came on stage to 'The Stripper' and if I remember correctly did 'Twistin' the Night Away' as an encore. I have seen Rod many times since, including a trip to Vegas for our 40th wedding anniversary, and seen many great shows, but nothing compared to that first time seeing Rod and the rest of the boys that night in 1972.

$5.25 was around an hour's wages for me at the time for those seats 20 rows from the front. We went to see Rod in 2018 and paid $200 a ticket for seats near the back of the stadium. To get seats 20 rows from the front now would cost well over $500! I wouldn't mind paying that if I was making $500 an hour, but as I am now 67 and retired it's a little bit beyond my budget.

Back in the UK, the Faces play a handful of gigs in October.

WINTER GARDENS
21 OCTOBER 1972, WESTON-SUPER-MARE, UK

I WAS THERE: IAIN LOCKE

I saw Faces a few times, and never in front of more than a crowd of three thousand. It was a completely unique experience as they were such a lads good time band that the girls loved. From the age of eight I started buying records and reading the *New Musical Express* and I was immediately captivated by London's Kinks and Small Faces along with the Stones, and of course the northern bands – The Beatles, The Searchers – and, truth be known, most pop songs of the day struck a chord with me. I started following Motown and blue eyed-soul and suddenly it was 1968 and something (as in Ronnie Lane) happened that changed my life.

In a circular album cover with a print of a tobacco tin with a logo was *Ogden's Nut Gone Flake*. It was wonderfully produced and the vinyl within just sent me happily humming, foot tapping and to this day reciting verbatim every word that came from the pens of (primarily) Marriott and Lane with the brilliant time keeping of Kenney Jones and Mclagan's Hammond organ completing this now maturing four piece powerhouse. As Ronnie Lane once said, something rather beautiful happened.

I became an avid follower of Mike Vernon's Blue Horizon Records and the bands on the label, particularly Chicken Shack (with Christine Perfect) and Savoy Brown. A friend was into John Mayall and the Yardbirds. We found out about Eel Pie Island in Twickenham and the bands playing there, one of which was Steampacket with Long John Baldry and a blues caller, one Roderick David Stewart. I started following them and heard about the Artwoods with one of the brothers – Ron, the youngest – playing blues-oriented sets. Jeff Beck put a band together with Stewart on vocals, Wood on bass, Micky Waller on drums and of course Beck playing guitar. *Truth* was released and I thought, 'Wow, this bloke sings the blues with feeling. The only other guy I've heard with such feeling is Marriott!' Then Marriott was hanging out with Frampton and he left the Small Faces reeling when he left to form Humble Pie. Beck was starting to alienate Stewart and Wood. Poor management prevailed across all the artists concerned.

I went to Windsor Horse Show once and Rod Stewart was there, with Dee Harrington. They cut a dash, and lots of onlookers were envious of the guy with the strange spiked hair accompanied by a leggy blonde.

Atomic Rooster were billed to play Weston's Winter Gardens but illness to Vince Crane forced a cancellation at short notice. I'm told the Faces needed a warm up gig prior to playing Wembley Arena and then the magical sign boards appeared outside the Winter Gardens, billing 'Faces' for one night only. 1,500 tickets were made available and they sold out in 24 hours.

Six of us drove the 24 miles to Weston. There were lots of tartan scarves, as Rod was wearing on the picture shoot for *Gasoline Alley*, and no support act. It was an 8pm starting time, but as ever they kept us waiting, not coming on until 8.45pm. The atmosphere was electric and incredibly intimate as they took the stage running on, smiling, shouting and communicating from the outset. Smoke was hovering above the crowd and condensation running down the walls as Stewart announced, 'A few ditties from our new album will be finely presented this evening, you lucky lot, but first here's one you may know, 'Maybe I'm Amazed',' which we all started singing along with. The band accompanied the audience and the vocalist, as if in disbelief that they've got us after just three minutes.

John Peel's love of early Rod and latterly of the band was a massive boost as the BBC reached out with Radio 1 in massive numbers. The press loved them and they recorded interviews that were often humorous and never serious. I think this endeared the band to many.

Warner Bros, realising they had struck a rich vein, promoted the band both sides of the pond to good effect, but perhaps the band and the record company asked too much of the songwriters, and when Ronnie Lane got pissed off with the hype, the end was nigh. From a fan's viewpoint the concerts were a celebration of rock 'n' roll, booze and having a great time. The band was always a bit loose and improvisational but that was the attraction. They were always late on stage and always had a few on board as a loosener. I saw them many times between 1971 and 1975 and believe they were the best live band on the planet!

KINETIC CIRCUS
22 OCTOBER 1972, BIRMINGHAM, UK

I WAS THERE: BOBBY HUNT

I was 14. The lad next door had a Jeff Beck album. He was going on about Jeff Beck, but I what I remember is hearing this vocalist. That's the first memory I have of hearing Rod Stewart's voice. It was just so different and so recognisable. Then I saw him singing 'Maggie May' live on Top of the Pops and I thought, 'Who is this guy strutting around the stage?' He was strutting around like a peacock, with that hairstyle, and so commanding on stage – a bit like Jagger with the Stones. You can't take your eyes off them.

Bobby Hunt met his hero at Villa Park

'Maggie May' was actually the B-side to 'Reason to Believe', and legend has it that a late night DJ in Cleveland, Ohio accidentally put the B-side on and the phone lines lit up and went absolutely crazy, with people saying, 'What's this song? We love it!' What is unique about 'Maggie May' is that it doesn't have a chorus. Other songs build up to a chorus and then have another verse and then another chorus. From there, I bought *Every Picture Tells a Story*. Rod having concurrent number one singles and albums in the UK and the US kept my interest in him.

The Faces were playing a gig in Birmingham at a place called the Mayfair Suite, under the original Bullring Centre in Birmingham. It was accessed via the bridge link which went to New Street railway station. I knew a couple of DJs in Birmingham, called Larry White and Brian Thompson (who went under the name of Brian T). They were the promoters of this gig. I remember turning up and I don't think there was even a queue for the tickets. And Brian said, 'We've just had the tickets arrive, but they're not quite dry.' They'd been printed on card.

It was about three quid to get in. It was a sell-out gig, and all standing. Rod was wearing a gold lame suit. 'You Wear it Well' had come out but I don't remember them playing it. One of the guys in there was a guy called Phil, who ran a record shop called Bailey's Records, which was also part of the old Bull Ring. He had a little stall set up selling Rod Stewart and Jeff Beck stuff and he said, 'If you come back here after the gig, I'll see if I can get you to meet the band.' When they came off stage they walked through the kitchen area to the dressing room. Phil called me over and I waited outside. When Rod came out he had changed into a bright red corduroy suit. Ronnie Wood was wearing a full-length Afghan coat. Kenney Jones and Ian McLagan were there too. The only one missing was Ronnie Lane. I don't know whether he stayed in the dressing room or had already gone off somewhere.

I got in the lift with them and Rod signed a football photo for me. When we came out of the lift, they got into a limo that was waiting for them, in which they had bottles of wine and a candelabra on this little table area. We followed the band to the Strathallan Hotel on the Hagley Road, but I got stopped on the door and couldn't get into the aftershow party.

I became a huge fan, buying everything and anything that was released. I was an obsessive fan as a teenager and travelled all over to see them. I remember seeing them in Leeds, and at the Reading Festival. When they reformed in 2015 and did a gig at Kenney Jones' polo club, my brother and I went and we stayed overnight. That was amazing, and quite emotional. That's probably the last time I will see them all together.

Just before my birthday in 1995, Rod was playing at Villa Park. We were event managing part of the night. Rod was due on stage about half an hour and I'd got myself a prime spot in the audience when a message came through the intercom system. One of the girls I was working with shouted, 'We've got a problem backstage. Can you come and help sort it out?' I thought, 'Oh bugger,' but off I went. I went down this corridor, heading towards the chairman's office, and they brought me into this room. I walked into this room and some of Rod's band members were there and I thought, 'What's going on?' And they opened the chairman's office and I walked in and there was Rod Stewart, just standing there. Because they knew it was my birthday and that I was a lifelong fan, my colleagues had set it up for me to meet Rod. He welcomed me with open arms. It was a really emotional thing. He was drinking brandy out of a cut glass decanter and he said, 'Do you want one?' I've never drunk brandy in my life but I said yes. I wasn't going to say no to Rod Stewart!

WEMBLEY FESTIVAL OF MUSIC, EMPIRE POOL
29 OCTOBER 1972, LONDON, UK

I WAS THERE: DEIRDRE YAGER

My sister saw the Faces at Wembley Arena when it was still called the Empire Pool. They were supported by the New York Dolls and the Pink Fairies. I was way too young to go, being only 12 in 1972 – boo hoo – but I still have the programme somewhere. And living through the Seventies meant that I lived through the best music and clothes ever!

I WAS THERE: JULIE HATCHMAN, AGE 15

I saw them live on many occasions. I first heard of them through my friend's older brother who used to play such great music, the Faces included. I would have been 13. I remember hearing *First Step* and loving 'Three Button Hand Me Down' and 'Flying'. I first saw them in 1972 at the Wembley Festival of Music. I just remember being totally overwhelmed by them and wishing I was right down at the front. I went to the show with my best friend and the aforementioned older brother. Then we went to just about every London gig they did. It must have been the music that got me into them as I wouldn't have seen them on TV. *Long Player* just blew me away. It's still my favourite. It was so unlike anything else I'd heard before.

Obviously, as a teen, I fell for Rod. By then I was also into the Stones and The Who but Faces were the band. They were so great live. There was nothing like it. I still have most of the ticket stubs. I saw all the Edmonton shows, Kilburn, Lewisham. I saw Ronnie Lane's last show. That was quite emotional, and also the last gig, where Keith Richards played.

We used to queue overnight to get to the front of the Sundown gigs. There would be 25 or 50 of us queueing overnight. I remember my mum bringing us sandwiches, bless her. It was brilliant, dashing to the front and holding onto the stage for dear life. We got so crushed that I nearly died, but I loved every second of it.

Julie Hatchman first saw the Faces at Wembley

I could see the Sundown from the top of our road. If we saw a concert advert go up, with FACES in six foot high letters, we'd forget about going to school. We used to run up there, wait until they opened and wait until we could find out when the tickets were going on sale. I always wished I'd taken a photo but I didn't even have a camera. Sadly the Sundown is long gone. I saw many bands there.

TOP OF THE POPS
15 NOVEMBER 1972, LONDON, UK

The band appear on the BBC Television programme to back Rod performing 'Angel'. Except for Ronnie Lane, who sends a cardboard cut-out of himself. The programme airs the following day.

The Faces begin a December 1972 British tour taking in 10 dates around the UK, opening in Dundee in Scotland and concluding at Manchester's Free Trade Hall on 23 December 1972.

CAIRD HALL
7 DECEMBER 1972, DUNDEE, UK

I WAS THERE: BILLY FILLON-PAYOUX, AGE 11

I was brought up in a children's home and my two loves at that age were football and Rod Stewart. I became a fan after 'Maggie May'. One of the staff at the children's home also liked Rod and the Faces, so he got two tickets to see them in Dundee – and took me! I remember it was just like being at a football match. And the concert lasted 90 minutes, just like a football match. I can't remember what they sang but I was hooked. I have seen Rod about 16 times over the years, at Ibrox Park, Hampden Park (twice), Glasgow Apollo (twice), Edinburgh Castle, Falkirk Stadium and about five times at the Hydro in Glasgow.

I WAS THERE: CAROLE LESLIE, AGE 14

I was hooked from the very first time I saw the Faces on *Top of the Pops*. Rod was brilliant but Ronnie was always my favourite – and still is! I started getting the *NME*, *Sounds* and *Melody Maker* to get as much info as possible about them, and my David Cassidy posters were soon replaced by Rod and the Faces. They were playing the Caird Hall. My friends Ruth and Elaine and I got tickets for our very first gig.

Carole Leslie was at the Caird Hall

I remember the tickets were all priced at £1 and seats were not allocated. We were so excited for weeks before and the day of the gig we were at school in the morning but went home at lunchtime to get ready. We told our mums a wee white lie, saying we were sent home early because of the concert. We rushed into town and the queue was huge because the seating was first come first served. Luckily for us, the queue was causing an obstruction and when it was split to get rid of the obstruction, they split it exactly at us. We ran up to the doors to start another queue and ended up in the second row. I don't remember the support but I do remember that as soon as the Faces stepped on stage everyone surged forward. I ended up on the shoulders of a stranger most of the night.

That gig ended up getting in the local paper as the seats were all damaged as everyone was standing and jumping up and down on the back of them. I am sure Elaine's mum was there too, but she was upstairs in the balcony, supposedly keeping an eye on us. I never caught a football but it was the most amazing gig and I am so glad I was there. *Ooh La La* was the first album I ever bought and, along with the Stones, the Faces are my favourite band.

I WAS THERE: DEREK KEITH, AGE 16

I first heard Rod Stewart when he was a band member with the Jeff Beck Group and really liked his voice. After that I bought Rod's album *An Old Raincoat*... I just really got into the Faces albums after that. The first time I saw them was at the Caird Hall, a concert I attended with Richard Melville. In those days there was no seating plan, so once the doors were opened you just made a dash to get as close to the stage as possible. We were lucky and got right to the front. Rod was wearing a yellow suit. The big thing for me was seeing Ronnie Lane, who I really liked and who I still listen to today. The crowd got very wild and everyone ended up on the seats. After the night was over,

Derek Keith (right) with turn ups

the first six rows were all broken with bits of wood and horse hair all over the place. The Faces were never invited back to play Dundee again.

I WAS THERE: LORNA BETT, AGE 16

I was in my house with my school friends the first time I heard 'Maggie May'. We were 14. A few weeks later, there they were on my parents' TV – the Faces. We had never seen anything like them. We were mesmerised. My friend Nancy and I fell in love with the band. That was the start of a lifetime of following the band. I saved up and bought every record I could – *Gasoline Alley*, *A Nod's as Good as a Wink*, *An Old Raincoat*... and so on. We loved them.

I was 16 when my parents finally allowed me to go to see them live. My friend Margaret and I travelled to the Caird Hall in Dundee and were in the third row. There they were, large as life, and colourful and loud – Kenney, Ronnie, Ron, Ian and Rod. I thought my heart was going to stop. That was it, I was hooked. We even missed the last train home and had to sleep in Dundee police station.

The next concert was at the Apollo in Glasgow, at that time Scotland's best venue. It was fantastic, a sea of Royal Stewart tartan. It was a party atmosphere and the band were enjoying themselves. The highlight of the night for me was seeing Maggie Bell strut on to the stage wearing thigh high black leather boots and joining in the chorus of 'Every Picture Tells a Story'. What a combination, Rod and Maggie. I loved the Faces. All of them. After I got married, I couldn't afford to get to the concerts but kept buying their music and read everything I could about them.

I was gutted when Ronnie Lane quit. I loved his presence and his voice. He was replaced by Tetsu. I liked him but he wasn't Ronnie. I cried when Ronnie died. Following the Faces felt like being part of a big family and Ronnie was part of that family. The band split soon after and we were devastated. We still followed Rod but it wasn't the same. No matter what musicians he had, we missed the band that was the Faces.

I've seen Rod over 20 times since. My partner, my brother and my sister-in-law have all met him. But not me, and I'm the fan! My brother's favourite band was The Who so we were delighted when Kenney joined them. He is an excellent drummer who stepped into Moonie's shoes and made them his own. It may sound stupid, but the Faces have been the soundtrack to my life. I love their music as much today as I did when I was that 14-year-old schoolgirl.

I WAS THERE: JOHN LOGAN

I next saw the Faces at the Caird Hall in Dundee and at Newcastle City Hall on successive nights. Caird Hall was mayhem from start to finish. Perhaps they were not used to staging rock concerts there. The band arrived late again, by which time the audience was at fever pitch. Rod was already a big star. The band's programme notes were classic Faces: 'Group members would like to announce and make it plain we may well be attired in the following dishevelment..' and then followed a list of songs with a footnote: 'Plus a few numbers if we are short… which three of us are!'

They opened with 'Miss Judy's Farm' and the audience went crazy. I was at the front and swear I saw the upstairs bouncing. It was a great but short set – under an hour and a half, probably due to the hall asking them to cut it short to minimise damage. There was damage to the first few rows of seats, with people standing to get a better view, and eventually the seats collapsed altogether.

After a climatic 'Twistin' the Night Away' and 'One Last Sweet Cheerio', they were gone, leaving the management to survey the damage. I gather it was some time before they had a rock concert there again!

CITY HALL
8 DECEMBER 1972, NEWCASTLE-UPON-TYNE, UK

I WAS THERE: JOHN LOGAN

The next night, they were just over the border in Newcastle. I had heard Ronnie Lane had taken to driving himself between venues in his Land Rover, rather than with the rest of the band. Was this the first signs of some disharmony? He only lasted another five months before saying 'I'm leaving the band', a stock answer from all the band whenever there was a dispute but usually not to be taken too seriously.

I decided to get to the City Hall early, to see if I could be enlisted by the band's roadies to give them a hand with the gear. I recall bringing in some lighting and some of the perspex stage panels they used to gaffer tape to the stage so that the lights reflected the band on to the stage. It was a great effect if you were upstairs. Pete Buckland was the Faces stage manager and became the road manager for the early Rod Stewart band after the Faces. He was a really affable guy, in keeping with the band's chaotic ethos, but very professional too. Beneath the throwaway, chaotic image, the band and the roadies took great time and pride in making sure the staging was good. There was no health and safety in those days. All you needed was a temporary road crew badge.

The gig was even better atmosphere than Dundee, which I didn't think was possible, and there was the same audience reaction when the band again hit the stage late. Vigrass and Osbourne were the support (Osbourne was a relative of Kenney Jones, I heard). It was a typical Friday night Newcastle atmosphere, with a few pints already down by time the band took the stage at around 9.45pm. It had been advertised as a 7.30pm start for the support act, and the roadies played the Phil Spector Christmas album whilst making last minute adjustments to keep people in the Christmas party mood.

It was a slightly different set to the previous night, as they played 'Memphis, Tennessee'. The City Hall had a large orchestra area behind the stage with steps for the orchestra leading up to the top of the hall and Rod used these to good effect for his more energetic stage antics. He announced a slow song that 'should be heard in the utmost seriousness' and they struck up 'I'd Rather Go Blind', Rod sitting with his legs draped over the stage, almost on the front row.

Rod had his multi-striped/multi-coloured suit on, Woody a striking bolero jacket, Mac was in black and Laneole was in his three piece with scarf. There were tartan scarves and 'Rod rooster' cuts everywhere. Newcastle audiences were renowned for their participation, but on this night they really excelled, with Rod trying to compete on 'Maggie May', 'Stay With Me' and 'Angel', his voice trailing away in disbelief at the noise the audience were making. 'Good vocals, Newcastle.' A compliment indeed from Rod.

I managed to grab one of the plastic Warner Bros footballs Rod was kicking out, with the band's next single, 'Cindy Incidentally', printed all over it. It was some reward for the hard work helping the roadies earlier. Rod said, 'Stuff the crap about the Faces blowing it by not playing long enough… we aren't going home just yet!' But they didn't get on stage until 9.45pm and people had buses to catch. They finished at 11.15pm, so an hour and a half set. Rod now plays a two-and-a-half hour set. Perhaps in 1972 they just hadn't rehearsed enough material to play for longer.

I WAS THERE: JOHN W BELL

My brother came home one day with a copy of 'Reason to Believe'/'Maggie May'. He was an avid single buyer and the single was yet to become a massive hit. My opinion on the gravel-voiced singer? 'This Rod Stewart can't sing!'

Next day at work, my workmate Doug, who had blond, collar-length, feathered, spiky hair, and who had been a Faces fan for a while, began to change my opinion, advising me to listen to more of their music. Rod's solo career taking off was helping the Faces build a huge fan base, which I soon joined. The next Saturday I spent some of my wages on the first LP I ever bought, *Every Picture Tells a Story*.

Thursday evenings became *Top of the Pops* time. I was totally overwhelmed by this fun time band enjoying themselves. It was Rod on the label, but we know it was the Faces that made him. My record collection soon increased with the addition of *First Step* and *Long Player*, and *Old Raincoat* and *Gasoline Alley* soon followed. I was 15 years old and in my first job, spending my own money and enjoying life. I was hoping one day to see the Faces live, growing my hair longer. I never achieved a Rod style. My hair was more like Plonk's and soon to become more like Mac's.

Then the day my dream came true; December 1972 at Newcastle City Hall. My first live gig. I was not disappointed. I had a good seat, and the City Hall is not a huge venue, with seating for 2,200. I was swept away. 2,000-plus Faces fans, with some Rod lookalikes. The stage was set, with a huge drum kit centre stage and a Steinway grand piano and organ to the left. My chest was heaving with the noise from the amps, Rod striding on stage wearing a striped satin suit, Woody in his toreador outfit, Plonk dressed immaculately. These five men playing familiar songs and some new ones they were trying out – 'Stay With Me', 'Miss Judy's Farm' and 'That's All You Need'.

My ears ringing and my body shaken when Woody finally stopped playing his amazing bottleneck slide guitar. I remember Plonk's bass thumping, Mac's keyboard playing and Kenney's 'I'm Losing You' solo, when the rest of the band left the stage. Of course, a few beverages were consumed. The good time band had come to town and we all joined their party. One memorable scene was when they played 'I'd Rather Go Blind' and Rod lifted his polystyrene cup to his lips as he sang the line 'when the reflection in the glass that I held to my lips'.

Soon the night was over. I had seen five extraordinary musicians together having fun, playing fantastic music and with the audience joining in. I believed this would last forever. Sadly, Rod's solo career was the downfall of the Faces. Yes, his success helped sell tickets, albums and singles. But *A Nod's* is one of the best rock albums of all time and there were tracks on Rod's albums and singles that were really Faces songs and which should have been on Faces albums. Rod's lack of enthusiasm for *Ooh La La* was the Faces' downfall.

OPERA HOUSE
10 DECEMBER 1972, BLACKPOOL, UK

I WAS THERE: SAM JOHNSON
I went to the Blackpool shows in both '72 and '73. We had great seats for both gigs, more or less central, and halfway back in the stalls. At the end of at least one of them, Rod and the rest gathered footballs from a giant sack or netting and volleyed them into the audience. I recall one friend recounting to others down the years that he caught one, but – 'liar, liar, pants on fire!' – like me, his hands remained empty.

I WAS THERE: ALAN PEARSON
I was a Small Faces fan and I read *NME* every week, so I was aware from when it was first publicised that Rod and Ron had joined the others. I loved the *Every Picture Tells a Story* album. I was 17 when that was released, and that was the year I started going to gigs. I saw them three times in Blackpool. They had a bar onstage on one tour, complete with barman serving them drinks. They were kicking footballs into the audience, the usual stuff. And they were much better live than on record.

LIVERPOOL STADIUM
12 DECEMBER 1972, LIVERPOOL, UK

I WAS THERE: STEPHEN AINTREE
I remember the queue stretching round the block. I must have got there in decent time, because I didn't have a bad place. I was in the centre, about halfway back. There was no reserved seating. I just remember them being brilliant. I still recall them kicking footballs off the stage into the crowd. I still have the programme, but it's in a box somewhere. Sadly, I don't still have the ticket. About 18 months later, I went to the same

venue to see Ronnie Lane's Slim Chance. This time there was no queue and I walked straight in. The place was half full, if that. I was always a big Ronnie Lane fan and I still play 'Debris' if I ever do a set anywhere. It's a tremendous song!

I WAS THERE: JOHN DUNN, AGE 12

It was the first concert I ever went to and can remember it very clearly. It was amazing. The Faces appeared briefly on the internal balcony of the stadium and the audience was looking across and cheering. Rod Stewart was singing about his heart, and putting his hand on his heart as he did so. The Faces kicked footballs out at the end; I would have loved to gotten hold of one of them.

I WAS THERE: STEPHEN WALSH

I saw them first at the Liverpool Stadium, with Ronnie Lane. I loved his look and more folky input. They were loose and obviously having a ball. Rod had had 'Maggie May' out as a single and that brought in the girls, but they also had a big male following being so laddish. The standout moments were Ronnie doing the intro to 'Maybe I'm Amazed' and the drum solo in 'I'm Losing You'.

I WAS THERE: JOHN WINDER, AGE 18

The Faces looked more glam pop than rock but they were great musicians and Rod had a great pedigree and a great voice. They were very different live from most bands at that time, in that they enjoyed themselves on stage. They put on a show and the Stadium gig was just that. The stage was perspex and I seem to remember a glitter ball. They kicked footballs into the audience and really got the audience going. Ronnie had a shiny silver Les Paul but that was for show. His playing was brilliant. They were great musicians, and probably one of the best bands at that time. The fact that they managed to transform a pretty grotty venue into a vaguely glamorous setting is testament to their charisma. But the top line was sheer, sometimes shambolic entertainment – they had a successful album and hit single behind them and Rod's solo career was taking off.

All in all, it's one of the best concerts I have ever seen. The fact that I remember it after all this time proves it!

I WAS THERE: MARC GAIER

I went to the 1972 concert at Liverpool Stadium and the later one at the Empire. The earlier one was the best as the band was in its prime and the venue was better. The stadium was a very basic spit and sawdust boxing/wrestling venue with no numbered seating. The earlier you got there, the better the seat but with a capacity of around 2,000 there no bad views. I don't remember a bad atmosphere at any gig because the seats were close together and most people were standing – it was rather like being in a football crowd. By comparison, arena gigs are so antiseptic, and watching on a big screen defeats the point of being there.

I must have queued – or joined someone who had gone earlier – because I was just a few rows from the front in the central section. It was a fantastic view and I could even see the infamous bar set up at the side of the stage where the band could be seen refuelling throughout the show. At that stage Rod Stewart was very much part of the band even though his solo career was flying. By the time of the Empire gig a year later, Ronnie had departed and the cracks were showing. It didn't help that I was in the circle at what is a cavernous venue. It paled in comparison to the Stadium gig.

I WAS THERE: JOHN HODGKINSON

It was during my autograph collecting days and I got Rod and Ronnie W to sign.

John Hodgkinson got Rod and Ronnie's autographs

TOWN HALL
14 DECEMBER 1972, LEEDS, UK

I WAS THERE: NEILL HALL

The first time I became aware of them was an appearance on *Top of the Pops*, when 'Maggie May' was number 1. I was 12 or 13 years old and they looked like they were taking the mickey out of everything, whereas all the other bands took themselves too seriously or had massive egos. When Rod and crew started kicking footballs around, that did it for me.

I only saw them twice. The first time was just after 'Maggie May' was released. It was at Leeds Town Hall, so it was a smallish venue with a capacity of between one and two thousand. Mr Lane was on bass. The second time was at the Queens Hall, Leeds during the *Ooh La La* tour. The Queens Hall was a terrible venue. It was the old tram shed in Leeds so the acoustics were non-existent and there was no seating that I can remember. By then, Tetsu was on bass and Long John Baldry was the support act. They came on to 'The Stripper' and I spent the entire concert hanging on scaffolding to get a view.

I sort of went off Rod when the Faces split (he got too melodic and/or commercial for me) and got into the Stones. They were quite serious but I thought Ronnie made them a bit more irreverent. I did see Rod on a solo stadium tour around 1990 at Old Trafford and he wowed the audience, but it was still not the fun time that the Faces had.

Neill Hall was won over by the Faces lack of pretentiousness

BRIXTON SUNDOWN
16 DECEMBER 1972, LONDON, UK

I WAS THERE: PERRY RIDLEY

The first LP I ever bought was Rod's *Every Picture Tells a Story*, in 1971 when I was 13 and following the success of 'Maggie May'. In the summer of 1972, I followed it up with *Never a Dull Moment*. My best friend at the time worked at WEA Records, and got me a copy of *A Nod's as Good as a Wink* and I was in love with the Faces. I always loved 'Debris' on that album, and still have my copy of this LP with the poster stored nicely inside the sleeve.

I had a poster on my wall for a few years in the 1970s of the rear cover photo of the models, again courtesy of my friend at WEA Records. Later in 1972 he got me a ticket for the show at Brixton Sundown (now the Brixton Academy) on 16 December 1972. I don't recall much about the show, but remember enjoying it. I wore my Stewart tartan scarf that I wore for most of the early 1970s. My friend had given me a tip off about the footballs being kicked into the crowd at the end of the show, and I waited for this. I managed to get one of the balls, despite sitting in the upper tier. This was stolen from me on the way out by some larger kids, who went on after and played a game on Brixton Road with my ball!

I WAS THERE: JEFF BYGRAVES

I was an avid fan of the Faces. I'm still a Rod fan, although I wasn't too on the old *American Songbook* stuff he did. I had the album *Ogden's Nut Gone Flake* and I loved Stevie Marriott's voice, but I wouldn't have said I was a fan of the Small Faces. I knew the more popular stuff like 'Tin Soldier' and 'Itchycoo Park'. I got into the Faces because of Rod's voice, but also because there was quite a lot of crossover in their music. They do rocky numbers but also 'Losing You', which was a Temptations number, and they'd do a Chuck Berry song, 'Memphis'. Rod came from more of a blues background, and the Faces appealed to me because they seemed to tie together a lot of these genres of music that I liked. I didn't think *First Step* was that great an album, but I stuck with them. When they brought *Long Player* out, that hooked me, and I loved *A Nod's as Good as a Wink…* and *Ooh La La*. My daughter is 27, and 'Ooh La La' is her favourite song. I've indoctrinated her.

I saw them in Brixton and Sutton, as I lived in the south London area. I have more vivid memories of the Brixton gig. It's what is now the Brixton Academy. At the time, it was called the Sundown because that and the Edmonton one were run by the same company.

I went to Brixton with Dave Thomas. I probably haven't seen him for 30 years, but we were best pals in those days. We went everywhere together. He was a great big tall guy, about six foot three, and he drove a Mini. He almost had to sit in the back seat to drive it. There were two great things about the Brixton venue – it didn't have any seats, so it was all standing, which was a real anomaly in those days. And at the back of the auditorium, they had small bars dotted everywhere. When everyone pushed forward, me and Dave just stood, pints of lager in hand, leaning on the bar and listening to the Faces. We looked at each other and said 'it doesn't get any better than this, does it?' For young 18, 19-year-old guys, that was it. It was just amazing. It was the perfect venue, perfect musicians. My best memories are of the Kenney Jones drum solos on 'I'm Losing You'. They probably lasted for five minutes and seemed to last for 15 minutes. It was just incredible. I've never heard drumming like that.

I saw the Mick Hucknall reunion show at Goodwood. I went purely because of the Faces being on the bill. It wasn't the same with Mick Hucknall singing, but he did a pretty decent job. Until I saw the Stones at the London Stadium in 2018, seeing the Faces was my favourite ever live gig.

Rod had a much rawer voice in those days. There wasn't anyone else singing like Rod back then, apart from Steve Marriot, and I preferred Rod's voice out of the two. I went off him a little but when he went into his blond 'Do Ya Think I'm Sexy?' phase. But I think he had some massive tax bill and he had to sing to pay the bills. It got him a new audience out in the States. And, at the end of the day, we all have to do what we've got to do to put food on the table. Although I think Rod's struggles are probably slightly different to ours.

EDMONTON SUNDOWN
17 & 18 DECEMBER 1972, LONDON, UK

I WAS THERE: BARRY KYME

I saw them three times. I don't remember much about the Weeley Festival (substances – ha ha!) whilst at Reading Festival in 1973 they were poor. (Ronnie Lane had left.) But at Sundown Edmonton in December 1972, they were glorious and this show is in my top three all-time gigs, along with Springsteen in 1981 and Brian Wilson in 2002. The gig was on a revolving stage, just like Boston Gliderdrome which I had been used to. The lights went out to total darkness for 20 seconds or so and then the lights blasted on and perhaps 20 can-can girls were doing their thing to the appropriate music. The stage did a sedate revolution and the lights went out again, this time for about ten seconds. Then the stage was back around with the band present. The lights blasted on and we were straight into a great version of 'Memphis, Tennessee'. That opening to a gig was the best I have ever seen, with footballs – the lot! Sadly, this is not the gig on YouTube.

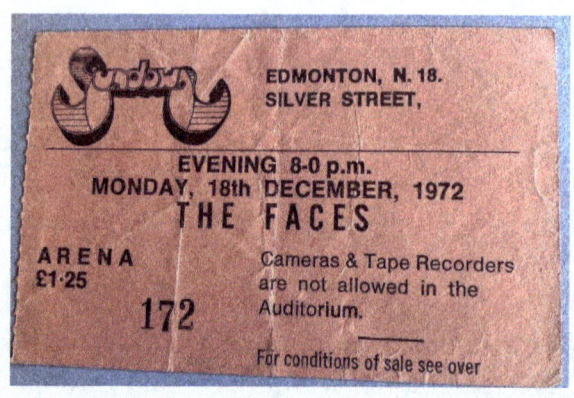
Barry Kyme remembers this Faces gigs as one of his all-time top three

I care little for Rod now, and haven't done for 40 years. Ronnie is still one of my heroes and he's a great player as it's about the song. RIP Mac. I'm so pleased I went to the Mick Hucknall reunion.

I WAS THERE: ALASTAIR RAYMOND, AGE 23

I saw them many times. The best one I can remember was the Sundown Edmonton Christmas gig, when they were so pissed I don't think they finished one number. They just kicked out a few footballs and attempted to start a new song. What a party! Mayhem! Rod carried Ronnie Lane about so much I think he forgot he was on his shoulders!

TELL EVERYONE: A PEOPLE'S HISTORY OF THE FACES

I WAS THERE: DEBBIE CRANFIELD

A friend at school had a spare ticket for the Faces at the Edmonton Sundown. I was 14 or 15, went along and I was hooked from that day. It was amazing, and totally riotous, like a big party. I loved the music and loved the atmosphere. I've been a fan ever since. I've seen Rod several times and he always delivers the best shows. I even waited outside his hotel in the freezing cold to meet him. He was with Britt Ekland at the time. He turned up at about 3am, said he had been at Tramps and that he would have had a drink with us but that he had to be up early to catch a flight. I was over the moon. My ex-husband was also a huge fan and had his hair cut at the same hairdressers as Rod in the late Seventies. Rod lives quite near me now and I often see him around. He's my hero!

I WAS THERE: SHARON BLAKE

I was at one of the Christmas shows. I was third row back at floor level, in a huge crush of fans. It was a great performance and one that I shall never forget.

I WAS THERE: PAULA JEAN VICTOR

I was at the front. I got crushed and was pulled out by a bouncer. I thought that was my night finished but he let me watch from the stage at the side.

I WAS THERE: JANET PAGE, AGE 13

I was there, two rows in from the front. I fainted half way through and spent the rest of the gig in the medical room.

I WAS THERE: PETER COALS, AGE 13

I was fortunate enough to see them four times, three times at the Edmonton Sundown and the final gig they did in England in 1974, at the Kilburn Gaumont State. December 1972 was my first ever gig and it blew me away – the noise, the energy and the atmosphere. The Sundown was originally a cinema called the Regal Edmonton and the downstairs section was the original stalls and then became standing only. There was this mad rush to get to the front and be as near to the band as possible.

I was there because of Rod's albums *Every Picture* and *Never a Dull*

Moment. I was not that familiar with the Faces' album material, but it didn't matter. What I remember is the presence and charisma of Rod Stewart as he threw the mic around the stage, Ronnie Wood with cigarette clamped in his mouth and me sharing a tartan scarf with a very attractive female who had green nail varnish on. We moved this scarf to and fro as 'Angel' was performed, and how I wish in those days I could have asked her for her number.

For all three Edmonton shows – I also saw them in the summer of 1973 and in December 1973 – you just sauntered up to the box office and bought tickets as it suited you. I still have my ticket stubs and programmes from the show. There was none of this nightmare of being confronted with exorbitant prices from ticket agencies or being asked for fortunes from the likes of Ticketmaster.

I WAS THERE: TONY EYRE

I saw the Faces at their Christmas show at what used to be called the Edmonton Regal in 1972, where they dished out many bottles of wine. Rumour was that during Kenney's solo on 'I'm Losing You', the rest of the band popped across the road to the pub opposite and sank a pint each. I was 16 or 17 and went with my ex brother-in-law. Standout memories are them all stumbling on stage with a bottle each and later them all leaving the stage, leaving Ronnie Wood playing the most scorching guitar solo for around 15 minutes.

I WAS THERE: LEN WEBSTER, AGE 18

It was a present from my parents because my birthday is in November. It was the first live show I had been to on my own. I had gotten into Rod via 'Maggie May' and *Never a Dull Moment*. I remember being elated by the gig and thinking that the time flew by and how it was all over

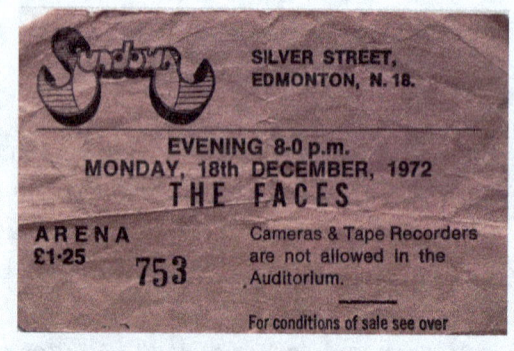

Len Webster saw the Faces twice at the Edmonton Sundown but has no memory of the second show

far too quickly. I also remember thinking that I needed to see more live music. Apparently, I saw them again in June 1973, because I have a ticket for that show too, but I have absolutely no recollection of going to it!

CITY HALL
22 DECEMBER 1972, SHEFFIELD, UK

I WAS THERE: PAUL BAMFORD

The first ticket I had to see the Faces was for a gig at Sheffield City Hall, in June 1972, part of a six concert mini-UK tour. I was 14 years old and beyond excited. My favourite band and my first gig! Alas, I went to school on the Monday morning of the gig, only to be told by one of my classmates that he had read in the *NME* over the weekend that the tour had been curtailed after the first night in Manchester. Apparently, Kenney Jones' pregnant wife had given birth early. Oh, the disappointment. I can still feel it now!

I didn't know it, but I would only have to wait six months until I finally saw the band live. In the meantime, I went to the City Hall to see Slade in November 1972 so Thin Lizzy, who were supporting them, became the first ever band I saw live.

Paul Bamford's Faces programme

TELL EVERYONE: A PEOPLE'S HISTORY OF THE FACES

The run up to Christmas 1972 was very exciting. My dad had promised to buy me my first ever pair of Levi's, and I had a ticket to see my favourite band on the Friday before Christmas. My mate and I travelled from our South Yorkshire mining village to Sheffield via two buses. I still remember the strong smell of patchouli oil on entering the Oval Hall, which for some reason it seemed fashionable to wear in those days. We watched the support band, Vigrass and Osborne (Gary Osborne was Kenney Jones' brother-in-law), and then waited in anticipation until the main event. I remember Chuch Magee and the other roadies were wearing black waistcoats with 'Faces' emblazoned on the back in yellow. Phil Spector's *Christmas* album blasted from the PA.

An hour passed and still no sign of the Faces. Rumours spread that the band hadn't turned up. The odd shout of 'Wally' – like patchouli oil, another quirk of the era – echoed around the hall. After another 30 minutes or so, we were told that the boys had been stuck in fog on the motorway but were on their way and should be on stage by 10.30pm.

Panic set in. Our last bus home was 11.10pm, so we would have to leave and miss most of the show. I came up with a solution though – a taxi! In those days, there were no mobile phones and we didn't even have a home phone. I had asked to be let out of the venue to find a telephone box (thankfully, they let me back in) in order to phone a neighbour to ask them to pop round to our house to ask my dad to leave me out some money to pay for a twelve-mile taxi journey home! Eventually the band walked on stage at 10.40pm to the strains of 'The Stripper'. Following a brief 'sorry we're late!' from Ronnie Wood, we were up and running.

In those days, with the Faces, seat numbers were irrelevant and me and my mate joined dozens of others in piling down to the front of the stage. I remember Rod using his mic stand to break up a scuffle.

The gig was everything I'd hoped for. The set included 'Memphis', 'Miss Judy's Farm', 'Angel', 'Stay With Me', 'You Wear It Well', 'Maggie May', 'Twistin' the Night Away', 'True Blue', 'Maybe I'm Amazed', 'I'd Rather Go Blind', 'Losing You' and a new song, 'Cindy Incidentally'. My favourite of the night, though, was 'That's All You Need'. By 12.10am, it was one last cheerio and they were gone.

A good time was had by all. It was a fantastic set and a memory I've cherished for 50 years. It remains special, as it was the only time I saw

Ronnie Lane with the band. Bless their cotton socks.

Suddenly my mate and I were back into the cold December night looking for a taxi, and hoping that my Dad had left some money out.

I WAS THERE: STAN STENNETT

They were supported by Fumble and Sutherland Brothers & Quiver. I had arranged with my parents for them to pick me up at 10.15pm, as this was a normal finish time for bands playing the City Hall and staying to the end meant I would miss my last train home. It was a cold, foggy, wintry night and the audience was alerted to the fact that the Faces plane had been delayed in London due to the fog… but they were definitely coming.

At around 9.30pm, the Sutherland Brothers & Quiver returned to the stage to play a second set and the crowd – fuelled by the bar – were in fine mood and weren't planning on leaving until the Faces had arrived and played! At 10 o'clock, the PA announced that the band had made it to Sheffield. Security had given up and (I suspect) gone home so I dashed out of the venue, spotted my parents' car across the road, and whizzed over to tell them to come inside.

As we went back into the hall the noise inside was incredible – pure drunken anticipation. I parked my parents at the back of the auditorium and made my way down to the front as the band came on stage to a tumultuous welcome, Rod in his striped glittery jacket. 'Thanks for waiting,' they went straight into the set. I'd like to tell you that I remember the set order but I honestly don't. My own favourite track, 'That's All You Need', made an early appearance, but other than that I can remember lots of drunken banter between songs and Rod missing his intros to songs… Alcohol had been – and was still being – consumed in large quantities. Footballs were despatched into the crowd and we closed with 'Stay With Me' and 'Maggie May'. Everyone went home close to midnight and Mum was chuffed to bits to have seen Rod live. Dad was less than impressed.

I saw the Faces a couple of years later at Leeds Queen's Hall, when Tetsu was playing bass. The Queens Hall was like a bus depot and that, coupled with the loss of Plonk, meant it just wasn't the same. God, I hate the big arena gigs and football stadia.

FREE TRADE HALL
23 DECEMBER 1972, MANCHESTER, UK

I WAS THERE: ERIC STEPHENSON

I saw them four times in Manchester between 1972 and 1974 and they were absolutely the best live rock 'n' roll show at that time. The memory I will cherish until my dying day is the smell! The venue held 3,000 but there were 2,600 females. I should have said – 2,600 wet females! Yeah, baby…

I WAS THERE: PHILIP MAHON

The second Faces show I went to was 23rd December 1972. I struggled to get a ticket but a friend's sister had a spare and sold it to me at face value – 95p (19/-). We arrived at the gig and the support was Vigrass and Osborne. It was Christmas and the atmosphere was incredible. They were about to release 'Cindy Incidentally' in the new year and they played it in the set and also as an encore. In the encore they kicked plastic footballs bearing the name of the single and its B-side. On the way home, we played football on the train and also through Bolton Street Station. We were flying from the excitement.

I WAS THERE: MELVIN KENYON

It was John Peel who first introduced me to the Faces. For a while at least, he was a big supporter and used to play their stuff and have live sessions on his show. And he appeared, as we all know, on *Top of the Pops*, miming with the band. I don't know what caused the falling out but I think there was one. Having no money, I used to record Faces stuff from the show on an old wireless transistor radio at night (complete with crackles) using a Bush cassette player and a small black microphone. I listened to it over and over again, until the tapes almost wore out. I particularly remember their rendition of 'Underneath the Arches' from that time! I used the same radio to listen to Muhammad Ali on American Forces Radio and it was on that radio that John Peel told me that Presley had died. I'm not sure what happened to it.

I loved the band because they were laddish and always seemed to be having a great time on stage, and the audience had a great time too. It was real good time music. Then, of course, they hit the big time with

'Stay With Me' and 'Maggie May' and, looking back, that was the beginning of the end. When the band broke up, I was devastated. I've been a fan ever since though that never translated to being a fan of Rod on his own.

I saw the Faces twice at the wonderful old Free Trade Hall in Manchester. It's a Radisson Hotel now and only the frontage is left. The first time I saw them was on 31st May 1972. I was 15 at the time and went with my mates Dicky (Richard) and Gas (Pete). The band were supported by Vigrass and Osborne, and Stumble (whoever they were). I don't remember too much about that show, although I still have the ticket which tells me I paid 80p. It being around the time of decimalisation, the ticket also shows the equivalent price of 16 shillings. I do, though, remember that we were at the front and Rod sang 'Angel' which was a new song to me and which appeared later that year on *Never a Dull Moment*.

Oddly, they were due to play the Free Trade Hall again just a few days later on 18th June so we caught the 24 bus from Royton, travelled down to Piccadilly and walked down to the venue near St Peter's Square only to see a notice saying that the gig was called off. That was the day of the terrible air crash in Staines, when a BEA flight went down and everyone on board was killed. Apparently, the band was stranded down south and couldn't get to Manchester in time. Perhaps even then Rod was enjoying his jet-setting lifestyle. We could hardly complain though, could we?

So the concert was rescheduled for the back end of the year – 23rd December – and, perhaps in recognition of the hassle, we were charged 75p that time – an old shilling less. I remember the gig well. We were right at the front and the support band was Byzantium. Oldham (Gas and I are still Oldham fans) and Rochdale (Dicky is still a fan) had played out a goalless draw at Spotland that afternoon, and Manchester United had been at home, so the three of us went straight from the game on the number 24 bus from Rochdale down to Manchester again, wearing our colours. The place was awash with football scarves and the crowd was just like a football crowd. Rod played up to us and kicked footballs around on stage and into the audience. The show was brilliant and I've read since that many aficionados regard it as their best ever show.

I loved the Faces and still do. I grew up with them. They had so many great songs. It's hard to pick a favourite but I loved 'Three Button Hand

Me Down', 'You Can Make Me Dance, Sing or Anything' and 'Pool Hall Richard'; maybe not the obvious choices. Great days.

I am the proud owner of one of Ronnie Wood's early prints which shows him alone on stage just as I saw him. It cost me 60 quid 25 years ago. It's worth a fair bit now but I would gladly swap it for just one night back at the Free Trade Hall watching the Faces.

TOP OF THE POPS
7 FEBRUARY 1973, LONDON, UK

The Faces perform 'Cindy Incidentally'.

PARIS THEATRE
8 FEBRUARY 1973, LONDON, UK

The Faces record an 'In Concert' for the BBC which isn't broadcast until 2003 (and then only by mistake) because the band sound too drunk.

The Faces first show of 1973 is in The Netherlands and is filmed for Dutch television.

POPGALA '73
SPORTHAL DE VLIEGERMOLEN
10 MARCH 1973, VOORBURG, THE NETHERLANDS

I WAS THERE: MARTIN VERGAIJ

I saw the Faces three times. The first time was in March 1973 during a two day event filmed for the television channel VARA and held in the Vliegermolen in Voorburg, near The Hague. There were many other groups on including Slade, the Eagles, Rory Gallagher, Chi Coltrane, The Who and Gary Glitter. There were no chairs, only places sitting on the ground, and I sat on the front row during the Faces. They appeared

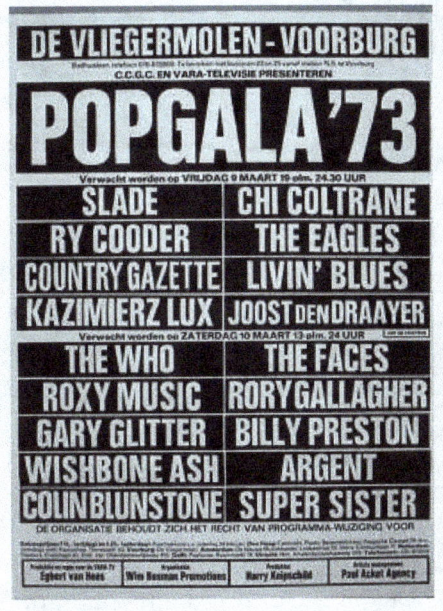

Martin Vergaij saw the Faces in Voorburg

on Sunday evening and played for about an hour. A lot of the TV footage has been lost but you can find some clips on YouTube. After the Faces came The Who, who were the headliners of the two day event. The Faces sat behind me on the podium to watch them. I had a small chat with Rod Stewart and Ronnie Wood. At that time, I didn't realise that almost 50 years later they would still be so big.

My second Faces show was in De Doelen, a big theatre in Rotterdam, later in 1974. Only the first ten rows of seats were occupied and they started an hour late. Rod and Ronnie Wood came on with a few liquor bottles in their hand. They were very drunk, but played great for 45 minutes before finishing with an a cappella version of Vera Lynn's 'We'll Meet Again'. They then went off never to return. I was a little disappointed that they played such a short show, but the little bit they played was great.

The third time I saw them I can hardly remember, but it was with Tetsu.

Back in the UK, the Faces play a handful of shows to promote the forthcoming album and as a warm up for their next US tour.

HIPPODROME
8 APRIL 1973, BRISTOL, UK

I WAS THERE: ANGELA HARVEY, AGE 14

It's 1973. I'm 14 and I bunk off school to queue at the Bristol Hippodrome for my tickets to see the Faces on their *Ooh La La* tour. My mum sews 'ROD' on my t-shirt in black sequins. I'm so excited that I can't eat my tea! My best mate Chris and I get dropped off in Bristol city centre. My mum and dad will pick us up after the gig. This is after I've managed to convince them to let me go – because my life depended on it.

The place is heaving and hot and noisy and there is excitement in the air. Rod is skinny, pale and probably well-oiled (all standard for an idol at the time!), chasing around, throwing the mic stand around with gusto. 'Stay With Me' 'Ooh La La', 'Angel', 'Maggie', 'Cindy' – all the album, one after another, are churned out by Ron with a fag in his mouth the whole time. Ronnie and Mac (bless them) and Kenney on the drums – mates on stage, giving it welly and having a ball. My eye is mostly on Rod – and nothing's changed since!

After the gig we go down Denmark Street, a cobbled alleyway at the side of the venue, to the stage door where a little gang of us wait in the dark and the cold for a glimpse of our idols, not giving a thought about Mum and Dad waiting in the (old) car. Mum had brought some hot water bottles to warm us up and one had burst, giving her a wet lap! I don't think it entered their heads that we were being groupies for the first time.

We are in for a disappointment though, as out of the gloom two young women in fur coats and sunglasses pitch up, only to be let straight in with the door shutting firmly behind them. It's Joanna Lumley and a mate. I won't tell you what we call them!

That was my first and last time seeing the boys together apart from on *Top of the Pops* or in the *NME*. I felt gutted when they split but that opened doors for Ron Wood and Kenney, still having it large, and for Mac and Ronnie to continue their own music. It's so tragic that their time was cut so short. In 2020, aged 75, Sir Roderick David Stewart finished a massive world and UK tour and he is still making headlines – some not so good!

Thank you, the Faces. The best £1.50 I ever spent!

OOH LA LA
RELEASED 13 APRIL 1973

Despite reaching number 1 in the UK album charts and the liner notes including a message to producer Glyn Johns saying 'see you in a year', Ooh La La proves to be the last Faces studio album.

It was a bloody mess. A bloody mess. But I shouldn't say that, should I? Well, I should say it in a few weeks' time. Not now. I mean, the public ain't gonna like me saying it's a bloody mess. It was a disgrace. Maybe I'm too critical. But look, I don't like it. One of the best tracks is one I don't sing on, and that's 'Ooh La La'. All that fucking about taking nine months to do an album like Ooh La La doesn't prove anything. But I'm not going to say anything more about it. All right? That's it.

Rod Stewart, talking to *Melody Maker*

LOCARNO
13 APRIL 1973, SUNDERLAND, UK

WE WERE THERE: PAUL ANDREW AND PETER SMITH

This turned out to be a very special night for a number of reasons. We were both crammed into a totally packed ballroom; you really couldn't move, and it seemed everyone who was into music in Sunderland was there. Before the support band had even taken to the stage, there was an atmosphere and a sense that we were going to experience something unique. The stars were aligned for a tremendous occasion. Rod had already enjoyed chart-topping singles and albums as a solo artist, and the Faces had the reputation of being the best live act around. Sunderland as a city was also buzzing. The football team had, against all the odds, just reached a cup final. That, and the rescheduling of the gig to fit in TV appearances for the band, only heightened the sense of anticipation.

Local band Beckett warmed up the crowd and there was a mood not only of excitement but one of celebration in the sweaty and intimate ballroom as we all waited for the Faces to take to the stage. The band appeared to an absolute roar from the eager crowd. We felt like we'd been standing in wait a long time, even though they hadn't particularly kept us hanging on.

The gig was raucous, energetic, raw and powerful. 'Maggie May', 'Maybe I'm Amazed' and 'Stay With Me' came and went, with everyone singing along. At times you couldn't hear the band for the hoarse voices of the audience screaming in your ears. For some reason, time seemed to speed up. We're not sure if they were rattling through the songs faster than usual, or if the tracks were carried along by the intensity of the atmosphere.

The legendary John Peel was the DJ for the gig. The camaraderie that night was such that he joined the Faces on stage at the end of the set. He is on record as stating several times that this was the best gig he ever attended. The band was also joined on stage by most of the Sunderland football team, who would famously go on to win the FA Cup a few weeks later.

This was a very special gig for many reasons and the best time we saw the Faces. It was the type of night where you thought it would always be that way. Things don't always work out like that, and when everything comes together, as with this gig, you cherish it all the more.

I WAS THERE: BRIAN BATEY, AGE 17

I saw them a few times. I was upstairs at the Locarno in Sunderland in 1973. In those days the stages were built with scaffolding. Rod had some Sunderland players on stage as they had just qualified for the FA Cup Final that year, which they went on to win. It was near the end of the concert and I climbed from the balcony onto the scaffolding at the top of the stage. Ronnie Wood was telling me to get down. When I

Brian Batey saw the Faces more than once

climbed down, I ended up behind the stage. One of the bouncers said I couldn't go anywhere until after the show. When the Faces finished, they walked past me so I asked Rod for his autograph. He did it on my forearm. If I had been brave enough, I would have got it tattooed but sadly I wasn't! I've regretted ever since.

My brother Thomas got me into Rod. I was 15 when he took me to the Mayfair in Newcastle to watch him. He said, 'I'm taking you to see a singer. He's absolutely fantastic.' We went, and he was. Sadly, my brother got knocked over and died on my 16th birthday and it's such a shame he never saw what Rod went on to do.

I WAS THERE: DAVE DICKINSON, AGE 15

I had discovered them via Rod's solo career, 'Maggie May', 'You Wear It Well', etc. – and I remember being blown away by 'Stay With Me' and getting *A Nod's as Good as a Wink*. I was 15 when I saw them in '73, after getting the *Ooh La La* album. They had cancelled the week previous (23 March 1973) and so the venue let everyone in for a Rod and Faces disco. They were introduced by John Peel on that tour and I remember it was a football match atmosphere. They were fantastic live, a proper bar room bluesy band. I went on to see Rod another five or six times but it was never as good as with Ronnie, Ronnie and Kenney.

Dave Dickinson saw the rearranged Locarno show

I WAS THERE: JANET SULLIVAN

I was there with my boyfriend Peter (now husband of 43 years) and my best friend Christine. We paid 75p for the tickets and, on the night, we were all very excited 16 and 17-year-olds and looking forward to the show. We were very disappointed when it was announced to the waiting crowd that Rod could not perform due to illness. Imagine our disappointment. However, we got a free night out in the Mecca and Rod and the boys turned up three weeks later and performed what was probably the best show I have ever seen. The three of us watched the show whilst standing on a table, hanging on to each other. Rod jumped around the stage as people threw tartan scarves at him from the crowd. Girls were fainting at the front and had to be pulled out of the crowd. They performed for an hour longer than billed and Rod had to strip off and squeeze the sweat from his black vest at the end of the show. It was a fantastic experience, and although I have seen Rod Stewart a few times since, this was the best and most memorable performance of the lot.

I WAS THERE: BRIAN PLUNKETT

I learnt of the Faces through my late elder brother who was a big fan. He saw the Faces at Sunderland Locarno and said that the gig was excellent and the atmosphere electric. I went to see them with my friend Michael sometime in '74. I recall Rod kicking footballs into the crowd and they did a reggae version of 'Maggie May' which wasn't much cop.

I WAS THERE: HENRY RACE

The next time that I saw them would've been early '73, when they played the Mecca Ballroom in Sunderland. Strictly speaking, it was called the Locarno Ballroom. This is the gig that John Peel says was the best he ever went to. There are different opinions about the date of this, as it's claimed to be the same day as Sunderland, who were in the second division, beat Arsenal from the First Division in the FA Cup semi-final to secure their place at Wembley. That game took place on 7th April, a Saturday, and Friday night was gig night at the Locarno, but in '73 the Faces were a big band, so if you were putting them on you would take what you were given.

It was a ticket in advance job and they sold out. My sister was a huge Rod Stewart fan; she used to have the posters and the stickers. About three days before the gig, I remember my sister in fucking hysterics because she couldn't find her ticket. I was quite fond of my kid sister so I said, 'Listen, I've seen them already. If you can't find it, you can have mine and you can go instead of me.' But she found it. She'd left it on top of the telly.

The place was absolutely heaving. It was up to capacity plus perhaps 200 per cent more. You couldn't fucking move. The Faces had a bar set up on stage and the band members would go to the bar between songs and get whatever they wanted, probably brandy. They also had a bunch of footballs on the stage which they kept kicking into the audience. The audience kept kicking them back! I can't remember anything about the set or if there was a support band and I can't remember who I went with. But there was no one to touch the Faces live. They were in their element. I saw the Pixies in the '90s and that was pretty fucking good, but other than that, it was the Faces at the Mecca.

I WAS THERE: JOHN W BELL

The Faces played Newcastle three times. They played City Hall twice, the first time being my first gig and the second occasion causing me to leave my sick bed whilst suffering a bad case of flu to join the queue for tickets that stretched around the entire City Hall building. Tickets sold out just as I reached the front steps to the box office. They also played the Odeon cinema, and again I was unable to buy a ticket.

In 1973 they played the Locarno Ballroom in Sunderland. It was the year Sunderland AFC reached the FA Cup Final. My good friend Tom accompanied me this time. We travelled by train to the city centre, walking the mile or so to the venue, and joined the rest of the Faces fans eagerly waiting to enter the venue. The doors opened an hour or so before the band was due on stage. For two almost 17-year-old lads, the lure of four bars was too much, and a few pints of Tartan bitter and Pernod were consumed. Big mistake.

To the left of the small stage our DJ for the evening was none other than John Peel. He was not too impressed when I handed him a photo of Rod for him to autograph.

As the band took to the stage, Rod was followed by some men dressed in suits. Rod introduced them as some of the Sunderland team. We crowded around the stage – there was no seating – and the fun began, with the band playing by now very familiar tunes and some new ones – 'Cindy Incidentally', 'Borstal Boys', etc. and an excellent cover of Free's 'The Stealer', performed as if it was a Faces original. Once again, we were witness to another wonderful musical party.

Soon the evening was over. Outside, we realised we had made no plans to travel the 15 miles home to Newcastle. The last train and bus had gone. Two slightly tipsy lads, we decided to walk. We were soon sobering up, but we were still singing. We had travelled about eight miles along main roads and it must have been about midnight when a car pulled up and a young lad kindly offered us a lift in his MGB GT. He dropped us off a couple of miles from home and, finding a phone box, I phoned my dad. Not at all happy, he came to collect us.

I WAS THERE: JOHN LOGAN

To my surprise (and joy) another North East gig was announced for April 1973 at the Sunderland Locarno, another ballroom gig similar to the Mayfair Newcastle one I'd seen in 1971. Half the Sunderland football team were there, having beaten Arsenal the previous week in the FA Cup semi-final. I think Billy Hughes, who was a Scottish international player, was a friend of Rod's

This was another great night. John Peel, the radio DJ who had been championing the band since they started, was at the gig and said it was the best gig he'd ever been to and I had to agree! They played some of the recently released *Ooh La La* album – 'Silicone Grown', 'Borstal Boys', 'Cindy Incidentally' and 'My Fault' along with Rod's 'True Blue' and the favourites – 'Stay With Me', 'Maggie May', 'Angel', 'You Wear It Well' et al. It turned out to be one of Ronnie Lane's last gigs, as he was gone later in the year, so I was pleased to catch him with the band again before he left. The band for me were never quite the same afterwards. Tetsu could never replace Ronnie's grinning face on stage.

I WAS THERE: JEFF SPENCE

It was great to watch a band grow from small clubs and pubs to playing on the mirrored stage for the 1972 Christmas tour. There was a feeling of 'we are all one' as they played and offered out bottles of Liebfraumilch (and not Mateus Rose, as some people claim). They smoked on stage and I got to swap cigarettes one night with Woody. Rod gave me a wine glass as they left Sunderland Locarno, not long before Sunderland played in the 1973 FA Cup Final. That was the night that the band had a lot of the Sunderland team onstage for a few minutes and then wished them luck in the match and dedicated the set to them. Contrary to popular belief, Rod did not play any of that night in a red-and-white strip.

I WAS THERE: TIM ACKLAM

My brother-in-law attended this gig with me. We remember it as being very good material, basically revolving around the hits, the Faces albums and, if memory serves, stuff from *A Nod's as Good as a Wink…* in particular.

The best live gig that I ever saw in my life – and I can say that quite categorically – featured the Faces. They played in Sunderland the night that Sunderland had beaten Arsenal in the semi-final of the Cup. The entire place was floating three or four feet above the ground and the Faces were the perfect band to capture the atmosphere. I'm not much of a dancing man myself, not got the physique for it really, but I ended up dancing on stage with them. Quite wonderful.

DJ & Broadcaster John Peel

AUDITORIUM
23 APRIL 1973, MINNEAPOLIS, MINNESOTA

The ninth North American tour kicks off in Minneapolis and winds up 15 shows later in Indianapolis.

MCGAW MEMORIAL HALL, NORTHWESTERN UNIVERSITY
26 APRIL 1973, EVANSTON, ILLINOIS

I WAS THERE: TERRY THOMAS

I was a senior in high school and a friend and I skipped school to go. Because we lived 90 miles or so from Northwestern, it was something of a trip to get there. I think I actually ordered the tickets by mail. Regardless, the opening act was a band named Jo Jo Gunne, a band I actually liked, and which had been formed by Jay Ferguson and other former members of Spirit.

The Faces put on quite a show and made the trip well worth it. They had a bar set up on stage. Back in those days, liquor on the stage wasn't unusual, but this was an actual bar. I think somebody said they had a bartender up there too, but I honestly don't remember that. The music was great. The thing with those guys was they had fun when they performed. I always considered their music a little ragged but that's not a criticism or a comment on their musicianship. That was how they did it – kind of the joy of raw, rough-edged rock and roll with a working class feel. I grew up like that so I was attracted to that so I always liked them and Stewart's solo work. The one song that still sticks in my head is 'Twistin' the Night Away', which was the final song of the set or perhaps the encore. They would have made Sam Cooke proud. Stewart was such a stage presence and I still remember him cranking that out.

Concerts now are productions, choreographed and scripted. Back then, they were more spontaneous, gut-level experiences and the best bands made connections with the audience, as if everyone was part of a common undertaking. Stewart, Wood et al could do that. It's still one of the half dozens best shows I've seen, and I've seen a bunch of them over the last half century.

I WAS THERE: DAVID MINICK

I saw Rod with the Faces at Northwestern University at the time of *A Nod's as Good as a Wink*. They were really great – and LOUD – and I remember Ron Wood with his stainless steel guitar. Fantastic!

I WAS THERE: ROBERT GORA

I was at that show. They took a break and wheeled a bar cart onto the stage.

I WAS THERE: SUSAN CANTY

It was the last tour with Ronnie Lane. Tetsu took over on the next tour. I was in the front row.

TELL EVERYONE: A PEOPLE'S HISTORY OF THE FACES

I WAS THERE: BILL CARLTON
I remember them kicking soccer balls.

WEXNER MERSHON AUDITORIUM
28 APRIL 1973, COLUMBUS, OHIO

I WAS THERE: CINDY BEBLAVY
I will never forget the energy... the place pulsed! It was the first time ever that I experienced such intense energy. I have been a Rod Stewart fan since that day.

COBO ARENA
30 APRIL 1973, DETROIT, MICHIGAN

I WAS THERE: JOSEPH HAMILTON, AGE 16
The whole band just rocked! They opened with 'Stay With Me' and did 'Every Picture' as an encore. I've seen all the great bands and I'd rank this show in the top three! (Later, I was lucky to catch Ron Wood play with Keith Richards as the New Barbarians.) I'll always remember the Faces and their raw and edgy blues.

I WAS THERE: DAVID JACKSON
I still remember that evening and what a wonderful time it was, from a great sold-out show to the party afterwards! We didn't have tickets so we purchased them outside. A guy told me his friend couldn't go so he had a spare ticket in the front row! The show was great and Rod played all the hits of the day and kicked footballs into the audience. I met an amazing girl named Jade at the show and she asked if I wanted to go to a party for the

David Jackson partied with the Faces post gig

band at the Statler Hilton in Detroit. I told my friends I would see them later and went with Jade to the party. We ended up sitting with Ronnie Lane talking about the show and other things, when a case of Remy Martin showed up and Ronnie poured us a drink.

At that point, I could hear a piano and voices in the hallway in front of the party. It was Rod and David Ruffin singing Motown songs and having fun. After the party, I asked Jade if I could see her again and she said she was going to London, England the next day. I lost her number and never saw her again.

I WAS THERE: MARIE RESNICK

I saw the Faces many times but the best is when I crashed the after party at the Cadillac Hotel in Detroit. My friends and I went to a Faces concert. Somehow, we found out where the after party would be and so we made our way to the Cadillac Hotel in downtown Detroit. We spotted Rod and his entourage leaving the restaurant area. We ran to try and get into the elevator, and got there just as the doors were closing. Rod was front and centre and caught my eye as the doors closed. I believe a hotel detective told us what floor they were on. We eventually made it into the suite. When we walked in, Rod was on the floor listening to a reel-to-reel tape of the show that was sitting on a coffee table. He looked up as we entered and said, 'Oh! I see you made it!' Of course, I was over the moon. Rod eventually disappeared and we stayed for a few hours. But it was so exciting to see my favourite singer of those days up close and

Marie Resnick was at the post gig party

personal and to know that he recognised me from the elevator.

The concerts that the Faces put on were always an event! We all glammed ourselves up and tried our best to get as close to possible to our heroes. The band was tight, Rod belted it out and shook his booty in his satin pants to thrill us all. It's one of my fondest memories.

I WAS THERE: MARTY BEAUDOIN, AGE 14

I got tickets with my sister and some of her friends. The entire stage was done up in white, including a wall of Ampeg amps. There was a second storey backdrop also done up in white, with a staircase that came down in the centre. They opened the show playing 'The Stripper' on the PA while the band wandered down the stairs and to their positions. Kenny Jones did an extended drum solo during 'I'm Losing You', where the drum riser lifted up and went about half way out into the auditorium. They played all the hits and it was a great show.

BOSTON GARDEN
2 MAY 1973, BOSTON, MASSACHUSETTS

I WAS THERE: BEVERLY DELAITE ATWOOD

I was at Boston Garden. The concert was great and I fell in love with Rod but I really don't remember a lot of it. That was kinda the problem in the early '70s – everyone got pretty loaded to go to concerts, which when I think back wasn't too smart After that concert, I stayed more sober so I could remember better.

I WAS THERE: LASKA MULLEN, AGE 16

The opening act was Peter Frampton. I remember Ron Wood looking like Rod, except with the dark hair, and playing amazing guitar. Rod came down a spiral staircase to 'The Stripper' song, taking off his shirt whilst drinking wine.

PROVIDENCE CIVIC CENTER
3 MAY 1973, PROVIDENCE, RHODE ISLAND

I WAS THERE: JERRY SOUSA, AGE 15

The first time I saw the Faces was in May 1973 at the Providence Civic Center. I was 15 years old, as were my companions Jimmy Sousa (no relation) and my cousin Steve Serpa. We started out in an upper tier with sidelong view, but that didn't last long. I had never been to a concert before. I just saw rock bands at local 'block parties', which were fairly common in the summers of the '60s and '70s, so what I saw looked like a spectacle on scale with a 4th of July parade, complete with marching.

My first memory of the Faces was watching Ronnie Wood and Ronnie Lane marching in opposing directions, back and forth, stage left to right, in time to the intro to 'Miss Judy's Farm'. Sound, lights and sequins had me pretty spellbound and I gravitated toward to the stage, at first on my own, but eventually joined by my companions. The better view was crucial in influencing my deepening decision about what I wanted to do when I grew up!

TELL EVERYONE: A PEOPLE'S HISTORY OF THE FACES

People were throwing reefers at Ron Wood in such volume and with such regularity that I assumed it was some sort of Faces tradition. Occasionally, Ron would sweep an arm along the floor and pick some of them up. This was good work if you could get it as far as I was concerned. I'd been playing guitar since I was twelve, but after that I doubled down on the practice with an eye towards living the life described in Faces lyrics. Travel the world, meet exotic women and get good and hammered.

The next vivid memory of that night was the kind of memory that stays with you for life and defines a person in your eyes. I went off on another meander and managed to find my way to just off stage left, as the band went into an instrumental passage to a song I can't remember, to find Rod Stewart heading offstage to dry himself with a towel. I just stood and stared. Rod noticed me and shouted 'Hiya, kid!' with a big smile, and I thought he must be the happiest guy on the planet.

I was back out on the main floor a short while later, chasing the soccer balls Rod was kicking during '(I Know) I'm Losing You.' I didn't get one.

The last vivid memory I have is charging the stage with a pack of other wild teens, so as better to hear 'Borstal Boys'. We formed a human dancing pyramid just off the forestage and I remember Ronnie Lane looking at us, smiling and shaking his head at how ridiculously exuberant we were. They went into the intro to 'Maybe I'm Amazed' immediately after Rod ceded the mic to Ronnie Lane, who refused to sing. We shouted 'sing Ronnie!' at him and Rod waved his arm over towards us to encourage Ronnie to sing, but Ronnie just looked over at us and smiled, shook his head and said 'no'.

I think that night I decided where my life was going, and so did Ronnie. The next time I saw the Faces was in 1975, with Tetsu on bass. He was good. He was fun. He did the marching and had a hilarious habit of falling on his ass while he was playing. He and Ron Wood kept dropping to the floor at the same time to lie on their backs, laugh and kick their legs. The Faces were the most fun band I have ever seen. I caught a silver ping pong ball that night. They had abandoned the soccer balls and were firing the silver ping pong balls from a cannon. That year I formed my first band. It was a punk band and a lot of the original '70s punks in my area were the same kids from the Faces concerts. You had the bourbon on your amp and you got hammered while you played and you fell down a lot. Because that's what we'd been taught and it was a good education.

I played in several bands as the years went on. I never really made it big on my own, but I got a slice of that life. I married a girl that worked for a promoter that the band I was with worked with in Edinburgh, Scotland, and moved here permanently in 2002.

Not too long later, my wife's aunt had a baby and a christening was set for a Sunday at their church and another communicant, who had just sired an heir of his own, needed that date as well. Our family's christening was rescheduled for the next week and our parish brother, Rod Stewart, got the coveted date for his baby. My wife's grandmother was absolutely livid at the affront. She didn't care who he was – she had the date booked first and was beside herself. I said nothing and smiled quietly to myself at what odd turns a life can take, and at the random situations that a vagabond life can bring.

I thought about going to Rod's baby's christening and shouting 'Hiya, kid!' as they brought the baby from the church, but figured I would just annoy his family and I'd already got him into enough trouble with Ronnie.

I WAS THERE: TOM BRUNEAU

There was so much great stuff coming out of England, and they were all pioneering. Zep, Jeff Beck with Rod Sewart, and then he with the Faces. That band was great in the beginning; it was absolute honky, rooster-strut rock. The scene was exploding. Everybody was fresh, the music was new, it was art. Nobody had burned out from the road yet. They weren't 'stars' full of hubris. They were young, and strong enough to recover from the serious drug abuse in eight or ten hours and still perform well. Then the alcohol took over. It always does.

The Faces played the Orpheum, Boston Common and Providence Civic Center. They were absolutely kick-ass, honky-tonk, bar room strut, and unparalleled at the time, except perhaps for Humble Pie with Marriot on a good night maybe. But around *Long Player* and *A Nod's as Good as a Wink* days? They perpetrated can-bashin', musical vandalism where ever they went, and they lived it.

Ronnie Wood is perhaps the best unacknowledged blues guitar player. The last time I saw the Faces with Rod Stewart was in Providence.

Ronnie played a quadruple length solo in 'I Wish It Would Rain' that was by any standard phenomenal, yet played few of those standard licks. I had dragged the harp player of the blues band I was in at the time down there – he hated the band – and his jaw was on the floor after that solo. I think there's a pretty good representation on the *Coast to Coast* live album. A lot of those musicians back then lived their music. Hendrix tripping his ass off and recording *Axis – Bold as Love*, the Faces with songs like 'Stay With Me', 'Bad 'n' Ruin', 'Too Bad' and 'Had Me a Real Good Time'. They were writing songs about their lives. It was a magical time, for five years or so, a true social phenomenon. And half a world away, at the same time, the Pig's machine, as it always has, was making hell on earth in the jungle.

Rod had already left the Faces by then musically, and they didn't want to be his backup band.

HAMPTON COLISEUM
5 MAY 1973, HAMPTON, VIRGINIA

I WAS THERE: BOB NAGEL, AGE 18

I was a senior in high school in a suburb of Richmond, Virginia when I first saw Rod Stewart and the Faces. Many of the top rock and roll acts came to Hampton, which was about 20 miles west of Norfolk, Virginia, and 70 miles east of Richmond, Virginia, so strategically situated to attract both markets. The capacity was about 11,500. I don't recall the attendance at that show, but it was probably not sold out.

I bought two tickets and originally intended to take a girl to the show but I was painfully shy about asking girls out, so I ended up making a deal with a buddy who also liked the Faces. I would give him a ticket (which probably cost $6) but he would have to drive. That way I could be sure I was 'primed' for what I thought would be a great show.

The Faces had just put out a new album, *Ooh La La*, which I had played incessantly in the weeks leading up to the show. To me it was their second album, following *A Nod's as Good as a Wink to a Blind Horse*. Intermingled with those two albums were Rod Stewart's *Every Picture Tells a Story* and *Never a Dull Moment*, which featured Ronnie Wood on guitar on many tracks. So there were four great albums and I knew that most of the songs they played would be taken from them.

I really don't remember anything special about the concert. I was thrilled to see Rod and Ronnie Lane front and centre. Rod's raspy voice was in full glory, and Ronnie helped out with most of the backing vocals. Ian McLagan, the underrated keyboard player, assisted on backing vocals. Interestingly enough, this was one of Ronnie Lane's last concerts with the Faces. And looking at a setlist from this show, I don't see any songs that he sings lead included. Kenny Jones kept a steady backbeat on the drums.

Bob Nagel was at the Hampton show

As a big-time rock and roll fan, music was life back then. The Faces had all the magic ingredients; great lead singer, electric guitar driven melodies, four guys who could sing or harmonise, and discernable identifiable lyrics. The Faces were always much bigger than just Rod Stewart. They come across as fun loving, imperfect musicians having a great time and taking their fans along for the ride. My favourite in the band was certainly Ronnie Wood. When the Faces were falling apart in 1975, I was pleased he joined my other favourite band, the Rolling Stones.

CIVIC CENTER
7 MAY 1973, SPRINGFIELD, MASSACHUSETTS

I WAS THERE: BRUCE GAYLORD, AGE 20

I was attending college and went by myself. I was seated on the right side of the stage. I liked them a lot but don't remember much except that Rod was throwing the mic around. I had *Ooh La La* but preferred *Every Picture* and *A Nod's*. They played tracks off both.

NASSAU COLISEUM
10 MAY 1973, UNIONDALE, NEW YORK

I WAS THERE: BEN HOCHBERG

I saw the Faces four times in the mid 1970s, all in the New York City/ New Jersey metropolitan area. The first couple of times they were advertised as 'The Faces', and the other times as 'Rod Stewart and the Faces'. Ronnie Lane was quintessential to the band and Tetsu merely a fill in. That's my opinion, but I think the recordings prove me right. The first time I saw them, they were supporting the *Ooh La La* album. During the show's intermission, there was a chorus line of girls entertaining on the stage, with music appropriate for that style. They did a whole dance routine and then the chorus line snaked off into the wings, except two of the 'girls' remained on stage; they turned out to be Rod Stewart and Ronnie Wood in chorus girl outfits. They played the rest of the show in those costumes.

INDIANA STATE FAIRGROUNDS COLISEUM
13 MAY 1973, INDIANAPOLIS, INDIANA

I WAS THERE: BRUCE DUMES

I saw the Faces several times in the early Seventies. One of the shows had The Doobie Brothers as an opening act. I was a massive fan of the two Ronnies, especially Ronnie Lane. Wood had the Zemaitis guitar in a Les Paul shape with mirrors stuck all over it. At one of the shows, I took some pictures with one of those plastic kid's 126 film cameras. I'm not especially tall and a giant guy next to me saw me with the camera and said, 'Here,

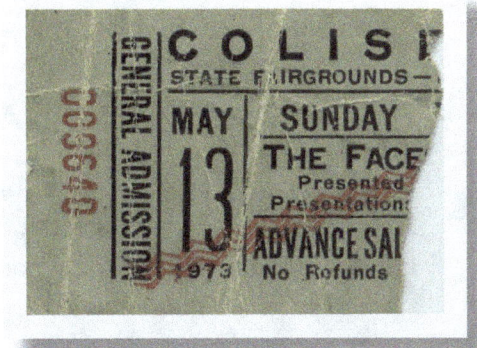

Bruce Domes saw the Faces twice in Indiana in 1973

I'll help' and lifted me up onto his shoulders before I could say a word! I had a perfect view of the stage from about 15 or 20 feet away. My buddy from school asked to borrow the pictures once, and I never saw them again. Who knows where the negatives went? Too bad, as I remember them as being surprisingly good.

The Faces were the best live band I ever saw, and I saw a bunch of bands. I made a list once of the ones I could remember: 115. The Faces didn't stray too far from the recordings, but everything sounded amazing. It was so much fun to watch Ronnie and Rod work the stage.

I WAS THERE: JEFF GIFFORD, AGE 17

I was a Rod Stewart fan in high school – his rough, slightly scraggly voice caught my ear. The vulnerability of 'Reason to Believe' caught my heart. Guys in my hometown Kokomo, Indiana didn't get vulnerable about love, though we all knew its twists and turns. 'Maggie May' was another one. I don't think everyone got the sentiment of that one and, as I recall, it was too much of a 'downer'. I liked both for the seemingly truthfulness belied in the lyrics. Later on, I discovered the connection between Rod Stewart and Faces. I liked some of the Rod Stewart songs for the most part particularly 'Stay With Me', but couldn't get the swing of the other guys' offerings. 'Stay With Me' was a favourite on the jukebox at the neighbourhood pool hall. I was impressed enough to seek out a couple of tickets to a Faces show in Indianapolis at the State Fairgrounds Coliseum.

I took my girlfriend. The seats were on the main floor, not the usual ones in the wings, or behind the stage that concertgoers from the outskirts of Indianapolis were commonly relegated to. I felt fortunate for the placing on the main floor and wondered, driving into Indy, if it meant there would be a smaller than usual crowd. This wasn't the case since, as far as I could tell, the Coliseum was full. The radio informed listeners that this show would be the last one of the Faces' North American tour and so I pictured a longer than usual set with encores and the band giving it their all as a tribute to the fans. I was really stoked for this concert, everything considered.

The opening band was a group with a couple of hits from their last album and a new album in the stores, the Doobie Brothers. 'China Grove' was new on the radio. They nailed that and their whole set was on the money. I remember thinking around this time that a band with the name Doobie Brothers was sure to be a flash in the pan. Folks five years older had groups like Deep Purple and Led Zeppelin to hang their hat on as bands they grew up with. My generation had the Doobie Brothers and Faces. Although the latter had been popular in England for a lot longer, they were more or less spring chickens in the Midwest.

Faces came out after the Doobie Brothers' barn-burning set and it didn't take long to realise they were all drunk, especially Rod Stewart as he dragged himself around the stage, pulling bottles from the crowd and taking swigs throughout the set. They did 'Stay With Me' and a slew of songs I didn't know as they stumbled and clamoured through 'til intermission. At intermission, one of the roadies asked for any young ladies who were interested in a party afterwards to please meet backstage now or after the show.

The second half was also rough and ragged. The crowd was taken in by all of the drunken mayhem and as the concert wore down the crowd revved up. I too got caught up in the moment. This wasn't what I expected but there was no denying the energy coming off the stage this night in Indianapolis. Even the songs I didn't know carried this lift, boost and raw energy that couldn't have been predicted beforehand.

After the encore, there was one more appeal for young ladies to meet behind the stage and the party that had been going on during the performance headed out the back door of the Coliseum as the happy, raucous crowd headed out front.

In the years after the Faces show I've thought about this night and wished I had paid more attention to Ronnie Lane. These days, it is Ronnie Lane that I go to for a shot of inspiration at my age. Funny how we change. *Ooh La La* back in the day was a disappointment to me (not enough Rod) but nowadays I regard it as a classic. Ronnie Lane and Pete Townsend were just this past week cleaning off the rear view mirror of my memories and taking me back for a dip in the Seventies. The wild affair of that concert back in 1973 is a window for me on a time when live music was a bit rawer, more spontaneous and less commercially oriented. A song on the radio was an invitation to a concert, where the band and audience bonded.

26 MAY 1973

Ronnie Lane announces he will leave the Faces. In an official statement drummer Kenney Jones is quoted in the NME: 'Ronnie obviously wants to do something of his own and there is no reason why we should stand in his way.'

Ronnie Lane's final shows with the Faces take place at the Edmonton Sundown in London.

EDMONTON SUNDOWN
1, 3 & 4 JUNE 1973, LONDON, UK

I WAS THERE: PAULA JEAN VICTOR, AGE 15

I went with a then friend who gave me the ticket. She was five years older than me and we had standing tickets and were lucky enough to be right at the front by the stage. I remember Rod kicking footballs into the crowd and my getting crushed into the stage. A bouncer pulled me out to safety and I thought that would be the end of my evening, but he allowed me to stand on stage, to the side behind the curtains, to watch the rest of the show. I'd lost my friend by this time and we each made our way home on our own. It wasn't too far for me, as at that time my parents lived in Angel House, just about five to ten minutes' walk. We also used to go to the Sundown for discos (God, I sound old) and the pictures (upstairs in the circle) as when it was the Regal it was just a picture house. It had a revolving stage.

I WAS THERE: YVE PAIGE, AGE 16

I first saw the Faces on 3rd June 1973 at the Sundown Edmonton. Ronnie Lane was still in the band. I was sweet 16 and went with my best friend, Sue, and her boyfriend. I took my tartan scarf that I'd bought on Walthamstow Market. It was actually two scarves sewn together to make a nice long one. We went down to the front of the stage. There were only five people in front of us. In those days, the floor sloped down as it was an old picture house and there were no barriers. The Faces were extremely late coming on as they had been down the pub, so by the time they came on we were packed in like sardines, stamping our feet, high on adrenaline and chanting, 'Rodney, Rodney!' The atmosphere was electric.

They rolled onto the stage saying something like 'let's get this done before the pub shuts'.

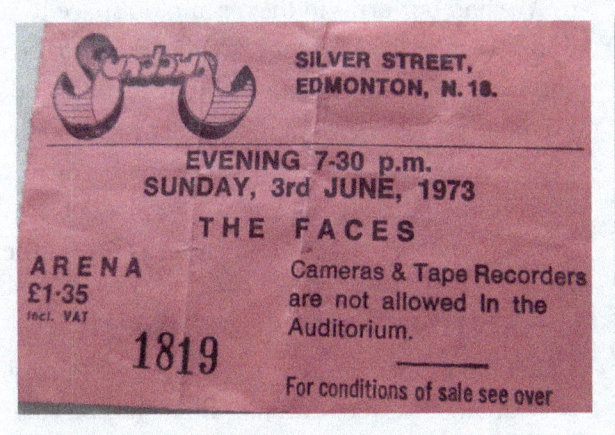

Yve Paige's ticket for her first Faces show

I don't honestly remember the set list, but more importantly was the feeling of being in the right place, where I belonged, watching a band I'd instantly fallen for musically. The one song that stood out for me was 'Angel'. Rod stopped the crowd. He was

I remember Rod singing a song and being surprised at the audience joining in. 'Hey, you lot know all the words.' But the most memorable three or four minutes were when the band started up 'Angel'. Rod started to sing and was so excited that everyone was singing that he started to conduct the audience to sing on command. 'Shhh, shhh,' he said. 'Just the left side sing… and now the right… now upstairs…'. Everyone got even louder, each section trying to outdo the other, and he was like a big kid who had won all the prizes at a raffle. 'Angel' remains to this day my top Faces/Rod track.

I'd never experienced such a magical time. The boys on stage were spell binding. Rod stole my heart, running around the stage. Ronnie Lane made me smile, Woody was just amazing and Mac bashing away at the keys was cute too. Kenney's drum solo must have lasted a good ten minutes before the rest of the band, laughing at the side and refusing to come back, ran on again, falling over each other and shouting 'Kenney Jones!' It all made it the most exciting gig I'd ever been to, and to be honest it's never been beat. Nothing and no one has ever surpassed my first Faces gig.

All the time, we were squashed up against the person in front and behind us. We had our arms in the air and no space to put them back down and were sweating like pigs, but that all added to the experience. Girls fainted and were being taken out via the stage, but we didn't want it to end. Finally, I remember them grouping together in a huddle, swaying as they sang 'We'll Meet Again' at the end and me crying because it was all over. They had brought the house down and we spent a good half hour chanting 'Rodney, Rodney' and stamping our feet to try and get them back.

I WAS THERE: ANNE WIDDOWFIELD

I can't remember where the venue was. I think it was North London. They were great, and were drinking Blue Nun on stage. I've always supported Rod. I just love him. I've seen him many times, once in St Louis where it rained all night. But we still enjoyed it.

I WAS THERE: ANNE WOODROFFE

I went with a friend on the bus from Enfield. It was great, with footballs kicked into the crowd. I remember loads of screaming girls packed in really tight, it being very hot… and going home deaf! I still have my programme. I saw Rod last year at Milton Keynes. He is still the best.

I WAS THERE: CAROL COULES

I have been a fan of Rod Stewart after I first heard his voice on a record called 'Baby Come Home', which he sang with PP Arnold. I carried on from there. My first concert was at the Sundown in Edmonton in 1973, after which I was totally hooked. That show included a man on the old-fashioned organ rising from the pit and having various items thrown at him – but he kept on playing! Then there was a stripper – a very large lady, I might add – who was cheered and booed and had cans thrown at her and she still carried on. Then there were dancing girls, who were nearly naked and who couldn't dance in time to save their life… Then the Faces came on and it was magic.

There was a bar on stage and by the end of the evening they were all pissed. But it was fantastic. After that I went with my then husband to every concert thereafter until about 1990. My husband left, so financially it was difficult for me to go to every one, but I managed to get to quite a few. Each one in the early days had lots of character and the naked girls were still there until the Eighties.

Rod's honesty on stage was also a factor which I liked. He came on once and said, 'I've got a shitty cold but I'll do my best,' and he did it well. I remember one concert at Earl's Court when he was with Britt Ekland. We came out and it had started snowing very heavily. The band and the fans and the coppers were having snowball fights. We joined in. Suddenly Rod and Britt drove right by us, waving to us all in his Roller. It was a great night.

ne's last gig, and that was emotional, as it was when he was ill and came on stage at Wembley to take a bow... The crowd went mad and gave him such a round of applause. It was very moving.

As Rod's concerts became more elaborate, the antics became less and he has gone from strength to strength. He is the ultimate showman. I met him and Penny once at a polo do in Epping. A friend of mine introduced me. Rod was still the joker, but they are a lovely couple.

I WAS THERE: DENISE GOLDING

I have been a Faces fan since 1971 and myself, Iris and Steve now run the Facebook group, *Faces: Had Me A Real Good Time*. My journey with the lads started a long time ago in the East End of London, where I was born. Always a Small Faces fan growing up, I was more than upset when they broke up. I was very sceptical at first when I heard that a band had formed from the ashes of the Small Faces. Little did I realise what a big part they would become in my life.

I first heard them on a John Peel radio programme. I sat on my bedroom floor with my tiny cassette recorder, frantically trying not to miss any of the mayhem that they were causing on set. That was

Denise Golding has been a fan since 1971

their appeal for me. As an East Londoner, they appealed to my love of cheeky humour and, dare I say, cockiness. As I listened, I could almost smell the beer and cigarette smoke.

Never before had I felt the passion for any other band as I did for the

Faces. The concert at the Sundown, Edmonton in 1973 was a magical thing; a night of raw, rowdy fun. Rod strutted like a peacock, always the arrogant front man, but that's what I liked about them. They were whipping the crowd up to a frenzy and they knew it. The party was on and drinks flowed, on and off the stage. A girl jumped on the stage and managed to grab Rod by the legs. She was quickly hauled off by security. Rod shouted to the girl, 'Give my regards to ya mother!'

Their set was amazing. Rod, all strut and groove. Woody's lead guitar. Ronnie, moving from side to side, with his chugging bass, Mac's keys gluing the whole sound together and Kenney's drums, the engine room of the band. Their closing tune was 'Memphis', which was an incredible choice. I was standing near the front, in the stalls. I looked up to the balcony and was shocked to see it bouncing – I mean, really bouncing – up and down. As the song built up, the balcony was moving so much from the stamping feet that I seriously thought it would collapse. The concert was reviewed the following week in one of the music papers and the journalist remarked that he thought there was going to be a serious accident, such was the force of those stamping feet.

They will always be my band. The sheer joy that they brought to their audience. If you were lucky enough to have witnessed the Faces in their full glory, then you had witnessed a party like no other.

I WAS THERE: PERRY RIDLEY

In March 1973 the Faces released *Ooh La La* and, thanks to my friend at WEA, I managed to get a copy a few days before it was released. I was able to get a ticket for one of the shows at the Sundown, Edmonton in June 1973. I can remember it was a long old journey from South East London to the North East of the capital. Again, although I enjoyed the gig, I don't remember much about it except that the band were extremely pissed on stage. The stage was set up all white, and was very

Perry Ridley was at the Sundown in Edmonton

bright. These gigs were Ronnie Lane's last with the band.

My main memory is arriving back at Liverpool Street and myself and my friends finding ourselves stranded as we had missed the last bus home. Fortunately, some police officers who questioned us as to why we were on the streets so late kindly gave us a lift back to South London. I still have the programme from this show, in mint condition and filed away in the sleeve of *Ooh La La*.

I WAS THERE: ROB RUCK

It was a great concert, with Rod and the band interacting with the crowd and kicking footballs into the crowd. It was extra special because it was Ronnie Lane's last gig with the band, and when it was announced all Ronnie said was, 'Where's me gold watch?' A special night.

I WAS THERE: TERRY HIRD, AGE 14

I am an Alice Cooper fan but I went to the Faces concert because my mates from school, male and female, all went. We had waited out the back for them to arrive and they all jumped out of a limo, except Rod. It was my first concert and I remember it was amazing. It was at the Sundown in Edmonton during the *Ooh La La* tour. We were up the front. We had a great time.

I WAS THERE: TONY WOOD

It was the *Ooh La La* tour. I went with my mate. His mum made us tartan scarves from material from Walthamstow market. I've seen Rod 20 plus times since.

I WAS THERE: RICHARD DAWSON

At high school in the 1970s, a group of us saved up our pocket money and took the long trip from Southend-on-Sea to Edmonton in North London to see our heroes. On arriving at the Sundown, we eagerly anticipated the gig in a packed hall having gained admission at 8pm. At 9pm, and with the stage set up with the band's equipment, the excitement was mounting. At 9.30pm, the show still hadn't begun. Finally, at 10pm a few footballs were kicked on stage and Rod and the boys appeared. My friends and I witnessed an extraordinarily good show and were in ecstasy for a whole hour, when we had to reluctantly leave in order to catch our last train home.

I WAS THERE: JONATHAN SEAR

I saw them four times and the best of these was at the Edmonton Sundown with Ronnie Lane. He had a rose in his lapel that I eventually discovered was peppered with a 'mixture' that Mac and Woody kept running over and sniffing. Bad boys!

I WAS THERE: MICK P (AKA SLRNR), AGE 14

I was at school when it was announced that Laneole would be playing his final shows at Edmonton Sundown. Fortunately, I only lived ten minutes away and school was five minutes further. At dinner break, I ran as fast as I could to meet with a huge queue of tartan and haircuts. There was a huge queue for tickets. By the time I got to the front of the line, I had met so many fans who had made this kid welcome. I was late back for class but detention was worth it.

The show came around. I was finally seeing the band I had loved for years. I met everyone from the queue and the atmosphere of my first live gig was electric. Up in the balcony, I thought it would collapse as the lads partied on stage. It was incredible, and remains the best day of my life. The can of pale ale I had been given didn't go down well. Arriving home an hour late from 'Scouts' a little bit frazzled and singing 'Angel' at the top of my lungs got me a severe bollocking from me mum. It was all worth it, and I can relive that awesome night as the show is now on YouTube.

My school friend's dad was a local copper and tells me he had to approach a fan around 11.30pm that night to keep the noise down. With that, the dude with the barnet went to hug the copper, dropped his bottle of wine and the blonde on his arm slumped to the ground. At this point, a member of the crew apologised profusely to the police officer and escorted a very drunk Rod back into the venue!

I WAS THERE: JACKIE MACDONALD

Me and my friends saw them live several times in different venues around London. They played at a venue called the Sundown in Edmonton, North London (long gone, it's now a Lidl) and this particular time they were playing three gigs in a week. We got tickets for every one. Then they added a fourth night, and I actually stood up a date I had for that night to go to the gig with my friends. It was an all-standing venue and we used to get there early so that, when the doors opened, it was a mad dash to get to the front, which we did every time. If you go onto YouTube and put in 'Faces Edmonton Sundown 1973', there

Jackie Macdonald remembers four nights at the Sundown when Ronnie Lane left

are good crowd shots of the front and we are in there. That was Ronnie Lane's final tour with the Faces, and everybody was throwing cards and flowers on to the stage for him. They were great times.

PALASPORT PARCO RUFFINI
16 JULY 1973, TURIN, ITALY

With Ronnie Lane having left the band, the Faces recruit Tetsu Yamauchi on bass and embark on a short European tour.

PALASSPORT
18 JULY 1973, ROME, ITALY

I WAS THERE: FABIO PONTI
I saw the Faces in 1973 in Rome and it was really a great show. I was with an important DJ from Italian radio and we both agreed that the man on guitar would have a great future. That 'man' of course was Ronnie Wood, and two years later he would join the greatest rock 'n' roll band in the world... The show was amazing, fun and the sound was the

best. It was a pity that Ronnie Lane wasn't in the band. I love the Faces. Along with the Stones and The Who, they are my greatest love in rock and roll music.

SOMMER ROCK FESTIVAL 2 RADSTADION
21 JULY 1973, FRANKFURT, WEST GERMANY

The show is introduced by Keith Moon, who plays tambourine on 'Borstal Boys'.

I WAS THERE: GARY DYCUS

It was the *Ooh La La* tour. It rained for two days but fans toughed it out. It rained all night so we sat with Parkas on. Next day, they announced 'don't eat the brown acid'. Someone was selling rat poison to the crowd. They were carrying people out behind the stage on stretchers. It was sad.

HARDROCK
29 JULY 1973, MANCHESTER, UK

I WAS THERE: PHILIP MAHON

The Hardrock in Stretford was Tetsu's first British gig with them. It had previously been a supermarket and also a bowling alley and it was a terrible concert venue. It was July and it was hot. They played a lot of songs from *Ooh La La* and some from *Nod* plus the usual selection of Rod's solo stuff: 'I'd Rather Go Blind,' 'You Wear It Well', 'Maggie May', 'Angel', 'True Blue', 'I'm Losing You', 'It's All Over Now' and 'Twistin' the Night Away'. Part way through the show, Kenney Jones collapsed through heat exhaustion and Gavin Sutherland took over on drums. He was obviously not a drummer and appeared to be daunted by the whole thing. When the drum break came in 'Twistin', Rod took over to do it before continuing to sing. Bloody hell, it was a hot night. Rod also sang, as the opening line to 'I'd Rather Go Blind', 'Something told me Denis Law has moved to Manchester City...'.

I WAS THERE: NEIL ROGERS

It was the first gig for Tetsu and the first gig for me. For some reason, I did ask myself if Rod Stewart was going to be there. The night was very hot and very sweaty. I didn't see the opening act (the Sutherland Brothers) but the Faces opened with 'Miss Judy's Farm'. I can't remember what they played after that, but after about half an hour Kenney fainted and was taken away. Ron Wood ended up playing his bass drum for about a minute or so. One of the Sutherland Brothers took over the drumming and they ended the show with 'Twistin' the Night Away'. Rod did the end paradiddle on the drums and that was it. They were on for just over 30 minutes. It was great. My first time and it was absolutely wild, but absolutely wonderful.

I WAS THERE: WILLIAM CARDEY, AGE 17

I went with four mates. It was packed and it was a very low ceiling. The drummer got heat stroke. I remember Rod hanging the mic over the heads of the crowd, asking us to sing 'Maggie May'.

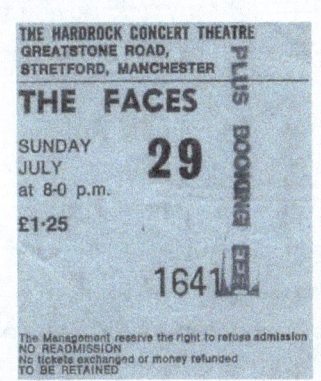

William Cardey was at the Hardrock in Manchester

KURSAAL BALLROOM
11 AUGUST 1973, SOUTHEND-ON-SEA, UK

I WAS THERE: CHRIS TURNER

I can remember everything about it because they were two hours late. The promoter came out and said, 'If you want to leave, you can have a refund,' but me and my mate stayed. We missed the last train home and had to walk eight miles at 2am but it was the best gig I ever went to.

I WAS THERE: MICHAEL MAYNARD, AGE 17

My attention was drawn to the Faces when I saw Rod Stewart on *Top of the Pops*. I was 17. Rod Stewart's 'Maggie May' struck a chord with me immediately. The backing band, I later learned, was the Faces. The band's performance was unlike any I had seen before. Someone threw a football onto the stage and Rod and Ronnie Lane had a kick about whilst 'playing'. The song itself was bouncy and catchy, and Rod's style of doing mic stand acrobatics made the whole show outstanding. I got the chance to see the Faces when I saw a bill poster on a wall in Southend, 'Rod Stewart and the Faces', live at the Kursaal.

The Kursaal was an old Victorian building that was the frontage of the town's funfair and its second most famous attraction after the pier. It was my first gig and the musical equivalent to losing my virginity. The whole event opened my eyes not only to the fantastic fun that was live music, but also the fun that was the Faces. They had their version of rock 'n' roll and the hit single 'Stay With Me' was the best example of this. I bought my ticket using my hard-earned money, saved from my part time assistant greengrocer's job with Fred Newman in Eastwood, which just happened to be next to an office run by architect Mick Karslake, who was to become Ronnie Wood's father-in-law when Ronnie married Jo.

I bought one of my first proper non-*Music for Pleasure* cheapo supermarket-sold covers albums, *A Nod's as Good as a Wink*, and played it over and over by leaving the arm up on the record player. The album opens with 'Miss Judy's Farm' and, although it wasn't a particularly commercial song, the vocals and that Faces sound were enough for me to love it. I also liked the way Ronnie Lane would sometimes do the main vocal. His song 'Debris' – the B-side of 'Stay With Me' and his finest work – made me realise the Faces were not just all about Rod Stewart, despite the publicity. The band was – and are still – my favourite band. 'Stay With Me' will be played at my funeral.

I was amused by the fun element of the band on TV. The fun was also evident on the album and onstage from the very first note the band played. It was clear that these guys were not only fun but also very drunk, which I thought was so cool at 17. I had never seen a frontman throw the mic stand in the air and catch it. Rod's style was unique, plus I loved the sound of Ronnie Wood's guitar. His style of playing that bluesy slide was superb.

'Stay With Me' was DJ John Peel's favourite song after 'Teenage Kicks' by the Undertones. With the line-up of Rod on lead vocals, Ronnie Wood on lead and rhythm guitar, Ronnie Lane on bass, Ian McLagan on keyboards and Kenney Jones on drums the picture was complete. These guys looked and acted as if they had been mates for years. Rousing shouts for more went up after the band left the stage and, yep, back they came. It was like getting out of a warm bath to get the soap, then getting back in. Heaven. Life would never be the same again.

I saw them again a year or so later after the release of *Ooh La La*. I actually got a train to London the day it was released because a mate said it would be a week before it was available in Southend. Man, I wasn't going to wait. The *NME* was giving away an introductory flexi disc, a thin bit of vinyl which had on it a snippet of several songs. How fantastic and thoughtful of the band, I pondered. One music paper declared the album as 'short but sweet' at just over 30 minutes long. They were right. It spawned the single 'Cindy Incidentally', a song I would listen to on Dial-a-Disc and then wait for the Sunday chart show to see where it was. Soon after, I bought the album which was another winner. Songs such as 'Sad and Lonely' and 'If I'm on the Late Side' showed once again the songwriting quality of the other guys in the band. Occasionally, an album filler would be on the track listing, none more bizarrely entitled than 'Skewiff (Mend the Fuse)', the B-side to 'You Can Make Me Dance, Sing or Anything'. It highlighted once again the band's approach to a tough and unforgiving business, and by using humour and Pythonesque out-of-the-box thinking, their style was just the ticket for me. Rock 'n' roll fun and, now and then, a sad lament.

I WAS THERE: COLIN PROMESSE, AGE 15

The Kursaal was a dance hall (my parents met there in 1952) with a sprung dance floor and that night we were literally bouncing. In '73 the amusement park was still active. We started queuing at 10am to be near the front when it opened in the evening. We were about 80th in the queue. I can still picture exactly where we stood. It was a red-hot summer's day and we all kept each other's places in the queue as we either went into the amusement park to ride the water chute or nip across the road to dip in the sea.

It was three days before my 16th birthday, and a great night for a 15-year-old Faces fan. We queued all day to get to the front, and smuggled in a bottle of homemade wine, syphoned off my dad's demijohns. (Home-made wine was a big thing in the '70s!) We all wrote our names and addresses on the blank label and proffered it up to the stage. Rod took it from us and necked it, but he never bloody wrote back to us to thank us, did he?

I am 99 per cent certain the review from the *Southend Standard* said something along the lines of 'Mr Stewart drank from a wine bottle proffered up from the crowd' – my first moment of fame – and 'not only are Mr Stewart's trousers so tight that you can tell on which side he dresses but so tight that you can tell on which day he goes to church!'

I think 14 is the musical age when you are hooked. That was 'Maggie May' for me. I still enjoy Rod Stewart and his music still resonates with me. Poignant tracks at different moments in my life underpin the togetherness I feel with him... But for me it was always the Faces. Like all good heroes and legends, they passed too soon. I recall being off work with a hangover and laying on the sofa moping with Radio 1 on when they announced the news of the break up. I was in mourning!

Since 1980, I've had a cassette tape that I've never done anything with. A girl I worked with in London brought in a vinyl LP. She said that a boyfriend who was a studio sound recordist had pressed this one album which he had recorded with a hand-held cassette recorder when he sat at a concert. I am guessing the concert was round about 1970. You hear Rod say, 'Ladies and gentlemen, I give you the Small Faces.' Ronnie Wood then leans into 'Flying' and Rod is on vocals. It is really raw and pretty rough! She maintains that it was the first gig for Rod when he joined the boys. I begged her to sell me the vinyl (to no avail).

I remember having my dad's massive 1970s earphones on, with a cassette player mic sellotaped to a broom handle and a tartan scarf tied to my wrist in the front room of our house with the lights off, whilst my parents were doing the weekly shop... or so I thought. I had *Long Player* at full volume in my head and I was belting out 'Maybe I'm Amazed' as a 15-year-old Faces front man when my dad switched on the light and all three of them were stood there wetting themselves... I hadn't heard them return.

Recently I went to see The Small Fakers, and in particular their Faces set. When Rod introduces 'Maybe I'm Amazed', he says, 'Here's one you may well know, you may not know, but if you don't know it, I really don't know where you've been. So you should know the tune. Here we go.' As The Fakers introduced the track, the lead singer started with the Rod intro. I had had a few so, as I have done about a million times in the past, I recited the same words as the lead singer. As the keyboards began, he turned away from the mic and said to me, 'Fucking hell, do you know EVERY word?' That was some 40 years after I bought the album. Of course I know every word!

I WAS THERE: JON PAUL SEIGEL

I was involving in promoting the gigs at the Kursaal and other venues in Southend. I remember the Faces gig well. The band arrived separately from Rod in a large vehicle and came in the back entrance, where usually a few fans gathered to get autographs. (There were no selfies in those days.) Rod arrived a little later but did not want to come in past the fans. Further round the back of the venue was a small door that led under the stage and into the back area of the hall, so we led him through and he joined the other members of the band. The concert was a sell out and the band were excellent. Straight after the gig, Rod left the same way and well before the rest of the band.

TOP RANK SUITE
17 AUGUST 1973, DONCASTER, UK

I WAS THERE: JOHN HEMINGFIELD, AGE 16

During the first few months of 1972, I was a 15-year-old lad searching for his musical identity. I liked an eclectic mix of popular music, a butterfly flitting between folk music, chart singles and a keen interest in Motown and Northern Soul. By early summer I was involved with my first steady girlfriend, who had a slightly older sister with a decent record collection which included Carole King's *Tapestry*. I remember listening to that album more than most.

John Hemingfield saw the Faces at Doncaster's Top Rank

The sister held a house party for her birthday sometime in May and I attended with a handful of Motown singles. The large living room soon filled with a bunch of older, cooler guys. (All older guys were cooler to a 15-year-old.) I noticed a couple of lads would take it in turns to jump up periodically and strut around the room with one fist in front of the mouth, the other around the pocket area, head bobbing back and forth like a demented rooster. I asked the guy beside me what it was all about and he told me that they were imitating the lead singer in the Faces. I was intrigued but not blown away. Little did I know that a seed had been planted.

A couple of weeks later it was my girlfriend's birthday and I took her to a record shop in Doncaster to buy her an album as a gift. She had her sights set on Slade or T.Rex but I suggested 'that Rod Stewart guy'. She agreed and I vividly remember being sat at the bus stop, looking at the double gatefold sleeve of *Never a Dull Moment*. In my ignorance I didn't know that most of the Faces were there between the goal posts in that photo.

Playing the album back at her house on her parents' hi-fi, I was totally blown away. My life had changed forever. I had found the music I truly loved and identified with. I became more of a Rod fan than a Faces fan at that time. With only a Saturday job I could not afford albums. Working in a clothes shop, all my spare cash went on clothes. I was one of the smartest kids out of school. Two tone Levi Sta-Prest and Ben Sherman button down collars, Harrington jackets and Crombie top coat were the order of the day. So it was that *Never a Dull Moment* got played to death – although I can't remember now whether I bought my own copy or acquired my girlfriend's.

In the autumn of 1972, I attended a field trip with the art class, drawing the rooftops of Robin Hood's Bay and the cliffs just north of Scarborough. One of the guys from the aforementioned party was on the trip and, one evening in the dorm room, struck up conversation about Rod. He educated me and said that I was misguided and that it was the Faces I should be listening to. He pulled a portable cassette player from his bag and proceeded to play *A Nod's as Good as a Wink*... Again, I loved everything that I was hearing. The rolling piano... the cloying guitar...the deep strong bass topped off with my favourite voice. Now I was a Faces fan and couldn't get enough.

Mum was a bit strait-laced and I was only allowed posters on one bedroom wall but it was covered in Faces and Rod posters. One was of Rod sat in an upright wicker chair and wearing bright yellow trousers with black socks and Jesus sandals. I couldn't get away with the yellow pants in a mining village but black socks and Jesus sandals became my trade mark. It worked for me, as my second steady girlfriend still remembers them, 47 years later. She is now my wife and live music partner of 43 years. (I still only wear black socks to this day.)

I started to dress more like a Face. I remember a blue crushed velvet suit with tulip lapels. I got sent home from school a few weeks before leaving for having a Rod haircut. 'But sir, don't you know who I am? I'm one of the Faces.' Dad dragged me to the barber's for a 'short back and sides' and the three button hand-me-down didn't quite look the same.

I left school that summer in 1973 and started work in the training centre of a Doncaster factory. By then, at the age of 16, I was getting into the town's nightclubs and the Top Rank had started booking chart acts. We had seen The Drifters and Jimmy Ruffin, etc., but fortunately for us, someone responsible for the bookings there had a little bit more ambition. When David Bowie was announced and I purchased a ticket with hundreds of others, little we know that we would be witnessing history. We watched Ziggy Stardust and the Spiders from Mars two weeks before Ziggy had to 'break up the band' at the Hammersmith Odeon.

Then to my delight the Faces Doncaster show was announced. I acquired my ticket for the princely sum of £1.50 and distinctly remember getting involved in a disagreement with a lad in the training centre who said that Rod would not be there because it only advertised the Faces. 'But Rod is the singer in the Faces!' I argued.

On the night in question, I remember sitting in a local pub having a couple of pints with a friend from school. I was keeping a low profile as we were only 16, but these were very different times. The excitement was building. Later we found a good vantage point on the balcony to the left of the stage in the Top Rank. I enjoyed the support act which was a group called Strider. The lead guitarist, one Gary Grainger, was very impressive and did not go unnoticed by Rod, who later employed him in the first incarnation of the Rod Stewart Band.

Rumour had it that this was just a warm up gig for the forthcoming tour with the new bass player. Dear old Ronnie Lane had recently left the

Faces and had been replaced by the Japanese bassist, Tetsu Yamauchi. On the night it didn't seem to matter. The crowd went wild when the boys hit the stage.

It was rough… it was raw… but it was fantastic. Sadly, we all forgot Ronnie was not there. All eyes were on Rod and Woody. I distinctly recall being impressed with the way Rod never stood still, using every inch of the stage. The bright yellow trousers (once again), the bang and clatter of it all, the football crowd style sing-a-longs. By this time, it had become more of a Rod show, with more glitter and sequins, flowing chiffon scarves and candelabra on the piano. The abundance of tartan scarves in the crowd indicated that most of the audience had now come to see Rod Stewart. Obviously, this was the reason Ronnie had left, and I much prefer watching the old recordings of the early days, when it was more chaotic and less polished, but it was still a great show. Just like Ziggy a couple of months earlier… Never to be forgotten.

I am so pleased I got to see the Faces live during their short lifespan. It inspired me to continue my support of Dear Rod and at least I got to see Ronnie on stage with the rest of the guys at Wembley Stadium in 1986 at the end of a Rod show, even though he was sitting down while someone else played bass.

The Faces were a breath of fresh air in my very structured life. Sometimes dishevelled and shambolic, all crash-bang-wallop, but often brilliant. They were full of fun and they didn't take themselves too seriously; a five-year party of laughs and giggles. We are still going to Rod's concerts all these years later. Well over 50 shows so far (including twice in 2019) but it all started back at that house party in 1972. The show cemented my love of the band and the music, which I still listen to regularly today.

I WAS THERE: FRANK HENSON, AGE 15

It was a warm up gig for the Reading Festival and Strider were the support band. Tickets were £1.50 each. When the Faces came on, they were all pissed and started kicking footballs into the crowd. They kicked off with 'Miss Judy's Farm'. I can remember a bit of a ruck in the crowd – the town drunks – and Rod had to tell the crowd to calm down. They did a great version of 'That's All You Need' with some brilliant slide guitar by Ronnie Wood. All in all, it was a superb gig for a 15 year old. I've seen Rod on his own over the years since and I'm afraid none of those shows get anywhere near to a Faces gig.

13TH NATIONAL JAZZ, BLUES & ROCK FESTIVAL
25 AUGUST 1973, READING, UK

I WAS THERE: CHRIS DODD, AGE 15

I was a 15-year-old Faces fan who had planned for weeks to go and see what, due to the Tetsu Musicians Union 'thing', could be my last chance to see Rod and the lads live on stage in the UK, at the Reading Festival. One by one my mates dropped out until I came to the realisation that I couldn't rely on other folks for my wants and needs. So, almost at the stroke of midnight, I swiped a bottle of fortified something or other and half a bottle of Whiskey Mac (whatever that was) from my mum and dad's 'cocktail cabinet' and set off alone for Crewe railway station.

I arrived in Reading about midday and found my way to the festival site by following the trail of empty shopping carts discarded along the way. I, as

The Faces were back at the Reading Festival just twelve months later

the lads say, 'Had me a real good time.' Rod and the lads were brilliant (and well worth the trouble I got into when I got home) and then it was all over. I slept on Reading Station, met a lovely girl from Sevenoaks and wrote to her a couple of times after, but I got remanded into the care of the local authorities shorty after and lost touch.

Reading wasn't the first time I'd seen them. I'd skived off school and queued up for tickets at the Free Trade Hall in my hometown of Manchester in December '72. The United team came on stage and my cousin flicked a ten pence piece up there to see if Rod and Denis Law, who were known to be on the thrifty side, would fight to pick it up. We called it the 'battle of the tight 'uns'. Sadly it remained unclaimed until a roadie picked it up after the encore.

I saw them again in July '74 at Buxton where I nearly choked to death on exhaust fumes while hiding in the boot of a coach after cadging a lift from the festival site back to town (unknown to the driver of the said coach!). Me and another weary traveller had to kick the boot door open before we passed out. I'd been down to Watford to see Rod play three songs at a thing for Elton at Vicarage Road in May of that year, so seeing the lads' full show plus the Memphis Horns was great and probably worth nearly dying of suffocation for!

I rounded out 1974 seeing them for what turned out to be the last time at Trentham Gardens in Stoke in December. Gary Grainger was in the support band, Strider, and the dirty twat kept spitting on everyone – a couple of years before punk and him joining Rod's band!

Rod and the lads meant so much to me then, as they still do today, but as a skinny awkward kid with scruffy hair and a nose slightly too big for my face, or a face too small for my nose. Don't worry, my face grew into it. Like a pair of school trousers, they fit you eventually! I was born in December 1957 in the Manchester and Salford Mission Maternity Home for unmarried mothers, probably another reason Rod and the boys felt like an extended family to me, a bit like Fagin and the Artful Dodger's gang-type thing. I'll be forever grateful for the Faces for making my life bearable back then and giving me a look and an attitude to copy and aspire to, important things for a lost kid then and probably still now.

I WAS THERE: CLIVE MARSHALL, AGE 18

Aged 16 and at school, I was a Suedehead listening to Motown and Reggae before growing my hair longer. Fashions changed and my musical tastes changed. I discovered Rod Stewart first, buying and listening to *Every Picture Tells a Story* in late 1971. I found out Rod was in the Faces so I bought *Long Player*, which I loved, and then *A Nod's as Good as a Wink* and *Ooh La La*. I thought the band were amazing. I saw them headlining at the Reading Festival on the Saturday night and they were excellent. Sadly, Ronnie Lane had left the band to be replaced by Tetsu, a Japanese bass player, but they were brilliant. Ronnie Lane was a great songwriter, with 'Debris' and 'Ooh La La' to mention just two songs. But all the band were great – Ronnie Wood, Ian McClagan, Kenney Jones. The clothes, the haircuts – they had it all. My favourite rock and roll band of all time!

I WAS THERE: MICHAEL KARL DENNING

Rory Gallagher was on the bill too! It was a bank holiday weekend and blisteringly hot. The Faces headlined, and followed the Sensational Alex Harvey Band and Status Quo, amongst others. What a fantastic day.

I WAS THERE: JIM WEAVER

I suppose you could say I was much like most mid-teenage boys of that era (I was 16 and a half in 1971) – spotty-faced, loving footie, beginning to have an appreciation of alcohol and not having a clue what I wanted to do when I left school. I enjoyed music, but no particular group or pop star was a firm favourite. I enjoyed some of The Beatles' music and had a liking for music from the Small Faces, the Kinks, The Who and some of the Stones' tunes, but I would not have described myself either as a Mod or a Rocker.

Little did I know that

Jim Weaver with wife Beverley and a very Faces-like barnet

Jim Weaver with Mac in 2008. The barnet is now long gone

my musical awakening was waiting for me just around the corner. It was in August 1971 that I recall hearing this song sung by a gravelly-voiced singer on the radio. The song I thought was rather good, and I particularly liked its mandolin intro and ending. And as 'Maggie May' broke into the Top 40, an appearance was made by Rod Stewart on *Top of the Pops*, accompanied by the rest of the Faces (plus John Peel). I was totally knocked out by the lads' performance. Not musically, as they were miming except for a very good vocal performance. No, it was the camaraderie and the antics that they got up to on that small stage in the BBC studio that bowled me over. From that moment, I was 110 per cent hooked.

A work colleague saw them at Birmingham's Rainbow Suite in late 1971 and said they were truly amazing. To this day, I regret not going to that gig. It was almost two years before I did.

The Faces were headlining on the Saturday of the three day festival, and my mate Rick and myself decided we would go. There was the added attraction for him of Status Quo, but I was only going to see one band. Our mode of transport was… our thumbs, as we had decided to hitchhike there and back. It took us seven hours to get from Birmingham to the site at Reading.

We stayed on the edge of the crowd, at the side, so we were quite far away from the stage and couldn't see much of the band. But I enjoyed it. My one abiding memory of the gig is Rod flinging the mic stand high up into the air. As it made its merry ascent, it started to rotate and to spin as well. At its highest point, it was totally upside down and as it descended, it completed its 360 degree rotation and was once more the right way up. I remember thinking this was quite special, although I can't remember if Rod caught it when it came back down!

Their set ended around midnight, after which we decided to start hitch hiking back home. To say that part of the plan hadn't been very well thought out was an understatement. Unable to hitch a ride, we ended up sleeping on a grass verge close to one of the main roads out of Reading. We finally arrived home in Birmingham around 5pm on Sunday afternoon.

I WAS THERE: PETER SMITH

I was back at the Reading Festival, and this year I hooked up with a large group of mates from town who had travelled down in a Transit van. I discovered Reading town centre, and the local pubs for the first time, and as a result missed some of the bands. We also discovered the bridge over the Thames, and spent many an hour watching people dive off it, which seemed crazy and a bit dangerous to me.

The Faces once again headlined the Saturday night. My memories of the Saturday are of Status Quo going down a storm, and the Faces putting

Reading Festival ticket

on another strong performance, but the real success of the day being the Sensation Alex Harvey Band. They were just about to release *Next*, and they started their set with 'Faith Healer', which was incredible, the intro throbbing across the field, slowly getting louder and louder like a weird electronic heartbeat. Alex was simply electric; the guy had no fear and took total control of the 30,000 strong crowd; he certainly made a lot of new friends that night.

The Faces performance was not quite as strong as the previous year. This was one of their first gigs after Ronnie Lane had been replaced by Tetsu. He was great, but you could sense that the band were losing their enthusiasm and that Rod would soon be on his way, with a solo career and superstardom beckoning. Lots of footballs were kicked into the crowd again. Everyone was still onside, and the atmosphere was one of pure enjoyment and fun, with the familiar festival figure of Jesus (Jellett) dancing naked throughout the whole of the set.

I WAS THERE: VINCE JAMES WANKLIN

I saw the Faces three times in 1973, at the Reading Festival in August but also at the Gaumont in Worcester in April and again in December, when Long John Baldry and Sutherland Brothers and Quiver were the support. For the Reading Festival, I got the train from Malvern in

Worcestershire on the Friday night when Rory Gallagher was headlining. The Faces were headlining Saturday. I remember Alex Harvey bollocking the crowd for throwing cans around. Quo were on top form. Then the Faces came on. The band struck up, and Rod threw the mic up for the first time, hitting the lighting gantry and putting the whole festival in darkness for 33,000 people for half an hour. Oops! I think Ronnie Lane's mobile studio was recording it all.

I slept by a fire in the arena all night and had my backpack nicked with all my gear in it. Luckily, I had my wallet and fags in my sleeping bag. I decided to hitchhike home, got out on the main road out of Reading – and found that thousands of others were all doing the same thing. But I was on my own and the first car that passed me was a bloke in a Fiat 500 who only had room for one, because he'd been playing in a big concert in London and had a tuba on his back seat. He took me all the way to Worcester, so I was back in Malvern and in the pub with my mates by noon.

BAYFRONT CENTER
15 SEPTEMBER 1973, ST PETERBURG, FLORIDA

The Faces embark on their tenth North American tour.

CAMERON INDOOR STADIUM, DUKE UNIVERSITY
19 SEPTEMBER 1973, DURHAM, NORTH CAROLINA

I WAS THERE: TERRY ANDERSON, AGE 16

I didn't know if I would get to go to this show or not, because my buddy David Enloe had the fuckin' flu and he was the dude I was going with. We were 16 years old and many miles from home. The tickets were $4.50. But David fought through his flu and we made it in through the rain. The opener we'd not heard much about – some Irish guy named Rory Gallagher. Him and two other dudes got up there and kicked everybody's ass. He brought the house down to a hush in a song about

Al Capone ('Ode Capone') – I mean to a hush! – and then kicked back in with all Hell involved! It was the most ass kickin' three piece I've ever seen, before or since.

Then it was time for our heroes, the Faces. Masters of Controlled Sloppiness. Well... about that 'controlled' thing? Not so much. What we witnessed was a great show, mind you, but not the show I was expecting. Number one: I was expecting Ronnie Lane on fuckin' bass guitar! Apparently, he had quit within days of the show and had been replaced with Tetsu Somebody. Well fuck! Where's Ronnie Lane? They were all terribly drunk (which I don't have a problem with, as long as you're entertaining) and they played fine for the most part, in between Woody falling down twice and Tetsu once. I remember the slow songs being especially great, notably 'Angel'. Rod sang that with his back mostly to the audience. Kenney played those pink, white and brown drums that you see on the back of *A Nod's as Good as a Wink...* He kicked a whole bunch o' ass! And my pal (later on), Ian McLagan, played beautifully. It was a great night of music, soul and inspiration. But it could have been so much more if Laney had've been there.

I WAS THERE: JOHNNIE MARSHBURN

The Faces were a great band. I was playing American football then, so by the time practice was over and I showered we were already running late. My friend and I arrived at the concert later than we had hoped. Rory Gallagher was doing his encore, 'Bullfrog Blues', when we got there. I was so disappointed that we didn't get to see Rory's entire set.

After Rory finished, the roadies for Faces went to work. A lot of the work involved placing liquor and wine bottles on the speakers and amps. They took the stage to thunderous applause. Rod was very fashionably dressed and had a drink in his hand. He finished his drink, launched the microphone stand into the air, caught it on the way down and began belting out 'Miss Judy's Farm'. Later on, while he was twirling the microphone stand around, he nearly hit Ian McLagan in the head. Ronnie Lane had to talk Ian into not walking off the stage. The night was perfect Faces. Gritty, raunchy rock and roll with superb musicianship, just the way God intended it to be. We also saw the band cruising by in their limos after the show. I wish I could remember more details but it was 50 years ago!

I WAS THERE: RICHARD MCDEVITT

I was in middle school – or junior high school as we called it then – aged 15 or 16, and already a big fan. The opening act was Rory Gallagher, and he was great, but I was squarely focused on seeing my guys so I was happy when he was finished. The stage set was something to behold. Amps and speakers were white not black, including a grand piano for Mac. And when they came onto the stage, someone – I forget who – kind of cartwheeled across the piano and came up holding a brandy snifter. It must have been Roderick.

I think they began with 'Miss Judy's Farm'. I do remember the crowd was ecstatic! And I quickly noticed that Ronnie Lane was not there... what? Where was Plonk? And who was that guy playing bass? I was not a big Free fan, didn't recognise Tetsu and, though he played fine, I was frankly disappointed.

I remember Woody playing what I would later learn was a Zemaitis guitar and he was amazing. But I couldn't take my eyes off them all. They sounded just as I expected, loose but solidly in the groove. 'I'm Losing You' and 'Stay With Me' were highlights but they were wonderful throughout. Kenney played brilliantly even though, as a basketball arena, the acoustics left something to be desired. The drums sounded great. Mac played and grinned. The time flew by and sadly soon enough they were done... I don't even recall if there was an encore. But I will always remember the moment when they came on stage. I had waited so long to see them. As a kid my options were limited in how far I could travel to see a show, so them being in Durham only nine miles away was like a gift. When I saw my heroes right there in front of me, I was amazed. And then they proceeded to tear the roof off the place. I wish that every young person that age could have a moment like that – it's transcendent!

MOODY COLISEUM
29 SEPTEMBER 1973, DALLAS, TEXAS

I WAS THERE: MIKE MCRAE

Ronnie Lane had left the band earlier that year, but Tetsu Yamauchi was a fine replacement on bass. We sat on the floor, near the stage. We had taken some mushrooms and had plenty of joints. What I remember most is that there was a bottle of whiskey on top of most of the amps. And they seemed to have so much fun, drinking and playing. And sounding great, as I recall.

DENVER COLISEUM
3 OCTOBER 1973, DENVER, COLORADO

I WAS THERE: BOB NAGEL

In June 1973 I graduated from high school and in late August I headed west to attend the University of Colorado at Boulder. As a freshman with no car, I still managed to go to quite a few good concerts in Boulder and Denver (35 miles away). Rod Stewart and the Faces were booked for a concert at the Denver Coliseum so a new friend and I hitchhiked there from Boulder. This show, just like the one in May, was a rock and roll delight, with one significant difference. Ronnie Lane had quit the band and was replaced by Tetsu Yamauchi. This didn't impact the show much, and it can be debated whether the band was better or worse with this change. I don't remember Ronnie Lane singing any lead vocals at the May show.

That was the last time I saw the Faces; they broke up in 1975 but their music still lives on in my car and house.

The album *Live Coast to Coast, Overtures and Beginners* was one of my favourites and I played it so much in the '70s and '80s that I had to buy a second copy, almost unheard of in my music world. In 2005, I emailed Ian McLagan through his website, asking if that album would come out on CD. He graciously replied:

Hi Bob,
Eventually Warners or Rhino will put out the four albums on CD with extra tracks singles etc etc, but not Coast to Coast as that's owned by Mercury.
Cheers, Mac

COW PALACE
9 OCTOBER 1973, SAN FRANCISCO, CALIFORNIA

I WAS THERE: ROGER CUADRA JR, AGE 19

The first time I saw them was October 1973 with Earth Wind & Fire opening and then Rory Gallagher. It was at the Cow Palace in San Francisco, the famous concert hall. Many famous bands played there, including The Beatles. I saw the Stones, The Who, The Kinks, Pink Floyd, George Harrison, Wings and Santana. I went with my late best friend, Brad, and another buddy. It was general admission so we got in early to get close.

I remember it was crowded up front and hot so I sweated a lot. It was a great show! Ronnie Lane didn't play bass, it was Tetsu Yamauchi. Ron Wood was on lead guitar and Ian McLagan played piano. He is one of my all-time favourite keyboard players. They played a great set – 'Miss Judy's Farm' was the opener and they played 'Too Bad', 'Stay With Me', 'Memphis, Tennessee', 'True Blue', 'Twistin' the Night Away', 'Cut Across Shorty' and 'It's All Over Now' amongst others. I also saw them twice in 1975, once at Cow Palace and once at Spartan Stadium in San Jose. Rod kicked soccer balls in the crowd at two of the shows. I saw Ron Wood again in 1975, because after seeing him with the Faces at Cow Palace, I also saw him with the Stones.

CAMPUS STADIUM, UNIVERSITY OF CALIFORNIA SANTA BARBARA
13 OCTOBER 1973, SANTA BARBARA, CALIFORNIA

I WAS THERE: DENNIS DONLEY

Rory Gallagher opened and played a stunning set. I remember for certain that he played 'Cradle Rock', because I remember him introducing it. The Faces were the drunkest I had ever seen a band on stage. (Several years later Warren Zevon topped them when opening for the Grateful Dead, and he was literally booed off the stage, rebuking the audience with a now-famous quote, 'You're nothing but a burnt-out bunch of acidheads.')

The Faces concert coincided with the arrival of a fresh batch of peyote buttons, so that was the drug of choice for the day. How did we know they were drunk? Well, they came with that reputation and gave every appearance of having over-indulged; a real clue to the extent of that was when Tetsu almost fell over on stage. Did it have a negative effect on their playing? Absolutely not – it simply added to the charm of their loose garage-band vibe. They were tight but loose at the same time. (In Zevon's case the alcohol degraded his performance.)

I wish I had kept setlists in those days. I'm pretty sure they played 'Stay With Me', 'Angel' and 'Every Picture Tells a Story'.

LONG BEACH ARENA
14 OCTOBER 1973, LONG BEACH, CALIFORNIA

I WAS THERE: LOUIS VARGAS

By 1973, the Faces were my favourite band and I saw them twice that year, with Rory Gallagher as the opening band both times. By the time they got back to the US in the fall of 1973, Ronnie Lane was gone, which I felt was a shame. Don't get me wrong, they were still a delight to see live. They were just not the same without Lane. At Long Beach Arena, Rick Grech came out and played violin on 'You Wear It Well'. That was pretty cool.

I saw them again at the Hollywood Palladium on October 18th. I remember them doing John Lennon's 'Jealous Guy' at the end of the concert, possibly the encore. When *Coast to Coast: Overture and Beginners* came out in 1974, I saw that part of it was recorded at the Palladium, and I thought how cool to be at a concert that was recorded for a live album.

The Faces return to the UK and embark upon a UK tour.

EAST HAM GRANADA
29 NOVEMBER 1973, LONDON, UK

I WAS THERE: PAUL VOLLER, AGE 15

I discovered the Faces through listening to 'Maggie May' on the radio.

I first heard it played at the local swimming baths in Barkingside. I recorded the song on my Philips cassette player when Rod was on *Top of the Pops* backed by the Faces with John Peel on mandolin. Back in those days, we had to hold a microphone close to the television and hope that Dad grumbling in the background wasn't picked up on the mic. I didn't realise at that time that Rod was the lead singer for the Faces. I played that song over and over. Then my sister-in-law went to work for Polydor Records in Ilford and used to bring home staff discounted albums by Slade and Rod Stewart, amongst others. I used to play them all whilst babysitting for her and my brother after school. She also got me copies of Rod's two earlier albums. Once I realised that Rod sang with the Faces, I started looking for their stuff and then I heard 'Stay With Me' on the radio and was hooked.

The first opportunity I got to see the Faces was at the East Ham Granada in November 1973. I went with two girls from school. We got dropped off and picked up by one of the girls' parents. We could only afford a ticket upstairs in the circle. The price was £1. Long John Baldry was the support act. The concert flew by. There was an unbelievable atmosphere and everyone in the audience knew every word to every song and didn't stop singing from the beginning to the end. It was like a football match. I don't remember anyone sitting down either.

Before I went to the concert, my eldest brother had told me not to bother. He said Rod Stewart wouldn't show up because he wasn't a member of the band.

KILBURN STATE THEATRE
30 NOVEMBER 1973, LONDON, UK

I WAS THERE: IAN LOGIE
In the mid Sixties and my own mid-teens I did not have a firm musical direction and simply embraced everything happening in very eclectic charts of the day, although I did have a strong liking for the Small Faces. When Stevie Marriott announced his intention to leave, a school friend with a father who owned an independent record store called Harlequin Records was able to give me background info on this Rod Stewart

character that was coming in as Steve's replacement. Within a very short space of time, I was hooked on the new line up but had to wait a while to experience it live for myself.

In 1970 I started work, conveniently halfway between home and Kilburn, which the Faces were to make a London home ground on any tour. And the Sundown Edmonton was also part of my regular journey to watch Tottenham home games, so when that became a favoured venue, life was cushty.

All the stories of a night at a Faces gig being chaos are more than justified. No band these days would get away with anything they did. To see the boys live was 'a night out with the boys personified' – the onstage bar, the cases of Blue Nun passed out to the audience, the missed lyrics and chords… yes, it all happened – and more!

One halcyon night at Kilburn State, the band arrived on stage late and in a condition that did not bode well. Starting with probably the most inept version of 'Stay With Me' ever, Rod announced, 'Well we buggered that up good and proper so now let's see what a balls up we can make of 'Cindy Incidentally'.' The fans loved it, unlike today's snowflakes who would head for the doors looking for money back and wondering who to sue for an emotional let down night!

The Faces gave me five golden years of madcap fun and allowed me to meet some amazing people. I wouldn't swap a moment.

I WAS THERE: PAUL BAKEWELL

Where to begin with the best live band ever? I saw them several times in London in the early Seventies, including at the Kilburn Gaumont, Edmonton Sundown, at the Oval supporting The Who and at the Buxton Festival. It's so difficult to describe a Faces concert in words, because you had to be there to fully appreciate it. There was always a buzz of expectation, but the real key was they were enjoying it as much as we were. They were sloppy at times but that somehow added to the charm. Sure, there were better more accomplished musicians and I've seen them all – The Beatles, the Stones, The Who and Zep – but it was the Faces that delivered in spades. They were unforgettable, yet you talk to people now and all they know is Rod Stewart! The Faces are rarely played on the radio or even mentioned, which is odd since at the time they were considered to be up there with the best.

I also saw the 2015 Hurtwood reunion. That was better than expected but was really too little too late. Interestingly, Rod's follow up show was good too when he played many old more obscure numbers. Newer fans walked out in disgust! The Faces career was far too short but so sweet.

'POOL HALL RICHARD'
RELEASED 7 DECEMBER 1973

'Pool Hall Richard', recorded just a few weeks before at Morgan Studios in London, is released as a 45 and reaches number 8 in the UK singles chart.

ODEON THEATRE
7 DECEMBER 1973, BIRMINGHAM, UK

I WAS THERE: JIM WEAVER

I saw them three times at the Birmingham Odeon, in December 1973 and then twice in November 1974. All three gigs followed the same pattern; meet up with mates in the closest pub to the gig, down three or four pints to get 'loosened up', get to the gig, join in with the crowd singing before the Faces came on – usually 'Rodneee, Rodneee' – and then the strains of David Rose's 'The Stripper' would blare out across the PA and on would walk the band to deafening noise from a raucous crowd.

At the '73 gig, Rod fell flat on his face as he made his way across to the mic stand – unbelievable, but a complete hoot. The Faces would basically whip the crowd up into a frenzy and much tartan scarf-waving (I had one of the long ones like Rod would wear) and congregational singing would ensue, along with falling off the seat once or twice during the gig. What used to irritate me, though, was when Rod would say, 'We got a long way to go, plenty more numbers to perform,' or words very similar and then we'd get two more songs and we'd hear 'we'll meet again, don't know where', etc. and then they were gone. No encores – that was it.

For the first gig in '74, I had purchased (at some considerable cost) a pair of brilliant white platform shoes and wore them for the first time to the Faces gig. I attended the gig wearing an almost white suit, white shirt, tartan scarf, newly highlighted spiky hair and white shoes. On inspection of the shoes the morning after, to my horror I noticed that they were more akin to looking like zebra shoes. Needless to say, they went straight into the bin!

QUEENS HALL
8 DECEMBER 1973, LEEDS

I WAS THERE: PHILIP MARTIN HOLMAN

I recall liking the singles 'Maggie May' and 'You Wear It Well', the latter encouraging me to buy my very first LP, *Never A Dull Moment*. This would be the summer of '72. I had been working that summer as a 16-year-old and got the money to start buying my own stuff. *Never A Dull Moment* was quickly followed by *Every Picture Tells A Story* and *Gasoline Alley* as I tried to pick up Rod's back catalogue. With my record collection growing with other genres, with LPs by such bands as Yes, Pink Floyd, ELP and The Who, the Faces remained a favourite for two or three years and I collected most of Rod's albums as they were released.

The favourite moment however was 8th December 1973, when the Faces UK tour came to the Queens Hall in Leeds. It was an underground car park with a stage. Concert columns could block the view. The standing surface was tarmac. Dead grotty, as George Harrison would say. But what an absolute joy. Rod was joined by Ronnie Wood (who I later saw with the Rolling Stones at Earls Court), Ian McLagan, Tetsu Yamauchi on bass (which was a shame, as I was hoping for Ronnie Lane) and Kenney Jones on drums, who I later saw many times with The Who following the untimely death of Keith Moon.

There was a huge feelgood factor about the concert, with plenty of tartan due to Rod's affiliation with Scotland. The tendency was to wear scarves around your wrist like the football supporters did in those times. The band came on with a load of footballs and kicked them into the crowd, returning them with glee if they found their way back to the stage. They played all their classics and the crowd sang along. The place was bouncing with band and fans almost as one. A joy.

Long John Baldry (who had discovered Rod, busking at a London tube station) was the support act. He was obviously a legend in his own right but the crowd was desperate for the main event. It's difficult to remember the set list as it was so long ago but they played the favourites such as 'Maggie May' and 'You Wear It Well' along with 'Cindy Incidentally', 'Angel' and 'Stay With Me', interspersed with blues numbers such as '(I Know) I'm Losing You', 'I Wish It Would Rain' and Etta James' 'I'd Rather Go Blind'.

It went on so long that we missed the train back to Bingley. We could only get to Shipley and then had to hitchhike the last three miles, getting home after 1am. But what a night. Happy days.

I WAS THERE: GRAHAM TAYLOR
It was £2.50 to get in. The band came on late after support from Long John Baldry but it was a stonking set!

I WAS THERE: NETTY WATTS
My husband, who was a big fan of Rod, and his friend queued all night for tickets, only to get moved on because a fight broke out and someone got stabbed. But they rejoined the queue and were able to get tickets. It was a fabulous night. I had recently had my son, who we named Ian Stewart, and I remember that Rod wore turquoise lycra. We went with my lifelong friend, Dave Mackenzie, and the concert was just beyond our wildest dreams.

I WAS THERE: PAUL RHODES
What a concert. I got a football but had to give it to a mob of girls!

I WAS THERE: BEVERLEY MIDDLETON, AGE 15
1973 was my year of daring to say 'fuck off school', so I decided to nick off school and go to Jumbo Records in Leeds on the train from Harrogate to buy tickets for Rod Stewart and the Faces. My hero was more important than school!

Dressed in a tartan outfit my mate had made, and which I'd borrowed (my mum liked Rupert Bear, so as a child most of my clothes were tartan, but these were much too small for me by this time), I got to the Queens

Hall and nipped into the queue with school friends who had been there since school finished.

Once inside the Queens Hall, it was a free for all but I eventually got to the front eventually. Long John Baldry came on first – good stuff – and then in a load of colour (no tartan) and all satin, lurex and footballs, Rod Stewart made his entrance.

The feeling was electric and the crowd went crazy. I only remember a few of the songs they played, 'Maggie May' being one of them. I got to the front of the stage and the roadies could see I was getting totally crushed. It was mayhem, and if I'd stayed where I was, I wouldn't be here now. I was hoping Rod might pick me out, but Ronnie Wood did. I'm a 'Mandolin Wind' fan and love a bit of tartan, but it was great to see Ronnie Wood playing. Of course, it was a new line up so not many of the old faces…

Rod, dressed in his satin and lurex, started kicking footballs off the stage. I'm sure it was cringe for the rest of the band. I didn't buy any merchandise. I was too tight, being a Yorkshire girl, and I had to get a train home with the rest of the tartan hordes. I've never worn tartan since. I didn't want to overdo it, as the Bay City Rollers were on the scene…

EMPIRE THEATRE
9 DECEMBER 1973, LIVERPOOL, UK

I WAS THERE: ALAN MCGINNITY, AGE 11

I was in my first year of senior school in Prescot and the first in the class to go to gigs. I went to the Faces with Tim Radleigh, who was two years older than me. My dad took us there and his dad took us home. Rod was wearing what looked like a blue chiffon number. Tetsu was on bass, and just about the only song I knew was 'Stay With Me'.

I WAS THERE: STEPHEN WALSH

After seeing them at Liverpool Stadium, I saw them again about a year later at the Empire in Liverpool. There was no Ronnie Lane this time – they were slick, loud and very flash, especially Ron Wood's Zemaitis guitars. The first gig was light-hearted in comparison. It was still like seeing the Stones but with a sense of humour, only by the time of the

Empire gig they were a slick backing band for Rod. It was still a great gig, but missing the light and shade of Ronnie Lane's input.

I WAS THERE: PAM LAKE

My friend Judith already had a couple of the singles, and then we bought 'You Wear It Well'. *Every Picture Tells a Story* was the big one for us. It was probably the first album that I absolutely loved. I remember all the tracks and everything.

I remember having to queue up for tickets for me and Judith, because she had started working and couldn't go for tickets herself. The second time I saw them, at Belle Vue in Manchester, her dad took me, her, her brother and his friend. Because we were quite young, only 14 or 15, her dad sat in the car and waited for us. We were very excited. We'd not been to Manchester before.

The music was so rocky it was great. They were the best band I ever saw live, without a doubt. There was emotion. They were chaotic and ridiculous, but huge fun and really musical. They were one of those bands that was a compilation of all the right people in all the right places at the same time; all talented guys individually but together they did something different. I don't know why we took to them. There was always lots of lads there and they were a bit 'Moddy', but I was never really a Mod. None of our friends liked them. But then I was never one who did what you were supposed to do. Donny Osmond was never my thing.

I don't remember being surprised the Faces were splitting, because we always knew Rod was gonna go out on his own. I think we thought it was a bit disloyal but we weren't broken-hearted. I loved Ronnie Lane too, and I saw him with Slim Chance at Liverpool Stadium, another amazing show. And I thought Ian McLagan was gorgeous. He superseded Rod for me.

FREE TRADE HALL
11 DECEMBER 1973, MANCHESTER, UK

I WAS THERE: PHILIP MAHON

The next show was a real cracker, 11th December 1973 and back at the Free Trade Hall. The support was Long John Baldry who was superb, with the late, great Sam Mitchell on slide guitar. They played a stunning version of Robert Johnson's 'Come on in my Kitchen' and even played 'Gasoline Alley', which was on Baldry's latest album.

The Faces entered to their usual 'Stripper' theme tune and kicked off with 'It's All Over Now'. If there is one thing I am consistent about, it is the best three rock 'n' roll songs I have seen live; 'Pool Hall Richard' is up there. What a night! Another point worthy of note is that part way through the concert Rod brought Denis Law on to the stage. The place erupted and rightly so when you consider the Lawman's status with both Manchester football teams. This was the night when Rod was awarded a gold disc for *Sing It Again, Rod*. This, I believe, was at a party in the Midland Hotel. An ex-girlfriend procured photos from the *Manchester Evening News*.

I WAS THERE: IAN RAGSDALE

I first saw them in 1973 at Manchester Free Trade Hall. I had a long Stewart tartan scarf and saw a fan with a Faces badge through his nipple! Denis Law came on and kicked balls into the crowd.

In '74 I went with a mate to see them again at Belle Vue, Manchester. There was no bus back so we spent the night at Piccadilly bus station and an all-night cafe with some lads from Yorkshire. I saw them again in '74 at the Buxton Festival, where I had a brief conversation with Rod at the side of the stage. They brought a white Steinway on stage for Ian McLagan.

I've seen Rod Stewart a few times in the last ten years, including what was left of Rod and the Faces at Hurtwood Park Polo Club in Surrey in 2015. I've been a big Faces fan all my life.

I WAS THERE: TONY RAINE

By mid-1973, I had dropped out of college and was working full time in a local record shop and going to concerts every chance I got; Bowie, Mac, Slade, Quo, Hawkwind, Mott, Heep, Yes, Lindisfarne, Curved Air and anything else that appeared locally. I was also (part time) dating a great girl who was a music fan but a bit older than me and hard to impress. That autumn, I saw The Who at Belle Vue in Manchester and travelling to Manchester, Liverpool and Blackpool for gigs was becoming a regular occurrence.

In November, I finally got a real date with the object of my affection by agreeing to take her and a friend to see the Faces at Manchester Free Trade Hall. My girl was mad about Rod Stewart at this time and while I had maintained a distanced interest in them, I was still curious to see them live.

The show that night changed my whole life. I had never seen such onstage energy, antics and great rock and roll – and a bunch of guys just having a bloody good time! From the opening notes of 'The Stripper', when front row audience members were lining up bottles of booze on the edge of the stage, to Rod and Woody looning around with Mac at the piano, the whole thing looked totally chaotic and yet totally entertaining. What I remember most was the feeling of inclusion of the audience in the lunacy. The Faces could throw a party like no other band and leave the audience feeling happy to be alive! This was a real change from most of the hard rock and heavier concerts I'd seen.

The sense of optimism and 'fuck them if they can't take a joke!' that that concert inspired in me has never left and has stood me well in my career as a concert producer. Every show I have worked or attended in all the years since has me looking for a bit of that magic. To see Rod Stewart bow down before footballer Denis Law that night, kicking balls to the crowd and joining the Tartan Army in singing 'Maggie May' was truly inspirational. I think the selection of songs in those days, from Sam Cooke and Temptations soul classics to Stones' covers and Faces and Rod's hits, showed a deep knowledge and respect for the music that had influenced the Faces. Those choices, both live and on record, made me dig deeper into the roots and history of popular music and still do.

I dated the girl for a little while after that but her heart was already given to Rod so I moved on. But I soon chopped my hair and began my quest to find a way into the music business.

OPERA HOUSE
12 DECEMBER 1973, BLACKPOOL, UK

I WAS THERE: ROBERT BOSWELL, AGE 16

I went to the gig in 1973 with two other people. I have many fond memories of the evening. The first think I remember was the support act. This was Long John Baldry and his band. Looking back, he was a fine blues singer but at the time the audience, myself included, were quite young and waiting for the 'pop' star, Rod Stewart. I sensed some boredom on the part of the audience during Baldry's performance and the best that can be said is that he was greeted with polite clapping, although I do remember enjoying his rendition of 'It Ain't Easy'.

The atmosphere changed when Rod and the Faces went on stage. It became one of bonhomie, drunkenness and audience participation. We all rushed to the front and the three of us were within feet of the band. I remember one fan passing McLagan a bottle of whisky, from which Mac took a drink. The bottle disappeared and the fan latter asked for the bottle back but McLagan said it was gone. Rod looked smaller than I imagined, and had a rather large nose. He did openly encourage people onto the stage who he then embraced before they were taken off by the security guards. He seemed to thoroughly enjoy becoming close to the audience.

Ron Wood also liked to get close. However, he was smoking and at one point spat a cigarette out and kicked the still-lit butt end right into the audience. Even then, I thought this was stupid as it could have gone into someone's eyes and resulted in some damage. But health and safety then was not what it is today. All I remember about Yamauchi and Kenney Jones was that they stayed at the back and looked somewhat disdainfully at the antics at the front.

Cigarettes apart, it was an excellent evening and one I fully enjoyed. I do wonder how drunk the band members were because the performance of all the band members was exceptional. It might all have an act just put on for effect. Either way it was a fully enjoyable evening.

APOLLO THEATRE
15 & 16 DECEMBER 1973, GLASGOW, UK

I WAS THERE: DEREK KEITH

I saw them again in 1973 and 1974. In 1973, myself and two guys called Charlie Downie and Alistair (Ally) Coupar headed off to see them at the Glasgow Apollo. The problem that night was not getting to Glasgow by train, but getting back at a certain time. If I remember rightly, all trains and buses were going on strike at 8pm but we were only interested in getting to the concert and would deal with getting home later!

The band came out to 'The Stripper' tune and I'm sure Rod was drunk, as he fell on his back when he came out on stage. But he managed to introduce Tetsu to the crowd. After the concert, we met a guy from Dundee so got a lift from him in an old Ford Corsair which we had to push out of Glasgow. Then we walked to Tealing, where we found a bus shelter with the intention of sleeping in it that night, but ended up clubbing together to get a taxi home.

ODEON THEATRE
17 DECEMBER 1973, NEWCASTLE-UPON-TYNE, UK

I WAS THERE: JOHN LOGAN

My next Faces gig was in December 1973 at the Odeon. With a capacity of 3,000 it was a larger venue than the City Hall. Long John Baldry, Rod's old mentor, was support. There were overnight queues for tickets this time, but these were always good natured and seemed part of the deal to get a precious ticket. I had seen David Bowie on his *Ziggy* tour and the Rolling Stones earlier that year, but they were not in same league as the Faces as a live event. I later heard they had grossed £100,000 for their UK December tour, the highest of any band that year, and that they were the second biggest attraction of the Seventies, behind the Stones. Considering they were really only around for five years as a UK touring band, that's a huge accolade.

WINTER GARDENS
19 DECEMBER 1973, BOURNEMOUTH, UK

I WAS THERE: DENNIS ROCK

It was like a party with posters and balloons handed out to the audience. They played past 11.00pm and the management pulled the plug on their electricity!

GRANADA THEATRE
20 DECEMBER 1973, SUTTON, UK

I WAS THERE: KEVIN MCNALLY

I remember queuing up at Lewisham for eight hours with my mate Steve. We didn't think there would be any left but we got four tickets. My reward was a ticket to see Led Zep at Earls Court. When I saw the Faces at Sutton it was a lot easier – I think I got tickets without any queue. I also saw them at Edmonton. I was 15. My mate Ralph got the tickets and it was a bit of a problem getting in as my ticket had been ripped in half. I was as drunk as a skunk and threw up as I was hanging over the railings, but it did me well in the end as I sobered up to enjoy one hell of a gig, with Rod kicking out footballs at the end. Great times.

I WAS THERE: COLIN BAKER

I guess there is only one place to start, which is where it all began… It was Saturday 2nd October 1971. I had bought Rod Stewart's 'Maggie May'/'Reason to Believe' that morning and was off to my mate's house for a small party with a couple of mates and some girls from school. I was 15 years old and was besotted with girls. One of my heart throbs, Alison, was at the party. It took me some while to pluck up the time to talk to her, but when I did, I asked her what she had done that day. 'I was up the High Street, and bought that great record by Rod Stewart,' she said. It was a sign, and the beginning of a love affair that still lives on to this day for both of us, and I believe it will until death do us part.

Alison loved Rod (and still does) as all girls seemed to. 'Well', I thought, 'I guess if a guy with that sort of hooter can get so much attraction, then there's hope for me!' As our relationship grew, so did the delving into everything around Rod and the Faces, including their albums. It was the Faces albums that appealed to me, although the first major gig I had been to see was Status Quo at The Greyhound in Croydon in early 1971. I fell in love with them at the time, but that rather died in 1977.

The urge for all things Rod and the Faces had me hunting for posters. I found three great ones down Petticoat Lane that Alison hung on her bedroom walls. We kept them for a long time and I thought they were in the loft, but I can't find them. But there is a lot of junk up there…

TELL EVERYONE: A PEOPLE'S HISTORY OF THE FACES

I had never considered taking Alison to a concert, but in 1972 we did venture to see Nazareth (she didn't like them) and Quo in Croydon (ditto). That must have stopped me searching for where the Faces might have been playing. If only we had the internet back then. I wasn't a big buyer of *Sounds* or *Melody Maker*, so failed to learn that the Faces had played in Croydon and in Sutton, local to me.

A year on and our dream came knocking. The Faces, sadly no longer with Plonk, were to play Sutton Granada on Thursday 20th December 1973. I had to go to work the day the tickets went on sale so I was reliant on Alison's brother Neil to buy our tickets. He queued with his school friend Trevor and, for the extortionate price of £1.50 each, got us our four tickets in the balcony.

How much do I remember so far back? It's slightly difficult to recall, but it was an experience I had never had before. Plus it wasn't only me. Alison also got the buzz…

As you looked down at the tartan hordes swaying and singing, it was like a football stadium. The atmosphere was almost a distraction, but the music blew me away, from the crowd singing 'Angel' to the fast and brilliant 'Stay With Me'. But nothing sticks more in the memory than their most recent release, 'Pool Hall Richard', although the masterfully melancholic 'I Wish It Would Rain' from the flip side of that single came close. The band were in full throttle.

They had been on stage for some time when, mid-song, Rod pointed into the crowd where there was some form of disturbance or scuffle and said, 'Any more of that and we are pissing off.' It was almost a cue to end what had been an amazing performance, because soon after they left the stage. I don't recall an encore, but it is now more than 45 years later. As we left what was our local cinema, the crowd were still swaying and singing as the adrenalin of what we had just witnessed created a party atmosphere on the streets.

I kept my ticket stubs in my wallet for some years after, only to foolishly leave my wallet at the petrol station just down from where the Granada was. Once I realised and doubled back, the people at the station claimed not to have seen it. There would not have been much money in the wallet, but the greatest loss has always been those two ticket stubs.

TELL EVERYONE: A PEOPLE'S HISTORY OF THE FACES

I WAS THERE: DAVID DALE

I saw Rod and the Faces at the Granada in Sutton back in December '73. I had just started going out with the girl I later married and she talked me into queuing up to get tickets, the only problem was it was an all-nighter. At about three in the morning, we got dragged into the police station opposite and asked what we were doing. When we told him, the copper didn't know who Rod Stewart was, but they gave us a cup of tea. When we got back out, someone had taken our place. It didn't matter as we got front row seats anyway. It was the first gig I'd been to, and we had a great time. True to form in those days, the Faces turned up an hour late.

David Dale and his girlfriend Caroline (later his wife) were Faces not Monkees fans

My wife died in 2015, but she would laugh to find someone was taking an interest in Rod and the Faces as they were such a big part of our early courtship.

I WAS THERE: ROBERT FROGLEY

During a period of intense study for our O levels in 1973, a few schoolfriends and I bunked off double English to queue for tickets for the gig at Sutton's Granada Cinema. At our next English lesson, we confessed and the teacher asked us if we felt that missing a valuable lesson for the sake of pop music tickets was worth it? We said that we thought it was, as we were unlikely to ever have another opportunity and, to her credit, she agreed.

Rod had just released 'Angel' and my abiding memories are of a huge illuminated angel on the wall behind the band – and the great music! And we did all achieve passes in the exams.

I WAS THERE: JOHN GRAY, AGE 13

I have been a Rod Stewart and Faces fan since September 1971, aged

11, and saw the band twice. It was on a cold Autumn morning in 1973 that I discovered the Faces would be playing just a mile down the road from where I lived. I was a paper boy waiting for my paper round to be made up when I spotted on the front cover of *Sounds* that the Faces would play the Sutton Granada on 20 December! I went home after my round and begged my mum to allow me to go. I was just 13. Not many people I knew at school were into the Faces, mostly it was Slade and T.Rex plus Sweet, Mud, Gary Glitter, etc. I never really rated any of them. But there was one mate I'd had since primary school and he agreed to come with me, despite seeming a bit reluctant to part with his £1.50 for the ticket.

I vividly remember entering the venue and noticing that most there were a few years older than me, probably in their mid to late teens. I was seated in the circle. Long John Baldry was billed as support but for some reason that I cannot recall he did not turn up and was replaced by another band that no one seemed very interested in. The excitement was total. I was wearing a Rod Stewart t-shirt and a tartan scarf. The door people remarked 'we've got some real teeny boppers here tonight' as me and my friend entered. I remember not being pleased at being described as such. I was a bit of a musical snob even at that age!

The band came on to the sounds of 'The Stripper' and I remember the entire stalls looked like a sea of tartan. Starting with 'It's All Over Now', I was amazed at how loud it was. I'd been to the venue many times, taken by my parents to see films like *Oliver!* and *The Sound of Music*, and expected the volume to be at a similar level. I was completely hypnotised by the band and, to this day, that night is the nearest I have ever come to what felt like an out of body experience. I was in a complete trance – nothing that had happened that day at school mattered and the next day at school seemed like light years away. The band finished with 'Pool Hall Richard'. Even up in the circle it was loud, and by the middle of the gig everyone was on their feet. It remains to this day the best gig I've ever been to. When I got home that night and went to bed, my ears were ringing.

I started the *Smiler* fanzine in 1981 which is still going strong although I now have little direct involvement.

I WAS THERE: BARRY MILLAM

It was so long ago – 1973 – and my memory is awful. The first time I saw them was at the Sutton Granada in Surrey and the second time was at the Lewisham Odeon. I remember the band being as drunk as us lot in the audience. They were never the tightest band in the world anyway, but for sheer party style fun the Faces were second to none. I was a massive fan back then, as were a lot of my mates at school. We all had Rod haircuts and tartan scarves. I remember when the band came on stage Rod said, 'Hello Sutton... where the fuck is Sutton?' I still regard it as one of the best gigs I've attended.

EDMONTON SUNDOWN
24 DECEMBER 1973, LONDON, UK

I WAS THERE: MIKE STENT

It was around August that I saw an advert for a Faces concert at the Sundown in Edmonton. Having been to see them there before, I knew that it would be a good night. The only way to get a ticket was to write a letter or go to the venue, so one Saturday me and a friend took the train to Edmonton station and did a pub crawl from Edmonton Green to the Sundown. This took a few hours and we were quite drunk when we arrived at the venue. Unfortunately, all the doors were locked and the place was in darkness. After knocking on the windows and doors, a lady appeared and asked what we wanted. We explained that we wanted tickets to the Faces concert in December and her reply was that we were too late and they had all sold out.

Not ones to give up, we persuaded her to open the door and started to plead with her. Eventually, she informed us that although the advertised concert had sold out there was speculation that there will be an extra concert on Christmas Eve and if we wanted we could pay her 'up front' and she will do her best to get us a ticket. We paid her the money (£2.50 a ticket, I think) and innocently left the building to catch the train home and get ready for going out.

I explained what we had done to my parents and my dad hit the roof, asking how could we be so gullible, two drunk teenagers giving an unknown woman £5.00 for a concert that may not go ahead?

Two weeks before the concert, a letter arrived containing two tickets for a Faces concert on 24th December 1973. They were premium tickets, on the front row of the balcony and about four seats from the centre. They could not have been better.

The night finally arrived and I arranged to meet my friend in the closest pub to Harlow train station. After a quick pint, off we trekked in our tartan scarves. The pub crawl started at Edmonton Green and again we arrived fairly drunk at the Sundown, just before eight o'clock. Once 'The Stripper' music started, we knew that the concert was about to begin and then there they were – the Faces in all their glory. Some really good songs were played and the concert was in full swing. About halfway through my friend needed the loo and at this point they were performing 'Twistin' the Night Away'.

The whole balcony was moving up and down in time with the music. Nobody seemed to realise that this could collapse at any moment. We panicked for about two seconds and then started laughing and just carried on.

An absolutely brilliant concert eventually came to an end and we left the venue. As it was Christmas Eve, most of the trains had stopped running and we realised we were stranded. Walking down towards Edmonton Green, our only option was to thumb a lift and hope for the best. After five minutes, a car stopped. The driver wasn't going our way but he was a big Rod fan and he duly drove us all the way home to our front doors.

An absolute brilliant night, but I often wonder what would have happened if the balcony had collapsed!

I WAS THERE: MICHAEL MAYNARD

A gig was to be held at the Edmonton Sundown in London. A mate picked me up and we duly set off. The crowd that was gathering featured many Rod lookalikes with bog brush hairstyles, red tartan loon pants and jackets. It was all new to me; this was only my third gig. The wait was a chore, but entertainment was provided by various ticket touts, programme sellers and merchandise stands. Lapel badges and scarves sold well. Sadly, my money had gone on the ticket and my half of the petrol money.

Once inside the dimly-lit Victorian theatre, the excitement was tangible and after what seemed like a lifetime, the lights suddenly came on and the can can music scratchily blared over the PA and then – bam! – real live scantily-clad female dancers slipped across the stage, showing a leg or two. I knew that this gig was going to be awesome, the reason being that the title of the latest platter was *Ooh La La*, a bit

of French inuendo and a fun title. The gatefold album cover opened up like the centrefold of *Playboy* and featured a girl in full stretch, making perfect material for an 18-year-old's masturbatory fantasy. Cheers lads! The Faces humour was also to be found on the front of the album, which featured a cartooned gentleman in top hat and what appeared to be an evening suit. By pushing down the top of the album, his mouth would move. You can't do that with CDs or an MP3.

The Faces were now more famous, more glamorous and more drunk. I watched every movement. One thing that other bands never seemed to do on TV was move much. But the Faces used to run all over the stage. Rod would run one way, and Ronnie Lane would have to step aside as Ronnie Wood was coming the other way. The stage show was a Friday night knees up down the local pub, a rowdy and riotous affair, only calmed by a Rod Stewart ballad such as 'Angel' or a Dylan song.

I WAS THERE: YVE PAIGE

My second Faces gig. I remember buying a pair of denim dungarees to wear with my tartan scarf as they were all the fashion at the time. We headed off to the Sundown for another night with the Faces, this time we knew what to expect. We were helped to get down to the front by a friend who was once a bouncer at the Lordship pub. He left us there and and retired to the bar.

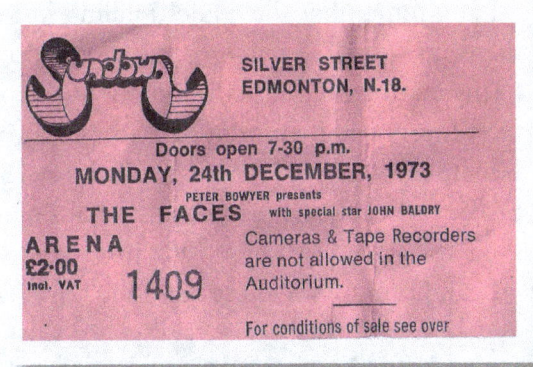

Yve Paige's second Faces show was at the Edmonton Sundown

The band were really late, like hours late. Well, it was Christmas after all. The chants of Rodney and the stamping feet went on and on forever, until they rolled on stage and the party began. The set list is a blur, but it didn't and doesn't matter. I was just having a party with the best band on the planet.

It was a repeat of the first show minus the dear Ronnie Lane and, yes, we missed that happy, jolly, little face laughing out loud. The sound of his laughing and the mucking about with the lads was so missed, but the show went on without him. Tetsu replaced him, but 'replace' is the wrong word. No one could replace Ronnie Lane with his cheeky smile and his humour. Tetsu just stood back and played, although I don't remember him moving, only propping himself up by an amp so he didn't fall over!

We had an organ playing before they came on, and the band were hours late. Their excuse was that they were down the pub. We had the can can girls, which I don't remember seeing at the first gig. I was stood in the same space I was before, maybe one row closer to the stage, and I was wearing a t-shirt and a pair of dungarees. Rod was all over the place and sang his heart out, and in true Faces style we all joined in. Again, a stand out memory is 'Angel'. We all put our arms in the air and swayed to the music, but by the time it was over we were so packed in we couldn't put our arms down again because we were so close together.

I also remember the confetti falling from the roof onto the stage and the front row. I was covered in it. We were so hot and sweaty that it stuck to my face, arms and hair and got in the pocket of my dungarees. I still have a very small amount of it to this very day. Once it was all over, I remember walking – or was I floating? – home down Edmonton High Street with a crowd of thousands, all singing 'Maggie May' at the tops of their voices. What a night! We just didn't want it to end.

I can honestly say these were the best gigs I've ever attended.

I WAS THERE: CAROL ROBINSON, AGE 15

I was 15 in June 1973 when I first saw the Faces in concert. After inviting me to go and see T.Rex at the same venue in December 1972, my school friend Jackie asked me if I'd like to see another concert at the Sundown. I was excited at the thought of going to see another live band. I loved the

TELL EVERYONE: A PEOPLE'S HISTORY OF THE FACES

Carol Robinson was at Edmonton Sundown and now has Rod's trousers

concert vibe and the thrill of the whole experience. I hadn't really heard much of Rod Stewart and the Faces until Jackie told me there was this great band and the lead singer was really good. I'd heard them on the radio and seen them on *Top of the Pops* – I was actually more into David Cassidy and David Essex at the time, and more of the Glam Rock scene than anything else – and liked 'Maggie May', 'Stay With Me' and 'Angel', so I thought 'yeah, why not?'. But my memories of this concert are a bit vague.

What I do remember is the second time I saw the Faces, on Christmas Eve 1973. After seeing them just six months before, and knowing their songs a lot more, I wanted to see them again. My sister Jean was 11 and loved being with both of us and spending time in Jackie's house playing records. She begged my mum and dad to be allowed to join me and Jackie at the concert and, after a lot of persuasion, they allowed her to go with us. In those days, you had to go to the venue to buy the tickets. I not sure if we walked the two miles to the Sundown, if one of our dads gave us a lift or whether we got the tickets from the box office on the night, but we paid £2 for standing only tickets, after paying £1.35 back in June.

Leading up to the concert, Jean and I went to Jackie's house every day after school where she played the Faces albums she'd bought with her pocket money in her bedroom so we could familiarise ourselves with all the songs. We loved every track. On one occasion in Jackie's bedroom, Jackie and Jean dressed up to look like Rod and Ronnie Wood, Jackie holding a handmade standing microphone and Jean with a rolled-up piece of paper in the corner of her mouth, emulating a cigarette. We then decided to make a banner to take to the concert and got some white cloth on which I wrote in big Seventies-style letters 'WE LOVE ROD'. I fixed two bamboo canes either end.

Early on the day of the concert, my dad drove me and Jackie to the Sundown to start queuing up. We weren't first in the queue. The doors were due to open at 7.30pm but we wanted to be as close to the front of the stage as possible. After a couple of hours, Mum and Dad brought us sandwiches and drinks to keep us going. We also took it in turns to look around the shops in the High Road for last minute Christmas presents. Around 6pm, my dad dropped off Jean together with our homemade banner and we offloaded our bag of Christmas presents. In those days, nobody minded anyone jumping the queue.

The excitement was building. At 7.30pm, the doors opened and we rushed into the venue to get a good position. We were right in the front, slightly to the left of the stage. They played Christmas songs before the Faces came on stage and we were dancing and singing along – we were so excited and happy to be there. The lights went down and finally, finally, the concert was about to start.

Twelve or so ladies dressed in can-can costumes came onto the stage and danced to the can-can. They went off stage and the band emerged from the wings. Ron Wood was on our side of the stage and Ron Lane on the other. Ian McLagan and Kenney Jones then appeared and then Rod, wearing his yellow satin trousers and yellow shirt and with a tartan scarf wrapped loosely around his neck, walked onto the stage with a beaming smile. He grabbed the mic stand in his usual fashion and kicked off with 'Angel', one of my favourites.

We danced and danced, singing along and waving our banner and Ron Wood shouted, 'Show it to Rod'. Well, that's what I thought we were doing! We were thrilled that Ronnie acknowledged us. They played all the songs we knew throughout the whole concert, with lots of banter and laughing along the way – in true Rod and Ronnie style. When they played their last song, they left the stage to chants from the crowd of 'Rodney, Rodney'.

Rod came back with a change of clothes, his hair all nicely blow-dried, and they sang 'Stay With Me', one of the best rock and roll songs of all time. When they sang the words 'don't say you love me', Ronnie bowed at us holding the banner... They finished the evening singing 'We'll Meet Again' a cappella style and that was the end.

We left the Sundown with bruises on our stomachs from being pressed up against the barrier. Our throats were dry, we had lost our voices and we were deaf from being quite close to the speakers, so all we could hear was a humming sound from the people chatting coming out of the auditorium. It's a shame we weren't allowed to take cameras into the auditorium. We still have the memories though. Our dad picked us up and we came home buzzing. What a night, what a fabulous night...

After seeing them at the Sundown on Christmas Eve 1973, we were already planning to book tickets for the next Faces concert, at the Gaumont State Theatre in Kilburn. Jean and I were now officially fully converted fans of Rod and the Faces. We saw the Faces in concert whenever we could and of course we were devastated when they finally broke up, but with Rod as a successful solo artist, Kenney Jones joining The Who, Ronnie Wood joining the Rolling Stones with Ian McLagan appearing with the band on occasions and Ronnie Lane starting his own band Slim Chance, they were (and are) still making great music.

I met Rod for the first time in 1981 or '82, whilst I was working for Barclays Bank in Palmers Green. A work colleague Neil knocked on my front door one evening asking if I wanted to meet Rod. Apparently, his dad knew Rod through football. Of course, I had no hesitation in saying yes, and so one winter's evening in the pouring rain, Neil's dad drove us and Neil's sister to Brighton in his Ford Capri straight from work. The traffic was diabolical, which was a shame as we were meant to meet Rod in his hotel room, have drinks and then travel with him in his limo to the Theatre Royal where he was playing. But we made it in time to go backstage in his dressing room.

Neil's dad knocked on his dressing room door and Rod opened it and welcomed us in. I thought I was dreaming. We were all introduced to Rod by Neil's dad and I met Rod's brothers too. The room was full of

Rod lookalikes and what seemed like journalists.

None of the other band members were there that I could see, but perhaps I was just too excited to notice. Rod came up to me and kindly offered me a drink and to help myself to any of the buffet which was laid out on the table. I asked for a Coke and he gave it to me. However, I felt a bit cackhanded as I had a plate of sandwiches in one hand and the Coke in the other. We had some photos taken which I kept in my handbag for years (they're now in a photo album). Rod dashed off to another room to have his hair wetted and blow-dried and then I heard him singing for a few minutes with the band.

The next thing I knew, we were ushered out to stand in the wings on stage. I stood by Neil, his sister and Linda Lewis (the then girlfriend or wife of Rod's guitarist Jim Cregan). She told me to take my coat off and put it with hers on some big black sound box which she sometimes sat on when she wasn't dancing. It was a shame I hadn't had time to change into my jeans – I was still in my work skirt and top – but I wasn't complaining. It was strange seeing Rod and the band perform from the side of a stage, and obviously we only had a side view, but who else can say they danced on the same stage as Rod? When I went into work the next day, everyone sang 'Sailing', waving their arms in the air.

About a week or so later, Neil came into work with a present for me from Rod (via Neil's dad) – it was a pair of Rod's yellow satin trousers. I tried them on when I got home and they were a 'snug' fit. However, they were a perfect fit for Jean, although she never wore them out. They still sit in a cupboard above my wardrobe. Who knows? Maybe they were the same trousers Rod wore when I saw him perform in 1973!

Jean and I met Rod again at his local in Coopersale, Epping a few years ago and he kindly agreed to have a photo taken with us. Jean and I have been to so many of Rod's concerts when he's been touring in the UK, the last one being in Brighton at the 1st Central County Cricket Ground in July 2019.

We saw the Faces 'reunion' in the grounds of Kenney Jones's Hurtwood Polo Club in Surrey on Saturday 23rd July 2011 – the same day Amy Winehouse died (with Mick Hucknall on vocals). Ronnie was a good friend of hers and he announced the sad news on stage. The remaining band members could still perform like they used to and it was, as expected, a great performance. I can't wait for the reunion album. We have been to many many different concerts over the years and seen some wonderful artists, but the Faces and Rod Stewart hold a special place in our hearts.

COAST TO COAST – OVERTURE AND BEGINNERS RELEASED 10 JANUARY 1974

This live LP, recorded at Anaheim and Los Angeles on 17 and 18 November 1973, is released. It reaches number 3 in the UK album charts and fails to make the US album charts. It is credited to 'Rod Stewart and the Faces'.

The Faces undertake an Australasian tour.

WESTERN SPRINGS STADIUM
27 JANUARY 1974, AUCKLAND, NEW ZEALAND

I WAS THERE: SETH BELL

They mostly played songs from *A Nod's as Good as a Wink*. It was the classic Faces line up plus Tetsu. It was a fantastic gig without all the security that we see today. Gigs in the Seventies were notorious for everyone getting wasted. The stand out track for me was 'Memphis'. It's ironic that Rod was in Auckland before Rachel Hunter (who he later met and married) was even born!

ROYAL RANDWICK RACECOURSE
1 FEBRUARY 1974, SYDNEY, AUSTRALIA

I WAS THERE: DAVE NEIL

I was a 16-year-old kid when I was first introduced to the Faces. You could hear 'Maggie May' on the radio. Rod's voice was so different to standard radio pop songs. I knew I was a fan. I was at a mate's place one night, sitting around playing some of his albums, when I came across

TELL EVERYONE: A PEOPLE'S HISTORY OF THE FACES

Every Picture Tells a Story and *Gasoline Alley*. My mate said, 'If you like these, you'll love this one' and out comes *A Nod's As Good As a Wink... to a Blind Horse*. I played that album over and over again, all night long. The following week I went down to The Record Bar, a record shop in Sydney, and lost myself in the Faces/Rod Stewart section. *First Step*, *Long Player* and *Nod* were all on my shopping list. I was a hopeless fan from that time on. Fast forward 45 years and nothing's changed. I'm a truck driver and there is always a Faces or Rod Stewart CD belting out the tunes somewhere on the highway.

They came to Randwick Racecourse in Sydney, Australia. The first act finished – Headband, a popular pub band of the time – and moved off the stage as the lights went down and the stage crew were scurrying about, setting up for the next act. The whole stage was covered with white plastic and the visual effect changed the whole atmosphere of the stage. A roar went up as the boys walked on. Kenney and Ian took their places, Tetsu got thunderous applause as he did a quick sound check, Ronnie Wood was fiddling with his shoulder strap, smoke in mouth, and then Rod ran on stage, slid across the plastic sheeting to the microphone and it was on...

They were on stage for what seemed an eternity, playing all the songs that we knew as well as a few of Rod's solo tunes. The last song of the evening was 'You Can Make Me Dance, Sing or Anything'. It's still one of my favourites. There were 30,000 fans that night, or so I was told. We were not disappointed. It remains the most memorable concert that I've ever been to. The solo riffs on 'Stay With Me' and Rod's sliding around the stage and mic tossing were real crowd pleasers.

They played two more shows in Sydney at the Horden Pavilion before moving on to Melbourne, Brisbane and then New Zealand. I remember the stories coming out later of the antics they got up to at the Seable Town House. This was a motel close to the city where all the big acts stayed. Apparently, there were parties, indoor football, drunken rampages in the corridors... the usual!

YouTube has a good selection of Faces tunes that I sometimes immerse myself in. I'm still a fan. Do I have a photo of me from back then to go with my story? No, I don't. But if Rod and I were standing side by side we'd look nothing like each other...

TELL EVERYONE: A PEOPLE'S HISTORY OF THE FACES

I WAS THERE: PETE WINSTANLEY

I first became aware of the Faces when a friend, Ian Parker, played me two tracks off Rod's second album, *Gasoline Alley* – the title track and 'It's All Over Now'. 'I like that,' I said and was informed Ron Wood played the guitars and both Ron and Rod were in the Faces. So I sought them out and looked through the magazines (a bit hard in Australia in the 70s; *Go-Set* was the Aussie music paper and the English ones were a month behind). 'Stay With Me' and 'Maggie May' were out within months of each other and I bought the albums they were taken from.

I was struck by Ronnie Wood's crunchy guitar style and I loved Rod's voice. Put Mac's piano in and Kenney and Laney (great bass player) and you have rock 'n' roll gold. Glam rock was in vogue but most of it was a bit poppy and/or 'girlie'. The Faces rocked on a bit. The odd article or TV clip I would see gave the impression they were having a great old time messing about with songs.

I recall a clip on *GTK* (a short ten-minute Aussie music magazine-type show) of 'Memphis, Tennessee' with Rod singing into a toy phone and leaping over a speaker to just make it to the mic to sing in time. And drinking and girls and 'going home' are referenced in the song, the very things for me, whereas heavy metal seemed mostly miserable and prog rock was Home Counties woosies singing about elves and fairies? Get lost. Faces ruled!

In 1973, an Australia and New Zealand tour was announced and me and my mate Trevor got tickets to see Faces at Randwick Racecourse supported by an Aussie group, Band of Light. We were 17 years old, still at school with part time jobs. We caught the train to Sydney (we had no cars) and made it to the race course. It was outdoors and several thousand were there. It was a warm night with a slight breeze, a bar onstage and then the Faces strolled on to a backing of 'The Stripper'. Mac boogied his piano, Ron crunched his guitar, Rod threw the mic and it was 'It's All Over Now'. It was... average. OK, it could have been better. The next song was 'I'm Losing You', awful by any standard. Next up to bat was 'Angel', which was not a hit in Australia and which fell a bit flat as hardly anyone sang along. Oh dear, not what I was hoping for.

The next song was 'True Blue' and I thought 'OK'. Then Rod half sang down the mic, 'Long distance information, shall we do that one?' 'Memphis' started. WHOOOA! What's happened? Something kicked in and we are awaaaaaay! We are rolling, rocking, collapsing in a heap, drinking onstage – all the Faces clichés. With an encore of 'Twisting the Night Away', Rod came on wearing a brown jacket and a brandy bottle in hand and said, 'Got someone's jacket on, don't know who's it is but I don't care.'

So the show ended and we were ecstatic. Then we got to the station and we had missed the last train. Trevor had a job as a car park attendant at a fair size multi-storey car park and it was his day to open up, so he had to pay $40 for a taxi home. It was worth it. 45 years later I can still remember that show.

SOUTH MELBOURNE FOOTBALL GROUND
3 FEBRUARY 1974, MELBOURNE, AUSTRALIA

I WAS THERE: PETE BARTER, AGE 20

I was a fan of the Small Faces, though I never got to see them play, and I had followed the transformation to the Faces. When Rod's *Every Picture* came out, it had almost as big an impact as when I first heard The Beatles. I purchased my ticket in September 1973 on hearing there was a Melbourne concert. Unfortunately, I had a serious problem with my heart and was hospitalised for surgery just two weeks beforehand. My op was on January 22nd, and as heart surgery was still very much in the pioneering stage, I thought I would miss the concert. In hospital I wrote to promoter Paul Dainty asking if there

Pete Barter saw the Faces Down Under

was any way he could talk the doctors into letting me out. (They were very reluctant.) He sent me the programme, some stickers and two posters. One poster was massive, and it was the same as the sticker. The other was a very interesting picture of Rod made out of shapes.

I really pestered the doctors and they allowed me out on the morning of the concert. It was a hot Melbourne summer's day, and halfway through I started losing blood out one of my drain tube holes. But I stuck it out! It was an awesome concert and I went back to hospital straight after

MEMORIAL PARK DRIVE
5 FEBRUARY 1974, ADELAIDE, AUSTRALIA

I WAS THERE: ANTHONY DEW, AGE 17

It was February 1974 in Adelaide so it would have been a hot night. The venue is a tennis stadium and looks a lot different now to how it did back then. It is next door to Adelaide Oval cricket ground and the River Torrens runs alongside it. Most of the big acts played outdoor concerts at 'The Drive' and the grassy banks of the river would be full of kids listening for free, armed with eskies full of beer. I listened to many bands that way.

As a kid from Middlesex who arrived in Australia in 1964 with my parents, I was 17 at the time of the concert. I had a sister four years older than me and she and her friends influenced the music I listened to. The Faces resonated with me as they were lads who grew up near where I came from, but also because they always seemed to be having a good time and they played great party music. They were never as technically proficient as, say, Pink Floyd or Yes, but their music rocked! The first album I bought with my own money was

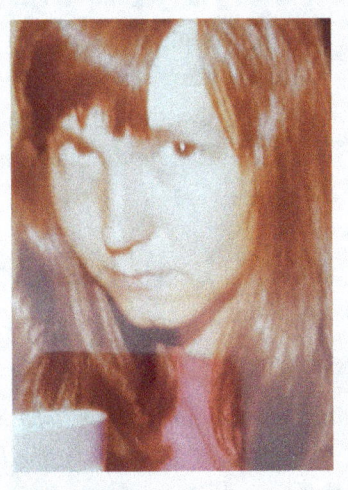

Anthony Dew was 17 when he saw the Faces at the Drive

Coast to Coast – Overtures and Beginners, which I still have. I can't even begin to remember the songs they played that night. I just remember my friends and I had a great night. I do remember Rod kicking balls out into the crowd and a lot of singing along by the crowd; we knew all the words.

HONG KONG FOOTBALL STADIUM HAPPY VALLEY
12 FEBRUARY 1974, HONG KONG, HONG KONG

I WAS THERE: ANDREW PATERSON
I saw them at Hong Kong Football Club Stadium at Happy Valley. It was a staid affair – Hong Kong audiences were renowned for their reserved behaviour although my recollection was that they were playing more to an expat audience than a local one. There was even proper seating on the pitch.

KOUSEINENKIN-HALL
15 FEBRUARY 1974, OSAKA, JAPAN

The Faces follow their stopover in Hong Kong with a short Japanese tour, playing Osaka and two shows at the Budokan, Tokyo.

MORGAN STUDIOS
APRIL 1974, LONDON UK

Rod is working on the tracks that will feature on his next album, **Smiler**.

THE WICK
APRIL – JUNE 1974, RICHMOND, UK

Ronnie Wood works on his first solo album, **I've Got My Own Album to Do**.

TELL EVERYONE: A PEOPLE'S HISTORY OF THE FACES

WATFORD FOOTBALL CLUB
5 MAY 1974, WATFORD, UK

I WAS THERE: VERITY BICKERTON

I must have first become aware of Rod and the Faces in 1971 when 'Maggie May' was number 1 in the charts in both UK and USA and his solo album *Every Picture Tells a Story* was also number 1 on both sides of the Atlantic. Rod and the Faces made several appearances on *Top of the Pops* and I recognised three of his band mates were from the defunct Small Faces. I became intrigued by this fun, sloppy band and Rod's voice, which was at its best then. I was 14.

I began to buy the *New Musical Express* to see if I could learn more and continued to buy it for the next six or seven years until Rod moved to the USA and became 'mainstream'. Sometimes, I bought the *Record Mirror* or the *Melody Maker* but I always went back to the *NME*. It seemed more serious and less popular.

I learned a bit about Rod, his history and previous music and wanted to hear more. I lived in rural Surrey and was still at school, so opportunities were limited and most of my good friends thought I was mad. Eventually, I managed to save pocket money to buy *Sing It Again* in 1973, a compilation of Rod's music. It was, I thought, a very good album. I loved it, my first 'grown up' LP. It had a distinctive album sleeve of a whisky glass. It was very innovative for the time, but it soon came unstuck. I recently saw a copy on eBay for £150!

I began to socialise a bit and obtained a Saturday job in Woolworths. So now I had some money and a boyfriend. He gifted me *Every Picture Tells a Story*, which took my knowledge to a new level. I also met a fellow Rod fan who was hard up and selling some of his LPs, so I bought *Never a Dull Moment* and *Ooh La La* for about 50p each.

With my new found wealth from my Saturday job, I then bought *A Nod's as Good as a Wink*, *Gasoline Alley* and *An Old Raincoat* and, a bit later, *Truth*, which Rod did with Jeff Beck. There's a fantastic version of 'Old Man River' on it, which most people have never discovered.

There was no internet to obtain information from in those days, so all my knowledge came from the *NME* and you could buy slightly discounted LPs by mail order with a crossed postal order. (No one in my family had a bank account, and few people had credit cards then.)

In 1974, Elton John (who I was also a fan of) announced a gig to raise funds for Watford Football Club, of which he was chairman. Rod was going to make a guest appearance and Nazareth would open. I had to go, so poor boyfriend had to come whether he liked it or not. I got two tickets with a self addressed envelope and crossed postal order, and we were set. We had no idea how to get there or back on a Sunday.

My parents (bless them) took us by car, dropped us off at Watford station and said 'see you here later'. I was off, although I hadn't a clue how to get back to the station (my boyfriend remembered). I still have the tickets, which were £1 each. We got to the stadium early and got a good spot at the front, but had to keep moving back as other people pushed in. I think my mum must have given us sandwiches for lunch as we certainly weren't going to move around and lose our place.

By this time, I had acquired several tartan scarves and Rod badges and cut my hair on top to copy Rod. (Mum realised when it was too late!) The weather was dry so we had a great afternoon. Nazareth were good, Elton played a bit and then Rod came on and did three numbers. The first one was 'Country Comforts'. I knew all the words and everyone sang along, waved their scarves and swayed. I had to sit on my boyfriend's shoulders, as by that time we were about halfway back. Rod looked straight at me and smiled so I was happy.

To finish, Elton sang 'Lucy in the Sky with Diamonds', his tribute to The Beatles. We exited the stadium and miraculously found my parents waiting parked near the station. I was so full of myself that I don't think I bothered to ask where they went for the day. I think they must have gone to St Albans.

RONNIE LANE'S PASSING SHOW
MAY/JUNE 1974, CHESTER, UK

I WAS THERE: SANDIE RITTER

I knew Ronnie leaving was coming once he left his wife, Sue, and went to Wales to be with Kate. It was obvious then that he was changing. I couldn't tell what was happening, because I didn't know him other than being a fan and just going to the concerts and saying 'hi' before they went on stage, but it was obvious that something wasn't right. And it's not surprising that he left because he wasn't recognised. Rod Stewart and Ronnie Wood are both very, very strong personalities and they just took over completely. And there were two of them and only one of Ronnie. Kenney just goes along with anything and Mac wasn't that much better. Mac couldn't see what was going on. It seemed to me that Mac was just partying with everybody else. He wasn't a big part of the songwriting in the Small Faces, and he joined the Small Faces later, so he probably wasn't aware of Ronnie's frustrations.

Rod suddenly had this success, and yes, there were problems in terms of what was going on his albums and what was going on Faces albums, but Mac had his life too. His marriage was breaking up and he had a young son. How much attention can you pay to everything? He said he was close to Ronnie but I'm not sure that he was. I'm not sure that any of them were that close to Ronnie at that point, because he was just doing his own thing.

None of them had gone off to live with a lawyer's daughter who was dressing up as a gypsy and living this hippie lifestyle. They were all staying in and around London being rock stars. So I don't think anyone could really see what was going on with Ronnie, and I don't think any of them realised that he had the onset of the illness that killed him. He may have known because of his mother, but he wouldn't have said anything. Ronnie was a very private person. He didn't share things with others until it was essential. I remember saying something to him once, and he said 'that's my business!'. Maybe his brother Stan knew, but it wouldn't have been public knowledge for a long time. And even if Ronnie had known himself, he wouldn't have wanted people to know.

I used to go and see Ronnie play after he left the Faces and I saw his decline. But during the Faces, it wasn't that obvious – at least, not to the audience. I could sense something was different from the side of the stage, but you couldn't really tell what was going on. I didn't realise until later about his frustration at not being able to have his songs on the albums. That only came out many years later.

I went to a few of the *Passing Show* gigs. I went to one in Chester. And I went to one in Reading, after which Billy Gaff drove me back to London.

I remember sitting in his house and we were watching a video when videos were still very new – and the last five minutes were cut off!

The *Passing Show* was great. It was wild. It was wacky. It was just fun. There was a clown. There was a comedian. There were one or two fire eaters. It was quite a spectacle. Then, of course, there was Kate dressed up in her finest gypsy outfit, dancing away. Ronnie was slowly bringing more of his music into it, writing songs and performing them.

Then came Slim Chance, which was really amazing, but unfortunately not too many people showed up at gigs by then. But the music was amazing, and Ronnie had the most fantastic musicians turning up to play with him, including Ian Stewart, from the Stones, and John 'Rabbit' Bundrick from The Who and Amen Corner. And he put out some amazing albums, much better than Rod, because by then Rod had gone completely Hollywood.

If Ronnie had been given more freedom on the albums, he probably wouldn't have left the band. Kate was his first wife's best friend and it was a pretty odd thing for him to go off with her. His wife, Sue, was a very different kind of person. She was much quieter. She had a solo career under there in Geneveve, and she was much more folk-oriented. She was more melodic and not rock 'n' roll at all. Kate was wanting to be this hippy gypsy person. She's a very, very strong character.

When they were living in Wales, she wouldn't even have a washing machine. She insisted on washing all the clothes by hand. That can't have helped Ronnie once he was diagnosed with MS, but he really liked that lifestyle. Roy Harper was a neighbour and they would hang out sometimes. That's how Ronnie ended up on Roy's *Valentine* album.

CRANBOURNE COURT, WINKFIELD ROW
SUMMER 1974, ASCOT, UK

I WAS THERE: CECILIA WALKER, AGE 19

I had the pleasure of meeting Rod Stewart. I was 19 and obsessively a fan. I discovered that he lived in Ascot in a mansion formerly owned by Lord Bethel, so I looked up Lord Bethel in *Who's Who* (this was 1974 and pre-Google and the internet). I asked a guy in Windsor if he knew the house. He said, 'There's the council estate and there's Rod Stewart's house and you have no chance of getting in.' We found the house, drove up the drive and there was a Lamborghini or Maserati outside. Alsatian dogs bounded up. Rod's then girlfriend, Dee Harrington, said, 'Come back in half an hour.' We did. Rod was resplendent in a yellow floral shirt, yellow loons… and carpet slippers like your grandad would wear! He was lovely, and made us all a cup of tea. I was struck dumb so my friends said to him, 'Cecilia is your biggest fan.' He gave us a guided tour of the house, we stayed for over an hour and we left with a signed photo. I got back to Bulmershe College in Reading, where we were all trainee teachers, rang my mum and screamed down the phone, 'I have just had tea and biscuits with Rod Stewart!'

The Faces first live UK appearance of the year is at the Buxton Festival.

BUXTON FESTIVAL
6 JULY 1974, BUXTON, UK

I WAS THERE: GRAEME HARTLEY-MARTIN

I first became aware of the Faces in about 1971 when, at the age of 16, I saw film of them on TV. I'm not sure what the song was, probably 'Stay With Me', but I distinctly remember being impressed by Rod sitting on the stage in front of Kenney's drums during a Woody solo. It was strange and esoteric to me as I'd never seen a performer do that. That sparked my interest, as it did in many other of my male friends. At the time I was working as an apprentice barber and I was soon overwhelmed by a rush of youths all wanting that haircut 'stepped in at the back and sticking up like a cockerel on top', which was of course modelled on Rod's barnet. Subsequently *A Nod's as Good as a Wink to a Blind Horse* was quickly added to my collection, and remains my favourite Faces LP to this day.

The first time I saw them was in atrocious weather at Buxton Festival in 1974 where, perhaps as a sign of things to come, they were billed as 'The Faces and Rod Stewart'. The line-up included a horn section, Tetsu on bass and Rod looking a bit poncy in a fluorescent pink blouse. I was pretty stoned at the time so I don't remember much of the gig, but I know I felt slightly disappointed because there seemed to be a lack of the boozy bonhomie that until Ronnie Lane's departure had characterised the band. Everything seemed a bit half-hearted and the refusal of the group to do an encore led to bottles and boos aimed at the stage.

Over the years, I became more familiar with the band's earlier output and although *Nod* remained a favourite, I still thrill to earlier classic tracks such as 'Three Button Hand Me Down', 'I'm Losing You', 'Had Me a Real Good a Time' and 'Maybe I'm Amazed'.

I WAS THERE: JAN HEDBERG

It was 1974 when I made a trip to England with my best friend, also called Jan, going abroad without our parents for the first time. We went by train. On the ferry from Oostende, we met Maggie Allison. She lived in High Barnet and we stayed at her place for three or four days. She happened to work for a company who sold programmes for the Buxton Festival and she spoke to her boss who wrote us a letter to show the staff up there. It said we would help out selling programmes – which of course wasn't true – but that got us in for free! We had two or three rainy days up there but we didn't mind. It was so nice to watch all the bands on stage, including a lot of groups we'd never heard of, like Lindisfarne, Horslips, etc.

I WAS THERE: TONY RAINE

My travels brought me to more memorable Faces shows in the early Seventies. In 1974, I was working in Bournemouth and saw the Buxton Festival advertised as taking place that July. Seeing the Faces alongside Humble Pie and Lindisfarne on the bill grabbed my attention. The threat of losing the job I had for taking time off to hitch up to Buxton meant nothing. I decided I'd take my chances on still having a job on Monday!

It was wet and cold festival site and I dined courtesy of the Hare Krishnas. I thoroughly enjoyed Humble Pie and the Faces, with the added bonus of the Memphis Horns. The highlight of my day was chatting to Woody, who scrounged a cig off me through the fence.

I WAS THERE: ROY SMITH

The Faces were my first festival headliners. I saw them at Reading but the really memorable event was up on a very windy Buxton moor. It was in the days before I was organised enough to have a tent or even a sleeping bag, so I was armed with just an oversized trench coat and it really wasn't warm enough overnight. Great gig though! I remember checking out the backstage area through a wire fence and seeing Ronnie Wood looking like he was taking some sort of home movie. I have no idea if that footage still exists.

Buxton Festival ad

I WAS THERE: JEFF SPENCE

I travelled to loads of Faces gigs. I remember the Oval in 1971 (God, was I scared of London then) when they supported The Who. I can still remember Rod's leopard print suit! And Buxton in Derbyshire, when they had a horn section that was (reputedly) the Memphis Horns. The main thing I remember about that gig was waking up to a very heavy frost on one side of the tent like it had snowed in the night. The day was decent weather but the nights were like the Arctic Circle.

The sets were lovely and sloppy, with lots of drinking and chucking the old mic stand around, and lots of pushing and shoving each other and moments of brilliant improvisation mixed in with the occasional 'jazz' notes. The introduction of the fairground/stripper lights in the '74 or '75 tour was a great touch that just embodied what we'd come to expect. Unfortunately, something changed about that time and suddenly Rod looked like he'd turned up in a chiffon negligee and said this was 'his people' and not 'ours'. None of us realised that at the time. He was a god by then and couldn't do any wrong, although extending 'Stay With Me' for Woody's solo didn't sit so well with me. That was the '74 tour, I think, and it replaced using 'That's All You Need or 'Plynth' as the vehicle for the extended solo. I also remember that Rod had to direct the spotlights off him and onto Woody, as he wasn't involved in that solo, but the spotlight stayed on him regardless.

The band still slid around the stage and raced each other to the back of the stage and then back to the front. Tetsu was in the band by then and anchored the band far more solidly than Ronnie Lane ever did. But we missed Ronnie and wanted him to sing the start of 'Maybe I'm Amazed' and stick those wandering bass lines in and give the band some of the old music hall magic.

But he was gone, and the band stiffened up musically and became a 'rock' band instead of a 'rock 'n' roll with soul' band. I still have my '72 tour programme and tickets. I have the postcard set from the '74 tour and the tickets for the '73 and '74 tours, and some other bits and bobs, but have lost a lot of memorabilia over the years. I keep all the tickets I do still have in frames.

I was gutted when the band broke up. I followed the Rod solo things for many years but gave up in the end when the rock 'n' roll stopped and the Vegas/*American Songbook* feel became the thing. I haven't been to see Rod since about 2012. I want to see real rock 'n' roll with a five or six-piece band playing a mixture of early stuff but it'll never happen. I go to see bands that have that ol' Faces feel – Dan Baird and Homemade Sin, the Black Crowes (when they were really good), the Quireboys and a few more. I don't think that any band really surpassed the Faces for a rambunctious good time and that after-hours sing-a-long feel. They were unique and sadly missed.

My wife, Mandie, is also a Faces/Rod Stewart fan and we sort of met because her parents had a pub that I used to frequent and we got chatting about her going to see Faces for the first time in 1972. She also borrowed a couple of my posters to decorate the walls in the back room of the boozer where we all used to hang out.

I keep my tickets in a frame at home, just for the memories.

I WAS THERE: MIKE WALTON

My first introduction to the Faces was my mum buying 'Maggie May' in 1971. It was number one and I played it and the B-side, 'Reason to Believe', to death. But T.Rex were the band I was really into at school aged 10. I listened to everything I could though, and one of my mate's big brothers was a massive Faces fan and used to play the albums to us. The first Faces-related record I bought was Rod's version of Jimi Hendrix's 'Angel'. Again, I played it and the B-side, 'What Made

Milwaukee Famous', to death.

I remember seeing a TV show in the same year called *Sounds for Saturday* and was blown away by the Faces' music. Everything about them was brilliant – the music, the haircuts (I've still got mine!), the clothes, the football-loving, bird-pulling image... everything.

I spent more time pestering my mate to borrow his brother's albums and bought my very own first Faces album, *Coast To Coast*, in 1974, and no matter what Rod says about this album, I still love it!

By the time Rod's album *Smiler* came out in the same year, my T.Rex album collection was tucked away in a K-Tel record selector and my Rod and Faces album collection was complete, along with the two Jeff Beck Group albums.

Nothing ever came close to Rod and the Faces after that. Unfortunately, my live memories are restricted to the reunion concerts, although I did attend the Buxton Festival in '74. But due to four cans of Tartan bitter for Dutch courage, the freezing weather (and I mean freezing), the threat of getting beaten up by what seemed to be loads of different sets of football hooligans and standing that far back, I don't really remember that much.

While I was getting memories from other attendees for issue 86 of *Smiler* magazine in 2005, Whispering Bob Harris backed up my memories telling us, 'Mmm... I only remember the horrible cold weather and the mud. So I must have been there.' Dee Harrington, who for some strange reason wore only a thin white sleeveless dress that was blowing about in the horrendous winds as she watched the set, told me, 'I don't think anybody remembers much about that day as the weather was so terrible. I only remember the stage with loads of scaffolding holding it up with the rain and wind blowing directly onto the stage.' But she did remember the drive home with Cyril, Rod's chauffeur, better: 'I kind of remember the day after on the drive back, Rod tying my shoes and clothes together whilst I was asleep for a joke as he was so bored!'

When I spoke to Mac about the concert, he did at least remember playing it, saying, 'My memory of this gig has more to do with conducting the Memphis Horns, who sat in with us that night. We had rehearsed with them the previous day, but I had to tell them which song we were playing and when to come in. I remember it was a miserable rainy night and we didn't have a great show, but I was thrilled to be on the same stage as Andrew, Wayne and James. Andrew and Wayne were The Markays, the horn section from Stax that played with Booker T and The MGs.'

After quite a few false music press promises, my next gigs ended up being three nights on Rod's 1976 solo tour. I was now 15 and getting to gigs was starting to get easier, plus I had now met guys like John Gray, Dom Murphy, Mick Pulchan and Martin Baker and many others who were known as The Rod Squad (later, *Smiler*), great guys who kept the Faces spirit alive at Rod concerts and who mostly ended up being friends for life. I have lost count how many times I have seen Rod live – it's literally hundreds. But his homecoming concert in '86 that ended with the short Faces reunion will always be my favourite ever, and this time I took it all in.

I WAS THERE: JIM WEAVER

My memory of this one is that the festival was out in the sticks somewhere close to Buxton, but it seemed like it was in the back of beyond. It was very wet, windy and cold for most of the day and evening. I thought it was a decent band performance, but with this gig I quite vividly remember that it was only a smallish type of wire fence that separated the crowd from the area that was to the side of the stage. Before the Faces came on, I observed a smallish man with a large mop of curly black hair, who was stage side of the fence, literally dragging a guy who was on the other side of the fence over it to the stage side and briskly marching him off and away behind the stage and out of sight.

I thought no more of it until I saw a picture of the small curly-haired man and it was none other than Chuch Magee III, Ron Wood's roadie. And then I started imagining all sorts of things that may have caused that incident to occur, and what might have happened to the unfortunate soul who had been dragged over the fence.

WE WERE THERE: JOHN HALL AND PETER SMITH

Forget glamping, forget Glastonbury's Pyramid Stage, forget even the most rudimentary amenities; this was about survival. You get the picture. This is outdoor rock and roll in the UK in the early '70s. Following the glory that was Woodstock, everyone wanted the experience and a few

TELL EVERYONE: A PEOPLE'S HISTORY OF THE FACES

people wanted to make a few bucks in the process. So, in the early to mid-'70s we had a series of multi day events, hosted by some unsuspecting landowner, with the promise of filthy lucre. Often poorly organised, and certainly subject to the vagaries of the good old British climate, there was a series of events, some grand in scope such as Weeley, Reading, the first Glastonbury festivals and let's not forget the Isle of Wight. Others were more modest and often forgotten. Names like

John Hall and Peter Smith were at Buxton

Bickershaw, the Great Western Festival (actually a very cool event) and the incredibly poorly named Hollywood Festival, held over a wet couple of days near the not very exotic, and appropriately named, Newcastle-under-Lyme in Staffordshire.

However, to rock and roll aficionados of a certain age, we simply didn't care. Get some good bands in a field which is difficult to access, with no amenities, and we were up for it. It was the adventure, the experience, the journey and of course the music. And so it was with Buxton. Booth Farm, located on the edge of the Peak District, sort of near the spa town of Buxton, hosted three such events. There was a one-day event in 1972, with a solid line up – Family, Steppenwolf, Uriah Heep, Wishbone Ash and Vinegar Joe, all stalwarts of the British rock scene. Slade and Curved

Air were also on the bill, but apparently did not play, with logistics, weather and facilities rather hit-and-miss to say the least.

The following year, another one-day affair took place, with another great line-up at an event also dogged by poor weather, mud, Hell's Angels and more mud. Who on earth decided to hold a rock festival here? So why not double the fun next year – and let's do two days this time!

In 1974, on Friday and Saturday, July 5th and 6th, at the same 'perfect' location, the third and final Buxton Festival took place. Friday headliners were Mott the Hoople supported by perennial festival favourites, Lindisfarne and Man, who were undeterred by a flooded stage, guitarist Mickey Jones saying to the crowd, 'We're all going to die soon anyway.'

With high hopes and much anticipation, my friend Peter and I (plus a group of mates) made our way separately to this ersatz shrine of music and general pandemonium. I drove from the Norfolk Broads where I had been holidaying with two mates, Rob and Kev. Peter had a simpler plan, driving down from the North East of England with his friend Gilly. He had been the prior year and knew what to expect – yet he still came again. He and Gilly arrived on Friday afternoon, finding the place cold and windswept. Not being the most prepared of festivalgoers, they didn't have a tent and planned on sleeping in their MG Midget, or in sleeping bags on the ground.

Seeing lots of people building makeshift huts from planks of wood, Peter asked them where they found the wood and they pointed to a storehouse in the next field. So off he went to retrieve some wood to build a much-needed shelter. He was leaving the store with some planks under his arm with a few other guys when they were stopped by a policeman, who asked where they were taking the wood. He bundled them all into the back of a police jeep and took them off to a temporary police cabin, set up for the weekend. Once in there they were searched, gave statements, made to wait for a few hours, and told that they

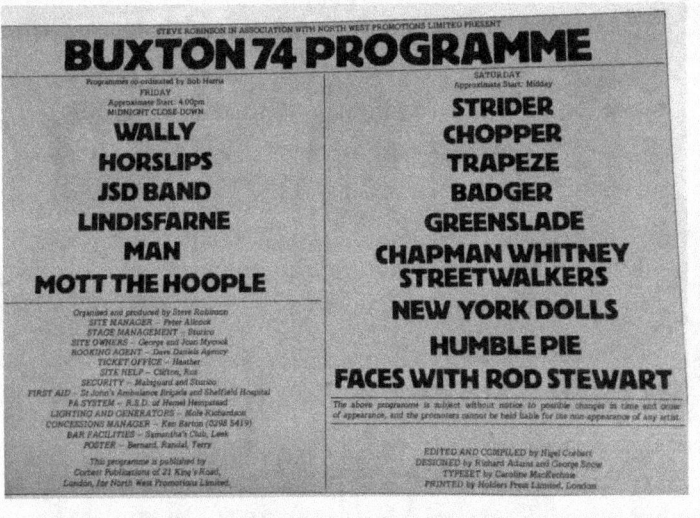

would probably be charged with theft for taking the wood. When the police did eventually let everyone go, they had to walk back to the site. Peter arrived back at the venue to find Gilly asleep by the car. The bands had started by that point, and they went into the arena and caught as much of the show as they could. Peter slept in the car and Gilly slept in a sleeping bag underneath it.

Me and my little gang fared a little better and caught most of the bands on Friday, enjoying a glorious performance by Mott the Hoople despite the grim weather. We slept in my car (actually my dad's car). The weather was cold and wet on Friday, while Saturday was mainly overcast and damp. Mid-afternoon, the Chapman Whitney Streetwalkers took the stage, featuring ex-Family members Roger Chapman and Charlie Whitney. Conditions were not on their side, but as they began to play the Family favourite, 'My Friend the Sun', the sun did in fact appear. The whole audience gave a resounding cheer.

The headliners took to the stage as dusk fell. The band were billed at this event as Faces with Rod Stewart, and also featured a horn section, perhaps a sign of things to come. The set featured material from both Faces and Rod's solo output, as well as the recently released *Coast to Coast* live album. By the time they took the stage, the dyed blonde, spiky haired, tartan contingent was very evident within the previously mainly denim clad rock audience. Many of them had perhaps made the journey on Saturday just to see Rod and the boys, and the ambience became more football match than rock concert. It was a shorter set than usual, and they opened with 'It's All Over Now' before moving into 'I'm Losing You', featuring an excellent and restrained drum solo from Kenney Jones. Rod introduced 'Angel' as 'the Denis Law song' (apparently, Denis was a big fan) and they played the Faces classics 'Pool Hall Richard' and 'Stay with Me'.

Late on Saturday evening, the adventure (or ordeal) came to an end. The crowd threw bottles at the stage when their heroes declined to play an encore. Ah, the good old days…

KILBURN GAUMONT STATE THEATRE
13 & 14 JULY 1974, LONDON, UK

The Ron Wood Band, featuring Ian McLagan on piano and organ, Rod Stewart on some lead vocals and Rolling Stone Keith Richards on guitar and piano, plays two shows to promote Ronnie's solo album.

The Faces play a one-off European festival.

JAZZ BILZEN FESTIVAL
17 AUGUST 1974, BILZEN, BELGIUM

I WAS THERE: CAMIEL VANLOFFELT
After seeing The Faces for the first time in 1971 at the Jazz Bilzen Festival and being blown away by them, the last time I saw them live was at the same festival three years later. The festival was originally started by American and British soldiers shortly after the second world war as a sort of distraction from their daily sorrows, being far from home, and a yearly bonus for the wonderful work they did in rebuilding Europe from the devastation caused by the Nazis. Bilzen is a small town in the province of Limburg, close to the borders of Holland, Germany, Luxembourg and France, and neighbouring bigger cities like Liege, Maastricht, Hasselt and Aachen. So it's very reachable for lots of people, which greatly

influenced its success. By 1974, the festival had grown out all proportion and drew huge crowds from across the borders.

In 1974, I was doing my national service in the Belgian army and I was not allowed to go out on August 17, when Rod Stewart and the Faces were scheduled to appear. But I had an appointment with a friend to go and see Rod and the Faces and there was no stopping me, so I 'jumped the wall' and made an illegal escape from the army. It cost me dear when I returned the following day, as seven weekends without leave was the penalty, but it was worth it.

The friend I'd made the appointment with had an accident that day and was going to be in hospital for a few days, so I went to the festival on my own. I don't remember all the fantastic bands that were on that day. but the last three were awesome – Kevin Ayers played a wonderful set followed by The Sensational Alex Harvey Band who played an immaculate hour and a half show, with girls with feathers in their arse and everything. They were good, funny and hard rocking and earnt an encore. There was talk in the crowd as to how hard it would be for the Faces to top that.

The awkward silence lasted more than 40 minutes before the announcer came on stage to announce that the Faces would be on soon. 'Maybe,' he teased, 'with Rod Stewart.' The crowd began to moan. 'You see,' my friend Roel said to his girlfriend, Rosine, 'that queer is not coming tonight.' Rosine was very smitten with Rod – she got wet from just looking at his picture – and Roel was very jealous. 'They will be better without him, anyway!' he blurted. Like Rosine, I hoped Rod would be there and that the announcement was a hoax.

'Ladies and gentlemen, THE FACES!' screamed the announcer. 'And a hobo,' he smirked. The Faces were, by then, a huge name in rock, certainly in Belgium. They stood in the same category as the Stones, Led Zeppelin and a very few others. The people went wild and cheered. Girls in the front fainted. And it hadn't even started yet!

Tetsu, Ron, Ian and Kenney leapt onto the stage. Three horn players followed and they immediately started playing 'It's All Over Now' before a man in raincoat and tartan hat ran to the white mic stand. He threw off his coat and hat and revealed the broken white clothing from the *Smiler* cover sleeve. It was Rod Stewart. Rosine screamed her head off and Roel watched her with dismay, but when 'It's All Over Now' rolled smoothly into 'I'm Losing You', he could resist no longer. He jumped and shouted and cried and hollered like there was no tomorrow.

Roel was lost, like the more than 20,000 others, in the magic that was Rod Stewart and the Faces. The real girl magnet came when Rod started 'I Wish It Would Rain'. There was fainting, screaming and pushing against the safety people. Rod made it worse by kneeling down and making the girls in the back come crawling over the heads of those in front of them so they wouldn't miss a thing. Some girls managed to run on stage and worked themselves over to Rod, who enjoyed it visibly. Ron Wood played an awesome guitar solo that lasted over ten minutes.

'Time for another slow song,' Rod screamed as they started 'Twistin' The Night Away'. The pounding drums, the rough guitar and Rod's unbelievably powerful voice set the crowd ablaze. Everybody, and I mean everybody, was dancing before the Faces decided to cool things down again with 'Angel'. 'Angel' was slow, heart-ripping and well sung and played. Ian's Hammond organ carried the song's masterful melody only to get cut off and turn in to an overwhelmingly loud 'Too Bad'. My friend, who was in hospital twelve miles from the festival, swears he could hear every note.

'Every Picture Tells a Story' and 'I'd Rather Go Blind' were played as a medley. Then it was time for Ron to do a song of his own. Assisted by Rod, they sang 'Take a Look at the Guy', which ended in a drum solo by the mighty Kenney Jones, at which point all the other band members decided to get a drink at the bar in the wings. Rod disappeared, returning dressed in black satin trousers and a bright orange shirt.

The taped barking of a dog signalled the start of 'Sweet Little Rock and Roller'. That's when the trumpet players came into action. This gave so much power, it was amazing. To my great delight, the next song was 'Dixie Toot'. With its complex melody lines, I was astonished that a band could play this live.

'Stay With Me' rocked the ground we stood on. Always a fantastic live song, this time it was sublime. And when you are amongst people going crazy and you think it can't get any better…

As the Faces played the first notes of 'Maggie May', it was total mayhem. On stage the Faces, the best live band of the moment, were playing, while in the crowd girls were tearing off their clothing, presenting themselves to the singer and the band. There were naked breasts wherever you looked. Rod threw himself on his knees and started singing 'You Send Me'/'Bring It On Home To Me' and the horns were again sublime. As they left the stage in a comradely shoulder-to-shoulder hug, the uproar was so loud my ears nearly popped.

For an encore, they played 'Had Me A Real Good Time', spun out for over 15 minutes, reggae loops and all. When this band left that night, everybody was convinced they had seen the best rock and roll band ever. The Faces were the only band that could challenge the Stones in those days. I think Mick and Keith knew it. That's why they lured Ronnie away from the Faces, in order to get rid of the competition. The rest, as they say, is history.

How do I remember this concert so clearly? Well, I had all the time in the world to write it all down during the weekends that I had to stay inside the barracks as punishment for my elopement. So the army was good for something after all.

UNKNOWN VENUE
10 SEPTEMBER 1974, ZURICH, SWITZERLAND

The Faces undertake a European tour, taking in 19 dates and winding up on 24th October 1974.

I'VE GOT MY OWN ALBUM TO DO
RELEASED 13 SEPTEMBER 1974

Ronnie Wood's solo album, featuring contributions from Rod Stewart and Ian McLagan, is released. It doesn't chart.

SMILER
RELEASED 4 OCTOBER 1974

Rod's fifth studio album reaches number 1 in the UK album charts and number 13 in the US.

MARTINIHAL
13 OCTOBER 1974, GRONINGEN, THE NETHERLANDS

I WAS THERE: RITA VAN DER STEEN, AGE 16

It was 1971. I was 13 years young and every girl in my school was in love with David Cassidy – except me. 'Maggie May' was played on the radio and I was immediately in love with Rod. His voice was completely different from all the music I had ever heard before. My best friend at school said her older sister had Rod's LP and

I had to listen to it! Right out of school, we got on our bikes and went to her house. Luckily for us, her sister was still at work and so we sneaked into her room and then the magic happened – *Every Picture Tells a Story*! Halfway through listening to it, her sister came in and yelled at us. We were in big trouble, and my friend wasn't allowed out of the house for two weeks, so I felt quite guilty and sorry for her, but it was well worth it!

From that day on, nothing was more important than getting that LP, and every penny was saved so I could buy it for myself. When I did, I was in seventh heaven. I played it about 3,000 times and drove my parents crazy. I bought every music magazine, and posters to decorate my room.

Then there was 'Stay With Me' by Rod and the Faces, and *A Nod's As Good…* I had just learned to speak English at school so I had no idea what the title meant. For me it was just 'a nod'. I loved that record, and especially the poster that was included with it. I loved the new music and also the old stuff. I spent my money on everything I could buy. My dad never understood why I only bought music by the same guy, and who had the voice of a crow. The Faces had something extra, that special kind of feeling, raw but with soul. They had fun together and I loved them all, except Kenney, who was kind of strange to me. It was nothing personal – it must have been because he was always in the back.

In 1972, Rod and the Faces came to play De Doelen in Rotterdam and I wasn't allowed to go. I cried all night and never forgave my parents. But two years later the Faces came to Holland again. I now had a boyfriend who was 17, so I bought tickets for me, him and his 19-year-old brother. We went by train, a journey which took two and a half hours. It was crowded outside and when the venue opened, we ran in and down to the front. We were in heaven – it couldn't have been any better. The stage was about one metre high so we could 'hang' on it. There was no security and no barrier, and no cameras were allowed.

I don't know what the opening number was, but it was so loud that I was immediately deafened because we were next to the giant speakers. It was overwhelming but great fun. We screamed and I even had a cry. Being so close to Rod, I could just have pulled him down from the stage. He was wearing tight, shiny yellow pants, a green glitter top and ballet shoes. I loved seeing Rod and Woody making jokes, Woody with a cigarette hanging on his lower lip. The stage floor was messy, with loads of wires everywhere, and I was on the lookout for anyone tripping over. There were glasses of whisky and water on the floor as well.

'Stay With Me' was very special because Rod sang my name. They also played '(I Know) I'm Losing You', 'Maggie', 'Debris', 'Jealous Guy' and much more, with Rod constantly juggling the microphone stand. I was in a bubble and the rest of the gig was one big blur and one big beep in my head, but I do remember Rod ending with the famous words, 'Thank you for your time, and your money.' Then the lights came on and that was it.

My ears were still not working as we went off to the train station. Everybody leaving the venue was in a cheerful mood, singing. We'd had so much fun. We got to the station at midnight, just in time to see the red lights of the last train home disappearing into the distance. We had no phone at my house, so we found a phonebooth and my boyfriend's brother called home. Their parents had already gone to bed, so my boyfriend's dad had to get dressed and cycle over to tell my parents that I was okay but that I was not coming home that night. Neither set of parents had a car, so nobody could come and collect us.

We walked the streets of this strange, unknown city. It was cold and we had no coats, but we were still cheerful and singing. Finally, we found a cheap hotel and, luckily, had enough money to be able to afford to stay there, three of us in two single beds with a nightstand in between. The hotel and the room were very scary, with squeaky old wooden floors and décor from the 1950s, with holes in the curtains and a yellow light hanging from the ceiling, It was like suddenly being landed in a Hitchcock film. I didn't sleep a wink, and kept my clothes and shoes on just in case we had to run, and because I was with two guys.

Next morning, we all had some kind of hangover, me from having had no sleep and worrying about having to face my parents and my boss, and my boyfriend and his brother from having too much booze! We all survived, but my mother did not trust me for a long time afterwards as she thought we had done it on purpose so that we could spend the night together.

OLYMPEN
24 OCTOBER 1974, LUND, SWEDEN

I WAS THERE: ANNKI ANDERSÉN GERDIN, AGE 15

I saw Faces live when I was young. They were quite unknown in Sweden but my older sister had been in England on a school exchange and got herself an English boyfriend (since, her husband of many years). He loved Faces and gave her *Never a Dull Moment* so when they came to Sweden we went to see them. It was a magical evening. They played in a small handball arena called Olympen in the small town of Lund and we were so close to the stage that you could touch them. I've been a huge fan of Rod Stewart ever since and been to many Rod concerts during the years, but nothing can beat that first one. We loved 'Angel' and 'You Wear It Well'.

Annki was 15 when she saw the Faces

The Faces conclude 1974 with a five week British tour, playing what will prove to be their last ever full UK shows.

LEWISHAM ODEON
15, 17 & 18 NOVEMBER 1974, LONDON, UK

I WAS THERE: TONY RAINE

I moved up to London that winter and saw the Faces once more at Lewisham Odeon, right after Rod's *Smiler* had been released and Rod had the USA in his sights. Ronnie Lane was building Slim Chance and I followed his career closely and realised what a major part of the Faces success he had been. That November, I met my wife (an American college graduate) and in 1975 I married and emigrated to the States, my own *Atlantic Crossing*. Since then, I've been lucky enough make a living in the concert business and continue to produce around 60 concerts each summer in New England. I'm still looking for some Faces magic at every show!

I WAS THERE: CHARLENE JAMES PATTISON, AGE 14

I was 14 when I saw the Faces. I had to take my Mum (or rather she took me). I wasn't allowed to go otherwise. I got into trouble for getting the tickets by lying to my parents about it!

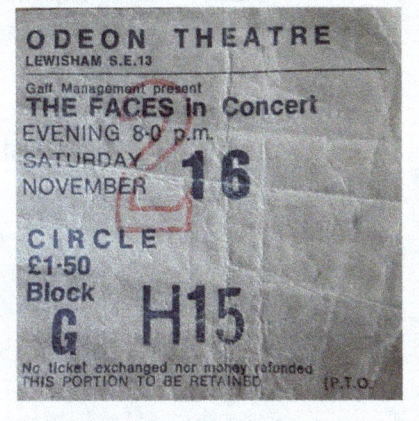

Charlene Pattinson had to go to the Faces gig with her mum

I WAS THERE: COLIN BAKER

I must admit we didn't travel around much. Even at our own young age, we were planning to marry one another so our money was being hoarded. However, when the Faces toured the UK again just under a year after that Sutton Granada show, the nearest venue they were scheduled to play was Lewisham. It's almost a stone's throw away and we go through Lewisham every time we visit the O2. Back in 1974, and not driving a car, the trains were the best option but you had to get to London first and then go back out to Lewisham. I should have talked to my dad more. He was a bus driver, and in hindsight that was probably a better alternative, as after the gig it would at least have got us back to Croydon.

We booked tickets for Saturday 16th November 1974, this time for myself and Alison. My brother's friend John and his girlfriend Joanna had tickets for the stalls, whilst my brother-in-law Neil and his friend Pete were in the balcony area. Being a Saturday, we didn't consider any issues. That was until we got to hear Rod had a sore throat and had cancelled the Saturday date and rescheduled for the Monday night. That meant going on a work day plus needing to go to work the day after. A disappointment at the time of the event, which still rankles a little now. However, it was not going to stop us.

We got to the Odeon in good time. I've never been much of a drinker, so I was not going to fall into the nearest pub like many seemed to have done, especially with my girlfriend in tow. Once the doors were open, and after buying a programme (which I still have, plus my ticket stubs) and a soft drink, we took our seats in the stalls. We had no idea where my brother-in-law was as we had come independently. All seemed calm at first, with very few people taking up their seats, but then as time passed that changed. The seats behind us were initially taken up by a group of lads (or as Kenney Jones would call them, 'herberts'). They would have their feet kicking the backs of your seat, but how could you react? Bill Barclay saved the day, though, because as soon as the action began on stage the herberts were off down the front.

After his short set, we were entertained by the group called Strider. I was very taken by them and enjoyed their music. But I was already becoming acutely aware of time drifting on, and the time that the last train back to London Bridge was due to leave Lewisham station.

The Faces lived up to their reputation of always being late to come on stage. That wasn't a problem when they appeared in Sutton the year before, but knowing you had to go to work the next day and get somebody's daughter home before you were deep into the early hours of the morning was another matter. We got to witness a brilliant evening, which was highlighted by Paul and Linda McCartney coming on stage to sing 'Mine For Me' (I would have preferred 'Maybe I'm Amazed', but the Faces own version of that song has always been brilliant) but then had to make the difficult decision to leave before they left the stage. Only when somebody recently shared a set list of the night did I realise that we only missed 'Twistin' the Night Away' in our dash to catch that last train.

TELL EVERYONE: A PEOPLE'S HISTORY OF THE FACES

The atmosphere inside the Odeon was just as it had appeared in Sutton. Although we didn't rush to the front but chose to stand, sing and dance in our allotted seats, we were closer to the crowd swaying and singing than we had been at the Sutton gig. The singing of 'Rodney, Rodney' and 'we want Rod' was like no other audience I have witnessed since (apart from Rod's early solo gigs at Olympia in the late 1970s, but that was probably much of the same audience that had followed the Faces).

Apart from 'Mine for Me', the song that still sticks in my memory almost 50 years later is 'You Can Make Me Dance, Sing or Anything'. Like 'Pool Hall Richard' and 'I Wish It Would Rain' in Sutton, it was fresh. That said, although not strictly a Faces number, 'I'd Rather Go Blind' always sends shivers down my spine when I hear it live.

Now, with so many clips and some concerts in full on video, you can recall the amazing way the band performed on stage. Their humour and rapport oozed into the fans. If the split in mid-'75 as Rod went solo and Ronnie moved from part-time to full-time Rolling Stone was heartbreaking, it was also inevitable.

The Faces and all their splinter factions left a mark on Alison and myself that still burns today, from seeing Rod perform solo around 35 times to seeing Mac a handful of times, the Jones Gang when possible and also the Rolling Stones, and let's not forget Slim Chance, Ronnie Lane's old band. And The Small Fakers and Faces Experience will give you a set from back in time that is worth every penny, even though it costs 100 per cent more than I paid for a ticket back in 1973 for Sutton Granada!

I always say that if I hadn't discovered the Faces, with all the concerts, records, videos, programmes, pictures, books and trivia attached to them that we have, I probably could afford one of Rod's old Ferraris. But look how dull life would have been. I guess you could call it Devotion… Just don't Tell Everyone…

I WAS THERE: VERITY BICKERTON

After my first taste of Rod, I had to see a full Faces gig so eagerly awaited the announcement of what proved to be their final UK tour that autumn. By this time, the boyfriend was an ex, but I made him promise to come with me to see the Faces. I was so selfish and horrible. I duly obtained two tickets for Friday 15 November from Lewisham Odeon, again with an SAE and crossed postal order. I actually obtained them direct from the Odeon. There was no middle person taking a large booking fee. The tickets were £1.50 each and I still have them, and the programme.

Mum and Dad decided they would take us. How Dad found the Odeon with no sat nav or even a map is beyond me. He dropped us off outside the Odeon and said 'see you here later'. The ex boyfriend and I decided we would go into the nearest pub and, of course, it was absolutely packed with the Tartan Army. We never got a drink but just stared in admiration at all the Rod lookalikes and their outfits. There was a fantastic atmosphere.

Inside the Odeon, we found to our delight that our seats were in the front row of the circle. We could not have had a better and unobstructed view. The concert surpassed all my expectations. It was loud, colourful, sloppy fun and I knew all the songs and sang along. After all these years it's still the best gig I've been to and the one I think of first. I was buzzing for days afterwards. Most of my friends hadn't even been to a gig and thought I was mad.

Afterwards, we met my parents parked up just outside the Odeon. Door to door service! Mum and Dad hadn't found much to do, so had walked into the Odeon, straight past the security staff, and somehow found the entrance to the stalls and watched some of the concert from there. So Mum had a closer view than I had. The security staff were too busy sorting out the screaming girls trying to get on the stage to challenge my parents. So Mum had a tale to tell her friends. And we were lucky to have tickets for the Friday, as the gig on the Saturday was cancelled as Rod had lost his voice.

The Faces broke up. Rod went disco and then mainstream, and although I have seen him quite a few times since, nothing has been as good as that Faces gig. I still listen to the old stuff all the time, *Every Picture* and before. But there's very little worth listening to after 1975.

I have seen a few Faces reunion gigs with Mick Hucknall, who was good, but with Ronnie Lane long gone and Mac also, and with Rod's voice certainly not what it used to be, it's sadly all in the past.

About 1983, I met Ronnie Wood in a pub with his family near where I was living. He had rented a large country house for Christmas. He gave me his autograph and was talkative and charming. I mentioned I had seen the Faces at Lewisham and he said yes he remembered the gig well. I doubt he did, but it was polite of him to say that.

Stupidly, I got rid of all my vinyl LPs several years ago so have had to get CDs or download old Faces and Rod music. The sound is not the same, and it was nice to have the original sleeves and poster pull outs and hang around record shops, which themselves are now mostly a thing of the past.

I WAS THERE: CAROLYN SIDDALL, AGE 17

I was living and working in London. From the North East, I went to the show alone. I often went to shows by myself. It was all about the music. They were a great group, real mates, and had fun on stage too. But I honestly don't recall any details. I was, and still am, music obsessed and I saw so many great groups. But I never remembered anything, even though I was always relatively sober and very much into the music. I would give anything to see again so many of those unbelievable concerts from the '70s that I just took for granted. I'd appreciate them so much more now.

I WAS THERE: HELEN WILLIAMS

My friend worked at the Lewisham Odeon and asked me if I wanted to work for three nights. I wasn't sure at first until she said who it was, when I jumped for joy. I sold programmes at the start of the evening and then ice creams at the interval, for which I got paid £3 an evening. I was working in the Northover at that time for £2 a shift, so was more than happy. We then stood at the front and watched the shows.

I WAS THERE: LASZLO NEMES, AGE 14

I don't know what it was about the Faces that caught my attention but they stood out head and shoulders above any other artist at that time. Apart from girls, music was the most important thing in my life and the Faces spoke to me in a language I understood. It was so much more than just a band – it was a bunch of mates having a really good time. I mean, what is better than being young and doing what you love more than anything else for a living, travelling the world, playing sold out gigs and sharing it all with your best mates? Everyone in that band was unique and slotted together like a jigsaw puzzle.

I remember seeing them on *Top of the Pops* and they just stood out. They were natural, relaxed and enjoying every second of what they were doing. It was the first time I saw two band members talking to each other and laughing while performing. At one point, a football bounced on stage and the band started passing it around to each other. I was hooked. I mean – they get paid to have this much fun?

Ronnie Lane was the reason I chose to play bass guitar. I had never heard anyone play bass like that. His bass lines were so melodic and off the wall in a fashion that almost said, 'Let's just play and see where this goes,' something that could also describe the attitude of the band he played in. One day, my 'kind of' girlfriend at school told me they were playing live the following month and we should go and see them. I was only 14 at the time and I begged my mum to let me go. She eventually said OK and off we went. I don't remember anything about how we got there, because what came next totally blew my mind.

It was my first live concert and I was not ready for the sheer volume and atmosphere but I was scooped up and carried off. Unfortunately, by this time Ronnie had left, so I never got to see him live, but I was still bowled over by what I had just seen. I walked out of that concert hall thinking, 'Now THAT is what I want to do for a living' and, luckily – I did. We missed the last bus home and started walking. After about 30 minutes, a police car pulled up and asked where we were going. We told him that we had missed the last bus and he said 'jump in' and gave us a lift home. I went on to have a very successful musical career of my own, with many great memories, but that night stands out more than anything and I can still feel the excitement now.

I WAS THERE: PAUL HOWARD

It was the winter of 1974. Me and my mates were 14 and 15 years old. We all lived in Eltham, south east London. The Faces were coming to our nearest half decent venue, Lewisham Odeon, about three miles away. Back in those days you had to turn up at the venue and be prepared to queue for your tickets a few weeks in advance of the gig. We queued up for six hours and the queue went right around the Odeon. By the time we got to the desk inside, we were starting to get pretty paranoid as to whether there would be any tickets left. Relief – we got them and not only that, they must for some odd reason have been selling the worst seats first as ours were right in the middle of the stalls, about eight rows back. Result!

Now the bad news... We duly turned up in our tartan and very excited. We had booked for the Saturday but as we approached the Odeon, a massive banner had been erected saying that the gig was cancelled as Rod was unwell. They postponed to the Monday, a bloody school night! To say we were gutted is an understatement. We went back to my mate's garage to drink beer, play *Smiler* and have a game of pool.

The following week off we go again. We arrived worried that Rod might still be ill but... no banner. Happy days! We took up our brilliant seats and, my God, what a concert. I've seen many, many massive bands since but for me that gig was truly the best. The raw energy coming from the stage was incredible. They were drinking and smoking, as was the audience, creating a blue haze just above our heads. The crowd absolutely rocked. Rightly or wrongly (it was rock 'n' roll), as the band finished with 'Twistin' the Night Away', either Ronnie or Rod thought it would be a laugh to encourage the people in the stalls in front of them to start ripping up the seats. (I'm sure they settled up with the Odeon after). A magical night and time in my life that I will never ever forget.

I WAS THERE: PAUL VOLLER

Having seen them live at East Ham Granada in 1973, I wanted more so I spent the money I got from my Saturday job on the rest of the Faces albums. In 1974, tickets went on sale for the Faces UK end of year tour. There were to be six concerts in London, three at Lewisham Odeon and three at the Kilburn Gaumont State. Very early on the morning that the tickets went on sale, I went to both places to queue up for tickets. Obviously, there was no online

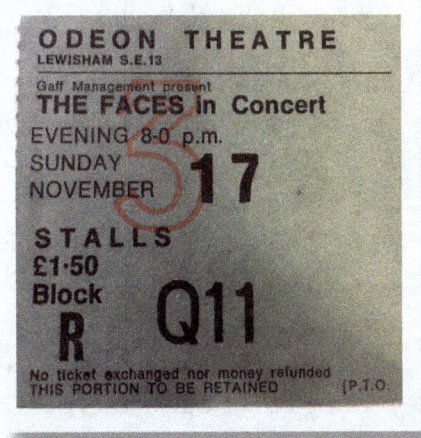

Paul Voller's ticket for the Lewisham Odeon show

booking back then – you had to physically line up to buy tickets – and I got two seats in the stalls for each of the six nights.

Every Faces fan remembers the concert at Kilburn on 23rd December as it was televised a year later on ITV. Keith Richard guested, and it was the last time the Faces played in the UK other than the one-off reunion gigs. However, my best memory of those six nights was the concert held at Lewisham Odeon on Sunday 17th November. I was 16 and I took my younger brother Derek, who was ten days shy of his 15th birthday.

I remember a lot about that concert. I remember the warm up act, Strider. I remember the comedian introducing the band. I remember pulling my younger brother to the front when the house lights went down and getting right up to the barrier. I remember feeling like I couldn't breathe, as every one behind clamoured to get closer to the band. I remember trying to get on stage and getting pushed back by the road crew. I remember my first taste of Blue Nun when one of the road crew handed me a half empty bottle for my trouble. Most of all, I remember the moment when the band walked on stage and opened with 'It's All Over Now' and the place went berserk. I also remember the Faces anthems 'I'd Rather Go Blind' and 'Angel', when Rod wasn't allowed to sing without the rest of us joining in. I came out of there in a euphoric mood, my ears ringing and feeling the best I'd ever felt.

My brother and I decided to go round to the stage door and try to meet the band. We were moved on by the road crew and, as a limo left the backstage area, we were standing on the main road. When it slowed, my brother stuck his head through the open window and had his tartan hat and hair ruffled by Rod. It had been such a wonderful night that we lost all track of time and missed the last train. We walked from Lewisham to London Bridge, got the night bus from London Bridge to Barking and walked from Barking to Hainault where we lived. We were almost arrested in Gants Hill when we were surrounded by police screeching to a halt and emerging from a Black Maria and telling us that they believed that my younger brother and I had tried to rob a jeweller's shop, even though we were wearing tartan with a tour programme sticking out of our pockets!

Because we weren't home until early morning, I wasn't allowed to go to the Monday night show which was a real shame because I heard that

TELL EVERYONE: A PEOPLE'S HISTORY OF THE FACES

Paul and Linda McCartney joined the Faces on stage to sing 'Mine For Me'. In the end I went to five of the six London concerts that year. All of them were brilliant but that night at Lewisham was magical. Still to this day my brother and I talk about that night.

The Faces were at their best when they were live. No one cared when they played a bum note, missed an intro or forgot the words. It was all part of the fun. It wasn't like watching a band. It was like a night out with your mates, where five of them always got up to sing and the rest of us always joined in.

I WAS THERE: THERESA TRIMBY

My then friend had bought me a ticket to see them for my 16th birthday. I was into reggae music and so didn't know anything about them. It wasn't my scene at all... However, upon seeing Rod and the screaming, etc., I passed out. The St John's ambulance crew carried me out and wouldn't let me back in so I had to listen to the whole concert from outside! 'You Wear It Well' stuck in my mind from that night. I was totally hooked.

I WAS THERE: GRAHAM WILKINSON, AGE 12

It was my first ever concert. I didn't think I would get in but I went with my sister and her boyfriend. The Faces played three nights. I wasn't at the one the McCartneys sang at. I remember it was very hot and very, very loud.

Jump forward to September 2015 and I was lucky enough to get tickets to the Hurtwood gig. I never ever thought I'd see them play live again, albeit it was just the three of them. It was incredible to watch them again.

I also saw Rod at the Cliffs Pavilion in Southend-on-Sea in 2019 where he performed in front of just 1,500 people. That was another fabulous night. And I was also lucky enough to meet him a few years ago whilst he rehearsed for three days at the Royal Opera House Production Park at Thurrock in Essex, where many bands practice before going on tour.

I WAS THERE: PERRY RIDLEY

My next Faces show came at Lewisham Odeon in November 1974. It wasn't the show that saw Paul McCartney join the band on stage. I was really looking forward to this gig as I had seen a fantastic David Bowie gig there in May 1973. I can remember leaving disappointed as it just was not the same without Ronnie Lane on stage, and that would be the last time I ever saw them. I was unable to get a ticket for the shows at the Kilburn State in December of that year. I was left to see out the 1970s listening to *Atlantic Crossing* – I cannot stand 'Sailing'!

I've never seen Rod live as a solo artist. I saw Ronnie Wood do a solo gig at the Theatre Royal, Drury Lane in March 2005. This was disappointing in that it lasted just over 80 minutes, and never really got going until Mick Jagger did a surprise vocal near the end of the show. Ronnie was also involved in an angry exchange with someone in the crowd, who requested that he perform a certain number. Perhaps it was one of the periods in his life when the demons have got the better of him. Kenney Jones sat in for a couple of songs at the end and that was a nice touch.

As a Father's Day present a couple of years ago, my son got me a copy of the book by Andy Neill, *Had Me a Real Good Time*. It's a fantastic read and a must for anyone with an interest in the band. It was quite sad and an eye opener the way the band disintegrated, but I look back on those days with great memories, and now have the whole of the Faces catalogue easily accessible on my iPod. My favourite is still *A Nod's as Good as a Wink...* and I play this at least once every couple of weeks.

Paul McCartney had written 'Mine for Me' for Rod. When Paul and his wife Linda turn up at Lewisham Odeon to watch the last of the three Faces concerts there, Rod calls them up on stage to sing along.

I WAS THERE: JOANNE STEVENS, AGE 14

I was at Lewisham Odeon when Paul and Linda McCartney came on stage and sang with the band. It was an amazing first gig for me, and no other since has really lived up to that night. The trip to the gig was organised by the youth club at my school, Stewards, in Harlow, Essex. I remember that it was £2.50, which included the ticket and minibus travel from Harlow.

Lewisham Odeon was a cinema, so it was a small venue and we were near the front. We had never heard of the comedian they had on the bill and he was an unusual choice for support, but he just held us with his guitar, singing, chatting – quite a feat considering that Rod Stewart and the Faces were to follow.

As soon as they came on, dressed in tartan suits, rocking out and singing as if the whole thing was just massive fun, I was hooked. rules in venues were pretty much non-existent then and we were all up on our chairs, jumping up and down and dancing. I have a very clear memory of Rod and Ronnie Wood singing together, with their arms around each other and laughing. When Paul and Linda McCartney came on stage and joined in, I wasn't even that surprised – it seemed just like all part of the magic. I wish I could remember what they sang but it is lost in the mists of time.

Getting up for school the next day was tough but worth it. My next gig, David Essex at the New Victoria Theatre, was such a let down. It was a massive venue so he was just a pin prick on the stage, and the support was useless and no standing up was allowed. But the memory of the Faces stayed with me and I still love live music. Just not in stadia.

I WAS THERE: JOHN GRAY

I was 14 in 1974 and very disappointed when the Faces didn't include Sutton on their tour. I had recently become friends with someone at school whose young trendy parents (in their thirties) liked Rod Stewart. Walking back from school with this friend one day, I stopped at his house and mentioned to his mum that Rod was playing live and showed her my copy of *Melody Maker* with a full page advert listing all the tour dates. I was amazed, as she seemed interested in going to Lewisham and pointed out that Kilburn wasn't too far to go either. Two days later, on a cold Saturday morning, she went over to Lewisham – about 13 miles away – and queued for tickets. I remember she mentioned how people waiting made remarks about her being 'a bit old to like Rod Stewart'. But she stuck it out ('some of those boys had knives' was another remark she made) and came back with circle tickets for me and my mate, his dad, herself and an uncle and aunt. I couldn't believe my luck!

On the night, I was picked up directly from school. My enduring memory of being driven through Lewisham that night is that everyone along the High Street seemed to be wearing tartan. I had a tartan scarf on, and sneaked in a tartan duffle bag in which I'd hidden a Philips cassette tape. I managed to record most of the gig and still have the tape. Strider were the support and passed me by a bit. Then a comedian called Bill Barclay came on. In the five minutes before the band appeared, he whipped the crowd into a complete frenzy. He got the crown chanting 'we want the Faces' which gave way to 'we want Rod'. The crowd sang 'You'll Never Walk Alone'. The atmosphere was electric. Those in the stalls were already out of their seats and crowding at the front of the stage. From my circle seat, I could see police helmets and St John's Ambulance men amongst the crowd. It was chaos down there.

Once again, the band staggered on to 'The Stripper', all of them strutting around the stage to the full song. They started with 'It's All Over Now', and songs from the latest Rod and Ron solo albums followed as well as the latest single, 'Dance, Sing or Anything'.

The gig was a replacement for the Saturday night gig that had been cancelled because Rod's voice had given out on the Friday. 'I'm sorry! I wasn't very well,' Rod said after the first song. 'I know it's Monday night and you lot will be going to work in the morning. But in these days of depression, music is the only way out, surely. I swear to God, I'll make it up to you.' I remember standing up to sing 'Angel', waving my tartan scarf high. When Rod sang to the audience between the chorus, 'I'll never ever leave you', I believed him. And I was right to – because he never has left his fans and, 45 years later, I still go to his gigs. Once again, I had that out of body 'who cares about school in the morning?' feeling.

Paul and Linda McCartney's appearance at this gig is well documented. Rod introduced them as 'my brother with one leg and my sister with the hump back'.

I never dreamed that would be the last time I would see a full Faces gig. I saw the 1986 and 2015 reunions, but they were augmented by so many additional musicians that it wasn't really the same. The feeling you got in 1974 was that it was five best mates making music and that they would never split up. They had a humour that both the glam rockers and heavier bands lacked. They were different. Of course, they did split up. I went on to follow them all as solo artists and in their various bands. And two years after Lewisham, I went to five of Rod's London Olympia dates that were, if anything, even more chaotic than the Faces in terms of audience misbehaviour and their refusal to use their allocated seats. But it wasn't the Faces, and I always wished I'd been born a few years earlier, and that the Faces had stayed together a few years longer.

I WAS THERE: MARTIN DAVIS

I was 14 when Rod hit it big with 'Maggie May'. I'd been fostered out until I was 13. I was a shy and quiet kid; my main passions were music football and fashion. I didn't really watch telly, so when 'Stay With Me' was a hit, I didn't connect it with Rod. Then I saw the Faces on the telly, and that was my band. I even looked at a bit like him, I thought. My mum was trying to reconnect with me and would spoil me with any fancy I took to, so she went out and bought all the Faces, Rod and Jeff Beck albums – anything she could find related to Rod. I was a super fan overnight.

Martin was at Lewisham Odeon

My mum wouldn't let me go to gigs until 1974, so there I was at the Lewisham Odeon on November 18. I remember queuing up outside and ladies thinking something Scottish was going on because of the sea of tartan. This was my local cinema, but it had never felt like this. It was like a football match with only one team playing, and with everyone supporting the same team. Rod even popped his head around a door to have a look at the crowd.

What a gig, what a band! Tetsu was no Ronnie, but they played great. I remember Woody passing out bottles of Liebfraumilch from the bar on stage. A bar on stage! Who else who would do that? I also remember Rod saying that the last train to London was going in ten minutes. No one moved. What a night, what a band. Oh, and Paul and Linda McCartney came on and sang 'Mine for Me' from *Smiler*.

What a night. I've had the Rod Barnet off and on since then. I had me a real good time

I WAS THERE: RICHIE DAVIES

The second time I saw them was at the Lewisham Odeon, with my late wife Esme. On the way there, it came on the car radio that the gig was postponed until a few days later so I turned the car around and went home. We went to the rearranged gig on (I think) the following Monday. We sat upstairs in the balcony, and I thought it was going to collapse, the place was rocking so much. I remember Paul McCartney and Linda coming on. I also remember a violinist playing. My mind may be playing tricks, but I think it was Jim Capaldi.

I also saw them at the Empire Pool, Wembley, with the New York Dolls supporting. They didn't float my boat that night, probably due to the fact that we were so far away from the stage. I saw Rod Stewart in concert at Twickenham ten or so years ago. It wasn't great. And I was in Las Vegas when Rod was at Caesar's Palace, but I never went. It's a bit too cabaret for me. I love my music raw, not overly-produced.

'YOU CAN MAKE ME DANCE, SING OR ANYTHING' RELEASED 22 NOVEMBER 1974

The Faces release their final UK 45. It reaches number 12. The single is billed as 'Rod Stewart and the Faces', and its full title is 'You Can Make Me Dance, Sing or Anything (Even Take the Dog for a Walk, Mend a Fuse, Fold Away the Ironing Board, or Any Other Domestic Shortcomings)'.

KINGS HALL, BELLE VUE
23 & 24 NOVEMBER 1974, MANCHESTER, UK

I WAS THERE: NIGE HAZLEHURST

The first record I bought as a serious collector was 'You Don't Have to be in the Army to Fight in the War' by Mungo Jerry. The second was 'Maggie May'. I then discovered Rod was actually part of a band called the Faces. I was 13. I bought 'Stay With Me' on the day it was released. I did the same with 'Cindy Incidentally' and had to ring round all the local record stores and departments until I found one that had it. I eventually got it from Brown's of Chester!

I finally saw the Faces live in 1974 at Manchester Belle Vue. I got the tickets by post. There were loads of fans dressed in tartan and Rod lookalikes at the gig. The band were late on stage and by then the audience were pretty drunk, and so, it appeared, were the band! But they were amazing.

'Bring it Home to Me'/'You Send Me' and 'Mine for Me' stick in my mind. Rod said he was more proud of the latter than any other song he had recorded. They were late on stage because of the traffic… it was a Sunday night! I have seen Rod solo many times since, and I've lost count of how many, but twice more with the Faces, in 1986 and 2015. 1986 brought tears of joy to my 'Face' to see them on stage together again.

I met Mac at The Boardwalk in Sheffield. I had to queue to meet him and I was shaking, which amused my daughter. His parting words were, 'See you at the Faces reunion.'

I WAS THERE: BOB H JACKSON

It was quite a strange night. My friends and I didn't even know they were on. We were at the Elizabethan Ballroom at Belle Vue, Manchester and there wasn't much going on in there. My mate said, 'I know how we can get in the King's Hall in Belle Vue,' which was about 100 feet away. We got in and it wasn't full so we sat down. My mate said, 'That's Rod Stewart on there.' We couldn't believe our eyes. They all looked pissed! The music, the sound, the atmosphere, the beer on stage – it was electric! It was the best freebie night out I've ever had, especially when they did my favourite song, 'You Can Make Me Dance, Sing or Anything'. It rocked. Ronnie has said he thinks it's the only time they did it live back then. His guitar work is fantastic on this one.

I WAS THERE: LESLIE MURPHY, AGE 16

I could only afford to attend one of two scheduled concerts at the Belle Vue venue and so I attended the second night. All along Hyde Road, Manchester that night, every pub was hammered out with people in tartan clothing assembled in fantastic spirits in anticipation of the evening's entertainment.

The atmosphere was electric and everyone was in good spirits, anticipating the performance of the band. When we finally got inside (nicely refreshed from several drinks), the area I was designated gave me a first class view of the stage and we all cheered, even when a roadie came on and tested the mics. Waiting in anticipation, we were suddenly treated to the sight of Ronnie Wood who came on stage left in only his underpants and holding a cigarette! Needless to say, he got a rousing cheer as he did a quick wave and exited stage right.

After what seemed like an eternity, 'The Stripper' was the introduction to the band coming on stage and, obviously refreshed by copious volumes of alcohol, they were magnificently shambolic and yet brilliant. All the songs were appreciated vociferously, with the crowd in high spirits matching the band's obvious enjoyment performing them. During 'Angel', several footballs appeared on stage and the band proceeded to kick them into the audience, raising loud cheers.

I was drinking in the atmosphere and I noticed Billy Gaff, the Faces manager, about three rows behind me. I signalled a big thumbs up to Billy after catching his eye, dressed up like a doppelgänger 'Rod'. He sent one of his security staff down to me and asked me if I'd like to attend the band's after gig party at the Piccadilly Hotel. Naturally, a chance to meet the band was a no-brainer and I agreed to make my way there after the concert. The big drawback with this was that about 20 people heard the security guy offering me this once in a lifetime chance, and they all followed me to the hotel! I couldn't dissuade them as everyone wanted this golden opportunity.

Arriving at the hotel, I was unfortunately unsuccessful in gaining access due to my entourage. Still, the best night of my young life was had that evening. It was unforgettable.

I WAS THERE: YVONNE HEYWOOD HAMBLETON, AGE 13

I saw the Faces four times, the first time at the now demolished King's Hall in Manchester. I was very young at the time. We were all decked out in tartan scarves and I used to wear a pleated skirt of the same fabric. They were the most exhilarating moments. Talk about excitement and feeling ecstatic. The adrenalin was flowing in my veins and I was feeling giddy.

The atmosphere was absolutely electric – you could've generated the whole building with light. Those five guys could whip the audience into a frenzy in seconds. Never before had I felt so much emotion at a concert.

We were screaming and bawling and dancing in the aisles. You were able to muscle your way to the front back then, so very different from today, where the crowd is set far back from the stage.

I probably went on my own as I was always the independent rascal. We had seats to sit on, which we ended up standing on throughout the concert, screaming our heads off. The venue wasn't so big so there was a really cosy familial atmosphere. Everyone had donned a piece of tartan of some description.

I saw Rod solo for the first time in years at Blackpool a few years ago, and have seen him again several times since. It was so surreal being amongst all the elderly people (including myself). I could not get my head around the fact that I'd been fast forwarded into the future and was amongst all the fogies! That was because there was no longer any shouting or screaming or a public display of passion and emotion.

I WAS THERE: PHILIP MAHON

The next two shows I saw were in November 1974, on the 23rd and 24th respectively. The opening act was a Scottish comedian called Bill Barclay followed by Strider who would provide the guitarist, Gary Grainger, for Rod's post-Faces band. Belle Vue was never my favourite venue. It was too far out of the centre and was not particularly good acoustically. Me and my mate camped out overnight for tickets and secured seats on the front row for both nights. Someone brought a flask of pea soup which was promptly renamed *Exorcist* soup.

The Belle Vue gigs were great but nowhere near as good as the Free Trade Hall ones. The exceptional moments were the times the played one of their best songs, 'You Can Make Me Dance, Sing Or Anything'. The set was mostly from *Nod*, *Ooh La La* and Rod's solo albums *Every Picture*, *Never A Dull Moment* and *Smiler*. Ronnie Wood also sang 'Take A Look At The Guy' and 'I Can Feel The Fire'. On entering, we were given discount vouchers for the albums to which were attached post cards. I wish I still had mine.

I WAS THERE: NEIL COSSAR, AGE 14

I was probably 14. I was so excited. We had really excellent seats. They all just stumbled onto the stage with cigarettes and wine glasses. They almost fell on stage, and then they just played and it was unbelievable. And the warmth, the love that they gave the audience was unbelievable too. They just seemed to be enjoying themselves so much. Ronnie Wood was wearing some really tight, bright yellow pants, and the next day I went back into Manchester to try and buy a pair for myself. I just thought, 'I've got to have a pair of pants like Ronnie Wood.' Luckily, I couldn't find any!

I was learning to play guitar at the time and for some of his slide work he used to use a perspex guitar and I'd never seen one before. And I was like 'wow', because I used to drool over all the guitar catalogues and stuff. I tried to buy a copy of what Ronnie had played but I didn't succeed. It was too expensive.

ODEON THEATRE
26 & 27 NOVEMBER 1974, NEWCASTLE-UPON-TYNE, UK

I WAS THERE: PETER SMITH

The last time I saw the Faces was at Newcastle Odeon in late 1974. The band were now massive and managed to sell out two nights. My mate Bill Gillum and I bought our tickets late and ended up with seats right up at the back of the rear circle, looking down on the stage. This was not a great view and we felt a little detached from the event as we looked down and watched the place going crazy along with the band.

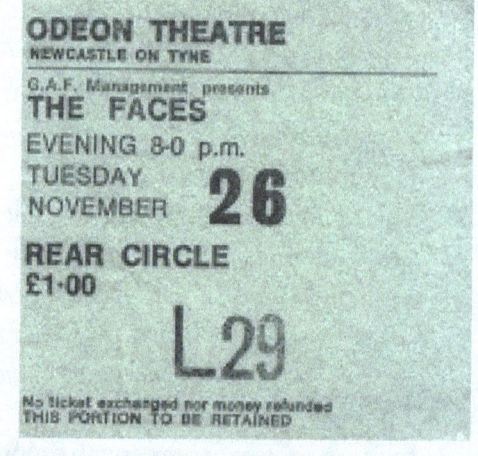

Peter Smith was at Newcastle Odeon

Support that night came from folkie comedian Bill Barclay and rockers Strider. The Faces were still fun; the crowd loved them and there was much singing along. Bill remembers members of the Newcastle United football team being present and sitting right down the front. Rod invited them on stage at the end and they joined him in kicking footballs out into the audience. This was the band at their commercial peak, and their performances were still lots of fun, but some of the craziness and looning around had disappeared along the way.

Rod was already dreaming of becoming a solo star, Ronnie was about to achieve his lifelong ambition and become a Rolling Stone, and Kenney and Ian would soon be rejoining the late great Steve Marriott in a reformed Small Faces. They always finished with 'Twistin' the Night Away', and I can still picture everyone walking down the stairs of the Odeon still singing along.

I WAS THERE: MARIE GRESSMANN, AGE 18

I was there with my sister Christine and two best friends, Eileen and Sheena. I was 18 at the time and working as a hairdresser. When we first heard that Rod Stewart was playing in Newcastle, we were over the moon and in no doubt that this was one of the greatest opportunities of our lives. We had to be there. We were great fans since first seeing Rod on *Top of the Pops* singing 'Maggie May' and we loved the unique sound and the stories he told in his songs.

The big problem was getting tickets. We were told that they were limited to two per person and that people would need to queue for them on a 'first come, first served' bases.

Sheena was going out with a lovely lad called Pete from Newcastle and he and his mate Lawrence kindly agreed to queue on our behalf. They ended up waiting all night in a queue and we were absolutely delighted that they each got two tickets. But a few days later, Pete's parents contacted Sheena and were concerned that their son, who was a good athlete and scholar, was put in a situation where his health could have been compromised for the sake of a couple of tickets. Looking back, it was totally understandable, and we hadn't really thought past our quest to get a ticket at all costs.

When we looked at the tickets, we were a tad disappointed to see we were only a few rows from the back, so would probably need a telescope to see Rod properly.

But, undeterred and full of youthful optimism, on that cold night we headed for Newcastle dressed in flared jeans and t-shirts. I remember wearing a thin cord jacket which I thought made me look so cool with my long dark hair and casual bag slung over my shoulder. We left our village, Esh Winning, at about tea time, got the bus to Durham and then the train to Newcastle.

When we got to the Odeon, there wasn't much of a queue and in we went. There was a singer and comedian on whose name was Bill (Barclay). He was good, but it was a hard job keeping us all entertained as all we wanted to see was the great man! I remember him singing a song that went something like 'does your hair hang low, does it swing to and fro…?', and I may have recalled this incorrectly, but I think he substituted some of the words for rude ones! People were getting up and down a lot and drifting into the toilets and foyer, probably just from boredom, as in those days you had no idea what time the main act was going to come on. It seemed customary to keep audiences waiting, perhaps to hype up the atmosphere. I had seen numerous good bands and it always seemed to take an age before they came onto the stage.

When Rod came on the stage, we were totally hyper. We stood up like everyone else and just rushed from our seats down the aisle on the left hand side. A bouncer stood with his arms outstretched in an attempt to administer some kind of crowd control but it must have been like King Canute holding back the tide and, inconsiderate young ladies that we were, we just pushed past him and stood at the front, not to be moved. So we got to watch from an incredibly close range and I literally couldn't take my eyes off Rod and the band.

Rod bounced onto the stage and the energy was amazing. He threw the mic, danced, sang, interacted with the crowd and even threw his slip-on shoes into the audience at the end of the night, so someone somewhere may well be putting them on eBay one day!

Some of the songs I hadn't heard before, such as 'Mine for Me', but when he sang 'Maggie May', it really did light up the room. I didn't want the night to end and loved every minute of it, so much so that I have never missed a gig in our city, when Rod has played on subsequent tours. In comparison to the places he performs in now, it was quite an intimate venue. The atmosphere, the novelty of such an unusual singing voice and the passion of the band made it a night on the town I will never forget. Sadly, my dear friend Eileen died quite young and I cherish the wonderful times like this, when we felt we were in the presence of one of our heroes.

I WAS THERE: JOHN LOGAN

The '74 tour was much more showbiz, with Rod, by then at height of his powers and it was more about him rather than him just being the vocalist of the band. Again, there were overnight queues to secure a good seat and this time there were two gigs on consecutive nights. Tartan scarves were everywhere in the audience.

Never knowingly underdressed, the band found Rod in a bright yellow satin bib and braces affair with a natty tam o' shanter which he took off and put back on at a whim. Ronnie was wearing his black jacket with feathers on the shoulders and they all seemed to be wearing ballet pumps.

The front ten rows of seats were soon reduced to a wreck with people dancing after a rush to the front as soon as the band came on to the strains of 'The Stripper'. It was another chaotic but immensely enjoyable night, with the band playing as well as ever. It was now a two hour show but it went very quickly indeed. The band had even turned up on time, for the first time ever when I had gone to see them.

The roadies were dressed smarter than a lot of bands I'd seen at that point, with smart waistcoats, and doubling up as bar tenders side stage whilst Kenney blasted away with '(I Know) I'm Losing You'. The PA blasted out the new single, 'You Can Make Me Dance' at the end of the 'Twistin' the Night Away' encore and them singing 'We'll Meet Again'. I recall thinking, 'Is this the last time?'. Ronnie was being courted by the Stones; his debut solo effort had come out that year with his Stones mates, and he'd played on their hit that year, 'It's Only Rock 'n' Roll'. As it turned out, I was correct. They lasted into the autumn of 1975 with a US tour, but Rod had already taken up residence in LA and released his *Atlantic Crossing* album, recorded at Muscle Shoals Studio, and with none of the Faces on the album.

I wore a specially made Stewart Dress tartan scarf to the Odeon show, an eight foot long number. During 'You Can Make Me Dance', I managed to throw it on stage from the front row. Rod spotted it, picked it up and put it on. I would have liked it back, but as it turned out I wouldn't need it. It was some 41 years before I watched another Faces concert, at Hurtwood Park in 2015. Straw boaters, like he sported on the cover of *A Night on the Town*, were the required garb for Rod's 1976 solo Christmas tour. He played four nights at Newcastle City Hall. I was there every night.

I WAS THERE: JOHN WATSON

At school in the early Seventies, there were two distinct music tribes – those that bowed to the hard rock altar of Led Zeppelin, Black Sabbath and Deep Purple and the group I belonged to, who followed the Faces, the Stones and a little local band called Lindisfarne. In a shared, safe territory between the two were Bowie, Lou Reed, Roxy Music and Iggy Pop. Thinking back, there was also a strange world inhabited by people in army coats, reading *The Hobbit* and listening to Yes and Genesis – but this was a comprehensive school on a council estate, far, far away from topographical oceans and satyrs.

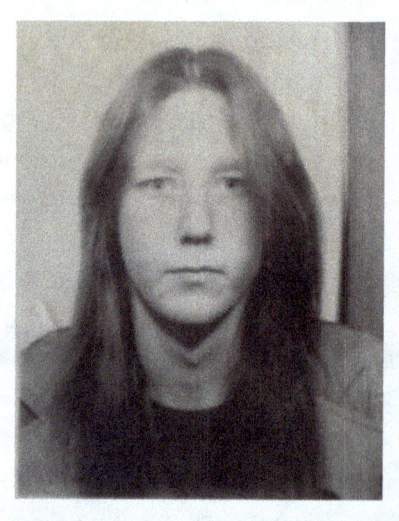

John Watson was at the Odeon

Everyone who followed the Faces, Stones and Lindisfarne shared something more than just the music – the hair, wearing your dad's old Fair Isle slipover and collarless shirts. The Faces in particular had a warmth that was absent from the hard rock gods – I doubt anyone saw Ozzy Osbourne play 'keepy uppy' with a football, before kicking it into the audience, as Rod Stewart did, or Led Zeppelin stopping half way through the misery of a 20-minute drum solo to have a singalong, which was something you took home from a Faces gig.

I was too young to see the Faces at their famous Locarno gig in Sunderland – I had to wait until November 1974 to see them at the Odeon Cinema, Newcastle. The Odeon was reserved for the 'big bands' as an alternative to the nearby City Hall. Ronnie Lane had left by then, and the Faces were at the height of their fame. I would later see Ronnie many times with Slim Chance, where he continued in the warm, folky way of the Faces.

I was about 20 rows back, but still close enough to feel the camaraderie the Faces were famous for – they seemed more like good mates, rather than distant idols from somewhere you were banned from. I don't remember the whole set list, but I do recall many of the songs that ended up on the Faces live album *Overtures and Beginners*, and its far better bootleg version, being in the set – 'Maggie May', 'It's All Over Now', 'Gasoline Alley', 'Stay With Me', 'Angel' and the farewell song, 'Twistin' the Night Away', which you could hear people still singing as they made their way back into the cold of a November night in Newcastle.

ODEON THEATRE
29 & 30 NOVEMBER 1974, BIRMINGHAM, UK

I WAS THERE: MICK BAILEY, AGE 16

I was 16 and still at school when one of the boys asked if I was interested in going to see the Faces at the Odeon. I was really into soul music but he assured me that I would enjoy it so I agreed to go. I borrowed a couple of albums from him and liked what I heard. His dad knew someone at the Odeon and got the tickets for us – about £2 each if I remember correctly. We were looking forward to the gig and it seemed that everyone we knew was going. A week before, the tragedy that was the Birmingham pub bombings occurred. At first, things were very much up in the air as to if we would be allowed to go, but eventually we were told that it would be OK.

When we got into the Odeon, some of the older lads told us to get to the bar because whisky was half price, but we went in and managed to get down to the front of the stage. The band came on and started to play. Ronnie Wood was nearest to us on stage and he bent down and passed a bottle of brandy to my mate who had a swig and passed it on to me. I passed it on and then Ronnie came back and asked for the bottle. Immediately, it was passed back through various hands to the stage, although much depleted. By this time, everyone was up on their feet dancing and having a great time. I looked up at the balcony and it was bouncing up and down, which looked a bit worrying but I was assured it was safe. Afterwards, we came out covered in sweat, ears ringing and voices gone, and we both said that we would have to see them again. A couple of gigs later, or so it seemed, the band had split and we never got a chance to relive seeing one of the best bands I have seen live.

I WAS THERE: DAVID GILCHRIST ELLIOTT
I was at the 1974 gig at the Odeon in Birmingham just after the pub bombings (the IRA terrorist organisation exploded two bombs in pubs in Birmingham on 21 November 1974, killing 21 people and injuring 182 others). It was a small crowd but a great show from the band.

I WAS THERE: NILES WORT, AGE 17
My story is the tale of two mates aged 17 who went to Birmingham the week after the IRA pub bombings to see the Faces at the Odeon. There was a very weird atmosphere in the city that night. There was a huge security presence going in and it was all very subdued. Until the Faces arrived… 'Fuck the IRA,' Rod announced, and – whoosh! – it was on with the show.

TRENTHAM GARDENS
1 DECEMBER 1974, STOKE-ON-TRENT, UK

I WAS THERE: JIM WEAVER
December 1974 and to Trentham Gardens, Stoke-on-Trent, which happened to be the third consecutive night I saw the group, two shows at Birmingham Odeon being the first two. Five of us travelled up the M6 in a smallish car and, as soon as we had parked up, we hit the bar. This was a gud 'un. There was a large crowd in the hall, it was standing only and we squeezed our way near to the front of the stage.

I recollect that musically this was a very good band performance but I don't recall any of the gigs I attended being poor, musically or vocally. The highlight of any Faces gig was their rendition of 'Angel', when much crowd singing and swaying was obligatory. It seemed to unite the crowd as one.

After the gig, we hung around a bit at the back of the building where there was some scaffolding. The scaffolding went up a couple of floors and someone said that it was very close to the Faces dressing room. One of our group started climbing it, and after four or five minutes he was back down with three-quarters of a bottle of Bacardi in his hand. He told us Woody had passed it out of the dressing room window to him. Maybe he had, or maybe it was a roadie. But Woody sounded better. On the way home, we imbibed that bottle. I only had a few gulps because I thought it was disgusting.

All in all, I saw the band six times live, and to this day they rank as the best gigs I've been to. I tend to say, when trying to put the other best gigs I've been to in an order, 'Well, whatever it is it starts off at number seven.'

I wasn't fortunate enough to meet any of the Faces when they were together back in the Seventies, but in later life I did have the great pleasure of meeting Rod once and Mac twice – both very affable gentlemen. Mac in particular was most engaging. It's just a huge loss that he departed this world much too early.

WINTER GARDENS
6 DECEMBER 1974, BOURNEMOUTH, UK

I WAS THERE: VINCE WELDON

I saw them two years running, at the Bournemouth Winter Gardens. These were pre-Christmas shows in December '73 and '74. Elton John had a walk on part for one of them. He'd allegedly flown back and just landed (I've always thought he'd said 'from Russia' but I can't find any evidence of this – he was in the USA in early December '74) and I think Rod introduced him as his old friend 'Sharon' who had arrived at Bournemouth's Hurn Airport and who wanted to say hello. There were lots of footballs kicked into the crowd. I was too far back to get one!

NEW THEATRE
8 DECEMBER 1974, OXFORD, UK

I WAS THERE: DAVID HALL, AGE 14

It was Rod, Ron, Macca, Kenney and Tetsu. Rod had his arm in a sling, and being probably the first live gig I ever went to, they blew my me away, especially Woody with his cigarette in the side of his mouth playing 'Stay With Me'. To this day, that song is my uplift song, and I love the drum solo by Kenney on 'I'm Losing You'. The theatre was probably 75 per cent men and boys, well-oiled and out for a great night. Underage drinking – ha ha! I had a green tartan cap that I threw on the stage and Rod wore it singing 'Stay With Me'.

OPERA HOUSE
10 & 11 DECEMBER 1974, BLACKPOOL, UK

I WAS THERE: ELAINE CORDON
I met Rod Stewart and the Faces at the Imperial Hotel on 11th December 1974. A school friend had found out where Rod was staying so a bunch of excited school girls ran up Blackpool Prom to the Imperial to hopefully see him and the band. As we arrived in the foyer, Rod was just coming down the stairs followed closely by the rest of the band. He stopped and had a chat with us and signed some autographs. I stood on the bottom stair and ruffled his spiky but ever so soft hair. He was wearing a red corduroy suit with a white frilly shirt underneath and he smelt divine.

I mange to get a kiss off Ronnie Wood but was to shy to ask Rod. Ian McLagan, Tetsu Yamauchi and Kenney Jones were also there – but to be honest we weren't interested in them! Rod excused himself after a little time with us and said he was entertaining some Manchester United players. As I wasn't a football fan then, I've no idea who that was.

Later that evening, we went to the Blackpool Opera House to see Rod and the Faces in concert. They were incredible and every time I hear the song 'You Can Make Me Dance, Sing or Anything' it reminds me of that magical night and a very special memory that I will remember for the rest of my life.

I've seen Rod a few times since, but nothing can beat that first time.

I WAS THERE: COLIN THOMPSON
I came out of rural Cumbria, which Radio 1 didn't reach. You had to rely on Radio Luxembourg to hear any pop music and you had to go

up a tree to get a signal for that. Even the TV reception wasn't that fantastic. A lot of people my age became aware of Rod and the Faces when they did 'Maggie May' on *Top of the Pops*, when they started kicking footballs into the audience. I was 13 or 14 at the time. That was a pivotal *Top of the Pops* moment. I really started to dig into them after that. I bought *Every Picture Tells a Story* and then *A Nod's as Good as a Wink…* and the singles and then started to backtrack into the older albums for both Rod and the Faces.

I went to see the Faces in Blackpool with a guy called Dave. I was 17 in '74 and at catering college. It was the last day of term at college. We did the show and went on to the year-end party after that. Strider were the support act and that was insanely loud. With the Faces, it was the drums. With a record, no matter how loud you play it, you never quite get that density of the drums, and that's what came through. Of course, we were catching the tail end in 1974. Ronnie Lane had gone and it was Tetsu, but it was still stunning.

For a very small glimpse of time, the Faces were the number one band in the world. The Stones weren't quite rocking it, The Beatles had gone. Just for a spell the Faces seemed to be everyone's favourite rock band. To this day, I still think 'Stay With Me' has got the best intro and the best outro and the best middle section of any rock song that's ever got into the top 10.

After that, Rod went walkabout. A whole bunch of us went off to see him in Newcastle City Hall in '76 with the *Atlantic Crossing* album. Whilst it was a great show, and I've seen some great Rod Stewart shows over the years, it wasn't the Faces. When you get the Faces live, with 3,000 people screaming, it's just bonkers. It was the loudest thing I've ever heard in my life.

APOLLO THEATRE
14 – 18 DECEMBER 1974, GLASHOW, UK

I WAS THERE: ERIC J SAWDEN

My girlfriend and I got tickets for this gig at the Apollo. We caught the afternoon train from Dumfries to Central Station in Glasgow. We had our tea and a couple of drinks near to the theatre. We arrived in plenty of time. We asked one of the staff, 'When does he (Rod) come on and how long does the concert last?' She said, 'He pleases himself. It could be 8pm or later and they play for two and a half to three hours depending on how much drink they have had.' Our last train back to Dumfries was 10.45pm.

Comedian Bill Barclay came on and did his bit, including his version of 'The 12 Days of Christmas'. Then it all went dark, 'The Stripper' tune started – which they came on stage to in those days – and the curtain came up and it started. It was loud, clear and just brilliant. They played the songs from *A Nod's as Good as a Wink...* plus a few others. It was fast approaching 10.30pm and we hadn't heard 'Stay with Me', 'Maggie May' or 'Reason to Believe'. We decided to stay until the end and get the early morning train. It was well worth it, as the remainder of the set was fantastic. By the time the concert was over it was after 11pm.

We thought we would try to thumb a lift home to Dumfries but only got as far as the outskirts of Glasgow. It was pouring down with rain by now. A very kindly taxi cab picked us up and dropped us back off at Glasgow Central Station. He didn't even charge us, as he said he had fond memories of being in Dumfries. There were about 40 Faces fans who had also made the same decision to get the next train home. One of them had managed to get a football so we all had a kick about in the station. When we got back to Dumfries the next morning we went our separate ways, back home or to work. I told my parents that I had spent the night at my girlfriend's house and she told her parents that she stayed at mine. To this day, none of our parents knew that we spent the night on station benches.

My girlfriend and I got married the next year and have been together for over 46 years (including engagement). We have seen Rod Stewart at least 35 times over the years including in Vegas. We've seen him perform with Status Quo, Gary Glitter and many more. Unfortunately, we have never got close to meeting him.

I WAS THERE: DEREK KEITH

The 1974 concert was also at the Glasgow Apollo so myself, Charlie and Ally headed off again to Glasgow, but this time in Charlie's car. We had a fantastic night and the band got the crowd built up into a frenzy as always. I remember they performed their new single at the time 'You Can Make Me Dance, Sing or Anything'. What an atmosphere!

I WAS THERE: KENNY HYSLOP

It was an excellent show. They kicked footballs into the audience when they took the stage. And they had a bar on stage, with a barman in a tux polishing glasses and serving them drinks. I was with Midge Ure. We were getting a band together, pre-Slik.

GAUMONT STATE THEATRE, KILBURN
21 – 23 DECEMBER 1974, LONDON, UK

I WAS THERE: YVE PAIGE

My third and final Faces gig. My best mate and I went with our boyfriends (and future husbands), taking the tube to Kilburn and walking down to the venue. They had introduced seats and we were halfway back in the centre. It was the first time we had seats (someone had died at a David Cassidy concert (at White City Stadium in May 1974) and good old health and safety kicked in big time, so along

Yve Paige was at the Kilburn Gaumont

came seats, barriers and security – ugh!). Sitting wasn't for me and I didn't like it. We stood and danced all night, but I missed the scrum down the front and the madness of it all.

I can't remember if the band were late, but we had the can-can girls as a warm up and I think someone was playing a piano which was raised from the pit. The Faces hit the stage and the rest was a blur. As always, it was an incredible evening and we came away unaware that this would be the last time that I would see them all together. I took it for granted my band would last forever. I was gutted when they split. I was livid that Rod dared to move to LA, and that Woody became a Stone. He will always be a Face, no matter how many years he's a Rolling Stone...

I WAS THERE: THOMAS CAPPAMORE, AGE 19

I saw them at the State Theatre, Kilburn in north west London a couple of days before Christmas 1974. The support act was Strider and I went with my brother after we had our mum get up really early a few weeks earlier to queue up to buy the tickets. We sat upstairs. Unfortunately, the Faces were poor; they came on late, played for only 30 minutes or so and did not come back for an encore.

I WAS THERE: GLEN MATLOCK

'Miss Judy's Farm' is a very inventive bass line. And that was my common ground with Steve (Jones) and Paul (Cook) in the Sex Pistols. When I overheard that they were looking for a bass player, I said, 'I play bass.' They said, 'Who do you like?' I said, 'Faces' and they said, 'That's our favourite band.' At my audition I played 'Three Button Hand Me Down', which got me the gig.

Not long after I met Steve and Paul, Ronnie Wood was doing his show at Kilburn Gaumont State and I went with my girlfriend. Keith Richards was playing with Ronnie, Willie Weeks, Andy Newmark and Mac. Keith was dressed as a pirate. We had cheap tickets upstairs and we went up a couple of flights too far. The lights weren't on because I don't think they had the whole place open and I thought, 'Oh no, we've gone too far.' Just as we were turning around to come down and go back down the stairs, there was a bit of a kerfuffle and Steve and Paul and their mates came down from the darkened bit, all covered in dirt and soot. They'd bunked in over the roof.

I love Rod Stewart. I think he's fantastic. I thought he was great in the band. I love bands when everybody's got a character. The Beatles, the Pistols, the Clash. You knew all of them, and it was the same with the Faces. And they were all fantastic musicians. It's all a bit edgy. The interplay between Ronnie Wood and Ian McLagan was fantastic. It doesn't need another guitarist. Mac was up there with Booker T as a Hammond player. And he was a fantastic pianist; as soon as you heard him playing the piano, you knew it was him. They don't even know it but as a band they were so influential on punk. If it wasn't for the Faces, Steve Jones wouldn't sound the way he sounds, with those guitars and that amp. If you listen to 'Borstal Boys', it's like a punk track and it happened well before punk. It was such a pleasure. It's a drag that they didn't do more. But Ron Wood got the phone call from the Rolling Stones.

I WAS THERE: ADAM PORGES

In North London in the early '70s, I used to knock about with mates. It was all about football (Chelsea one week, Arsenal or Spurs another), shopping together for clobber, and sharing music. The Faces and The Who were my two favourite bands by then. I had a copy of *A Nod's as Good as a Wink* and loved the front and back covers.

Adam Porges was into football, clothes and music back then

I'm not sure where it came from – I probably swapped it for a pair of brothel creepers or similar, as you did back then! I remember a few of us listening to 'Cindy Incidentally' over and over at a mate's house and loving it (still do) and buying *Ooh La La* the day it came out.

Alas, I only saw the Faces with Tetsu on bass. There was a huge amount of tartan in the audience and more than a few Rod lookalikes. It's perhaps more of a wish than a real memory but I seem to remember a bar on the stage and the band helping themselves to drinks. There were definitely footballs being kicked into the crowd and huge singalongs for 'You Wear It Well' and 'Maggie May'. It was a superb atmosphere and great fun.

I WAS THERE: STUART LANGSBURY

I first got into the Faces with *A Nod's…* I loved that album. Then Rod released *Every Picture* and I was hooked. As a 17-year-old living ten miles from Reading, my first ever gig was Faces headlining the Reading Festival in 1972. I remember Rod wore a sparkly silver jump suit. I then saw them at Brixton Sundown in December of that year and at Edmonton

TELL EVERYONE: A PEOPLE'S HISTORY OF THE FACES

Sundown the following October. I then saw them in Kilburn on 23 December 1974 on their last UK tour, for *Ooh La La*. I remember this gig most fondly. I passed my driving test the week before so I borrowed an Austin 1100 from the garage I worked at part time, drove to the gig with my girlfriend – and parked outside the door!

Stuart Langsbury was at the Kilburn Gaumont

The support were a great little band called Strider (whose guitarist Gary Grainger was later to spend some time in Rod's band). I got down the front for the Faces and the gig was like a party. They had a bar onstage and were clearly well oiled! Rod's *Smiler* album hadn't long been released, and when they did 'Sweet Little Rock 'n' Roller', Keith Richards came on – he had played guitar on the album version. It was just an amazing night and, sadly, their last tour of the UK before they split.

I've seen Rod virtually every tour he has done since, and the Stones too (Woody is a bit of a hero of mine). I saw the Wembley gig in July '86, when the Faces reunited at Rod's show with Bill Wyman on bass. A clearly unwell Plonk was sat in a chair and loving it all.

I WAS THERE: SIMON JACOBSON

I first encountered Rod Stewart in the summer of 1971. I was working in Marylebone High Street in London's West End. I was going to lunch, and stepped off the pavement into the road without paying much attention. I became aware of a car on my right hand side that had to stop very quickly. There was a squeal of breaks and a car horn. When I looked up, there was a sports car, which was extremely close to hitting me. The driver

Simon Jacobson met Ronnie Wood backstage

was smiling and indicating to me to continue to cross the road. As I nodded my appreciation, I recognised Rod in his Marcos!

Fast forward to December 24, 1974, at the Kilburn Gaumont in London. Directly after the Faces had ended their set, I managed to get invited backstage and to talk very briefly with Rod. I said that the gig was great, and he thanked me. I then mentioned the Marcos incident, which after a moment or two, he recalled. Laughing, he said as he was leaving, 'Well, you're still here mate. Merry Christmas!' And he was gone.

A few minutes later, Ronnie Wood was leaving. Although he didn't have time to talk, he was fine with having a photo taken.

I WAS THERE: PETER COALS

I queued up outside the theatre for about five hours on a Saturday in order to purchase tickets. It was a real sense of achievement when I was clutching them. I am pretty sure the gig itself was Christmas Eve (December 23rd) and the band came on later than was expected. 'Rodneeeeee' chants echoed around the arena, even though his full name is Roderick. Tetsu was obviously playing bass then. Keith Richards was on stage (I'm not totally sure why, other than the close friendship which was developing between the Stones and Ronnie Wood). There was a small string section of men dressed in dinner jackets which looked incongruous. They played on certain tracks and there were rumours that Mac was not happy they were there. The set list was shorter than expected – I guess because they were late on stage – but it was a magical night full of raw energy and it will be etched in my memory forever.

The rendition of 'We'll meet again, don't know where, don't know when…' felt sincere and genuine. I did not realise this was the last time I would see the band perform; it was a great pity they did not tour again before Mac died.

We missed the last tube to Walthamstow Central on the Victoria line and had to be content with a train terminating at Seven Sisters station, from where we eventually hired a taxi home from a miserable man who resented being disturbed on Christmas Eve. The experience of attending the gig made my Christmas that year.

I had several girlfriends before I met my wife and she started accompanying me to Rod Stewart gigs. I've now seen him 113 times. I was never fortunate to take a girl to see the Faces or Rod Stewart before meeting her. I coerced two different male friends to go to these Faces gigs; they were not massive fans but I am guessing my parents would not have let me go on my own.

It is Rod's stage presence and the relationship with Ronnie Wood which I so miss, along with the tartan drum kit of Kenney Jones and the Steinway piano for Mac, who often seemed to have his back to the main action and was constantly turning around as he thumped the keys. The sound and the musicianship may not have been as slick as the current Rod gig experience, but there was a raw energy and absorbing atmosphere which left you breathless and which will never be repeated.

I WAS THERE: SANDIE RITTER

I was at the Kilburn gig where Keith Richards joined them and it was weird. Sitting in the audience you knew it wasn't quite right but you couldn't pinpoint what was wrong. But for me things were never the same when Ronnie Lane left and Tetsu joined. The energy wasn't the same. The enthusiasm wasn't the same. Maybe at that point, Rod and Ronnie had to go out there and create more enthusiastic energy, because Tetsu was very laid-back. Personally, although it was still a lot of fun going to the concerts, I would say that when Ronnie Lane left the Faces ended. Ronnie Lane had this amazing energy. He had a powerful stage presence. And then it was gone. Tetsu was rather insipid by comparison.

My mum and dad came into the dressing room afterwards and Keith was slumped in the corner of the room. My mum came in saying, 'Who was that ugly bloke on stage with you?' I said, 'Mum – he's carrying a gun and a knife. What are you going to do?'
Ian McLagan

'YOU CAN MAKE ME DANCE, SING OR ANYTHING' RELEASED 22 JANUARY 1975 (USA)

The Faces final single is released in the United States.

WAR MEMORIAL AUDITORIUM
11 FEBRUARY 1975, SYRACUSE, NEW YORK

The Faces embark upon their eleventh US tour.

WINGS STADIUM
12 FEBRUARY 1975, KALAMAZOO, MICHIGAN

I WAS THERE: BLAIR HOLBEN

Rod produced a small whiskey flask from his jacket, said, 'I deserve this', took a swig and then put it back. Kenney did a drum solo on his custom tartan-finished Premier kit and I remember walking around during it and thinking he was not too good – funny that, because now he is one of my favourite rock drummers. Rod bowed his head over low at one point and his hair looked like someone took large hedge shears and just chopped it all – very straight – across! Then, when he threw his hair back, there was his famous shag haircut... After they finished playing and the house lights came up, they played 'You Can Make Me Dance, Sing or Anything' over the PA.

COBO HALL
14 FEBRUARY 1975, DETROIT, MICHIGAN

I WAS THERE: RICHARD B KELLEY

In the winter of 1975, I was a high school senior in Toledo, Ohio, making poor-to-middling grades in everything but art. This while I was working part time at the local underground record store and head shop. I was a bit of a latecomer to the cool kid crowd but my gal pal, C, kept me tight because she enjoyed my art and music enthusiasm and attempts at humour. C had plenty of boyfriends and flaunted herself for the attention, but none of those favours were directed at me. I was more of a buddy when C needed permission from her parents to do something that required help from a slightly older, responsible friend. C was also truly and madly in love with Rod Stewart and was convinced that one day she would marry him. Or so she claimed.

As Rod's popularity grew, his solo albums continued to outsell his efforts with the Faces and, unremarkably, there was a part of his audience that really didn't understand that the Faces even existed in their own right. By 1974-75, they were merely Rod's back-up band. C was one such fanatic, good-naturedly complaining that Ron Wood had no business wearing his hair like Rod – or even looking like him.

The Faces themselves didn't seem to care much as long as their handlers kept them plied with brandy, ale and babes. Their shows had always been ramshackle affairs and were becoming more so.

It was into this atmosphere that Rod and his cohorts returned to the road in the winter of 1975. There was no album to flog, so the tour was merely christened *Faces on Tour*. In a series of one-nighters, the group warmed up in Rochester, New York, and opened the next night in the new Wings Stadium in Kalamazoo, Michigan. The first major market of the run and a longtime Rod Stewart stronghold, going back to the Jeff Beck days, was Detroit.

The Faces hadn't played the city since 1972 and Rod had only gotten more huge in the meantime. C had a way with the boys and I was no different. She got what she wanted and in this case she just had to have me accompany her and her friend V to the 'Rod Stewart concert' in Detroit, or her and V's parents would not allow either 17-year-old young lady to attend. I was a year older and an apparently responsible guy, and Detroit was a big, scary place that out-of-towners feared. 'If Richard goes with you, then it's all right' were the parental marching orders. C and V paid for my ticket and plied me with beer, not that I needed any cajoling. Hell, I loved the Faces even if I couldn't convince C that they were as viable as Rod himself.

They picked me up at 6pm, threw me in the back seat of V's car with the promised six pack and we were off. None of us had ever been to Cobo Hall but it wasn't hard to find the place. (The building is still there though the arena has been razed and retrofitted as an expanded convention centre.)

In those days, hard tickets were sold at outlets throughout the vicinity of the show. C. had purchased our tickets from either a Travel Agency or department store in Toledo who were given a nifty block of seats. These would have sold quickly in today's computerised systems where everybody is competing for the same ticket but instead the seller (fifty plus miles away) had a couple rows at center ice, eye level with the stage! VIP stuff today. In researching this missive I found that Welsh rockers, Man, had apparently opened the evening's proceedings but I don't recall them. I think we arrived as the lights were going up on their set.

The Faces were fashionably late so we had plenty of time to observe the hard partying going on throughout the tall, U-shaped arena. That Detroit audiences take their rock and roll seriously is not hyperbole. Kiss recorded most of their breakthrough album, *Alive*, at Cobo Hall the following spring and J Geils Band and Bob Seger would soon follow suit. For Valentine's Day a heart-shaped sign had been professionally hand painted and hung over the stage. It said 'FACES LOVE DETROIT' and the feeling was most assuredly mutual.

A little after 9pm, the lights went down and a bawdy, horn band version of David Rose's 'The Stripper' provided the walk-on music for Rod Stewart and the Faces as the crowd roared. As the lights came up, Rod said something like, 'It looks like we're home,' swung the mic stand with a flourish and the band stormed out of the gate with 'It's All Over Now' which, in retrospect, might have been a harbinger for the Faces in the months to come. As the band tore through the old Bobby Womack and the Valentinos number, my first thought was, 'What the hell is Rod Stewart wearing?' A bright yellow jumpsuit with high flourishes on the shoulders still haunts my memory! He reminded me of Glenda the Good Witch from *The Wizard of Oz*. My second thought was that girls were screaming and crying, British Invasion-style. I'd been going to concerts for a few years at that point, but had only witnessed such behaviour on the old *Ed Sullivan Show*.

With Rod's help, Ron Wood followed the opener with 'Take A Look at the Guy' from his solo album released the previous year, and being in Motown, the Faces usual showstopping version of '(I Know) I'm Losing You' followed, but it sort of crashed and burned. The drum solo was too long and the ending just sort of fell apart. Nonetheless, it received the biggest applause of the night thus far. Rod used the occasion to doff the weird top he was wearing and remind the audience of the Faces history in

Detroit, including their riotous appearances at the fabled Eastown Theater.

To settle things down and perhaps save Rod's voice, the group carried on with a medley of Sam Cooke soul numbers from the *Smiler* album, and Chuck Berry's 'Sweet Little Rock and Roller' followed, sounding much like the recorded version and beginning with recorded dogs barking and driven by Ronnie's raunchy guitar.

Working backward in time the Faces next delivered 'I'd Rather Go Blind' from Rod's prior solo outing, *Never a Dull Moment*. The audience howled impatiently throughout the quiet Etta James number. It was followed by 'Angel', which allowed Rod to engage the audience in a singalong. We were now seven songs into the show and the Faces had yet to play a song from any album credited to the Faces! It had been all Rod (and Ron) all night, not that anybody really cared. That log jam broke with the next song, a raucous take on 'Stay With Me', which evolved into a Ron Wood solo guitar segment including a bit of 'Motherless Children', played like the Eric Clapton version from the previous year. This begat a slide and lead guitar tour-de-force, the likes of which Ronnie never performed again after he joined the Stones. A portion of 'Gasoline Alley' from Rod's second solo album segued into the run and then Ron returned to his six-string master class which evolved back to a repeat of the 'Stay With Me' finale. When the Faces were on, they were on, and they most definitely were on that night!

Things settled down again with another return to Rod solo. After the pyrotechnics of 'Stay With Me', the audience didn't have much patience for the lovely 'Mine for Me' which closes *Smiler*. As solo turns were again being doled out, Ronnie took the energy up quite a few notches with 'I Can Feel the Fire' from his solo debut. Rod pretty much hijacked the song, singing most of Ronnie's lines and the missing Jagger and Richards vocal parts heard on the original recording.

The Faces kept the energy at maximum, returning to their own oeuvre with 'Too Bad'. Band and audience alike were now riding a runaway train as the Faces, without missing a beat, shifted to a supercharged take on Rod's *Every Picture Tells a Story*, rocking it harder than the LP version. Rod then instructed the audience to give themselves a round of applause, and as Ronnie began the chugging intro to Sam Cooke's 'Twistin' the Night Away', announced 'this will be the last one'. The song was sloppy, jaunty and joyous and ended without the ending, the band simply waving and walking off. After the obligatory encore break 'You Wear It Well' and of course, 'Maggie May' ended the night. In taking their bows the band sang a brief snippet of 'We'll Meet Again' (some sunny day).

It seems the Faces were generous with Detroit, perhaps throwing in a couple of numbers rarely heard elsewhere. What they didn't do was play much in the way of Faces music. Four songs of the 16 performed could be found on a single Faces album and they played nothing from *Ooh La La*.

On the way out, I bought my first ever concert t-shirt, and I still have it. Reflecting the shift in the Faces fortunes, the graphic proclaims 'ROD STEWART Faces Tour' and shows two pictures of Rod the Mod, a larger one with him alone and another with the band. I wore the shirt through college, finally packing it away about 1980.

The Faces trek continued into spring and with it came word that Ronnie Wood would stand in for the departed Mick Taylor on the Rolling Stones tour which would traverse North America in June and July. He was referred to as a guest but there was no doubt he could hold his own with the self-proclaimed 'World's Greatest Rock and Roll Band'. Ronnie looked and felt right even if he didn't have the virtuoso skills of Taylor, even if he did temper his own style ever after.

CAPITAL CENTER
15 FEBRUARY 1975, LARGO, MARYLAND

I WAS THERE: MIKE LOVE, AGE 20

I'd liked the Small Faces and heard Rod Stewart on Jeff Beck's albums. Then I heard 'Mandolin Wind' on my brother's copy of *Every Picture Tells a Story*. The concert I attended was at Capitol Center in Landover, Maryland, a sports arena and entertainment venue which has since been demolished for commercial redevelopment. I went with a big group and can't recall exactly who was there. The Faces with Rod on vocals were really tight, playing energetically and well performed tunes. They had a very bright stage environment using hundreds of clear light bulbs that were placed as fancy, almost burlesque-like fashion. Rod was Rod, dressed in tuxedo-like costumes and maybe a matching top hat. At least one of his costumes was bright yellow and he sported a yellow boa – outrageous, but not so over the top. Mostly I remember the excellent performance of 'Stay With Me'. They nailed it and I think it may have been that same set of songs they recorded for their live album from that time period.

I WAS THERE: CHRISTOPHER QUINN

I hadn't yet turned 11 when my siblings all went to see Elton John. I was an Elton John fan but my parents wouldn't let me go. So when my sister asked me if I wanted to go and see the Faces, I said yes and my parents agreed my siblings could take me. I didn't know who Rod Stewart was, but I was dying to go to a concert. I borrowed my sister's records and started listening to them. Capitol Centre was the first arena in the DC area. We had stadiums, but this was a new 20,000 seat arena. It was a big deal to go there. We were sat up high and had a bird's eye view of the stage. Susan Ford, daughter of the President, was at the show. We could see her sitting on the side of the stage. 'That's her!' Blue Öyster Cult opened the show. We'd never heard of them. *On Your Feet or On Your Knees* was their new album and they pretty much played that. The Faces came on to 'The Stripper'. Rod was wearing a yellow tux. I remember them playing 'Stay With Me' 'Sweet Little Rock 'n' Roller', 'Angel' and 'Maggie May'. They played everything I wanted to hear. Three guys right in front of us were passing a bong back and forth. My sister's friend's younger brother, Marty, was a year or two older than me. I think we both got a contact high from the bong these guys in front of us had. I can remember Marty playing piano on everybody's head on the way home.

I saw Rod and the Faces later in October, at the University of Maryland, and I don't remember anything about the show other than hating the opening act, Brian Auger and his Oblivion Express. They were awful. But the first records I ever bought were straight after that first concert; Elton John's *Greatest Hits*, and *Smiler*. It was that concert that decided it for me that music was what I wanted to do. I grew up convinced I was going to be a popstar.

CIVIC CENTER
16 FEBRUARY 1975, PHILDELPHIA, PENNSYLVANIA

I WAS THERE: SAM MCCLAFFERTY

Out of 350 concerts I've seen this is the only one I saw at the Civic Center. There had been rumours for weeks that Lynryd Skynyrd were going to open for them so there was quite a buzz in the crowd. Sadly, it was just a rumour and instead Duke Williams and the Extreme opened. But the Faces put on quite a show, one of the best I ever saw.

INTERNATIONAL AMPHITHEATER
18 FEBRUARY 1975, CHICAGO, ILLINOIS

I WAS THERE: PATRICK DANIEL DEANE, AGE 21

One of the most fun concerts I remember. Ronnie Wood on the edge of the stage played the opening chord for 'Twistin' the Night Away' and started out real slow. It went on for over five minutes, teasing the audience and everyone going nuts, like being edged before the climax... Then – bam! – the song starts and everybody was screaming and 'twisting'. Then confetti started to rain down on the stage, at least three feet of it. The band were playing, kicking around, falling in it, and then huge fans behind the stage blew clouds of confetti into the crowd. There were real hot French waitresses pushing drink carts around the stage, making drinks and serving them to the band, Rod kicking soccer balls into the crowd, bagpipers walking around the audience... Fun, fun, fun...

I WAS THERE: PAUL DUBIEL

I saw the Faces two or three times at the Chicago Auditorium, once at the Ampitheater and also in Puerto Rico, at the Mar y Sol festival. At first impression, Rod and Ron Wood both had the same haircut, Me and my friends called it 'chicken head', and began to cut our own hair the same way. The Faces also had very stylish clothes, which were not normal in the early Seventies, but the best thing about them was the fun they had playing with each other and with the audience. They were often asking what song we wanted to hear next, which created a very intimate feeling with a huge group, which I have never seen before or since. They were like 'we're your friends' and it was as if they were performing just for you!

Halfway through the show they had a bar on wheels, full of liquor. They began drinking and passing out bottles of wine to the audience – glass bottles and not a single person was injured! Why should we be, we were all together having a good time with thousands of strangers who were now our friends. I miss those days... What the hell happened?

The band was tight, rocking and loud, which was very similar to the Rolling Stones' honky tonk style at that time, but with more heart and soul. Something else that struck me was the humbleness displayed by such a talented group of musicians. Rod was the leader, but he was never arrogant and everyone got a solo...

CONVENTION CENTER
20 FEBRUARY 1975, INDIANAPOLIS, INDIANA

I WAS THERE: SID GRIFFIN

In 1975 I saw the Faces on both their spring tour and then again on their autumn tour in South Carolina. They were fantastic and, of course, in between these tours Ronnie Wood went out with the Rolling Stones on tour. So I saw Ronnie play live four times that year, and it was obvious to me he couldn't be in both bands at once. Musically speaking, you would never have guessed that the band that I saw in spring 1975 and in autumn 1975 was going to disband.

Yes, behind the scenes we knew Ronnie Lane had been unhappy and had left and we now know Ian MacLagan was unhappy at the situation. Kenney Jones was furious that Rod Stewart didn't want to gig in 1974, and told the media Rod's decision not to gig cost him something like £100,000. But when you saw the band onstage, either at the spring or autumn gigs, you would never have guessed there was any dissent in the ranks. They were terrific.

In the spring, they were performing songs from Ronnie Wood's autumn 1974 new record, *I've Got My Own Album To Do*, where they did things like

TELL EVERYONE: A PEOPLE'S HISTORY OF THE FACES

'Take a Look at the Guy' and 'I Can Feel The Fire' and they did some songs from Rod Stewart's *Smiler* LP, like 'Sweet Little Rock and Roller'. I remember they did that and of course they did the Sam Cooke medley with the live string section onstage, arranged by Jimmy Horowitz. For me, the string section was too much, a kind of a bridge too far, but it was interesting to see a 20-piece string section on stage and you could hear it in the auditorium. It was not drowned out by the loud rock and roll guitars.

There was no band on earth that ever drew you into their show more than the Faces. There were bands which played a very warm inviting music before, and there were bands which had a stage show which drew you in. Witness Bruce Springsteen, the Replacements, NRBQ and some others… I like to think the Long Ryders did too, as we were all Faces fans top to bottom. But there was never anything quite like the Faces to me. They did not play *at* their audiences as most rock bands do, they played *for* and *with* their audience, drawing them into the show.

There are only two things which these days remind me of a Faces concert. The first is a really good football match in between two Premier League or Championship League rivals. If you've ever been to one of those football derbies between rivals, where everyone is singing and the atmosphere never stops, never wanes, never slows, then you've been to an event which is like a Faces concert. The other thing that reminds me of a Faces show is the atmosphere at a prize fight. I imagine most people reading this have never been to a professional boxing match, but if you have and you know what it's like when the fighting heats up and everyone is on their feet in a crowd and screaming, then you have also experienced something like a performance by the Faces back in their early 1970s heyday.

I have seen many a fine concert since, witnessed many an exuberant rock and roll performance since, but I have never seen and heard recreated the vibe, the tenor or the feeling you received from a Faces performance. And I do not expect to ever have that feeling or experience again. It was sadly never really captured on record, but *A Nod is as Good as a Wink…* has moments where it's captured on record. Before McLagan died, he was working with the late Gary Stewart at Rhino Records in creating from live tapes the ultimate Faces live album. Now that both gentlemen are gone, I guess we'll never hear it. May McLagan, Ronnie Lane and Gary Stewart rest in peace.

TELL EVERYONE: A PEOPLE'S HISTORY OF THE FACES

I WAS THERE: JEFF MILLER

My fraternity brothers and I were all big fans of Rod Stewart and Faces. My female guest for the evening tossed a bar of soap up on stage and Rod picked it up and rubbed it over his body as he performed. After the show we went to the Hilton where they were staying. As they walked from the limo into the hotel, my 'date' said, 'Mr. Stewart, I really enjoyed your show.' He commented, 'Thank you, love.' She then said, 'Save energy, shower with a friend.'

Jeff Miller and his friend Jane got to party with the Faces

That was the caption on the bar of soap. Rod then said, 'You and your friends can meet me at the bar.' We gathered up another couple and went to the bar. Rod was nowhere to be found.

As we were walking out, I saw Rod on the house phone. We went over to him and he was on the phone to Ron Wood's suite. My date was very short and had a bustline out to South Bend. Rod was looking her up and down and said, 'Woody, Woody. You've got to get down here and look at these tits!' We eventually joined them at the bar. About 3am, the bartender quit serving us as last call was 2am. They said, 'Fuck you! We could buy this place. Let's go trash the pool!'

After throwing furniture into the pool, Ronnie looked at me and said, 'It's time for you to go' and told my companion, 'You're coming with me.' Ronnie ended up taking my 'date' on the road with them for about three months. When she returned, I heard all the stories. She had a wild time! I've read Keith Richard's biography and several of the names mentioned there I recognised from her stories. I won't say in what capacity, but I recognised them just the same!

She'll never forget her time with Faces. Neither will I. It was an awesome concert! Faces kicked ass. What a hard working band! A few years later I went to a Stones concert in Chicago. I ran into her there. I asked where she was going when the lights went down. She said, 'Right in front of Ronnie.' He recognised her and we were both invited back stage. He remembered me as well and thought we might have gotten married, but we were just friends. She's a great friend at that and we both have special memories from that night back in '75 and from seeing the Stones in Chicago as well!

CIVIC CENTER
21 FEBRUARY 1975, CHARLESTON, VIRGINIA

I WAS THERE: GARY PLANTS, AGE 20

I only saw the Faces this one time and I've seen Rod probably 15 times since. It was a real rock and roll show and the venue was pretty much sold out. It held 12,000 to 15,000 people, depending on the concert. The show was festival seating, which was popular at that time. There were no chairs on the floor in front of the stage, so if you bought floor seats it was first come, first served. I was at the concert with a girl I had dated for a couple of years and we were in the middle of calling it quits, so not the best of times. I remember there was an abundance of pot at the concert. It was everywhere. One thing that is still very much in my memory about the show is that, when everyone started chanting for 'Maggie May', Rod's reply at the time was 'I don't have to sing it if I don't want to… and I don't want to!' That kind of stung a bit, and at the time I thought 'what an ass'. Later on in the show he did sing it, and things were better after he did. I've been a big fan ever since.

Gary Plant thought Rod wouldn't sing 'Maggie'

CIVIC CENTER
23 FEBRUARY 1975, CHARLESTON, VIRGINIA

The Faces earn a lukewarm review: 'Faces Know Place: Behind Rod Stewart'.

MADISON SQUARE GARDEN
24 FEBRUARY 1975, NEW YORK, NEW YORK

PHILIP CACCIAPAGLIA, AGE 16
Blue Öyster Cult was the back up. The Faces had a completely white stage – amps, rugs, everything matched! They had a full bar set up on stage and when they entered, 'The Stripper' tune was played. They played most of what was on *Overtures and Beginners*. I was so stoned I can't believe I remember it all, but they were a favourite of mine!

I WAS THERE: BEN HOCHBERG
After the '73 show, I saw them three times in 1975, firstly in February when Blue Öyster Cult opened for them at Madison Square Garden. I didn't know what all the fuss was about BOC, but the Faces were great.

In August they played Roosevelt Stadium in Jersey City, New Jersey. Lynyrd Skynyrd opened and were excellent. When Ten Years After came on, it was right after Alvin Lee had decided to play electric music again after his stint doing mellow stuff with Mylon LeFevre and George Harrison. TYA blew the house down. In contrast, when the Faces came out, they were disappointingly lacklustre. There was an echo off the back of the stadium that seemed to annoy Rod, and they couldn't keep up the high energy level set by Skynyrd and Ten Years After.

In October they played Nassau Coliseum again. It may have been during this show where the band took a break for an extended drum solo by Kenney Jones. There was an actual bar set up on stage with a bartender. Everyone but Kenney went over to the bar and enjoyed some drinks right there on stage while he played. When Kenney indicated that his solo was coming to an end, the rest of the band waved him off and continued their drinking, leaving poor Kenney to improvise some more.

CIVIC CENTER
25 FEBRUARY 1975, PROVIDENCE, RHODE ISLAND

I WAS THERE: SARAH LOCKWOOD DONAHUE

I saw the Faces in 1975. That was a long time ago. My twin managed to get autographs from Rod, Woody and Tetsu, and all the Stones (including Woody) in June 1975 in Boston. I've seen Rod 17 times since.

I WAS THERE: PETER D'ERRICO

I saw the Faces twice in 1975, at Providence Civic Center and again in October at the Boston Garden. For the February date, several of us slept out in front of the venue months earlier to be the first ones to purchase tickets. We were in the front row on Woody's side. He wore the shirt with the black wings that night and we caught a few of the silver ping pong balls!

The October show was a bit more 'Rod' as it had the back catwalk which was across the rear of the stage. Rod would go there to sing to the crowd. Jesse Ed Davis was the second guitarist that night. I also saw Woody in June of that year, as he played with the Stones at Boston Garden.

THE FORUM
3 & 5 MARCH 1975, LOS ANGELES, CALIFORNIA

I WAS THERE: PATRICIA PALERMO

It was the beginning of new ways to sell tickets. I had a friend, Duane, whose father worked at or ran one of those new ticket agencies. He got us great seats, centre, not too far back from the stage. I caught a soccer ball the Rod kicked out. I think he had a dozen or so. The guys behind me were trying to wrestle the ball from my hands. Duane was a big guy and he got them to leave me alone. The soccer ball had marks from Rod's boots. I kissed them. And I held onto that ball like it was a baby. Thugs in the parking lot tried to get the ball from me too. It was later stolen from the Newport Beach, California house I rented with friends. That was a sad day, losing my prized possession. I loved Rod and Ronnie and all the Faces. I found it shocking at first when Ronnie left to join the Stones, but he and Keith were so good together.

I WAS THERE: LOUIS VARGAS

In early 1975, the Faces played several shows in southern California and I went to three of them. There was no new Faces album so they toured on Rod's *Smiler* album and Ron Wood's first solo album. They played two dates at the Forum with a day off between shows. On the first night, I sat in the sixth row just off centre stage. It was a great concert and I got some really good photos. At the very end, a ton of small silver ping pong balls fell from above onto the front of the stage and into the crowd. I scooped up a few, keeping one and giving the others away. I found out much later that the silver balls were meant to symbolise pinballs and it was Rod's way of saying that he was meant to sing 'Pinball Wizard' in the movie *Tommy*, not Elton John.

The next day, between the two concerts, me and a couple of friends heard that the Faces were staying in Beverly Hills so we left school early and headed over to the Beverly Wilshire Hotel. We were there for only a few minutes and who do we bump into but Rod himself! We talked with him for a few minutes about the concert the previous night and how we were going the following night. I got an autograph from him. He was pretty cool. The next night I had fourth row centre and my two friends had first row centre. It was another great concert!

Two nights later, on Friday March 7th, a bunch of us from school piled into two cars and drove to the Swing Auditorium in San Bernardino to see the Faces. The Swing Auditorium is a large metal barn converted

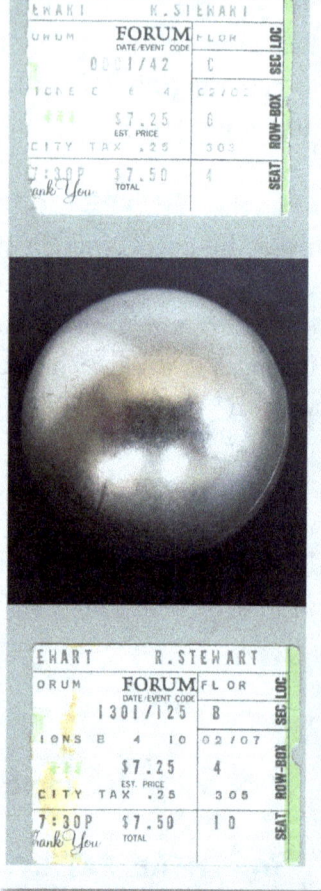

Louis Vargas caught two Forum shows

into a concert hall and it was hot as hell in there. It was a great show but what a sweatbox! It was a standing room only show so I got up to the front. I hadn't brought my camera because I was pretty happy with my Forum photos, and I wanted to enjoy the show without my camera.

I WAS THERE: MAUREEN MASSARELLA, AGE 16

It was my first concert and I fell in love with both Rod and the whole concert experience. I've seen Rod over a dozen times since. I started taking my son to concerts when he was four years old. When he was 16, Rod played at the Staples Center in LA and I spent hundreds of dollars on the two tickets so we would be up close. As I was 16 when I first saw Rod, it was fantastic that, when my son was 16, Rod was in town.

Maureen saw Rod when she was sweet 16

HEC EMUNDSON PAVILION
12 MARCH 1975, SEATTLE, WASHINGTON

I WAS THERE: WALT BRICKER

They were touring the *Smiler* album. Rod was wearing a shiny purple three-piece suit and Ron had on black pants and the black waist coat with the feathers on the shoulders. I didn't recognize the *Smiler* songs yet but they did '(I Know) I'm Losing You' with a long drum solo and also 'You Send Me'/'Bring It on Home to Me'. The final song was 'You Wear It Well', going straight into 'Maggie May'. They had a giant mirror ball and what looked like about a million chrome ping pong balls falling over it. There was no encore. Foghat opened.

NOW LOOK
RELEASED 2 JULY 1975

Ronnie Wood's second solo album, featuring Mac and Kenney but also Keith Richards, is released. It reaches 118 on the Billboard 200.

'SAILING'
RELEASED 8 AUGUST 1975

Rod's choice of 'Three Time Loser' as the UK single from his forthcoming album is overridden by Warner Bros. 'Sailing' reaches number 1 in the UK singles charts, stays there for four weeks and goes on to be Rod's biggest selling UK 45.

ATLANTIC CROSSING
RELEASED 15 AUGUST 1975

Rod's sixth solo album is released, recorded at Muscle Shoals Sound Studio. It's the first solo Rod album with no other member of the Faces on it.

CIVIC CENTER
19 AUGUST 1975, ASHVILLE, NORTH CAROLINA

The Faces embark upon their twelfth and what will prove to be their final tour of North America. Jesse Ed Davis joins the line up as an additional guitarist and a twelve-piece string section, hired in each city the band plays, appears on stage for 'Angel' and the 'Bring It on Home to Me'/'You Send Me' medley.

THE SCOPE
20 AUGUST 1975, NORFOLK, VIRGINIA

I WAS THERE: SIDNEY LOWE JR

My love for rock starts and ends at the concert watching the Faces, the best band ever, with my future wife. They weren't exactly your average band. They were sloppy and out of time but loud and, oh God, did they hit the spot with me? I loved all five of those guys. I still remember they played 'Ooh La La'. What a great show. I only got to see the Faces once, but I've seen Rod Stewart over 20 times. I'm still a die-hard Faces fan, and I also love the Small Faces. Rest In Peace, Steve Marriott.

CLEVELAND STADIUM
23 AUGUST 1975, CLEVELAND, OHIO

I WAS THERE: MICHAEL NEISER

This show was billed as *World Series of Rock* and was one of a series held in Cleveland between 1974 and 1980 at the Municipal Stadium, sponsored by radio station WMMS out of Cleveland. We partied in the stadium parking lot the night before. It rained like hell up until show time. I remember it was a very hot day, with lots of people at Red Cross stations, but it was a great concert. Mahogany Rush opened with a wonderful rendition of 'The Star-Spangled Banner'. Blue Öyster Cult and Aerosmith had a great choice of tunes and energy but Uriah Heep were a bit of a let down.

Michael Neiser remembers 'the best show I ever attended'

People began doing somersaults down the nets behind home plate and climbing the foul poles. When Rod and Faces were about to start, darkness had set in and the shenanigans of the crowd continued. Rod strutted out on stage to begin but everyone's attention was focused in the other direction. He left and came back out again, getting everyone's attention this time. They were great, and well worth the ticket price of $10. I remember the sound wasn't the greatest, but back then that was commonplace at big open air shows. It's very easily the best concert I ever attended.

I WAS THERE: RICK MENARD

Mahogany Rush opened followed by Blue Öyster Cult, Aerosmith, Uriah Heep and then the Faces. Both Mahogany Rush and Aerosmith were fantastic which pushed the Faces to put on a phenomenal show. It rained that day and the guys got a little wet but they soldiered on. Another show we saw was at the Cobo Hall in Detroit. Every show we saw the Faces play was great. At one they had an orchestra with them and Rod spent a lot of time leading them. At another, they had a bar and a bartender serving them, and a white stage

MYRIAD CONVENTION CENTER
28 AUGUST 1975, OKLAHOMA CITY, OKLAHOMA

I WAS THERE: DARREN KNOX

I saw the last Faces tour, with Tetsu Yamauchi and without Ronnie Lane. Either the band, or maybe just Rod, made a grand entrance to the music of 'The Stripper' over the PA. I recall the soccer balls and a lot of glitz. 'Sailing' had been released and they played it, 'Stay with Me', and – of course – 'Maggie May'. That's about all I remember.

ANAHEIM STADIUM
30 AUGUST 1975, ANAHEIM, CALIFORNIA

I WAS THERE: LOUIS VARGAS

The Faces paid a second visit to California in 1975 but were playing stadiums. I'm not fond of stadium concerts – but it was the Faces. Fleetwood Mac were opening, Loggins and Messina were second on the bill and the Faces were headlining. I got up to about 20 feet from the stage during Loggins and Messina. When they finished their set, it took forever for the Faces to get onstage. I found out later that their equipment truck had broken down and they had to rush and get rental equipment. The minute the Faces hit the stage, the crowd rushed forward. During their whole set it was a case of survival down in the front of the stage, with a lot of pushing and shoving going on. I noticed that Jesse Ed Davis was playing guitar along with Woody. The set had changed only slightly from the concerts in March. I enjoyed the concert, but it was hell in the front of the stage.

I WAS THERE: SEPP DONAHOWER

The band would be in tour buses. Or, when they were big, they would charter a plane. They had varying transportation modes, and as the promoter you are a separate entity. You're catching the redeye flight and you're on your own schedule. You're not in the plane with the band. You've got to get there before they come there, get the hall ready, get the union crews ready for when the truck shows up with the gear and get the show set up. You've got to run the show, settle up with the box office and pay everybody. The band is long gone before you leave the hall.

Peter (Buckland) would be with the band primarily, rounding them all up, getting them in the cars, getting them to the hotel and sending away the undesirables. That's the typical job of a tour manager; the same job that Richard Cole would do for Led Zeppelin, the same gig. Peter would also make sure the light and the sound was set up correctly, and we would collaborate with Peter to make sure everything was perfect. We were pretty good promoters, so everything ran pretty smooth. That's why we became a big company quickly. The bands don't deal with flakes. If you don't have your act together, they'll find somebody else.

We only had one real crisis I remember, and that was when we had Anaheim Stadium filled with about 50,000 people and the band's equipment and the sound equipment hadn't showed up yet because the truck broke down. And the audience were fed with two or three hours of excuses. That was like a crisis date. The band were probably having a nervous breakdown by the time they had to perform. We didn't know if we were going to have a riot and the stadium would collapse. We were just praying that we would get through the day.

Being a promoter is brutal, especially if you're doing it night after night. You can understand why stimulants might have become popular when you're on the road.

When we put them on at the Forum in Los Angeles, they put on a hell of a show and they really owned the audience. That was an 18,000 capacity show. They would get an audience into a fever pitch. They were a real high energy band.

When the Black Crowes came out, I thought they must've gone to some Faces shows, because they sounded almost like the Faces live. The Faces live were better than their albums.

BALBOA STADIUM
31 AUGUST 1975, SAN DIEGO, CALIFORNIA

I WAS THERE: BARON URIAS
I saw them in Berdoo on the release of *A Nod is as Good as a Wink… to a Blind Horse* and later at Balboa Stadium in San Diego. They headlined a bill that opened with Lynyrd Skynyrd and Fleetwood Mac, who introduced Lindsay Buckingham and Stevie Nicks as brand new members, along with Loggins and Messina whose big hit at the time was 'Your Momma Don't Dance'. Their whole stage was in white – the stage, the amps, the grand piano. And they had a 12-piece string orchestra in tuxedos and the four horn players from Tower of Power. Rod wore silver and mauve silk PJs and a pink feather boa. He sang 'I'd Rather Go Blind' with so much soul that people in the audience, me included, were weeping. The Faces were working class yobos with a keen ear for their roots. It was a party when they played, and a rollicking good time.

MADERA SPEEDWAY
1 SEPTEMBER 1975, FRESNO, CALIFORNIA

I WAS THERE: LOUIS VARGAS
A few days after seeing them in Anaheim, me and a couple of friends drove up to Fresno to the Madera Speedway for another Faces concert. This is one of the strangest line-ups I have ever seen. The Faces were headlining with Black Sabbath second on the bill, Lynyrd Skynyrd third and Fleetwood Mac bottom. It took the roadies forever to set up Fleetwood Mac's equipment, and by the time they set it up there was not

enough time for the band to perform. They had to tear down Fleetwood Mac's equipment and set up Skynyrd's equipment. Those were some pissed off roadies!

By the time the Faces hit the stage, most of the crowd were exhausted. It was a long day. Because of that, it was nice and mellow in the front of the stage. I enjoyed the concert much more than Anaheim.

SPARTAN STADIUM
6 SEPTEMBER 1975, SAN JOSE, CALIFORNIA

I WAS THERE: KEVIN BUSHMAN

I met them backstage when I was 12 or 13 years old at Spartan Stadium, when War opened for them. War's harmonica player, Lee Oskar, was married into our family and when they played local shows I would get to go. For this one, I got to show up with them in the limo and went backstage. I saw the Faces and couldn't help but think, 'Man, these guys sure have big noses. And lots of make up!'

HONOLULU INTERNATIONAL CENTER
9 & 10 SEPTEMBER 1975, HONOLULU, HAWAII

I WAS THERE: JIM NARDI

I had graduated from high school the previous spring and this was only the second or third arena concert I had been to. I'd been a big fan of the band for several years. I recall Ron playing one of his Zemaitis guitars and it just looked so cool under the

Jim Nardi's version of Ronnie Wood's guitar

HOT FUN IN THE SUN No. 2

Rod Stewart FACES

WAR

PETER FRAMPTON

EAST BAY STROKE

**SATURDAY SEPT. 6.
SPARTAN STADIUM**

MorningSun Productions

OPEN 10 AM   MUSIC STARTS AT NOON

Tickets: $7.50 in advance; now at all BASS outlets, Pacific Stereo and Montgomery Ward stores; ASUC—Berkeley; Bullock's—Palo Alto; Banana Records—Sutter St., San Francisco; Munters Music—Livermore, Discount Records—Reno; San Jose Box Office, All Macy's stores; Neil Thrams—Oakland, Peninsula Box Office—Los Altos; Book Mark—Freemont, Santa Cruz Box Office. For BASS information and reservations dial T-E-L-E-T-I-X or (408) 246-1160. Please, no bottles, cans or alcoholic beverages.

PACIFIC PRESENTATIONS

lights. I couldn't afford the real deal, but I did pick up the Samick version down the road; still one of my favourite guitars to play today.

COLISEUM
27 SEPTEMBER 1975, CHARLOTTE, NORTH CAROLINA

I WAS THERE: SKIP THOMPSON

I saw them on their last US tour in 1975. The stage was kinda like two levels, with staircases on each side. The upper level had an entrance way and, as the song 'The Stripper' was playing, they made their entrance through the door opening. They then paired off and made their way down each stairway. And when they were ready to go, Rod went up to the mic and said, 'Saturday night in Charlotte, it's got to be good.' They opened up with 'Memphis, Tennessee'. Britt Ekland was sitting at the side of the stage. A girl threw a bracelet up on stage and Rod picked it up and tossed it to Britt. They rocked and rolled like crazy.

Skip and Mac

I also met and got to know Ian McLagan. He would come through town playing gigs. And I always made a point of having a good chat with him after each show.

SPECTRUM
1 OCTOBER 1975, PHILADELPHIA, PENNSYLVANIA

I WAS THERE: DIANE VOLPE

I loved the whole Mod scene and fell in love with The Who and Small Faces. I can't tell you how many times I saw The Who and wrote for a fanzine in the States called *Who's News*. Unfortunately, I never got to see the Small Faces but was thrilled when the Faces came to Philly in the '70s. I was in my late twenties and went a number of times with close friends who loved British bands. What I remember the most from Faces shows is that you never sat down. You were always dancing in your seat and singing so loud with Rod that your voice was hoarse by the time you left. The shows always left you euphoric... a natural high. The last time I saw them in Philly was bitter sweet, because I knew they were retiring as a band.

I WAS THERE: LYLE BECKWITH

I was eleven years old when I heard 'Maggie May'. I got into Rod and then I realised that Ronnie Wood and a lot of Faces played on his solo albums, and so I got into the Faces albums. I was in my formative years, just getting into music, and the energy they had just struck a chord with me. I loved that they sang about things that I cared about when I was 13 or 14 and growing older – girls, drinking, having a good time, cars.

Lyle Beckwith remembers a fun show

The whole thing was upbeat and not dark or heavy like a lot of rock songs. They were uplifting and fun and it was all about having a good time. They were just a tad older than me and gave me a vision of what it might be like to be older and having fun. I only saw them live once, on the last tour.

I lived way up in rural Pennsylvania, about an hour north of Philadelphia, so whenever there was a concert we'd have to go into Philadelphia to the Spectrum, where the hockey team played and all the concerts were held.

All my soccer buddies from high school were into the Faces, so a bunch of us went down with a couple of our girlfriends. Our seats were on the first overhang tier, stage left, and right on the railing. One of the guys' girlfriends was sitting on the railing, just leaning over and watching the warm up. As soon as the lights went out for the Faces to come on, I physically picked her up and moved her back and grabbed that seat. So I was just hanging over the railing watching.

There was so much energy, it was so much fun. I was overwhelmed. I was singing along with every song. I was wearing a *Peaky Blinders*-type cap. I wore it everywhere. I wore it to soccer games, where I'd keep it on the bench and put it on when I came off the pitch at half time. I wore it when I drove – I had an old Austin Healey back then – I just wore it all over the place. When the Faces came on to do their encore, I threw that cap down onto the stage. It was the only tribute I could do to the band to show how big a fan I was.

I remember Rod running all over the stage. Bruce Springsteen must have taken lessons from him, because that's the only concert I've seen that has the same kind of energy as a Faces concert. The word that keeps coming back to me is fun. They were just fun.

ASSEMBLY HALL, UNIVERSITY OF INDIANA
3 OCTOBER 1975, BLOOMINGTON, INDIANA

I WAS THERE: GLENN MOORE

I saw the Faces farewell tour. The J Geils Band opened. The sound was bad. The echoes were bad. But it didn't ruin the show. J Geils' opening set was powerful and set the bar high, and I saw Ronnie Wood at the side stage, watching intently. So J Geils really rocked and Rod Stewart gave a tip of the cap to them as the Faces took the stage. They seemed to be having a good time as I watched them. One of the highlights was 'I'm Losing You'. Kenney Jones' drum solo on this song really brought down the house and was followed by extended applause. Of course, they did the classics, with the crowd cheering songs when they had played just the first few notes. My friends and I really enjoyed the entire show. I was just starting to play guitar at the time and I watched Ronnie and J Geils closely. Ronnie had some great tone and didn't play that many notes, but played just the right ones. Except for the echoes, it is one of my favourite shows ever.

UNIVERSITY OF NOTRE DAME ATHLETIC & CONVOCATION CENTER
4 OCTOBER 1975, SOUTH BEND, INDIANA

I WAS THERE: MARK MCINERNEY

An acquaintance of mine played back-up violin at that concert. J Geils opened so it was a great concert with two soon-to-be famous front men and two outstanding guitarists, J Geils and Ron Wood. Are the Faces in the Rock and Roll Hall of Fame? J Geils aren't!

SPORTS ARENA
7 OCTOBER 1975, TOLEDO, OHIO

I WAS THERE: RICHARD B KELLEY

As the Stones summer tour ended in a cloud of conjecture about what really happened when he and Keith Richards were busted in rural Fordyce, Arkansas, Ronnie returned to the Faces for another US run. The Faces line-up was a bit different, however, as journeyman guitarist Jesse Ed Davis was added to the band. Jesse was a Native American who'd kicked around the British music scene for a few years as a utility player for Eric Clapton, John Lennon, George Harrison and other luminaries. It was thought he had been brought in to provide a level of focus and professionalism to the Faces, who couldn't always be depended upon for musical consistency. They would be promoting Rod's all important Warner Bros debut after all. There were said to be some shows on that fall run in which Ronnie sat out, leaving Jesse Ed to play all of the guitar parts in this new, and now crumbling, version of the Faces.

A two night return to Detroit was scheduled in October and one night at the Sports Arena in Toledo, Ohio, just fifty miles south. I was still working at the underground record store and head shop and we were selling tickets to the show, now clearly billed as Rod Stewart and the Faces. The Detroit shows, with a capacity of about 12,000 (back at Cobo), were sold out or close to doing so, while the Toledo show was doing modestly well with maybe a little less than a thousand tickets left in a 5,500 capacity venue.

Among my duties at the record store was returning the cash and any unsold tickets to the arena box office somewhere around 4pm on the day of a given show. In so doing, I was rewarded with a pair of comps to that night's performance by the box office manager. I was looking forward to seeing the Faces for the second time that year, when suddenly one of the store owners stormed out of the office shouting, 'The shit's gonna hit the fan! The Rod Stewart show has been cancelled!'

We never did learn why the show was pulled, literally three hours before the doors were to open, but it wasn't the best of times in the Faces world in the fall of 1975. The band broke up shortly thereafter, with Rod Stewart bitchily proclaiming they 'couldn't keep it going with the guitarist on permanent loan to the Rolling Stones' or some whine to that effect. Ironic given his outsized importance in what had originally been a band of equals.

In the years since, Faces reunion albums and tours have been rumoured but never come to fruition. With just three surviving members, all well into their seventies, it's a good bet it'll never happen and likely just as well. What the Faces captured in a few short years was lightning in a bottle, unique and unrepeatable. Five guys walk onto a concert stage...

CIVIC ARENA
9 OCTOBER 1975, PITTSBURGH, PENNSYLVANIA

I WAS THERE: DENISE GOUGLER CUBAKOVIC, AGE 16
It was festival seating, where you sit on the floor and there were no chairs. It meant you could walk up to the stage anytime you wanted. It was my first concert ever and I will never forget it! I even partied with the roadies and a little with Rod in the hotel room after.

BOSTON GARDEN
13 OCTOBER 1975, BOSTON, MASSACHUSETTS

I WAS THERE: KEITH REXFORD, AGE 16
I saw them at the old Boston Garden. Keith Richards was playing with the band, basically auditioning Ronnie Wood for the Stones. It was a great show.

THE OMNI
19 OCTOBER 1975, ATLANTA, GEORGIA

I WAS THERE: JOHN LEE DOZIER

The Omni was a big venue for rock concerts, although the acoustics were not good there and the best shows were at the Municipal Auditorium and the clubs back then. The Omni's capacity was around 20,000 and I saw Jefferson Starship, Santana, The Who and Robin Trower there, as well as the Faces. I don't think Rod Stewart ever stopped moving on that huge stage. He dressed in all white, like the orchestra. It was a very energetic concert. Ronnie Wood was the driving force of the band, and it was him I really went to see, but Rod Stewart was a hell of an action-packed entertainer (even though I was never a big fan). The chicks loved him back then. There was talk of Jeff Beck joining them for this show as a special guest. That didn't happen but overall it was a great, energetic show.

I WAS THERE: RICK FREEMAN

Flash forward to 1973 and 1974. Ron Wood and Keith Richards had become friends. *I've Got My Own Album to Do* was my favourite. I played it so much, trying to figure out who played what. The fact that there were no credits drove me insane. It was only years later that the credits were released. Of course, the rest is history. I knew, no matter what the Stones were saying or doing, Wood was going to be in the band. The Stones toured here in 1975. I saw them four times. At times I felt Ron overplayed some of his solos but he was learning. As Ron had said, he planned to be a member of both groups.

That fall, the Faces toured with an orchestra. I saw them in Atlanta. *Atlantic Crossing* had just been released. They also had Tetsu on bass, Jessie Ed Davis on guitar and – at the show in Atlanta – Bobby Womack on guitar and backing vocals. It was a great show, but the chemistry and camaraderie was gone, with very little interaction between the members of the group. I think Rod and Ron had both already left the band in reality and were just finishing out the tour. As much as I loved the show, I knew the end was near. Of course, Rod Stewart went on to become one of the largest selling artists ever. His *Songbook* albums made him enough money for him and countless generations of Stewarts.

Ron is by far one of the best guitar players around. Listen to his brilliant playing on the Stones' *Blue and Lonesome*. I have listened to every Stones concert since they started back touring in 2012. His playing is sublime. No bum notes. People forget he was only one of three people to ever play on stage with Led Zeppelin. I have listened to the encore he played on. His 'duel' with Jimmy Page should be required listening to any aspiring student of music. Ronnie Lane's bass playing rivals anyone's. He sounded like a second guitar player and I loved his voice. Ian McLagan was and is the best rock 'n' roll keyboard player, even when he toured with the Stones and Dylan. I thought Kenney Jones was a great choice for The Who, and is one of my fantasy drummers with any group I imagine playing together. Unfortunately, he had the unenviable task of following Keith Moon.

COBO ARENA
21 & 22 OCTOBER 1975, DETROIT, MICHIGAN

I WAS THERE: MARK REICHARD

It was their last tour. Woody had already toured with the Stones that summer and Rod knew that he was going to be joining the Stones permanently, so that was that. I don't remember too much about the show except I thought they were pretty sloppy and generally didn't give a fuck. My impression is that they were a really great live band in the early Seventies. But by '75? Not so much.

They were very popular in Detroit, which was one of the first cities in the US where they really got a foothold. They played a big festival in West Michigan in 1970 called Goose Lake, I think about 200,000 people came. They had a lot of Michigan bands like the MC5 and the Stooges. One of my DJ friends said Rod and Woody were very nice and loved Mateus Rose (of all things). Detroit audiences loved bands that rocked hard and tried to be really entertaining. J. Geils was like that. No matter how big the audience, the Faces made it feel like you were in a bar and we (including the band) were all friends.

TELL EVERYONE: A PEOPLE'S HISTORY OF THE FACES

I WAS THERE: RICK EARNEST, AGE 24

By 1975 Rod was becoming a star in his own right, so I would speculate that many came just to see him. I remember it was packed. They were already pretty drunk when they hit the stage but performed a loud and rowdy set that included 'Maggie May', 'Stay With Me' and 'Every Picture Tells a Story'. By the end of the show, they were over the top, with Rod kicking soccer balls into the crowd. I also saw them at Goose Lake, a Woodstock-like festival in Michigan, in 1970. That one I don't remember as well…

I WAS THERE: TIM MARKO, AGE 16

I don't remember much about the concert other than the stage and piano were all white. There is a short video of that concert on YouTube.

I WAS THERE: BRUCE KAHN

Me and three friends made the hour drive from Eastern Michigan University to see what we knew would be the last appearance of Rod Stewart and the Faces here in Detroit. We were aware of the bickering going on within the band due to Rod doing his solo stuff and Ronnie Wood joining up with the Stones, but we still expected to see a top flight show and

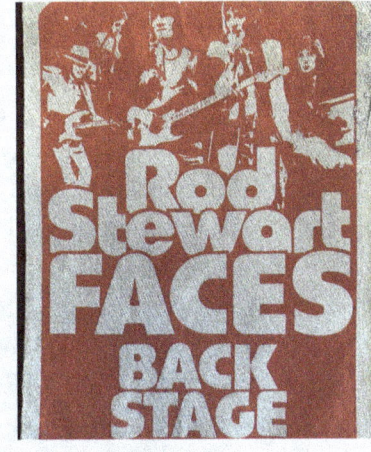

we got just that from one of the best rock bands of all-time. One of our group said that she knew the band would be at the Sheraton Southfield hotel afterwards, where many other bands stayed when playing the Motor City. She wanted to meet Ronnie Wood in the worst

Bruce Kahn's backstage pass and with Ronnie Wood

way, so we decided that at the risk of staying out all night and sleeping through our classes the next day, we'd go over there.

After a couple hours in the hotel bar, we decided it wasn't going to happen, plus we overheard someone saying that Woody had gone to an after show party at someone's house. While leaving the hotel, we ran into Rod and his then girlfriend Britt Ekland. We said 'hi' and started a conversation with him that lasted about five minutes. He was cordial and signed a programme that I had purchased outside the arena. He asked where it had come from and told me it wasn't official. Britt liked the picture in it of him laying on a mirrored stage, so he wasn't too upset about the fact that it was a bootleg item. Having been satisfied with running into some of rock's royalty, it was back to campus for us.

The next day, I managed to make it to one of my morning classes that one of our group, Brian, had with me. We talked about how great the show was and the experience of meeting Rod afterwards. It was at that instance that we both had the same idea – let's get the other two and try again to meet up with Woody. We didn't have tickets in hand for the show that night, but if we could at least have a drink with the 'new Stone', that would be good enough.

We went to the hotel mid-afternoon and called up to Woody's room. He answered and I said how great it was to see the Faces one last time and that we'd like to buy him a drink. He said to hang tight in the bar and he'd be downstairs. We went in the bar and parked it at a table, which turned out to be one where the late Bobby Womack and his manager were sitting. Womack was brought on the tour by Wood in response to Rod having Jesse Ed Davis playing in the band.

We had a drink with Bobby and his manager and talked about the friction within the band. Woody walked in with his assistant and sat down with us to have a drink. He ordered a straight Jack and a Jack and ginger ale and offered me one of them, since my glass was empty. They both looked the same to me and I ended up grabbing the Jack straight up. We chatted with Woody for about an hour and he asked if we were going to the show that night. I told him we didn't have tickets. He asked us if we wanted to go, and because I had put down a few cocktails and wasn't paying total attention, he asked again if we wanted to attend the gig, and I once again said we didn't have tickets.

He said, 'Bruce, I didn't ask if you had tickets, I asked if you want to go to the show tonight.' I got it together and I told him we would love to see it again. It was back downtown to Cobo Arena to see the Faces one last time, but for this one, we stood side stage as we had backstage access for the night. We were able to chat with Mac and Kenney beforehand, and it was an experience not to forget.

Bobby Womack told us to come back to the hotel to continue the party, which we did. While sitting in the bar with him, he got summoned upstairs to mediate a disagreement between Rod and the rest of the band. It was bad enough that it threatened to break them up before the tour was over. After an hour, Bobby returned to the bar to tell us that things were simmering down, but that he had more repair work to do with them to ensure they'd get through the last dates of the tour. We all understood and thanked him for taking the time to hang with us. It was once again time to head back to campus with some unbelievable memories that we'll have for the rest of our rock and roll lives. Long live the Faces!

I WAS THERE: CHARLESETTE HADDEN

The Faces were huge in Detroit. I probably saw 20 Faces shows. Detroit used have a radio station called WABX. Russ Gibb (who came up with the whole 'Paul is dead' thing about McCartney) was a DJ there and I remember sitting on my parents' front porch when he played the first song off *The Rod Stewart Album* (*An Old Raincoat Won't Ever Let You Down* in the UK), Rod's first album without Jeff Beck. It was the beginning of a very long love affair for me.

Russ Gibb was getting in contact with bands that no one had heard of, like the Faces and Led Zeppelin. Promoters brought them into Detroit and bands wanted to play at places like the Grande Ballroom because there was a kind of awakening that their music was going to be huge. And a Detroit audience was a really good audience to put that music in front of, as opposed to going to a city that just didn't get. It was a testing ground to see what the reaction was.

I was around 15 or 16, on the edge of being too young to be at the Grande, but I went anyway. My best friend in Detroit ran the Grande, so whether we were supposed to be there or not nothing was going to stop us. We'd go to see bands and there would be like ten people in the audience standing there. You knew that these people were going to be huge and it felt like you had an inside secret, walking in and seeing nobody else there.

They played the Eastown Theater with Spooky Tooth and shortly after they were playing stadiums and hiring limousines. It really caught on very quickly, between *The Rod Stewart Album* and *A Nod's as Good as a Wink…* It was a vast difference, and almost two completely different genres in terms of the way the tour was structured.

I love to sleep, and we went to a party after one show and everybody was having a very good time. All I wanted to do was go home to sleep, but I couldn't go without the person who needed to drive me home. So I went around, gathered up everybody's coats and went to sleep underneath the dining room table. And when I woke up, everybody was gone. I have no idea what happened! The people were probably looking for their coats. I never thought about that before.

By the time Rod was dating Britt Ekland, the Faces were huge. They were staying at the Hotel Pontchartrain in downtown Detroit. There was an escalator as you came into the hotel and everybody that was invited had to go up the escalator Riverdale stayed at the bottom just waiting for anybody to come down. I looked at my friend and I said, 'I just want to go home.' Everybody was getting drunk. Everybody did a lot of rum and Coke. My friend said 'all right' so I got on the escalator. I didn't realise that my criss-cross top became crisscrossed coming down the escalator. That was one of the more embarrassing moments of my entire life.

It was an odd evolution from the beginning of the time when we first saw them until they started doing the biggest stadiums. Obviously, the structure of having access to Rod and all of that changed. The band were very protective towards me because of my age. They always knew when the line was going to be crossed, and shovelled me out so I never got to see any of the really good stuff. The music seemed more real then, rather than produced.

You were always looking to see what they were going to be doing. I was really drawn by the way they looked. Everybody suddenly had a Rod Stewart haircut, like a male version of Farrah Fawcett, and some did it better than others. I went to Redford High School. It was notorious for having the best drug dealers in the city. There'd be a lot of people milling around and wandering around the school who thought they were rock 'n' roll bands and they all had the haircut. Rod is lucky that he's kept his hair this long.

They were fantastic times, and great clothes. I had an obsession with the clothing for anybody that was in a band. And Rod had a fabulous look. The Faces had a weird kind of part-hippie-part-glam style about them. There was the Jimmy Page-type pants, which were very sleek, and they had the trademark hair that none of us had seen before.

Ron Wood and Rod really did make the Faces a band. I don't identify Ronnie as a Rolling Stone and I never figured out why he just departed the Faces. He was just as successful with Rod and the Faces.

FORUM
24 OCTOBER 1975, MONTREAL, CANADA

I WAS THERE: DAN SIOUI

My ticket cost $6.50. I was a teenager and had of course consumed a few beers but I remember a lot of the show. Tunes I specifically remember are 'I'd Rather Go Blind', 'Jealous Guy', 'Love in Vain', 'You Send Me'/'Bring It on Home to Me', 'Maggie May' and 'You Can Make Me Dance'. I also remember Rod put on a good show in spite of being a little too drunk. We were seated on the side of the stage and saw Rod throwing up behind a set of speakers during the encore. But I enjoyed the show in spite of Rod's upset tummy! My buddy Sean was drinking a mickey of Southern Comfort during the show and offered it up to Ronnie Wood who without hesitation accepted the offer and took it. It's Sean's claim to fame!

I remember Ronnie performing a blistering solo during 'Love in Vain' but the one thing that sticks out in my memory more than anything is the start of the show, with Rod slowly stripping off his scarves and shirt, etc. to the tune of 'The Stripper'. And there was an orchestra of some note playing along with the boys, although I don't remember how many songs they joined the band on. I wish I could have seen the band when I was a few years older. I grew to appreciate the other members of the band, in particular Ronnie Lane, later and continued to be a big Stewart fan after the break up and saw him perform many times in the following years. But he was never really able to replicate that rollicking camaraderie the Faces had and I am so grateful to have seen the band before the break up.

I WAS THERE: JOHN BEKAVAC, AGE 15

How lucky I was to see them as my first concert ever as a 15-year-old? The cost of the ticket was $4.50 (Canadian). My seating was about five rows above the floor, close to the stage. The opening act was Heart, who were promoting their debut album, *Dreamboat Annie*. The show was awesome and energetic. Rod must have booted a few dozen soccer balls towards the audience, and seeing Woody on guitar was a bonus. I just wish I kept the ticket stub. Not long after, Ronnie joined the Stones and it was all over for the Faces. I was lucky to see them near the end.

MAPLE LEAF GARDENS
27 OCTOBER 1975, TORONTO, CANADA

I WAS THERE: MALCOLM MARTIN

It started in grade seven. The first song I heard was 'Itchycoo Park' by the Small Faces. My neighbours were older than me and I got access to their record collections so I found out about the Small Faces and the Jeff Beck Group. Then 'Maggie May' was on the radio and that was huge. Every day at lunch, I had French fries and gravy and listened to 'Maggie May'!

The Faces played Toronto in '71, '72 and '75. I was a huge fan of the Stones and they were very reminiscent of the Stones for me; flamboyant, with lots of outfits, lots of drinking and lots of cover tunes – 'Maybe I'm Amazed', 'It's All Over Now', 'Maybelline'. A great British rock 'n' roll band.

I met Woody once. In the summer of 1975, he was on loan to the Stones. I saw the Stones four times that summer and they played Toronto twice. We saw them the second night, and we'd already determined what hotel they were at. After the show, I drove to the Windsor Arms in downtown Toronto, not far from Maple Leaf Gardens, and there's the limo with Keith and Woody getting out. So it was, 'Holy shit, step lively boy and you're gonna catch them.'

It was a small hotel with only three or four floors, and so I just started doing level by level. I heard music blaring and it was 'Fingerprint File', on which Woody played bass. So I knocked on the door and, sure enough, Woody opens it. 'Hi, how ya doin'?' So I got his autograph and mentioned that I had caught the last couple of shows. I invited myself in and he said 'no' and slammed the door in my face!

I went downstairs and there was Ian Stewart standing there and nobody knew who he was, so I walked up to him: 'Stu! Blah blah blah…' There were other fans and groupies standing around, and these girls were saying 'who's this guy?'. Stu's talking to me, and he's got that lantern jaw, and he goes, 'Nobody recognises me because my hair is longer.' And I'm going, 'yeah, that's it. That's why!' Jagger was there, Anita Pallenberg. I had brief 'hi, how are you?' encounters with them. Anita had a skintight silver satin jumpsuit on, unzipped to the navel. I was following her around, saying 'take me to Keith'. 'No.' 'Take me to Keith!' 'No!'

I was disappointed as hell with the '75 Faces show because Ronnie Lane wasn't there. Tetsu was barely able to stand up, he was so drunk. They also had Jesse Ed Davis, which I understood because Woody wanted a second guitar player after playing with Keith. But there were too many people on stage, and because they were always loose the timings seemed to be off. It wasn't working, and they didn't have enough original material.

Ronnie Lane would write a song and he would have the whole thing down. Beginning, front, back, verse, chorus, bridge. Everything was there. And if Woody played something Rod liked, he'd say, 'That's a good riff, remember it.' And eight out of ten times he would, and they'd build a song around it. And you had the back and forth with Rod's solo career. I remember Mac saying, if it was a Faces track, 'Let's take the piano off.' 'How dare you?' But if it was a Stewart solo track, 'Sure, no problem. We can do a retake.' So there was always that struggle going on within the band. And they had been burned by Steve Marriott leaving, so the three Small Faces were mostly anti-lead singer.

Plus there was the heavy Britt Ekland influence on Stewart. The face make up was too much in my opinion. The Faces weren't a glam band. They were British rock 'n' roll and should have been treated as such. I like my meat and potatoes in my music, something I can sink my teeth into. Don't go all frilly on me. And, of course, then Rod went off to Hollywood. LSD – lead singer disease – is what I call it. They get full of themselves and off they go. It's happened in my band a million times. You bring them in. They're not so good. You nurture them for six months, they turn into Godzilla and then leave.

You had to see the Faces live. They were so much better live than in the studio. If they'd taken it a little more seriously and done a lot less drinking, they could have put together a definitive album. They never had a *Who's Next*, a *Sticky Fingers* or an *Abbey Road*. It was always, 'Yeah, pretty close.' Overall, they never lived up to their full potential in my mind. Maybe it was doomed from the beginning, but it was good while it lasted.

They only did three or four shows after Toronto and that was it.

I WAS THERE: IAN THOMSON, AGE 14

My sister bought *A Nod is as Good as a Wink to a Blind Horse* when it was released and I would sneak into her room and play that album whenever she was out. I was hooked. I followed them, along with The Who, my whole young life.

When I hit high school I also hit that magical age where

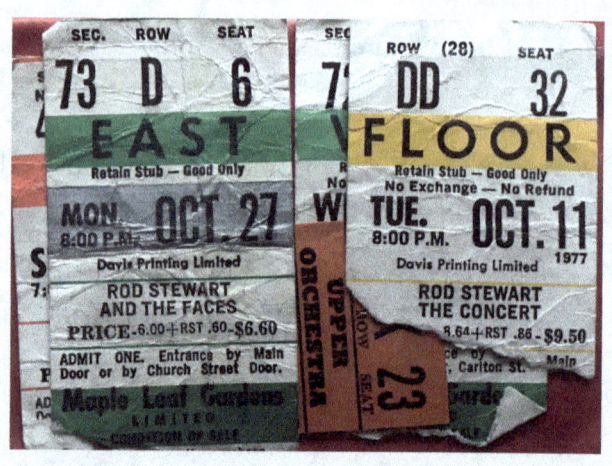

Ian Thomson's ticket for 'Rod Stewart and the Faces

your parents allowed you a lot more freedom so heading downtown Toronto to Maple Leaf Gardens to see shows became a ritual. I saw many bands there but the Faces who were billed as Rod Stewart and the Faces (which also pissed me off) was one of my all time favourites.

I went there with two friends from high school and a mitt full of hash to make sure we had a good time. We sat in section 73, which was more than halfway along the seating, so it was a good ways away from the action. Maple Leaf Gardens was not the best place to see bands. It had a lot of echo issues from the concrete, and the seating was not ideal for where the band played. However, I was in heaven. I am a guitar player, so my eyes stayed on Ronnie Wood the whole time. I was too young to remember how they played and the hash probably helped in that regard.

I was angry with them all at the time they broke up, because that's what you did when your favourite band breaks up when you're 14. I didn't want Ronnie Wood to join the Stones. I wanted things to remain the way they were.

MAPLE LEAF GARDENS
27 OCTOBER 1975, TORONTO, CANADA

I WAS THERE: RAY CANALE

I saw the Faces three or four times back in the day. I'm originally from Aberdeen but I moved to Canada when I was a young lad. I was 16 years old when I heard 'Maggie May' for the first time. A friend from high school got tickets to see the Faces in 1971. I hadn't put two and two together and didn't realise Rod Stewart was in the Faces. I went to the concert with a girl and with the pal and his girlfriend. I had to leave early because the father of the girl that I took the concert wanted her home at a certain time. So I missed the end of the bloody concert, the encore and all that.

Paul Burford had a hairdressing salon on Yonge Street in downtown Toronto called House of Lords. They had a big sign in the window with a picture of Rod Stewart advertising 'Stewart cuts', so I went in there one day and got my first Rod Stewart haircut. I developed a friendship with Paul and, through him, met this guy named Ewan Dawson. Ewan and Rod were very, very good friends from way back. Ewan had moved from London to Toronto. I met Ron Wood through Ewan, at the House of Lords, in 1975.

That fall, the Faces came to Toronto once again. We found out they were staying at the Royal York Hotel, so after the show me and a couple of pals rushed down to the Royal York Hotel and hung around the lobby. The lads walked through the front door and Rod began walking up the steps. I went over to him and said, 'Where have you been?' He looked at me and I said, 'You haven't been in Toronto for such a long time.' He said, 'Well, we've been busy, busy.' I said, 'Have you seen Ewan Dawson?' and Rod said, 'I imagine he's in the pub. Come down to the pub with us.' He invited me and my two pals to the bar in the Royal York Hotel.

In the bar, we all sat down. Rod was sat next to me and Ronnie Wood was sitting in the other seat. I remember them pulling this English girl's leg, talking about how Canadians are all such good tennis players. She said 'why is that?' and they said, 'Because it snows so much here in Canada. They play tennis in the summer and they use the tennis racquets as snowshoes to get around in the winter.' That cracked me up. I remember Rod getting up and they were just singing a little song together. There was a really good-looking girl there and Rod reached over her shoulder and grabbed her by the tit. You couldn't get away with that today!

Rod bought us all drinks and then, at the end of the evening, they all decided they were going to a party with this Ewan guy, so we all walked out the front of the hotel. Everybody was getting into cars and I distinctly remember all four of them squeezing into this Volkswagen bug. I was stood outside the hotel and I waved as the bug pulled away. They were very close to the end of the tour and I remember thinking that this was the last time the Faces were ever going to play in Toronto as a band, and the last time we were ever going to see them as a band.

Over the years I've met Rod a couple of times. My mum's uncle in Aberdeen had a good friend called Rick Simpson who became a very good friend of Rod's. So I managed to get tickets to a few of his concerts and meet him, and I actually travelled all the way to Aberdeen once, when Rod played in Aberdeen with his band for the first time. I flew all the way there just to see that concert, in my hometown.

STADIUM
31 OCTOBER 1975, CHICAGO, ILLINOIS

I WAS THERE: THOMAS ROBERT LANGFORD
Ronnie Wood had just got off his first tour with the Rolling Stones and he was wearing the same red leather suit he'd worn with the Stones, One of the highlights was that Jesse Ed Davis was on guitar, and he'd appeared on *Atlantic Crossing*, still one of my favourite Rod albums. They performed 'Three Time Loser', 'Sailing' and , I think, 'Alright for an Hour', as well as 'Sweet Little Rock and Roller' from the *Smiler* record. Jesse and Ronnie worked so well together. I wish they'd made a live album of that tour.

LABOR TEMPLE
1 NOVEMBER 1975, MINNEAPOLIS, MINNESOTA

The Faces play what is to be their last ever show.

I WAS THERE: LEON LAUDENBACH, AGE 19
I was 19 at the time, going on 12. We were playing the *Ooh La La* record all the time. The Stones and the Faces played in the summer and fall of that year, and my friend and I drove up from St Cloud, Minnesota for both shows. Ron Wood played with both bands, which was incredible to witness. I still believe that he is vastly underrated as a guitar player and songwriter.

We made it to downtown Minneapolis okay, but I was so drunk and stupid we were yelling out the window every other block, asking where the Minneapolis Auditorium was. I think Labor Temple was another name they used for it.

I never got to see Ronnie Lane play with the Faces but Tetsu Yamauchi did a great job. They had the addition of Jesse Ed Davis to beef up the sound, although I don't think that was ever needed. They entered down a white staircase with the theme song 'The Stripper' blaring. That really got the crowd roaring, and they opened with 'Memphis, Tennessee'. They played some new ones, 'Three Time Loser' – a Rod Stewart recording – and Ron Wood played 'Big Bayou', neither of which I'd heard before. Both were rocking. The energy went through the roof on 'Sweet Little Rock 'n' Roller' and 'Losing You'. It's just my two cents, but I think the Faces did the most credible covers of a Chuck Berry tune amongst their peers.

There was a bar and a bartender on stage that served drinks during their performance. The whole band retired to the bar during Kenney Jones' drum solo on '(I Know) I'm Losing You'. They also played 'Miss Judy's Farm' which has such driving guitar, something you don't hear from Ron Wood in his role with the Stones.

The biggest shame about that era is that they didn't continue on for one or two more records. It fell apart with Lane's departure. There aren't bands like the Faces any more, playing to enthusiastic crowds like that. 'You Send Me' came towards the end of the night, and nobody brought Sam Cooke alive like Rod. It was a great show, and a great memory. I loved that band.

We ran out of gas a mile away from my friend's place on the way home. I was dumb as shit.

Years later, I got to meet Mr Lane at the Caboose Bar in Minneapolis. He was ravaged by his battle with MS and I saw his wife literally pick him up and put him in a chair behind the mic. He was an unbelievably soulful man. I don't think his condition should have allowed him to be there that night, but his love for music and his delivery of those great songs meant you couldn't stop him. I got his autograph on a business card. His hands were shaking and I shouldn't have put him through it, but he smiled the whole time. I kept that card in my wallet and lost it when my wallet was stolen. That sucked.

The Faces know that I'm with 'em, you know? And the Stones know I'm always there when I've got that time off… I've always thought of meself as a member of the Faces for the duration… I don't want to make the choice, particularly. **Ronnie Wood**

ROD QUITS THE FACES
18 DECEMBER 1975, LONDON, UK

Rod Stewart quits the Faces after six years, making the announcement at a press conference and blaming his guitarist 'being on permanent loan to the Rolling Stones'.

I WAS THERE: SANDIE RITTER

I don't think Rod had it in mind to go solo. The press said 'that was it' when Ronnie went off to play with the Stones, although Ronnie was saying that he could do both. It might have worked temporarily, but he would've had to have made a choice at some point. And he always said he knew he was going to be a member of the Stones. That was his ambition forever. So, if he was going to choose between the two, that was what he was going to choose. I felt he compromised his playing doing that. Once he joined the Stones, he wasn't playing at the same level as he was playing in the Faces. But I saw him on his solo dates in 2019, and I realise now that he's learnt a lot from being around the Stones. When the Faces did a rehearsal, it was just 'let's play a few numbers' and that was it. I had VIP tickets for the 2019 solo tour and we got to see the rehearsal and you can see how vigilant Ronnie was about everything. He wanted to practice little things here and there to get it right. It was so professional. It was so impressive, but so different to the Faces.

RONNIE WOOD JOINS THE ROLLING STONES
23 APRIL 1976, LONDON, UK

Ronnie Wood is officially declared a member of the Rolling Stones.

A NIGHT ON THE TOWN
RELEASED 18 JUNE 1976

Rod's first solo album following the demise of the Faces tops the UK and US album charts and yields two number one singles, 'Tonight's the Night' in the US and 'I Don't Want to Talk About It'/'The First Cut is the Deepest' in the UK.

CITY HALL
14 – 17 DECEMBER 1976, NEWCASTLE-UPON-TYNE, UK

I WAS THERE: GARY CONSIGLIO

I got a job as a steward at Newcastle City Hall and worked all four shows that Rod played there in December 1976. That was a stellar band, with three guitarists – Gary Grainger, Billy Peek and Jim Cregan – and Carmine Appice on drums, Phil Chen on bass and John Jarvis on keyboards. The musicians who played his solo shows were far superior to the Faces, but after the Faces I thought most of Rod's new material was crap.

I WAS THERE: GARY LUTHER

I saw the Faces live at Newcastle Odeon in 1973 and twice the following year at the same venue. I had a poor version of 'the haircut' back in the day and lived next door to a dressmaker who made me satin jackets, tartan jackets, scarves, etc. I saw Rod loads of times after he went solo – he nicked a Scottish lion rampant flag off me at Newcastle City Hall in 1976. He took it on stage the first two nights and gave it back, but kept it on the third night. I still went on the fourth night but I never got it back.

I've only ever spoken to Rod once, at a gig in Holland organised by the *Daily Mirror* Pop Club, and after he'd already left the Faces. I remember he turned up to meet people in a brown fur coat. He looked like a grizzly bear – but with a better haircut! I lost a bit of interest after 'Do Ya Think I'm Sexy?' and although I got a bit of interest back later, he has never matched the Faces days.

Rod's childhood home was at 507 Archway Road in London. (The house is no longer there as it's been demolished.) I pinched the chrome door numbers – 507 – off the front door in either 1975 or 1976. Aged 17 or 18, I was on a course in London and made my way over there, complete with screwdriver. I remember I crashed my car on the way back to my digs in Stanmore. I guess that's karma! I kept the door numbers for years in a fake leather glasses case in my bedside drawer. I've no idea what happened to them…

OAKLAND-ALAMEDA COUNTY COLISEUM
18 JULY 1984, OAKLAND, CALIFORNIA

I WAS THERE: DAVID CARON

I saw Rod Stewart but not with the Faces (I wish I did). My wife worked at Fantasy Records in Berkeley and knew Queenie at Bill Graham Presents who got us front row seats at the Oakland Coliseum. Rod was great live! My wife was not a big fan until he came over in front of us, sat down on the edge of the stage and sang '(If Loving You is Wrong) I Don't Want to be Right' to my wife. He was singing right to her and I thought she was going to melt right down to the floor!

FIRS HALL
14 DECEMBER 1985, WINCHMORE HILL, UK

I WAS THERE: TRUDIE MAYNARD

I first saw Rod Stewart in concert at Wembley in the late Seventies. I went with a friend from school. We nearly missed our last train home. All the fans in the train were singing Rod's songs. I was stood holding the pole in the middle of the train singing when the train suddenly jolted and I lost my grip on the pole. I ended up sitting on some strange bloke's lap, not once but twice!

I became an avid fan of Rod Stewart. I was lucky enough to meet him personally at his private family party for his mother's 80th birthday at Firs Hall in Winchmore Hill. My ex-husband worked there, and one weekend he phoned me at home and said I should get to Firs Hall as soon as possible. I said, 'Why, what's so important?' and he said, 'There's a famous person here called James Stewart.' I said, 'Why would I want to see him, for God's sake?' Then he told me it was Rod Stewart, so I raced round the house to get ready, found some money and booked a taxi. It was a very foggy night. The taxi driver thought I was mad, travelling about in the fog, but it was well worth the journey. I was able to join in the party celebrations with no questions asked as to who I was, but I think they knew who I was connected to. I was able to join in the party and somehow ended up dancing with Rod in front of me, doing the conga.

I also met him at his local pub in Epping but he declined to have a photograph taken with me. He probably thought I was stalking him, as I was turning up in different places!

WEMBLEY STADIUM
5 JULY 1986, LONDON, UK

I WAS THERE: SCOTT GOLDSMITH
I saw Rod at Wembley Stadium when the Faces reformed for a few tracks. They wheeled Ronnie Lane on stage in his wheelchair. The Faces are my favourite band of all time, and my first memory of them is 'Pool Hall Richard', at the age of nine. I still have the original 45.

I WAS THERE: WENDY HUDSON
I started at the back of the pitch when the support was on, and by the time Rod came on I was at front. I am a five foot tall woman and I just kept saying 'excuse me, excuse me' until I got to the front. When Ronnie Lane came on, the emotion was overwhelming. It was the best day ever, and I still can't hear 'We'll Meet Again' without getting a lump in my throat.

I WAS THERE: ANDY MILLER
Rod Stewart played a concert at Wembley Stadium and the Faces came on and played a short set; Ronnie Wood, Kenney Jones and Ian McLagan. Ronnie Lane was suffering badly with MS so couldn't play, but he sat on a stool and provided backing vocals. Bill Wyman played bass. The deal was that my girlfriend at the time (now my wife) wanted to go and see Rod Stewart at Wembley, and I said I would only go if she would go to a concert the following week, where the headliners were Queen.

I WAS THERE: DAVID ISAAC
When Rod Stewart brought out 'Maggie May' in 1971 and I saw him and the Faces on *Top of the Pops*, I just loved it. I loved the organ played

by McLagan and they just looked like a lads' band, and so different from other bands and all the glam rock stuff. I bought Rod's first solo album, and obviously the Faces played on all that, and then I got a couple more of his albums and again it was mainly the Faces playing on them. I saw them on a BBC2 *In Concert* TV programme and they were really down-to-earth guys, playing live in the studio, and I just fell in love with them. I thought they were absolutely brilliant. When Ronnie Lane left and Tetsu came in, they just didn't seem the same band and I could see the split coming. I never got the chance to see them live, which I was really disappointed about. But I did see Rod, and I might sound a bit sad, but I've seen him about 29 times! He's a great entertainer.

David Isaac (left) was at Wembley

But I always wanted to see the Faces, and in 1986 they said they were reforming. I knew Ronnie Lane was ill but they were going to reform them back on the stage and I just had to be there. Four of us went to Wembley for the day – myself, my ex-wife, my brother-in-law and my sister. I've seen loads of people. I've seen Springsteen and even Pavarotti when it comes to that, but it was great to know I could actually go and see the Faces. I knew Ronnie Lane wasn't going to play, but they said he was going to make an appearance and I thought 'how brilliant is that?'

The heavens opened up and it rained like you wouldn't believe. My sister was wearing a widely knitted jumper that went down to just below her hips. By the time the rain stopped, it was down to way past her knees. But we were down the front and we didn't worry about the weather. It was a great day.

Rod did his own thing and then he brought the Faces on and Bill Wyman took the place of Ronnie Lane. Poor old Ronnie came on in a wheelchair and Ronnie Wood, being a bit mischievous, tried to lift him up and carry him, and more or less dropped him. I felt a bit embarrassed for Ronnie Lane actually.

I think it went on a bit longer than it should have done. And Rod kept saying, 'It's not raining, honest. It's not raining.' That was easy for him to say. Rod did Wembley Arena three nights in a row after that because he felt so bad about it raining.

In the early days, they just always looked like they were having a ball and that's what I liked about them. They may have been half-drunk but they still played really well. That thing about letting the audience sing half the songs is something Rod did with the Faces, and in the Seventies not a lot of bands did that, starting that singalongaFaces. And then when he did his own thing, it was singalongaRod.

Just before they split up, there was tension between Rod and Mac. Mac was a little peed off that Rod was getting all the attention. It wasn't the Faces anymore. It was Rod Stewart and the Faces, and unfortunately that got to Mac a little bit.

I WAS THERE: MICHAEL MAYNARD

When they split, I felt as if I had lost a friend, a mate, someone who would lift my mood or enhance it. In 1986, Wembley Stadium was to be host for a Rod Stewart concert, 'I may go to that,' I debated, until it was billed as a Faces reunion. Bingo, I just had to attend.

80,000 people crammed into the hallowed stadium. It was a 2pm to 10pm show. Some of the bands were okay; The Blow Monkeys, whose lead singer probably needed protection after he ridiculed our Rodders (whatever happened to him?), and Feargal Sharkey. 'Teenage Kicks' and 'Stay With Me' on the same bill? I hope John Peel was there.

Out flounced Rod, only to fall flat on his backside. It had been raining and the stage was wet and, had there been Facebook back then, that would have gone viral. Like the true pro he was – and is – he laughed it off in true ex-Faces member style. I cannot recall his first few songs or even much of his set. I was too busy thinking, 'Where is the Faces reunion?', especially bearing in mind Ronnie Lane had MS. Was I beginning to regret my purchase? Would I have rocked up had the Faces not been there?

'And now, please welcome… The Faces!' Yes, get in! Ronnie Lane was wheeled onstage, Ronnie Wood tried to get him to stand up, almost dropping him. I'm not sure what came first, the chair incident or the one song that I would venture most of us came to witness for old times' sake, but they played it. There was the opening frantic attack from Ronnie Wood and then, after the first three bars, the major punctation from Kenney Jones, playing like his life depended on it, and the floodgates duly opened:

Stay with me
Stay with me
For tonight you better stay with me

80,000 throats, as raw as Rod's, and tonsils bulging. Yes boys, we all want to stay with you.

KAWASAKI CLUB CITTA
3 MARCH 1990, KANAGAWA, JAPAN

I WAS THERE: MASATOSHI SHOJI

I've seen every member of the original Faces line-up play live, but not all at the same time. Ronnie Wood appeared with Bo Diddley at Nakano Sun Plaza in March 1988 and 'Around the Plynth', 'That's All You Need' and 'It's All Over Now' featured in the set. Then Ronnie Lane came to Japan in March 1990 on his *Just for a Moment* tour and played the Kawasaki Club Citta, in Kanagawa. He was using a wheelchair. His set included 'Debris', 'Ooh La La' and 'You're So Rude'. Mac was part of the band and there were a lot of Mods there! Around 1991, I had a ticket to see Steve Marriott play at Club Quatro in Shibuya, Japan but the gig was cancelled. He died soon after.

I WAS THERE: DON HARVEY

When I was in Austin in 1990, I joined Ronnie's band for his last tour, a tour of Japan called *Just for a Moment*. It was the only time I played with Ronnie. I owned a studio at the time called the Austin Rehearsal Complex. Mac lived in Los Angeles back then, which he called 'Shakytown', and he came to Austin to rehearse with the band and then we took off for Japan. On the Japan tour, Ronnie had to be carried on stage because his MS was so bad at that point. He probably weighed 90 pounds. I didn't know Ronnie when he was healthy. I only knew the Ronnie that was sweet as sugar, just the sweetest guy. That Japanese tour was one of the most fun tours ever. Mac's sense of humour was incredible. We had a great time on that tour, and Mac and I became friends and we stayed in touch.

Don Harvey (centre) with Mac and Ronnie on Ronnie's *Just for a Moment* tour of Japan

NATIONAL EXHIBITION CENTRE
10 APRIL 1991, BIRMINGHAM, UK

I WAS THERE: MARK HUNT

I grew up with the love of the Faces and Rod Stewart through my brother, Bobby. I'm a massive, massive Rod Stewart fan and I've been to 104 Rod Stewart concerts. The first one was at the NEC in 1983, and every time Rod played Birmingham, I probably did all of the concerts. I managed to get backstage once, and it was a complete fluke. I didn't have a ticket so I went along on the day and tried to buy a ticket on the door, as they'd often be selling them right up until the concert started. On this occasion, the concert had already started. A friend's sister was working behind the counter. She recognised me and said, 'Are you looking to buy a ticket?' I said I was and she said 'wait there'. When she came back, she gave me an envelope and inside it was an 'access all areas' pass so I went and sat in the arena, about six or seven rows from the front.

Everybody in the two rows I was in had the same triple A pass, so when the curtains went down for the interval – Rod used to call it half-time – all of these people I was sat with said 'come on then' and we went backstage and there was a buffet on. I was just milling around, eating sandwiches, for about half an hour. Bob Stewart, one of Rod's brothers, was there so I went up to him and said hello and we started to chat. I was talking to him for about five minutes. Then Rod (and Bob's) sister Mary came over and said, 'Come on, we'd better go back to our seats.' Bob said, 'I'm not going back to my seat. I'm going to the side of the stage.'

The music started for the start of the second half and Rod Stewart came out of the dressing room and was walking towards me. I put my hand out and he shook my hand and carried on straight up the stairs and back on stage. Bob said to me, 'Come on, we'll go round here,' so I went and watched the show from the side of the stage with him. I couldn't believe how close I was to Rod, my idol. He kept coming over to the side of the stage, laughing and winking at Bob, and at one point Bob nodded to Rod and gave him a football, which Rod then gave to me. That's one of four footballs of his that I've got.

I also met Rod when he did a book signing in the little local bookshop in his village in Epping Forest. There were probably only 100 people there because it was quite low-key. Rod was just signing his name in the books and not writing any dedications, but I brought along a 1945 model railway book I'd bought off the internet, 1945 being the year Rod was born. When I got to the front of the queue I said, 'Rod, I've got you a present,' and he looked at it and said, 'Bloody hell, that's fantastic.' And he looked at the year and said, 'It's even more fantastic,' and he told Penny about it. He said to me, 'What's your name?' He signed the book to me and another two copies as well.

DEATH OF RONNIE LANE
4 JUNE 1997, TRINIDAD, COLORADO

Ronnie Lane passes away after battling multiple sclerosis for nearly 20 years, the same illness that had afflicted his mother. Rod and Ronnie Wood had helped pay his hospital bills.

OLYMPIC TORCH CONCERT, THE MALL
26 JUNE 2004, LONDON, UK

I WAS THERE: PETER SMITH

Tickets were given away free through a ballot for this concert to mark the arrival of the Olympic Torch and The Mall was transformed into a huge open-air venue holding 70,000 people. It was impossible to get anywhere near the stage, but video screens had been erected along its length to show the concert and the progress of the Olympic torch as it was carried through London. The concert included a three song set from Rod, featuring the cast from *Tonight's the Night* (a big West End success at the time) on 'Sailing' and 'Rhythm of my Heart'. But the concert also featured Rod with his old Faces mate Ronnie Wood on guitar for 'Stay With Me'.

We were stood right at the back of the crowd, watching it unfold on a screen, and may have had a better view if we'd been watching the live TV broadcast back in Sunderland. But the atmosphere was great and, judging by the excitement in the audience, I wasn't the only one to appreciate the momentous reuniting of two musical legends. It was great to see the two of them performing together again, even if only for a few moments, and it brought back many happy memories of seeing the Faces in the early 1970s.

FIVE GUYS WALK INTO A BAR...
RELEASED 20 JULY 2004

A Faces box set, curated by Ian McLagan, prompts renewed talk of a Faces reunion.

In the middle of a song, I'd hear a Ronnie Lane bass lick and I'd look over at him and smile. I just kept him in mind ever since then... With Glen it suddenly becomes the Faces because he's playing those very important Ronnie Lane bass parts.
Ian McLagan, talking to *Billboard*

ROYAL ALBERT HALL
25 OCTOBER 2009, LONDON, UK

The Faces, with Simply Red vocalist Mick Hucknall substituting for Rod, play a charity concert in aid of the PRS members benevolent fund. It sparks speculation that the Faces will reform, with a different singer if necessary.

We've been waiting and waiting for Rod to say yes; now he's finally said no. He's busy doing other shit. So we're gonna do it. I'm 64, for chrissakes. If we don't do it very soon, one of us is gonna check out.
Ian McLagan, talking to *Billboard*

VINTAGE FESTIVAL
13 AUGUST 2010, GOODWOOD, UK

I WAS THERE: GLEN MATLOCK

I hadn't seen Mac for donkey's years because he'd moved to America but we used to get on like a house on fire when he'd played with The Rich Kids. He was on the radio in London doing the *Roundtable* programme so I called the radio station up and I said, 'Ere, give Mac my number when the show's finished.' I drove out of town and the reception went and then I was on the ferry to the Isle of Wight when the phone rang. It was Mac, and we picked up where we left off. We hooked up in town and I said, 'What are you doing?' He said, 'I don't know. Springsteen keeps calling me up and offering me good money but…' so I said, 'Well, what do you really wanna do?' He said, 'I want to reform the Faces.' Ronnie Lane had passed away by then. And I said, 'Listen, you know that I know that you know that I know that you know that I'm the right bloke for the job? Put a word in for me.'

It didn't happen for a while. Mac was trying to court Rod to do it, and I don't really know what went on there, but they ended up getting Mick Hucknall to do it. Mac called me up and said, 'Are you sure you're up for this?' and I said, 'Mac, I know those songs backwards. You know, I learnt to play listening to them.' He said, 'Oh great.' I said, 'Yeah, it's forwards I have trouble with.' And he laughed. I think that's what actually got me the gig.

It was great rehearsing with them. I had read about how when Ronnie Wood got the gig with the Stones, Clapton and Jeff Beck were having a try out and were winding him up, saying 'We're better guitarists than you are.' And Ronnie said, 'But I'm the right bloke.' And when he went in there, instead of waiting to be told what to play, he said, 'C'mon, let's do that blues song you used to do down Eel Pie Island.'

When I started rehearsing with the Faces, they said, 'What are we gonna do?' and I said, 'Let's do 'You Can Make Me Dance'. Ronnie went, 'I can't remember how it goes.' So I was stood there with Ronnie going, 'Well, I think it goes a bit like this …' Actually being in the room with him at Kenney Jones' house down in Surrey, just watching Ronnie slowly getting his chops back together, was great. I think I brought something to the table there. But you don't really need to do much more than play Ronnie Lane's fantastic bass lines.

The Vintage Festival at Goodwood was our first proper gig. We were doing 'Losing You' with the drum solo and the band goes off. I'm standing at the side of the stage with Ronnie and he said, 'What d'ya reckon?' I said, 'Great, but you know what? I've never been in a band that does a drum solo before and I bet in the old days you used to go off for a bit of this, that and the other. And you had the bar set up on the stage. We're both on the wagon now. That's all a bit redundant.'

Ronnie said, 'I know what. Keep Kenney's attention,' and he snuck off behind the drums. On top of his amp, Ronnie had a big bottle of Johnson's Baby Powder which he'd put on his hands for when they get sweaty. He comes back and he says, 'I got it.' I said, 'What are you going to do with it?' He said, 'You watch. Keep him playing.' So while Kenney's playing and I'm keeping his attention, Ronnie sprinkles this Johnson's Baby Powder all over these two kettle drums. And then he comes back and he says, 'Okay, let's get him to do it.' So we get Kenney to go round the kit. He's looking at us funny as we go, 'Around the kit – not that way, the other way,' and finally he gets on the timpani – doom, doom, doom, doom, doom! – and – pfoof! – this big cloud of Johnson's Baby Powder goes everywhere. And Ronnie says, 'That's why you have a drum solo.'

It was great being on stage with them. My biggest buzz ever was the last gig I did with them, in Japan. I used to pretend to be in the Faces, standing in front of the mirror when I was 14 years old. And there I was, in front of 50,000 people, playing in the Fuji Festival. That was the highlight of my career. Mick Hucknall's great, but he's not Rod Stewart. I would have loved to have done it with Rod.

I WAS THERE: GRAEME HARTLEY-MARTIN

In 2010 I attended the Goodwood Vintage Festival where the (partially reformed) Faces headlined. Ronnie Wood, Ian McLagan and Kenney Jones were joined by Mick Hucknall, who took the place of Rod, while Glen Matlock became Plonk Lane for the evening, even to the extent of copying Ronnie's characteristic marching-on-the-spot style. I must admit I was dubious about Hucknall taking Rod's place but he actually performed excellently on a tight-as-a-drum comprehensive set that included songs from *Long Player*, *Nod* and *Coast to Coast*.

A few years later, the band undertook another reunion gig at a polo club in Surrey, which I didn't attend due to the £80 ticket price. Having seen the video footage, I must say the Goodwood line-up had the edge. (Sorry, Rod.) I still love to see footage of the band at their peak and contend that, between 1970 and 1973, they were the best rock band in the world.

FUJI ROCK FESTIVAL '11
30 JULY 2011, NAEBA, JAPAN

I WAS THERE: MASATOSHI SHOJI

Rod Stewart played Yokohama Arena in April 1994 and Mac was the keyboards. The set included several Faces-era songs including 'Cut Across Shorty', 'Reason to Believe', 'Handbags and Gladrags', 'Maggie May', 'Sweet Little Rock and Roller' and 'Twistin' the Night Away'. And in 2011, the Faces came to Naeba in Japan, with the original members Ronnie Wood, Ian McLagan and Kenney Jones as well as Mick Hucknall of Simply Red on vocals and Glen Matlock of the

Sex Pistols on bass. Since Mick, not Rod, was the singer, the Faces also played a few Small Faces tunes such as 'All or Nothing' and 'Tin Soldier'. Although it rained really hard just before they came on, it was an amazing night.

UNIVERSITY MEDICAL CENTER
3 DECEMBER 2014, AUSTIN TEXAS

I WAS THERE: JON NOTARTHOMAS

I first met Mac around 2004. With Napster and streaming services, I was really disillusioned at the prospect of making a music and writing career work. For the first time in my life, I'd decided to cease pursuing music and performing as my first endeavour and had gone back to school at St Edwards University.

But some of the people I knew had friends in Austin. I'd worked with Scrappy Jud Newcomb and with Don Harvey, who at that point was Mac's drummer in the Bump Band. Don's a realtor as well and had helped me find a house. Don and I had driven out to some house and he was excited about going out on the road on one of Mac's first tours with the Bump Band. And I casually said to Don, 'Man, I'm so starved of not playing and not being out on the road.' He said, 'Why don't you come along and be the driver? You could sit in!' I replied, 'Sit in with Ian McLagan? I'm in!'

I didn't sit in, but I did go on the road with Mac. He and I hit it off pretty well from the start, and for a couple of years I became the default tour manager. Even from those first gigs, Don had asked me to look over the money and the receipts and different things, and Mac began to rely on me as part of the group. We had no idea what it would develop into. I became part of the entourage at that point. Mac wasn't touring for months on end, just a few weeks here and there. He was a real fixture in Austin and real proud of being in the Austin music community.

Mac and Kim had moved into Keith Moon's Malibu house for a while after Keith passed away. But those were troubled times for Mac. He never felt at home there. The earthquakes unsettled them. He had a lot of bad habits at the time. He admitted that he pretty much blew the advance of the *Troublemaker* record up his nose.

Mac came to Austin because Ronnie Lane was here and he thought he would reconnect with him, but no sooner had Mac arrived than Ronnie said he was moving to Trinidad, Colorado because he couldn't handle the heat. As soon as Mac and Kim were in Austin, they got their house and Kim was immediately gardening. Things were in bloom and they just loved the environment here and felt at home for the first time. Mac loved the fact that nobody troubled him or bothered him in Austin. He got given a couple of honours in the first couple of years of being here for being a Texas musician, which he was super proud of.

He was always wanting to get back together with the Faces, but there was a tension between him and Rod which is odd when you saw these guys always being such jokesters – 'taking the piss of out each other' as Mac would say. It always struck me as a little odd that it became more personal between those two. Mac would get frustrated with every Rod record, because Rod would talk about getting the Faces back together, and it seemed like it was just rhetoric to put intrigue into whatever record he was trying to sell.

Mac was very excited when there was talk of them actually getting back together, but it's tricky when you have the notoriety, and the lawyers and the managers involved. How many collaborations in the music world haven't happened because of managers and lawyers getting in the way and wanting to bat for their world class artist?

Mac championed the Rhino box set, *Five Guys Walk Into a Bar*. He was super proud of that work, and he wanted the Faces to happen again and he really thought it would be great. But sometimes Mac would say the wrong thing and inevitably it would get back to Rod, or there'd be some other animosity which would cause tension. At one point, they did get together and do rehearsals with Rod, and apparently it went great. I remember discussing it with Mac and there was so much tension, but it was all around managers and such and such that was getting in the way. I was saying to Mac, 'You just have to get into that room with the guys. I'm sure it's going to be the same old magic and camaraderie that you always had.'

But they got together, rehearsed a few songs and then Rod or his manager decided that he wasn't going to do it. But they didn't discuss it and the others were waiting for an answer forever. They ended up hearing via the *Jimmy Kimmel Show* or whatever, with Rod just laughing it off. 'I'm not going to get together with those drunks.'

Mac really felt that jab. Those little Rod insults really came across. John Langford had a radio show in Chicago and a frequent joke that Mac would have if the subject of retirement came up was, 'You know what they call retired musicians, John? Rod Stewart.' It was funny, but it got back to Rod and it would always cause animosity. Mac still had a little bit of a temper and could be a bit volatile at times. But you could talk to him about just about anything.

At the point at which Kim was killed, my relationship with Mac wasn't good. I was nervous to even call Mac for a couple of days after it happened. Scrappy, the Bump Band guitar player, and Mark Andes and the guys had gone out there, but I held back. But at the memorial service we had at Zilker Park, Mac came over and gave me a big hug. I said, 'Mac, I'm so sorry.' And what I had assumed to be potentially the end of our working relationship turned out to be the beginning of it. All he knew and all he wanted to do was to perform and play. I think he even played at the Lucky Lounge that week that Kim died. He said 'I need to play' and he played for Kim.

Those first couple of tours afterwards were a little rough. We'd get back to the hotel room afterwards and he'd want me to hang out and have a Guinness with him, and there were a lot of tears and a lot of hugs. He needed a friend to get through that time, and it just happened to be me. A couple of those tours were booked in haste and were really not profitable. They were very stressful, and Mac was still in mourning and was getting angry at a lot of people.

At one point I blew up in a way that I don't think Mac was used to. He wasn't used to too many people other than Kim responding to him and really letting him have it. But I let him have it, assuming I'd probably be fired from the group. I said, 'Mac, I don't need the money. I'm not playing in this band. I'm doing this because of the love of the guys.' I said to him that perhaps he was making a mistake in how he was getting to the Faces and his attitude towards Rod. I said, 'You brag about the fact that you would cross your arms when Rod would play 'Hotlegs' and refuse to play it. If anyone did that in your band, you know they'd be out.'

He listened to me and I somehow won his trust to become a voice of reason and honesty. But Mac wouldn't take any shit from anybody. One time he was pissed off because somebody from Rod Stewart's fan club got his personal phone number and called him wanting to talk. He didn't appreciate that at all.

We were playing in Houston that night. This was the last year of his life and he was definitely wanting the Faces thing to happen. I said, 'You really ought to think about Rod being your best friend and think of him in that way. Forget all the animosity and the slights and all those things.' 'I do, I do. There's no animosity.' 'Mac, we're coming from a show and the last person in line was the woman who runs his blog or his fan site. And you called him a fat-nosed cunt. That's why the Faces aren't getting back together. How is that not going to get back to Rod?' He would get pissed off but later he would say, 'I heard you. I know what you're saying.' He realised he was not exactly being his own best friend and the champion for the cause that he was working for. He really wanted to have another tour or another get together with the Faces, and have it just be spectacular.

Every year we'd have a Bump Band Christmas party. And Mac was going to be meeting up with Los Straitjackets and Nick Lowe in Minneapolis for the start of a Christmas tour. I wasn't there because I was driving back from seeing my brother in Atlanta, but I'm told the Christmas Party that year was probably the best in 20 years of those parties with Mac. He said, 'Everybody's talking about the future or the past. What about the right fucking now?' That was the last toast.

I was home the next day when I got a call either from Jo Rae, his publicist in town, or Ken Kushnick, who was managing Mac at that point. They said, 'Have you seen Mac?' And I said, 'No, I haven't heard from him yet.' Mac called me daily. 'Well, he didn't make rehearsal.' I said, 'That's odd. Did he check into his hotel room?' 'They said, 'Yes, he's just not answering his door.'

And I said, 'Call them back'. Mac had had a stent put in because he was having a heart attack about a year earlier. When he had the stent fitted, the hospital was insisting that they wheel him out in a wheelchair because of liability, etc. But Mac refused to get in the chair. They signed him out the day after his stent was fitted and he stood up out of his chair, did a little dance and said, 'I'm dancing out of here.' He was full of life.

A couple of weeks before, he'd had his yearly check up and he kept telling everybody he was feeling great and everything was good, but he may still have been on blood thinners. I said, 'Call them back. They need to go into his room and check on him. Tell them that he has a potential heart condition and be sure he's OK.' They called back and said, 'He's not in his room. The bed's not disturbed.'

I started thinking about it and I said, 'Who checked into the hotel? Was it the tour manager?' Because the tour manager could have checked in for the whole entourage. And it occurred to me that we had booked a separate room the night prior. So I said, 'Was he in the room before?' I started piecing it together. 'No, he never checked into that room.'

I think Jo Rae had said Mac's flight was delayed. Well, if he got stuck in Dallas or Denver, he knew where the Irish pubs were and he'd always send me a picture of himself with a drink. And I hadn't heard from him at all so I thought 'that's odd.'

I called Jo Rae and had him call Lonnie, an old Korean and Vietnam vet from across the street who would look after Mac's house. Mac would take his car and park it at the airport so I said, 'If Mac's car's in the driveway, tell Lonnie he needs to go in and check on Mac.' Lonnie went over, and Lonnie's daughter and son-in-law were both paramedics and didn't live too far away.

I got in the car and drove the twelve miles from my place. As I was driving on the 130, I remember seeing an EMS come down one of the tributary roads and I thought, 'Oh man, that's not good.' I drove up to Mac's house and the EMS and police were right behind me. Lonnie's daughter and son-in-law had found him in the tub.

I remember going upstairs in his place and feeling a little panicked. They were trying to revive him on the floor. There were things all over and the bathroom was cluttered but they had tried to pick him up and they were moving him. They had called the Medvac to fly out to his place in Manor. The Medvac helicopter landed out in his front property and they were going to take him. They were asking for his wallet, so I was frantically looking for his wallet and trying to let them know that he'd had a stent and that he had some medications. His bag was right there by his bed and I had to rifle through it looking for the medication.

They were carrying him out. He was unclothed but I remember seeing his arms and his leg kinda kick in, almost as if he was having a little seizure. And I remember thinking, 'This is good. At least he's alive. Something's going on.'

They flew him to Seton hospital in Austin. I called my girlfriend and we drove into Seton to meet up with him there. And I reached out to his son, Lee, and let him know what was going on. But when we got to the hospital, we checked in right away. He had had a CAT scan and one of the doctors asked if we were family and so on and so forth. And I said that we were speaking with family and we were his first connections in Austin. We were taken into a side room and the doctor came in and said Mac had had a severe stroke. While he potentially could recover, he'd likely need 24/7 care and probably be in a vegetative state. It was a hard thing to hear.

I'd been with him that time he went to the hospital for the stent, when they really should have raced him in because he was having a heart attack. The good thing about that was that we were very clear about what Mac wanted. He had made Jo Rae and myself promise that if he ever had something debilitating or had to be on life support or whatever, he did not want to live that way. We had to promise not to do anything. So we knew we had to let him go.

The only concession we made was that they agreed to hold off on disconnecting the ventilator until Scrappy – who had just arrived in Marfa, Texas, about an eight hour drive from Austin – could get back and a couple of Mac's other friends could be there.

So we gathered a lot of his closest friends from Austin and we played a few songs. Mac's foot and hand kept moving at times. That had to be muscle memory. If you ever watched Mac playing organ or piano, he had this funny dance and he was constantly working the volume pedals or turning it on and off with his foot. And, of course, he was playing the piano with the expression pedals.

I don't know if anything registered with him but we played Booker T and the MGs' 'Green Onions', 'Glad and Sorry' and 'Honey Bee' by Muddy Waters. Mac passed in the middle of that. How many times did I play 'Glad and Sorry' with the Bump Band or with Mac privately? Somehow that song really rang out clearer in that moment than it ever had.

Mac and Bobby Keys had been in touch those last years. I recall Mac having a phone conversation with Bobby. We were driving into Syracuse while Mac and Bobby chatted and I recall Mac reassuring Bobby that Bobby would get better and be back out with the Stones. Bobby had stated he wasn't going out with the Stones, who were about to play Australia. In the frantic time at Mac's house when they were moving him out on a gurney, I was getting his things together. I was trying to find his wallet, where I knew he had his meds. It was chaotic and I couldn't find it, but I eventually discovered his pants hung by the bedroom door. When I picked up his phone, I noted a message on his home screen – a missed call from Bobby Keys. Bobby had died within hours of Mac having had his stroke. I guess the call was actually Bobby's wife, letting Mac know he'd passed. Two Stones sidemen passing so close together…

That last year of Mac's life might have been one of his better years. It brought him a new lease of life. He was a great guy to hang around with. He was always saying how lucky he was and how much he loved life. Even in those last couple of years, when he was playing some little honky tonk joint in west Texas to 30 or 50 people, it didn't matter. Whether he was playing for several thousand people or playing for 20, he'd still give it his all.

I've become the point man for Mac in a lot of the world. I'm still helping his son deal with the estate a little bit. It's funny to look back at it now and realise how good pals we'd become. I really miss the guy.

I WAS THERE: DON HARVEY

When Ronnie was becoming more ill, Mac and Kim decided to move to Austin and Mac tasked me with putting together a new Bump Band. Mac moved here in 1994, and I played with him for 18 years, and 'managed the unmanageable' for five. I say that completely in jest, because he would admit he was unmanageable.

Mac and I had really hit it off on that Japan tour, and I thought I was really special, but that's just how Mac was with everybody. Everybody thought they were really special with Mac. But we became very, very close. As his drummer and his manager, we spent an enormous amount of time together.

My son Adam has the same birthday as Mac, and when we would rehearse at Mac's house, his wife Kim would babysit Adam. They had a really special bond. I remember Kim really fondly. She was so wonderful, a very elegant lady. They were supposed to be coming over to our house for dinner on the day she died in the car crash. Mac called me up from the scene. He was hysterical. I couldn't go alone, so I picked up Scrappy, the guitar player from the Bump Band, and we went together to be with Mac. That was an horrific day. Life was hard after he lost Kim. There were some really rough days. He was broken.

Don Harvey with Ronnie Wood, Mac, Kenney and (back row) Simon Edwards and Scrappy Jud Newcomb at the Marquee Club, London

Mac and I made five or six records together. I left the band two years before he died – we had a falling out – but we made up about six months before he died. We really had a wonderful time together at our annual Christmas party at a pub in Austin, which was held on Thanksgiving because he was going to be going on tour with Nick Lowe, and we had hugs and we made up. I was gonna be playing some gigs with the Bump Band again and then he died three or four days later. That was really tough. That was the very first time in my life that a very, very close pal of mine died.

The Bump Band played loads of Faces songs, but it was part of Mac's history. He shared the Faces with us. I listened to Kenney's parts and utilised many of Kenney's parts, but I just made it my own. Mac never asked us to play a song just like the Faces played it. That would've been a drag because then we would be like a cover band with Ian McLagan. And that's not what it was.

Mac was really quite obsessed with getting the Faces back together. He and Ronnie were very close, and he and Kenney remained good friends, but Mac and Rod had a falling out. I don't know if the failure to make a reunion happen was because of their relationship, but at one point it got really close. Mac went to LA to visit and Rod invited him over for dinner and invited Jerry Lee Lewis over too, because Mac was such a huge fan of Jerry Lee. It was a kind of a making up thing. Mac was really super happy about that.

HURTWOOD PARK
5 SEPTEMBER 2015, EWHURST GREEN, UK

I WAS THERE: NIALL CORBETT
On Christmas Eve 1976, I saw Rod at Olympia in London. This was another great show and the band were all great musicians, but it was not the same. I missed the Faces and especially Kenney Jones, one of my all-time favourite drummers. Hurtwood Park in 2015 was billed as a Faces reunion and featured Rod, Woody and Kenney, with other musicians to complete the band. I enjoyed it, but I knew it wasn't the same. In reality, it couldn't have been. No Mac or Ronnie Lane. The looseness was still there but the feeling wasn't. I came away feeling faintly cheated. I'm sure that many didn't and loved it. Maybe they weren't there in the early Seventies. Maybe it was just me…

I WAS THERE: JOHN LOGAN
The Faces reformed in 2009 with Mac, Kenney, and Woody, with Mick Hucknall as vocalist, but I had to be content with YouTube footage as I didn't see any of these gigs. Hucknall is a fan, apparently, and coped admirably with the songs. But a Faces without Rod, I think most would agree, isn't really the Faces.

I saw the 2015 reunion, this time with Rod, at Kenney's polo club, Hurtwood Park. This was a cancer awareness gig Kenney had organised. It was a good day out, with other performers like Paul Carrack, Midge Ure and Steve Harley's Cockney Rebel. The Faces came on last, at around 9.15pm, and played a typically ragged 45 minute set, kicking off with 'Feel so Good'. Rod got it wrong, saying it was a Muddy Waters number when it's a Bill Broonzy song.

They also did 'You Can Make Me Dance', 'Sweet Little Rock 'n' Roller' and the obligatory 'Stay With Me'. It was fascinating to see a Faces audience again, as they were a very different crowd to a Rod solo concert. Some were clearly Rod 'Do Ya Think I'm Sexy?'-era and onwards fans seeing Faces for the first time. But Rod immediately became the Faces lead singer again, inhabiting a different persona to what you'd see at one of his own concerts since the Faces disbanded in 1975. The old camaraderie was still there, but I did find myself looking over to stage left and the space normally occupied by Mac. It was sad to see that he wasn't there after him wanting this reunion for so long.

A Faces gig was a mix of the Marx Brothers and The Last Night of the Proms with a little bit of *Match of the Day*, New Year's Eve and a good night at the pub all thrown in for good measure. The Faces sang the songs, played the games and collapsed in a heap exhausted at the end… leaving you like a good party should, wishing you could go to another one the next night. As a live act, there was nothing like them before they got together, nothing like them when they were together and nothing like them since.

There's been talk of a reunion tour for many years now. Let's hope Ronnie and Rod can clear their diaries and make it happen before they leave the room for good. Two sets of fingers and one throat is better than nothing. As for being too old now, well, so am I. But that 2015 reunion gig involved a mammoth 13 hour return trip to Surrey in the car for me and a friend, all for a 45 minute set. And it showed me that the magic of the Seventies is still there now, even though they are all actually in their seventies. You can't polish a turd but you can sprinkle it with gold dust!

I WAS THERE: BRIAN REES

What a day that was. My missus is a bit younger than me. I said, 'I'm gonna go.' She got the tickets. I think there were only 5,000 of them. All the hotels were booked. She said, 'Look, we'll drive down, I won't drink, and we'll drive back.' I said, 'You're joking, ain't ya?' She said, 'I know it means a lot to you,' so we drove down and we drove back. We knew they were going to play, but we didn't know how long a set it was going to be. There were rumours it might only be a couple of songs, or maybe four songs. And it was bloody cold, so it was like, 'Christ, what are we actually gonna get here?' For me, there was still that worry that it might all be hype and perhaps it would just be Rod doing some solo stuff. So when they actually stepped out it was, 'Christ, this is actually happening.' I was right down the front. I remember Ronnie Wood shaking his fingers, saying, 'It's cold, ain't it?' But what a great day. We were there dead early. We soaked it all up. I was in tears of joy throughout it all. It was just incredible.

I WAS THERE: WAYNE PHILLIPS
It was a strange gig. We had polo to start with, and then Scottish pipers before Paul Carrack, Midge Ure and Steve Harley all did a few songs. Annie Nightingale then introduced the main event, the Faces. I was in my element watching them. A fantastic day, all in all. Only seven songs, but well worth the journey up from South Wales to see them.

I WAS THERE: PAUL BAKEWELL
The first single I bought by the Small Faces was 'Lazy Sunday', on a school trip. And I was familiar with the Jeff Beck Group; *Truth* was one of my favourite albums. The first time I saw the Faces was on a programme called *Sounds of the Seventies*. They did three numbers off of *Long Player*, and I was so impressed I went out and bought the album from a stall on Romford Market. I had a quick chat with the guy and I said, 'What's the deal with the Faces?' He said, 'Yeah, they're really good band.' That led me onto their back catalogue, which was their first album. I finally got to see them in '70 or '71. I saw them five or six times. I can't recall the first time. I just remember them being a great feelgood live band, one of the best. I've seen them all – The Who, the Stones, Zeppelin, and I saw The Beatles when I was younger – but this was something else. I've never seen anything better since. I saw them at The Oval, second on the bill to The Who. The Who were good but the Faces blew them off the stage. And I saw the last Ronnie Lane show, in Edmonton, where they had the can-can girls. I remember Ronnie Wood sliding across the stage during his solo on 'Plynth' and his silver Zemaitis coming unplugged as he did so. He just plugged it back in and carried on playing.

The best thing about it was that you were guaranteed a good time. We used to have a few drinks beforehand. It was a drinking, 'laddo' culture. There weren't many girls there. They were sloppy players, but it just held together in a good sort of way.

I went to the Hurtwood Park reunion, which was good, but it wasn't quite the same. They only did about an hour, and they were lacking Mac and Plonk. Two weeks later, I saw Rod at Hyde Park and he played all the obscure numbers, which I really liked. It wasn't a greatest hits show, and he made that clear from the start. Hundreds of fans were just storming out disgusted because he was doing a lot of stuff the Faces used to do.

I was really looking forward to *Coast to Coast*, but it doesn't come across on CD or vinyl. You had to be there. They were just the best thing live. Technically, other bands might have been a lot better, but they took themselves far too seriously. You felt that the Faces were just having a really good time. And I don't just want a repeat of what's on the album. I can go and play the album for that. I want something a bit special, and the Faces always delivered that. It was like magic, like pixie dust.

I WAS THERE: YVE PAIGE

I never made it to the Wembley concert in 1996, due to having a new daughter and life. And Ronnie Lane died, so I never got to see him again. I last saw Mac in 2014, at the Half Moon in Putney, four months or so before he passed. I was at the three shows they did with Mick Hucknall standing in for Rod, and to give the boy his due, he did good. He was humble and worked his socks off…

I was at the last Faces gig for Prostrate Cancer in 2015 at Hurtwood Polo Club. I was down the front and even had a little 'Rodney!' shout out. It was a great time to be alive, to relive a small touch of those days gone by. My memory is of Rod cutting 'Sweet Little Rock and Roller' to start again and Woody saying, 'Why? I ain't gonna play it any different!'

The Faces… bring something out in (Rod) that his solo shows never will. For decades he has resisted this reunion, but by the time they finished their short, seven-song set, he looked and sounded like a man who had rediscovered his purpose. I hope he doesn't make us all wait another 40 years to do it again.

Daily Telegraph review

TELL EVERYONE: A PEOPLE'S HISTORY OF THE FACES

I WAS THERE: SANDIE RITTER

There was nobody like Mick Jagger in the Faces, both as a front man and as businessman. Mick had a vision and went down that road with that vision. No one in the Faces had that vision. What has Kenney done since The Who ended? He hasn't got that drive to be successful. Mac put some great solo stuff out before he died, but he didn't really have the personality. Even though he was building quite a following, he could've built on it more. When the Stones played in Austin, he was the support act. Somebody could've pushed him to be the support act somewhere else, like LA or New York, where he would've been noticed more. When he was in the Stones, he asked for more money so he didn't continue being in the Stones. He knew what Mick was like, and that if he asked for more money he would probably be fired.

They've left it way too long. Rod doesn't have the personality for it any longer. I saw him in LA in 2019 when Jeff Beck joined him on stage and it was very disappointing. Jeff Beck's great, but Rod is just a Vegas act now and he couldn't do the songs very well. When they did 'Ain't Superstitious', he would sing 'dogs begin to howl' and then make those howling noises. Jeff Beck was doing his guitar thing and Rod was just saying 'woof woof'. He wasn't even singing, and he can't blame cancer for that because he could sing in a different vocal range. He does that on other songs. His heart isn't in it anymore.

I saw the Faces at Hurtwood Park when they did a few songs and it was 'alright'. But to be honest I prefer the Faces when I saw them with Mick Hucknall singing. It was more rock 'n' roll then, with Glen Matlock on bass, because Glen was a fan of Ronnie Lane. He actually took up bass guitar because of Ronnie Lane.

I know Kenney and Ronnie and Rod keep talking about how they're going to do the Faces again, but I just can't see how. I don't know what keyboard player they'd find who can play like Mac played. The only other person is Nicky Hopkins and he died years ago. Mac's playing was quite unique. And, unfortunately, Rod won't use Glen Matlock. He wants his own bass guitarist, which is a shame because Glen fits better. Glenn sometimes plays at Small Fakers reunions. Glen was a Small Faces fan too, so he's earned the right to be there. When they did 'Maybe I'm Amazed' and he was on bass and Mick Hucknall was singing, Glen had remembered all of Ronnie's movements and facial expressions. He was reliving it while he was playing. It was really heartwarming. I was remembering it as it was then. It's not going to be the same without all that. It's just gonna be more Vegas sort of stuff.

I don't know why Rod would do it now. He turned it down a number of times when Mac was alive, unless it's just because he's friends with the other two. He's not friends with the members of his own band. They are a lot younger than him. It must be quite nice to think, 'Oh, I'll go on tour with my friends.' Kenney would love to do it. I remember him saying, when he came to see Mac play, 'I want to play arenas, not small clubs like this.'

Some of the songs they wrote were so sexist. We didn't think of it that way at the time, but when you listen to lyrics now you think, 'Oh my God.' Even hearing them saying that now makes me want to cringe. Society has moved on from there. But I never sat down and listened to the Faces records then. For me, it was about seeing them live.

I WAS THERE: DEE HARRINGTON

I couldn't say how many Faces concerts I went to altogether – over 20 but not as many as 50. I went to festivals like The Oval, but there were a lot of venues. They were always great. The crowd loved that kind of atmosphere, and they were quite upbeat with the stuff they played.

Irwin Steinberg had signed Rod to Mercury Records. I don't think everyone realised Rod had a separate record contract. Some fans may have thought it was all part of the Faces, but Rod didn't just branch off on his own. He was always doing it, and his career was so enormous. *Every Picture* was an unbelievable record, and Rod was Irwin's baby. Irwin made life very easy for Rod, and Mercury would do generous things like send up a limousine just for him. That was their generosity and their way of saying thanks to Rod. Irwin came to visit us in the house. He bought me a pair of antique gold earrings. It was a very nice gesture but Rod had earnt them a fortune! There would always be a representative turning up at shows from Mercury Records along with Warner Brothers, which was the band's label.

One of the first things Rod ever said to me was, 'What you've got to do is not listen to any of the Faces' wives.' I thought, 'That's a bit strange.' But in the end, I realised what he meant. Not that there was anything that terrible, it was just this Rod 'thing' – the massive record sales. The attention on him was huge. It was very hard for everybody. It was a situation that nobody set out to create and when something like that happens, you just have to learn to deal with it. Rod's career was like a rolling stone that rolled and rolled and rolled and you couldn't stop something like that – and why would you? You can't say, 'Oh well, I'm not going to be a solo artist and sell less records' just because it might piss a few people off.' That's not the way it goes after you've been planning to do this for the last ten years.

I became aware of how the rest of the band couldn't deal with Rod's success. The wives were always a bit fed up. I think it was down to the fact that Rod earned so much more money. But his name put bums on seats! His career gathered momentum and just exploded, and then everybody was left dealing with the explosion. Promoters wanted to put 'Rod Stewart and the Faces' on the billboards. They wanted to sell the venue out. Those people are not there just for the music. When you've been number one for six weeks with a single and an album on both sides of the Atlantic and you're playing Madison Square Gardens, they're not going to leave Rod's name off the bill. He wasn't stomping around going, 'I want my name on the top.' It wasn't anybody's doing. It was the way the industry worked. The music business is exactly that – business.

The other Faces would say things like 'you kept all the best songs for your album' which of course wasn't true. The Faces music was a bit different to Rod's solo stuff. But they overlapped because Ronnie would be there with his guitar. Rod and Ronnie have always had a good relationship and it looked good and sounded great. And the Faces were a good time band.

Rod had probably been writing some of those songs on his solo albums long before they came out. He might have been writing some stuff when he was with Jeff Beck. He wrote 'Maggie May' with Martin Quittenton. He wasn't sitting down writing a song an hour before we went to the studio with the Faces and then saying, 'Oh, I'm not gonna let you have it.' He was never like that. I think if you asked Rod now, he'd say, 'Oh my god, it was so much hard work to try and come up with so many songs.' Writing is a creative thing and it doesn't always happen all at once. Rod would be singing stuff and playing guitar and working on things all the time.

Another problem was that the Faces as a band and Rod as a solo singer had the same manager in Billy Gaff, so Rod was sometimes put into compromising positions. I remember he started going and seeing other managers. I asked him, 'Why do you want another manager?' 'Well, you know, I might just need to have somebody on my side.'

I remember Ronnie Lane saying to Rod, 'You look like an ageing queen.' I was really upset by it and at the time I thought, 'Oh my god. That was so terrible to be saying that. You're meant to be a unit.' For me, it showed great animosity and unrest, which obviously never got repaired.

And, of course, Ronnie Wood was born to be a Rolling Stone and Rod was probably always going to be a solo artist. Ronnie was always there with the Stones, and he was always there with Rod before that. The Jeff Beck Group was a real stepping stone for Ronnie's career, being with Jeff Beck, Rod and Micky Waller, and then going on to the Faces with Rod.

The Stones would be hanging out in Ronnie's house long before he joined their band. Keith Richards used to live in the cottage at the end of Ronnie's garden. They were in each other's pockets all the time. I'd look at Ronnie and think, 'You are a Rolling Stone. Now you've found your home.' And, of course, he's been there ever since.

Rod was struggling to survive in the Faces, where everyone was unhappy. He had a lot of work on – he had two albums a year, the Faces had one – and a lot of work goes into writing, recording and to promoting those albums. And you've got to have a life.

It's a shame that it ended like it did but it ended the way it needed to, with Ronnie with the Stones and Rod being a solo artist and in control of his own destiny, rather than having to pussyfoot around anyone or upset anybody. Because Rod's not that type of person. He feels guilty about things – 'should I have done this?' – and he's very non-confrontational. He's not a bolshie 'oh, fuck you I'm gonna do this' type of person.

Rod had been working on his career for a long time before he ever knew any of the Faces. Right from when he was a beatnik, through his time with Long John Baldry and Steampacket, he never stopped working towards that goal. He was a Mod, and it was the clothes, and it was the scene in London. He just went on and on and on until he reached the point where he made the record. It's not five minutes' work for somebody, it's a long haul.

Rod's obviously had some mad times in his life and he has produced a lot of not great music but also a monstrous amount of incredible music. I was very lucky to be there. The Faces had a fantastic career and sold bucketloads of records, and did what they loved most of all – playing live. And they all had a damn good time. And the best thing about it for me is that Rod and I are still friends.

I WAS THERE: JOHN PEEL

And you may have seen in today's paper that Rod and the Faces have finally parted and gone their own separate ways. I don't think that comes as a great surprise to anyone, but it's very sad nevertheless, because although there may have been better bands musically, I don't think there's ever been a more enjoyable band, and I for one am very sad to hear it.

ABOUT THE AUTHOR

Richard Houghton lives in Manchester, UK. He divides his time between writing books about music (and especially collecting fan memories of seeing classic bands in concert), walking his dog Sid, watching Manchester City FC and Northampton Town FC and… listening to classic rock bands, including the Faces and early Rod Stewart. Check out his website at *richardmhoughton.com*.

Did you see the Faces live? Or have you got any memories of any other legendary rock acts? Please send them to Richard at iwasatthatgig @ gmail.com.

TELL EVERYONE: A PEOPLE'S HISTORY OF THE FACES

SPECIAL THANKS

Special thanks to the following:

William Adamson; Philip Andrew; Colin Baker; Paul Bakewell; Paul Bamford; Tony Bartolo; Simon Bates; Penny Bearcroft; John Walton Bell; Seth Bell; Don Bennett; Paul Bent; Verity Bickerton; Joar Bolme; Tim Brackley; Mark Brady; Paul Brenchley; Martin Burgin; Ray Canale; Luther Center; Dave Chant; Steve Chouteau; Paul & Linda Churchill (Dronfield, Derbyshire); Martin (the face) Clements; Peter Coals; Lyn Collin; Richard Titch Cook; David Cooper; Herman Daldin; David Dale; Aad de Winkel; Andy Dean; Anthony Dew; Brian Dewhirst; Chris Dodd; Paul Dubiel; Stephen Dudley; Bruce Dumes; Brian Duncan; Paul Evans; James Feeney; William Fillon-Payoux; Brian Finlay; James L Fisher; Rick Freeman; Howard Gardner; Des Garrahan; Denise Golding; Gary Goodwin; Michele Poppo Gormley; John Gray; Peter Green; Marie Gressmann; Vincent Griffin; Dennis 'Pudgie' Gwynne; John Hall; Ruth Angelika Hannuschka; Julie Hatchman; Robert Hayward; Nigel Hazlehurst; Andrew Height; John Hemingfield; Mark Herd; Ben Hochberg; John C Holcomb; Brian Howell; Karin Ingram; Simon Jacobson; Jenny Joannou; Bruce Kahn; Derek Keith; Richard Kelley; Melvin Kenyon; Aidan Kidd; Mary Jane Kilpatrick; Stuart Langsbury; Matthew Lee; Neville Lee; Carole Leslie; Iain Locke; Pauline Lever; John Logan; David Logan; Ian Logie; David Long; Charles Longley; Roger Lund; Gary Luther; Bill Lynn; David Lyons; Ian Macdonald; Tom Mann; A Ma-Nu; Donna Manus; Annabel Marshall; Gareth Millard; Nigel Charles Molden; Jim Moore; Steven Morris; Baz Mort; Gary Mort; Leslie Murphy; Dominic Murphy; James Nardi; Stephen Nixon; Sue Oates; Jon Christian Opøien; Mary O'Sullivan; Julian Page; Yvonne Paige; Mark Paszkiet; Charlene Pattison; Mark Pawlick; Alan Pearson; David Pett; Jamie Pipe; Gary Plants; Brian Plunkett; Gerard Rafferty; Ian Ragsdale; Brian Rees; Brian Rickard; Perry Ridley; Carol Robinson; Angela Rodda; Jon Rogers; Mr SR Russell; Elaine Salmons; Lavinia & Tullio Schivella; Shirley Sheehan; Charlie Shillibeer; Masatoshi Shoji; Andrew Siddall; Katrina Smith; Trevor GH Smith; Susie Smith; Peter Smith; Ms M Spence; Nigel Spooner; Paul Stennett; Tore Styve; Janet Sullivan; Tim Sullivan; Glen Tolley; Chris Townsend; Joan Unwin; Camiel Vanloffelt; Louis Vargas; Martin Vergaij; Paula Victor; Paul Voller; Johnny Walker; Jacqueline Walker; Mike Walton; Robert Warr; Steve Warren; David Waters; Alan Watters; Michael Watts; Eric Weitzmann; Stephen Weston; Andrew Whiles; Kelvin White; Webb Wilder; Graham Wilkinson; Helen Williams; Carol Wilson; Mick 'Monsta' Wood; Niles Stephen Wort; Rob Yalden.

www.ingramcontent.com/pod-product-compliance
Lightning Source LLC
Chambersburg PA
CBHW072043110526
44590CB00018B/3013